Contents

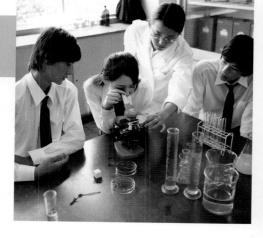

Foreword

As an author of an elementary Japanese textbook for college students, I am keenly aware of the difficulty of writing an elementary textbook. It is time-consuming, energy-consuming and creativity-consuming. Writing an elementary Japanese textbook for high school students must be much harder than writing the counterpart for college students, because it involves a host of age-adequate considerations peculiar to high school students.

Adventures in Japanese has been prepared by highly experienced and knowledgeable high school teachers of Japanese, Hiromi Peterson and Naomi Hirano-Omizo, who know exactly what is teachable/learnable and what is not teachable/learnable for high school students. They know how to sustain students' interest in the Japanese language and its culture by employing so many age-adequate, intriguing activities with a lot of fun illustrations. The grammar explanations and culture notes provide accurate and succinct pieces of information, and each communicative activity is well-designed to assist the students in acquiring actual skills to use grammar and vocabulary in context. In short, *Adventures in Japanese* is an up-to-date high school Japanese textbook conceived and designed in a proficiency-based approach. Among many others, it comes with a teacher's guide which is intended to help a novice high school teacher of Japanese teach Japanese in a pedagogically correct manner from day one.

I am pleased that at long last we have a high school textbook that is both learnable and teachable, and very importantly, enjoyable. I endorse *Adventures in Japanese* wholeheartedly.

Seiichi Makino
Professor of Japanese and Linguistics
Department of East Asian Studies
Princeton University

What is an ideal Japanese language high school textbook? Is it one from which you can enjoy learning Japanese? Is it one which encourages you to communicate successfully in the language? Is it one which opens doors for you to experience Japan, its people, and its culture?

As teachers of Japanese, we have tried to design a text from which you will have fun learning, and one which will encourage you to continue your study of Japanese, a truly exciting and dynamic language!

While keeping your interests foremost in our minds, we have also incorporated the overall goals of our Japanese language curriculum into the writing of our text. These goals are:

1. To create a strong foundation of the Japanese language through the development of the four language skills: speaking, listening, reading, and writing.

2. To strengthen, in particular, your conversational skills.

3. To deepen your understanding of the Japanese people and culture through the study of the language and the many aspects of Japanese culture.

4. To encourage a rediscovery of your own language and culture through the study of Japanese language and culture.

5. To encourage the growth of culturally sensitive, globally aware, responsible world citizens.

These general goals align with the Japanese language national standards and create a foundation upon which to build should you choose to sit for the AP® Japanese Language and Culture exam. More concretely, these are areas that you can look forward to learning as you progress through Volume 1 of this textbook series. We hope you will enjoy learning Japanese and discover the excitement of exploring a new culture.

Topics
Topics which appeal to students such as yourselves were selected. Situations which you are likely to encounter in your daily lives are used in this text. By the time you complete this text, you will have learned how to introduce yourself and others, identify and locate objects, discuss your daily activities, describe things and people, talk about your family and your home, discuss school (subjects, grades, extra-curricular activities, friends and teachers), express your likes and dislikes as well as your strengths and weaknesses, describe your physical ailments, and much more!

Can-Do Statements
Each lesson starts with a set of Can-Do Statements and two to three Performance Tasks that set the goals and expectations for the lesson. At the end of the semester, you will have an oral proficiency interview with your teacher based on these tasks. At the end of each lesson, you will also find a Now I Can... self-assessment checklist to help you determine if you have mastered all of the learning goals for that lesson.

Vocabulary and Language in Context

Vocabulary was also selected carefully. Basic vocabulary and vocabulary essential to discussing the topics are taught. Many are vocabulary words which students in our previous classes have found important to know and have enjoyed using. Traditional Japanese expressions, i.e., *"Doomo sumimasen"* as well as those less commonly found in traditional basic texts but frequently used in daily Japanese conversations, i.e., *"Ganbatte!"* abound in this text. The Additional Vocabulary section gives you extra vocabulary which you may want to use.

After the additional vocabulary, you will find a short Language in Context section, which uses the vocabulary and sentence patterns of the lesson in short reading activities without *romaji*. These sentences are models of real-life communication you can use.

Grammar

We have organized the introduction of grammatical structures so that you will be able to systematically build from the very basic to the more complex. We have also made an extra effort to recycle previously-learned structures throughout the text to provide opportunities for you to review them. On completing this text, you will have the grammatical capability to:

1. Describe actions and objects affirmatively and negatively in the present, future, and past tenses

2. Ask and respond appropriately to questions

3. Form simple compound sentences

4. Make suggestions and extend, accept, and decline invitations to do things

5. Make requests and ask for and grant permission to do things

6. Express your wants and preferences

Finally, we avoid using complicated grammatical terminology and have kept our explanations simple. Each grammar explanation is followed by model sentences with audio available, and practice exercises to help you master the grammar point.

Writing

At the end of Volume 1, you will have learned to write and correctly use *hiragana* and *katakana,* two of the basic Japanese writing systems. Your text provides romanization (English spellings of Japanese words) through Lesson 4. In Lesson 4, dialogues, vocabulary, and grammar explanations will use romanization, but the grammar exercises will stop. Thereafter, it is assumed that you will be able to read *hiragana*. Romanization is provided for *katakana* up through Lesson 8.

Kanji

In addition to *hiragana* and *katakana*, you will also learn to write 60 *kanji*. You will begin learning to write *kanji* in Lesson 3, and will learn approximately six *kanji* every lesson thereafter. All 60 *kanji* that you are expected to learn will appear in dialogues and vocabulary sections throughout the book with *hiragana* readings above them. Once you have finished a lesson, it is assumed you will know how to read and write the lesson *kanji*, and readings will no longer appear. Starting in Lesson 6, *kanji* used in each lesson will appear in grammar exercises and activities.

There are also additional *kanji*, called **Recognition Kanji**, beyond the 60 taught in Volume 1; these *kanji* are meant only to be read at this point, and you will learn to write them in later levels.

Adventures in japanese 1

アドベンチャー日本語

Hiromi Peterson & Naomi Hirano-Omizo

4TH EDITION

CHENG & TSUI COMPANY

Boston

20 19 18 17 16   2 3 4 5 6 7 8 9 10
Second Printing 2016
Published by
Cheng & Tsui Company
25 West Street
Boston, MA 02111-1213 USA
Fax (617) 426-3669
www.cheng-tsui.com
"Bringing Asia to the World"™

Adventures in Japanese Vol. 1 Textbook, 4th Edition
ISBN: 978-1-62291-056-4

The *Adventures in Japanese* series includes textbooks, workbooks, teacher guides, audio downloads, and a companion website at **cheng-tsui.com/adventuresinjapanese.**

Visit **www.cheng-tsui.com** for more information about *Adventures in Japanese* and additional Japanese language resources.

Printed in Canada

Photo Credits

front cover ©iStock.com/tuk69tuk; Radu Razvan/Photos.com; Level 2 ©SeanPavonePhoto - Fotolia; Level 3 ©ULTRA.F Getty Images; 19, 81, 121, 155, 219, 319, 347, 379; ©Imagenavi; 25(t, l) Getty Images/Polka Dot RF/Photos.com; 25(t, r) John Foxx/Getty Images/Photos.com; 28(b), 226 Getty Images/Photos.com; 28(m, r), 62, 67, 86, 97(l), 199(b), 247, 399 Jupiterimages/Getty Images/Photos.com; 33, 43(t) Rich Legg/Getty Images/ iStockphoto/Photos.com; 39 Anthony Brown/Getty Images/iStockphoto/Photos.com; 43(b) Ippei Naoi/Getty Images/iStockphoto/Photos.com; 44(l) Getty Images/Photos.com; 44(r) Cathy Yeulet/Getty Images/Hemera/ Photos.com; 48, 112, 186, 254, 318, 378, ©iStock.com/-WaD-; 49, 100, 115, 141, 172, 187, 227, 243, 251, 255, 292, 297, 355 (b), 363 ©AsiaStock www.fotosearch.com; 52(l) Aleksandar Bedov/Getty Images/iStockphoto/ Photos.com; 5(r) Getty Images/Photos.com; 59(t, r) PhotoObjects.net/www.jupiterimages.com/Photos.com; 80, 150-151, 218, 286, 346, 408-409 hichako/Getty Images/iStockphoto/Photos.com; 83, 203, 205 Catherine Yeulet/ Getty Images/iStockphoto/Photos.com; 87 Yuko Hirao/Getty Images/iStockphoto/Photos.com; 91(l) Edward Bock/Getty Images/iStockphoto/Photos.com; 91(r) Denis Raev/Getty Images/iStockphoto/Photos.com; 92 ©iStock.com/WebSubstance; 94 Tetsuo Morita/Getty Images/iStockphoto/Photos.com; 97 (r), 108 Comstock/ Getty Images/Comstock Images/Photos.com; 99 keko-ka/Getty Images/iStockphoto/Photos.com; 101 zhu difeng/Getty Images/iStockphoto/Photos.com; 119(l) wong sze yuen/Getty Images/iStockphoto/Photos.com; 11(r) vitchanan/Getty Images/iStockphoto/Photos.com; 126(r), 167(b), 214(m) Getty Images/iStockphoto/Photos.com; 135(b) ganjarelex/Getty Images/iStockphoto/Photos.com; 135(m, l) runin/Getty Images/iStockphoto/ Photos.com; 135(t) Acky Yeung/Getty Images/iStockphoto/Photos.com; 139(l) Nathan Watkins/Getty Images/ iStockphoto/Photos.com; 145(l) zhang bo/Getty Images/iStockphoto/Photos.com; 145(r) SantosJPN/Getty Images/iStockphoto/Photos.com; 146 Rudyanto Wijaya/Getty Images/iStockphoto/Photos.com; 151 violet-blue/ Getty Images/iStockphoto/Photos.com; 154 ©iStock.com/MsEli; 160(b) Matteo Mazzoni/Getty Images/iStockphoto/Photos.com; 160(l) Noraznen Azit/Getty Images/iStockphoto/Photos.com; 161 Hiroyuki Akimoto/Getty Images/iStockphoto/Photos.com; 164 (l) Stockbyte/Getty Images/Photos.com; 164(r), 196(l) George Doyle/ Getty Images/Photos.com; 167(t) suchoa lertadipat/Getty Images/iStockphoto/Photos.com; 178 Brent Bossom/ Getty Images/iStockphoto/Photos.com; 181(b) Juergen Sack/Getty Images/iStockphoto/Photos.com; 181(m) Marija Yurlagina/Getty Images/iStockphoto/Photos.com; 192 Yasuno Sakata/Getty Images/iStockphoto/Photos. com; 193(b) Patryk Kosmider/Getty Images/iStockphoto/Photos.com; 193(t) Artsem Martysiuk/Getty Images/ iStockphoto/Photos.com; 196(r) Kuznetsov Dmitry/Getty Images/iStockphoto/Photos.com; 199(t) satoyan/Getty Images/iStockphoto/Photos.com; 200 Yasuno Sakata/Getty Images/iStockphoto/Photos.com; 202(l) ccharleson/Getty Images/iStockphoto/Photos.com; 202 (r) Alexander Gatsenko/Getty Images/iStockphoto/Photos. com; 206(r) Hongqi Zhang/Getty Images/iStockphoto/Photos.com; 207 kennosuke/Getty Images/iStockphoto/ Photos.com; 208 (m) Juergen Sack/Getty Images/iStockphoto/Photos.com; 208(t) Aloysius Patrimonio/Getty Images/iStockphoto/Photos.com; 212(l) mocker_bat/Getty Images/iStockphoto/Photos.com; 212(r) Hyperion-Pixels/Getty Images/iStockphoto/Photos.com; 225 ©KPG_Payless/Shutterstock/vinhdav; 237 yuanyuan xie/ Getty Images/iStockphoto/Photos.com; 251 © Perseomedusa - Fotolia.com 273 ©iStock.com/Jprescott; 287 © AG- /Getty Images 368(b) ©iStock.com/JJ Gutierrez; 369, 370 Sakarin Sawasdinaka/Shutterstock

Culture

Understanding culture is essential to learning a language. We have thus included many cultural explanations in the form of Culture Notes. Each of these Culture Notes also contains an activity to help deepen your understanding of Japanese culture and compare and contrast it to your own culture. Lessons in culture can also be drawn from many of the illustrations and photos. In addition, Language Notes will help you understand elements of the Japanese language that may be very different from your own language, such as counters and word order.

Every other chapter also includes a Japanese Culture Corner which gives you a chance to further compare your culture with Japanese culture. You are encouraged to find answers through research by using various resources available to you, including the Internet, reading materials, or people from Japan!

Project Corner

Japanese culture includes many crafts and games. This text introduces origami (how to make a balloon, a box, a crane), songs *(The Elephant)*, the making of rice balls and *mochi*, games *(karuta, gomokunarabe)*, tongue twisters, and a Japanese folk tale *(Rolling Musubi)*. More Project Corners are available on the companion website at **cheng-tsui.com/adventuresinjapanese**

Review Questions and Text Chat

After every lesson, there is a list of common questions related to the topics covered. You will ask your partner these questions in Japanese and your partner will answer you without looking at the textbook. You and your partner will take turns asking and responding. You should pay attention to speed, intonation, and pronunciation as these factors matter in communicating successfully and will be assessed by your teacher. You may also practice or check your answers using the audio. If you need to review, page numbers are provided to help you find the relevant material.

There is also an AP®-style Text Chat review activity. You will respond to text messages from Japanese students based on prompts, modeling a real-life text chat exchange on topics related to the lesson.

It is our hope that upon completing this volume, you will be able to communicate successfully at a very basic level, orally and in written form.

One piece of advice from your teachers:
The key to success in the early years of foreign language study is frequent and regular exposure to the language. Take advantage of class time with your teacher, use your lab time effectively, and keep up with your work. Learn your material well, don't hesitate to try it out, and most of all, enjoy! And, as the Japanese say,

"Ganbatte!"

Ken and Emi are U.S. high school students learning Japanese. In *Adventures in Japanese Volume 1,* you will study Japanese with them, as they practice speaking the language with each other and learn about Japanese culture.

KEN Ken Smith is one of the main characters in the *Adventures in Japanese* series. In Volume 1, Ken is just starting to learn Japanese as a freshman at a U.S. high school. Ken is half Japanese from his mother, who speaks the language well, though his father does not.

Ken is an avid sports fan and athlete. He excels at several sports and also plays the guitar. Ken is laid-back, but his kind and caring nature is obvious from his interactions with friends and family.

EMI Emi Taylor is the other main character of Volume 1. She and Ken meet on one of the first days of school as freshmen. Like Ken, Emi is a beginning student of Japanese. Her family is from the U.S., and she is the first in her family to learn a second language. Although Emi is not an athlete, she enjoys sports and loves to watch movies and read books.

As their freshman year progresses, Ken and Emi become good friends. They often have lunch together, celebrate birthdays, and attend other school activities with their friends—all as they practice Japanese.

Meet the Rest of the Characters
Throughout Volume 1, Ken and Emi will meet several people who help them learn Japanese.

TANAKA-SENSEI
Ken and Emi's
Japanese teacher

AKIKO
A Japanese student
visiting America

MR. ROBERTS & MR. JONES
The two owners of a local store who learned
Japanese while living in Japan—students
often practice speaking Japanese with them

BEN An older student
that Ken knows from
school—he is also
learning Japanese, and
works part-time at a
local cafeteria

In *Adventures in Japanese Volume 2,* Ken and Emi will continue to learn about Japanese language and culture as they make many more friends including Mari, a Japanese exchange-student. In Volume 3, they will experience Japanese culture first-hand as they study abroad in Japan.

The following sections outline the ACTFL-World Readiness Standards for Learning Languages* and other standards, and how activities in *Adventures in Japanese Volume 1* align with them. While this is not an exhaustive discussion, it will inform you, the teacher, about how standards may be met in Volume 1. A full **Scope and Sequence,** as well as supplemental materials including audio and other resources, is available on the companion website at **cheng-tsui.com/adventuresinjapanese**.

I. Communication
Communicate effectively in Japanese in order to function in a variety of situations and for multiple purposes

1.1 Interpersonal Communication. *Learners interact and negotiate meaning in spoken, signed, or written conversations to share information, reactions, feelings, and opinions.* Students practice speaking with one another and the teacher on various topics, often in realistic Communicative Activities which require the exchange of authentic information, such as phone numbers, birthdays, or descriptions of people. Students are tested using review questions which require proficiency in asking and answering questions on a variety of topics, and engage in simulated written communication through Text Chat activities. Students ask for and give information, state preferences or opinions about food, clothing, prices, classes, gifts, family, times, etc.

1.2 Interpretive Communication. *Learners understand, interpret, and analyze what is heard, read, or viewed on a variety of topics.* At this level, students listen regularly to audio exercises. They listen to and respond to questions from their teacher and classmates on a daily basis. They also gain reading skills through reading dialogues, e-mails from Japanese students, and authentic materials such as menus, weather maps, and posters.

1.3 Presentational Communication. *Learners present information, concepts, and ideas to inform, explain, persuade, and narrate on a variety of topics using appropriate media and adapting to various audiences of listeners, readers, or viewers.* Students have several opportunities at this level to do presentations. They include singing songs, such as *Zoo-san,* presenting short speeches as part of Culture Notes activities, and making longer presentations using multimedia in Extend Your Learning activities.

II. Cultures
Interact with cultural competence and understanding of Japan

2.1 Relating Cultural Practices to Perspectives. *Learners use Japanese to investigate, explain, and reflect on the relationship between the practices and perspectives of Japanese culture.* Culture Notes cover a variety of topics that demonstrate Japanese patterns of behavior as well as how they are reflected in the language. For example, students are introduced to the concept of *uchi/soto* by different family member terms and are taught about the differences between the use of *ohayoo* versus *ohayoo gozaimasu.* In addition, students learn many expressions and gestures commonly used by the Japanese, and show how language and non-verbal actions communicate politeness. Students also are exposed to many Japanese activities, such as *karuta, gomoku narabe,* sumo, as well as songs and storytelling.

* Reprinted with permission from *World-Readiness Standards for Learning Languages* (2014), by the National Standards in Foreign Language Education Project.

2.2 Relating Cultural Products to Perspectives. *Learners use Japanese to investigate, explain, and reflect on the relationship between the products and perspectives of Japanese culture.* As students use this volume, they will learn to prepare rice balls and *mochi,* fold *origami,* practice using chopsticks, and play *jankenpon,* among other activities. Through these activities, students are expected to draw conclusions about the nature of these traditional arts and how they are representative of Japan. Activities in the Culture Notes also encourage a deeper understanding of Japanese cultural practices and products.

III. Connections

Connect with other disciplines and acquire information and diverse perspectives in order to use the language to function in academic and career-related situations

3.1 Making Connections. *Learners build, reinforce, and expand their knowledge of other disciplines while using Japanese to develop critical thinking and to solve problems creatively.* Japanese Culture Corners at the end of every other lesson encourage students to research topics of Japanese Culture associated with a variety of fields including geography, sociology, and economics. Special "Connect" activities in each lesson also encourage students to use their knowledge of Japanese to answer questions involving other career-based disciplines. In addition, students learn about cooking (*mochi* and *musubi*), music (songs), art (origami), and math (numbers and computations).

3.2 Acquiring Information and Diverse Perspectives. *Learners access and evaluate information and diverse perspectives that are available through Japanese and its culture.* At this level, students learn to recognize distinctive Japanese practices, such as their sensitivity to weather, climate and seasons, the frequent use of *aizuchi,* unique eating practices, ways of counting on one's hands, standards of beauty, use of proverbs, etc. Students are also made aware of many of the cultural distinctions through the cultural Extend Your Learning corner, for which they must acquire information about a number of diverse topics.

IV. Comparisons

Develop insight into the nature of language and culture in order to interact with cultural competence

4.1 Language Comparisons. *Learners use Japanese to investigate, explain, and reflect on the nature of language through comparison of the Japanese language and their own.* Language Notes teach students about differences between Japanese and their native language, and encourage them to make comparisons to their own language. For example, students will learn to differentiate between using *ohayoo gozaimasu* and *ohayoo,* and how they convey different levels of politeness not found in the English "Good morning." Students learn that counting in Japanese means learning different counters (classifiers), depending on the physical nature of the objects being counted. Finally, students are given numerous examples of loan words written in *katakana,* which students can compare to words from which they were derived in English and other languages.

4.2 Cultural Comparisons. *Learners use Japanese to investigate, explain, and reflect on the concept of culture through comparisons of Japanese culture and their own.* Students receive a good dose of comparative culture by engaging in the Japanese Culture and Extend Your Learning projects that follow every other lesson. The Culture Notes and activities also provide information about Japanese culture while encouraging students students to compare it with their own. For example, on the lessons about school, students learn about the different school calendar, the system of *senpai/koohai,* large class sizes, the role of homeroom, uniforms, and preparation for college entrance in Japan, and are encouraged to consider how each of these topics is perceived in their own culture. Other topics which offer ample points for comparison in the Culture Notes include lifestyles, holidays, foods, and sports.

V. Communities
Communicate and interact with cultural competence in order to participate in multilingual communities at home and around the world

5.1 School and Global Communities. *Learners use Japanese both within and beyond the classroom to interact and collaborate in their community and the globalized world.* At this level, students are able to share their learning and skills in Japanese through presentations of songs, skits, and stories if teachers provide such opportunities outside of the classroom. They may also use Japanese as they explain food preparation *(mochi* and *musubi)* or other activities (using chopsticks, origami, sumo, *gomoku narabe)* to their families.

5.2 Lifelong Learning. *Learners set goals and reflect on their progress in using Japanese for enjoyment, enrichment, and advancement.* In this volume, students engage in many activities that may lead to lifelong enjoyment and enrichment. They include games and crafts such as origami, making Japanese snacks, using chopsticks, paper sumo wrestling, *gomoku narabe,* and *karuta.* Students' use of the Internet to search for information about Japanese culture will also introduce avenues that they can employ to learn more about the language and culture of Japan. Can–Do Statements and self-assessments also encourage students to set goals and reflect on their progress throughout their life.

Common Core State Standards

The Reading, Writing, Speaking and Listening, and Language skills acquired and practiced every day in the Japanese language classroom align with the Common Core Anchor Standards for English Language Arts & Literacy in History/Social Studies, Science, and Technical Subjects. Additional activities and questions with the Common Core icon encourage students to read texts closely; to write to explain, to persuade, and to convey experience; and to understand the purpose behind communication. Students will write narratives portraying the meaning of Japanese proverbs, draw comparisons about practices, products, and perspectives in U.S. and Japanese culture, and closely read Culture Notes for details and main ideas.

21st Century Skills

Adventures in Japanese encourages students to develop 21st Century Skills and achieve technology and media literacy through activities and research. These skills are emphasized in activities with the 21st Century Skills icon, and in special activities at the end of each Japanese Culture Corner. Students will research Japanese culture online, prepare multimedia presentations, and learn to critically view a variety of media.

We hope the preceding information has been helpful in providing you, the teacher, with ways in which *Adventures in Japanese Volume 1* meets national language standards. The ultimate goal of the authors of this text, however, is one that supersedes meeting standards. It is our wish to nurture students who grow to love the language and culture of Japan and integrate it into their lives so they may eventually contribute to a more seamless relationship between our nations. We hope that with their appreciation for and understanding of language and culture, they will be better prepared to lead us into a more peaceful and harmonious world.

Acknowledgments

Adventures in Japanese was developed thanks to the efforts and contributions of countless people in the Punahou School community and beyond. We gratefully express our appreciation to all who contributed in any way, even if we may have failed to mention them below.

First and foremost, a warm thanks to all of our students who have contributed directly and indirectly to the development of the text. They have provided us with a purpose, motivated us, taught us, given us ideas and suggestions, and encouraged us in many ways.

We acknowledge Professor Emeritus Seiichi Makino of Princeton University, who has graciously written the foreword, conducted workshops for us, and offered us much support and encouragement throughout the project. We thank Professor Emeritus Masako Himeno of Tokyo University of Foreign Studies for her generous guidance over many portions of the text and for her valuable suggestions and support through the years. She has also graciously and painstakingly edited many portions of the new version of the text.

We express our gratitude to our illustrators, former Punahou student Michael Muronaka, former colleague Emiko Kaylor, and former student Mark Bailey. We also thank Shinji Nakatani for his more recent artistic contributions to our text and for the photos he took and edited in Japan. We also credit him for creating a menu for us. We are grateful fo Yusuke Fujisawa and his students of Tosajuku School, Masumi Takabayashi, Reiko Hatsuya, Christina Tamaru, Chihoko Tanefusa and Deai for their photo contributions. We thank Jennifer and Abraham Tokunaga of Hanabata Days Photography for their photo editing of many of our most recent photos. We appreciate the new illustrations and recording of *Omusubi Kororin* provided by Nayu Terasawa as well as her help in updating some of our text material. We acknowledge the assistance of students Amanda Nakanishi and Megan Ishii for the coloring of the illustrations in the text.

Our thanks are extended to present and former Japanese language colleagues at Punahou School who contributed to the writing of the text, to the creation of supplementary materials, and for suggestions for improving the text: Junko Ady, Jan Asato, Linda Fujikawa, Elaine Higuchi, Emiko Kaylor, Hiroko Kazama, Carin Lim, Emiko Lyovin, Naomi Okada, Carol Shimokawa, Michiko Sprester, and Misako Steverson. We also acknowledge Janice Murabayashi, a former Social Studies colleague, for writing the questions on Japanese culture and Kathy Boswell, a former English colleague, for naming our text. Our gratitude is also extended to Miyoko Kamikawa, who assisted with the translation and interpretation of the *karuta* cards. We thank Wes Peterson for generously sharing his technological expertise and support throughout the project.

We also thank former director Carol Loose, media design specialist Linda Rucci, Martha Lanzas, and other staff members at the Punahou Visual Production Center for their many years of assistance with the early compilation of the text.

We recognize Ms. Roko Takizawa and the Shobi Music College in Tokyo for the most recent production of the final editions of the audio recordings. Contributors to the audio recordings include Aruno Tahara, Mahiro Inouye, Sho Mizumoto, Rin Miyano, Mai Aoki, Mizuho Isaka, Miki Tominaga, Yukari Hino, Akane Yamagishi, Keisuke Iwamura, Fumiaki Takano, Takumi Takamatsu, Shunya Nagano, and Koichi Makishima. We acknowledge Harry Kubo for his contributions as the English speaker on the audio recordings. In particular, we express our gratitude to those who have supported in audio recordings of previous editions. We express our gratitude to David and Robin Furuya, Misa Uyehara and students Ashley Imai, Masa Sakamoto, Reo Nagai, Arissa Cheng and our Punahou colleague Junko Ady and her husband Jeff Ady. We extend our thanks to Mr. Takuro Ichikawa for the use of the recording of his musical presentation.

We are grateful to Akemi and Shiyo Sakamoto, who have assisted us in many ways, including arranging for members of the Yuhigaoka High School Music Department to assist us with music recordings and providing us updates on new aspects of Japanese language and culture.

We appreciate the work of members of the Yuhigaoka Music Department for sharing their musical talents and technical expertise. They include Nobuko Yamamoto, Fumio Mikami, Shinichi Katayose, Shinichi Tanihiro, and many student volunteers. We thank Ryne Kimura for his recording of the *"Hitotsu, Futatsu…"* Song.

 For helping to create multi-media activities for this and previous editions, we thank Jan Asato and former students Brandon Yoshimoto and Kevin Takasaki, Aaron Kobayashi, Ashley Tomita, Grant Kondo, Serine Tsuda, Reona Ono, David Woo, Justin Pyun, Mark Kuioka, Glenn Shigetomi, Kazuki Sakamoto, Brandon Lam, and Jeff Sult. We extend our deepest gratitude to them as well as to Junko Ady, Shioko Yonezawa, Hiroaki Uchida, and A1 Sound Effects for their assistance.

We thank Yukie Maeda for allowing us the use of her business card for our *meishi* lesson, and to Keiko Ogawa for the use of her family photo. We are grateful to the many students and friends who served as models for photos in the newest edition of the textbook.

We are grateful to all of the administrators at Punahou School for their support of our textbook efforts through the years. Finally, we express our appreciation to our families for their unwavering support of our efforts in every aspect of the development of *Adventures in Japanese.*

Hiromi Peterson and Naomi Hirano-Omizo

- **New Full-color Design with Up-to-date Photos and Content**
  - The new full-color design of *Adventures in Japanese* 4th Edition is easier to read and easier to navigate.
  - More photos bring Japanese culture to life.
  - Updated vocabulary reflects changes in technology and in Japanese society.

- **More Practice**
  - New grammar exercises have been added for each grammar point.
  - New authentic materials provide students with real–world reading practice.

- **Improved Pacing**
  - Now with 12 lessons instead of 16, pacing and instructional flow have been streamlined, making *Adventures in Japanese* easier to complete in one year.
  - New introductory lesson allows teachers to introduce *hiragana, katakana, kanji,* and pronunciation at whatever time best suits their class.

- **Clear Expectations**
  - Can Do statements and self-assessment checklists have been added to each lesson so objectives and expectations are clearly defined. Review Lessons are available for download on the companion website at **cheng-tsui.com/adventuresinjapanese.**

More Kanji
Additional instruction of over 60 *kanji* provides students with a stronger foundation for continued study and AP® exam preparation.

New Student Audio
New audio recordings for Vocabulary, Language in Context, Grammar models, review questions, audio activities, and Culture Notes are available for download from the companion website at **cheng-tsui.com/adventuresinjapanese.**

New Common Core Activities
Additional activities aligned with the Common Core State Standards (CCSS) for English and Language Arts are included throughout the textbook. Found with the Culture Notes, these activities encourage students to read critically and write narrative, informational, and persuasive responses.

21st Century Skills Activities
Students extend their learning about cultural topics by using technology to do research, create presentations, and improve their language skills and cultural competence. Students will also practice critical reading and writing skills aligned with the CCSS.

Connect activities
Students use Japanese to practice skills in other career-based disciplines, including math, statistics, science, and social studies.

Recycling
Recycling of key grammar structures and vocabulary is now clearly indicated.

Introduction
Japanese Writing Systems and Pronunciation

Three Japanese Writing Systems

Until Japan came in contact with China, Japanese was a spoken language only with no writing system of its own. The Japanese adopted Chinese characters to express their language in writing. This Chinese form of writing is called *kanji*, which literally means "Chinese characters." *Kanji* is now one of three systems the Japanese use to write their language. *Hiragana* and *katakana* are the two other systems. The latter two are phonetic systems (meaning they are based on sound), whereas *kanji* is a semantic system (meaning it is based largely on meaning).

Writing Japanese Sentences

Kanji		Hiragana		Katakana
私は	たいてい	学校へ	バスで	来ます。
Watashi wa	*taitei*	*gakkoo e*	*basu de*	*kimasu.*

Translation: I generally come to school by bus.

Modern Japanese sentences are made up of a combination of *kanji*, *hiragana* and *katakana*.

- *Kanji* is usually used to write words which carry important meaning like nouns, verbs, adjectives, and some adverbs.
- *Hiragana* is used to write parts of the sentence that do not convey the main idea of the sentence, such as the conjugated portions of verbs, adjectives, or nouns (tenses, negations, etc.); particles; interjections; most adverbs; and other parts of sentences.
- *Katakana* is now used mainly to write words of foreign origin, or names of foreigners.

Origins of Japanese Writing

Both *hiragana* and *katakana* are derived from *kanji*. For example, to express the "ka" sound, the Japanese took the *kanji* 加 (also pronounced "ka" in Chinese), and modified it into a more stylized form, か, which is the *hiragana* symbol "ka." *Katakana* also grew out of *kanji*, but it is a representation of a portion of a *kanji*. For example, for the same "ka" sound, カ was taken from the left portion of the *kanji* 加 and became the *katakana* カ.

Kanji can be pronounced in several different ways depending on the context. Chinese pronunciations are called *on* readings, and native Japanese pronunciations are called *kun* readings. For example, the *kun* reading of the *kanji* 山 (mountain) is *yama*, and its *on* readings are *san* and *zan*.

Origin of Hiragana

Hiragana are Japanese phonetic characters. There are 46 basic characters. *Hiragana* strokes are not straight but slightly curved, because *hiragana* was created by the Japanese during the Heian period (794 – 1192) from the cursive style of *kanji* (Chinese characters).

Writing Hiragana

It is important to follow the correct stroke order so you can write *hiragana* faster and in better form. The sequence of strokes are shown by the numbers on the page at right. Each number is the beginning of the stroke. Each stroke generally starts from left to right and/or from top to bottom. There are three ways to finish a stroke:

a blunt stop ー   a hook ㇁   a tail し

The way each stroke ends is clear when *hiragana* is written with a brush, but it is not as obvious when written with a pen or a pencil. There are also several printing fonts, which differ slightly in appearance. The following charts are all read top-to-bottom starting from the rightmost column.

W	R	Y	M	H	N	T	S	K	
ん n	わ wa	ら ra	や ya	ま ma	は ha	な na	た ta	さ sa	か ka	あ a	← / a / line
		り ri		み mi	ひ hi	に ni	ち chi	し shi	き ki	い i	← / i / line
		る ru	ゆ yu	む mu	ふ hu/fu	ぬ nu	つ tsu	す su	く ku	う u	← / u / line
		れ re		め me	へ he	ね ne	て te	せ se	け ke	え e	← / e / line
	を o	ろ ro	よ yo	も mo	ほ ho	の no	と to	そ so	こ ko	お o	← / o / line

Particle

P	B	J	G
ぴゃ pya	びゃ bya	じゃ ja	ぎゃ gya
ぴゅ pyu	びゅ byu	じゅ ju	ぎゅ gyu
ぴょ pyo	びょ byo	じょ jo	ぎょ gyo

R	M	H	N	T/C	S	K	
りゃ rya	みゃ mya	ひゃ hya	にゃ nya	ちゃ cha	しゃ sha	きゃ kya	YA
りゅ ryu	みゅ myu	ひゅ hyu	にゅ nyu	ちゅ chu	しゅ shu	きゅ kyu	YU
りょ ryo	みょ myo	ひょ hyo	にょ nyo	ちょ cho	しょ sho	きょ kyo	YO

Hiragana Stroke Order

Begin writing each stroke starting at the location of the numbers.

	W	R	Y	M	H	N	T	S	K	
ん N	わ	ら	や	ま	は	な	た	さ	か	あ A
		り		み	ひ	に	ち	し	き	い I
		る	ゆ	む	ふ	ぬ	つ	す	く	う U
		れ		め	へ	ね	て	せ	け	え E
	を O (Particle)	ろ	よ	も	ほ	の	と	そ	こ	お O

Japanese Writing Format

Japanese was originally written vertically on a page starting from right to left. Many Japanese books are still printed in this way. Therefore the front cover of a Japanese book opens from the opposite side of a Western book. Recently, Japanese is sometimes written horizontally as is English and books written this way open the same as Western books. Japanese writing paper is often in "blocks" instead of "rules" or "lines" like in English. Each character takes up one block.

1. Vertically: Start from the right-hand column and read down, then return to the top of the next column on the left.

2↓	1↓
ご	あ
ざ	り
い	が
ま	と
す	う

2. Horizontally: Read across from left to right, as in reading English.

1→	あ	り	が	と	う
2→	ご	ざ	い	ま	す

Japanese Punctuation

1. まる *maru*　　　　　　。　　Period: It is used always at the end of a sentence.

2. てん *ten*　　　　　　、　　Comma: Unlike English, there are no definite rules for using commas. Japanese people use commas where they normally pause in speaking.

3. かぎかっこ *kagikakko*　「」　Quotation marks

4. There is no question mark in Japanese.

5. Each punctuation mark occupies its own block.

Position of punctuation.

A. Horizonally

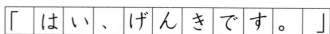

B. Vertically

「
は
い
、
げ
ん
き
で
す
。
」

Origin of Katakana

Katakana is a phonetic alphabet. Each *katakana* character was made by simplifying or taking a portion of a *kanji* which represented the corresponding sound. For example, the *katakana* カ *ka* was taken from the *kanji* 加.

What is Katakana used for?

Katakana is now used mainly to write words of foreign origin or names of foreigners. It is also sometimes used as a device to call attention to certain words (i.e., in advertising, announcements, etc.) and to write onomatopoetic expressions.

Difficulty of Katakana

Katakana looks easy to foreigners, but *katakana* may be harder to learn than *hiragana* and *kanji*. *Katakana* words are created from the spelling or the pronunciation of foreign words. The way a Japanese person perceives foreign words is often different from the way a native speaker hears them. There are some foreign sounds which do not exist in the Japanese language, i.e., "th," "f," "v," "r / l," "t," etc. Similar sounds from the native Japanese sound system had to be substituted for these sounds. For example, the English "v" sound often becomes a "b" sound in Japanese.

	W	R	Y	M	H	N	T	S	K		
ン n	ワ	ラ	ヤ	マ	ハ	ナ	タ	サ	カ	ア	A
		リ		ミ	ヒ	ニ	チ chi	シ shi	キ	イ	I
		ル	ユ	ム	フ	ヌ	ツ tsu	ス	ク	ウ	U
		レ		メ	ヘ	ネ	テ	セ	ケ	エ	E
	ヲ o	ロ	ヨ	モ	ホ	ノ	ト	ソ	コ	オ	O

(Particle)

P	B
パ	バ
ピ	ビ
プ	ブ
ペ	ベ
ポ	ボ

D	Z	G	
ダ	ザ	ガ	A
ヂ ji	ジ ji	ギ	I
ヅ zu	ズ zu	グ	U
デ	ゼ	ゲ	E
ド	ゾ	ゴ	O

P	B
ピャ	ビャ
ピュ	ビュ
ピョ	ビョ

J	G	
ジャ	ギャ	YA
ジュ	ギュ	YU
ジョ	ギョ	YO

R	M	H	N	C	S	K	
リャ	ミャ	ヒャ	ニャ	チャ	シャ	キャ	YA
リュ	ミュ	ヒュ	ニュ	チュ	シュ	キュ	YU
リョ	ミョ	ヒョ	ニョ	チョ	ショ	キョ	YO

Additional Katakana Combinations For Foreign Words

F	D	T	TS	CH	J	SH	TH	GW	KW	V	W	Y	
fa ファ			tsa ツァ				tha ザァ	gwa グァ	kwa クァ	va ヴァ			A ア
fi フィ	di ディ	ti ティ								vi ヴィ	wi ウィ		I イ
	dyu デュ									vu ヴュ			U ユ
fe フェ			tse ツェ	che チェ	je ジェ	she シェ	the ゼェ			ve ヴェ	we ウェ	ye イェ	E エ
fo フォ			tso ツォ				tho ゾォ		kwo クォ	vo ヴォ	wo ウォ		O オ

Writing long vowel sounds in katakana

Write a | following the character you are lengthening if you are writing vertically, or ー following the lengthened character if you are writing horizontally.

Example: チ and チーズ (cheese)

チ
ー
ズ

Katakana Stroke Order

N	W	R	Y	M	H	N	T	S	K		
ン N	ワ	ラ	ヤ	マ	ハ	ナ	タ	サ	カ	ア	A
		リ		ミ	ヒ	ニ	チ	シ	キ	イ	I
		ル	ユ	ム	フ	ヌ	ツ	ス	ク	ウ	U
		レ		メ	ヘ	ネ	テ	セ	ケ	エ	E
	ヲ O (Particle)	ロ	ヨ	モ	ホ	ノ	ト	ソ	コ	オ	O

What is Kanji?

The word *Kanji* means "Chinese Characters." *Kanji* are Chinese characters that are used in Japanese. They are an essential component of the Japanese written language. Most *kanji* have several different pronunciations. Those pronunciations are called readings. They draw from both the original Chinese (*on* readings) and the native Japanese vocabulary (*kun* readings). To master the use of *kanji* you need to learn to write and recognize characters, as well as learn when each reading is used. Although it can appear complicated at first, *kanji* is an essential and important part of the Japanese language.

What Kanji will I learn?

By the time you finish the complete *Adventures in Japanese* series, you will have learned all of the 410 *kanji* you need to succeed on the AP® Japanese Language and Culture Exam. In Volume 1 of *Adventures in Japanese,* you will learn to read and write 60 basic *kanji*. These *kanji* have been selected and arranged to build as you learn. First you will focus on simple, commonly used characters. As your Japanese improves, you'll learn more complex *kanji*. At this early level, you will learn several vocabulary words in *hiragana* that are normally written in *kanji*. In higher levels, you will learn many new *kanji* used in vocabulary you have previously learned.

How will I learn Kanji?

Kanji will be introduced starting in Lesson 3. Six new characters will be introduced in each lesson of the Textbook. In the *Kanji* section of the *Adventures in Japanese* Workbook, you will practice reading and writing the characters you've learned.

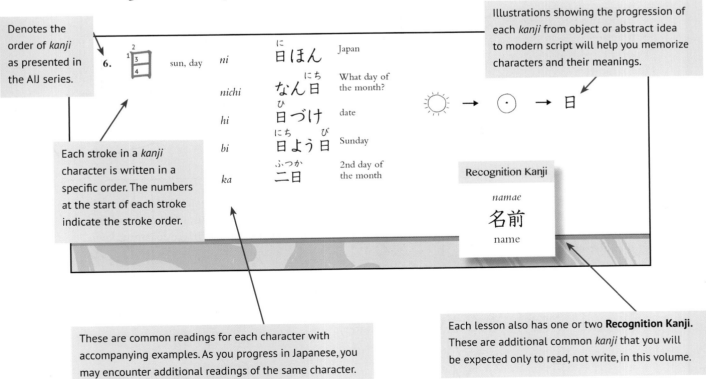

Denotes the order of *kanji* as presented in the AIJ series.

Illustrations showing the progression of each *kanji* from object or abstract idea to modern script will help you memorize characters and their meanings.

Each stroke in a *kanji* character is written in a specific order. The numbers at the start of each stroke indicate the stroke order.

Recognition Kanji

namae
名前
name

These are common readings for each character with accompanying examples. As you progress in Japanese, you may encounter additional readings of the same character.

Each lesson also has one or two **Recognition Kanji.** These are additional common *kanji* that you will be expected only to read, not write, in this volume.

When will I learn Kanji?

Some *kanji* will appear in gray below *hiragana* in vocabulary sections, including Lessons 1 and 2. However, you will not be expected to read or write any characters until Lesson 3, when all 60 *kanji* in Volume 1 will begin to appear in dialogues. Whenever a *kanji* appears, it will have *hiragana* readings over it to help you learn the character. Once the *kanji* has been formally introduced in a lesson, the readings for that *kanji* will disappear.

Once it has been formally introduced, the character will begin to appear in grammar examples and activities in subsequent lessons. Starting in Lesson 6, characters will appear in grammar examples and activities in the same lesson where they are introduced. This will provide more practice in context. Characters that will be learned in that lesson will appear in black text in the Vocabulary section, instead of gray.

Types of Kanji

English Term	Japanese Term	Explanation	Examples
Pictographs	象形文字 *Shookeimoji*	Stylized representations of actual objects	山 *yama* (mountain) 木 *ki* (tree) 月 *tsuki* (moon)
Ideographs	指示文字 *Shijimoji*	Representations of abstract concepts and ideas	一 *ichi* (one) 上 *ue* (up) 中 *naka* (inside, center)
Compound Ideographs	会意文字 *Kaiimoji*	Combinations of two simpler characters that together represent a new meaning	林 *hayashi* (forest) 明 *akarui* (bright)
Compound Semantic-Phonetic Ideographs	形声文字 *Keiseimoji*	Combinations of two or more simpler characters (called radicals), one of which represents the sound of the character, and the other the meaning. 80% of *kanji* belong to this type.	時 *toki* (time or hour) Composed of 日, indicating meaning associated with time/day and 寺, indicating that one of the readings is *ji* 読む *yomu* (to read)

Common Radical Types (部首 bushu) and Examples

Kanji is often made up of multiple parts derived from simpler *kanji*. These parts are called radicals, and can represent a semantic (based on meaning) or phonetic (based on sound) element of a character. Knowing the most common radicals and where they appear in a character can make learning *kanji* significantly easier.

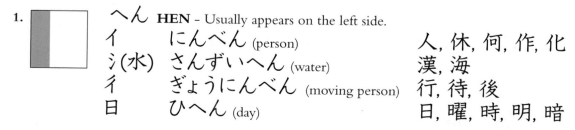

1.   へん **HEN** – Usually appears on the left side.
    イ　にんべん (person)　　　　　　　人, 休, 何, 作, 化
    氵(水) さんずいへん (water)　　　　　漢, 海
    彳　ぎょうにんべん (moving person)　行, 待, 後
    日　ひへん (day)　　　　　　　　　日, 曜, 時, 明, 暗

女	おんなへん (female)	女, 好, 姉, 妹, 始
木	きへん (tree)	木, 校, 林
言	ごんべん (speech)	言, 語, 話, 読

2. つくり **TSUKURI** – Appears on the right side.

| 斤 | おのづくり (ox) | 新, 所 |

3. かんむり **KANMURI** – Appears at the top.

宀	うかんむり (u-crown)	家, 字, 安, 室
艹	くさかんむり (grass)	花, 英, 草
雨	あめかんむり (rain)	雨, 電, 雪
亠	なべぶた (cover)	高, 文

4. あし **ASHI** – Appears at the lower half of the *kanji*.

| 心 | こころ (heart) | 心, 思 |
| 儿 | ひとあし (legs) | 先, 見, 兄, 元 |

5. かまえ **KAMAE** – Surrounds the *kanji*.

門	もんがまえ (gate)	門, 間, 聞
囗	くにがまえ (country)	国, 四
气	きがまえ (steam)	気
匚	はこがまえ (box)	区, 医

6. にょう **NYOO** – Starts at the left and flows under to the right.

| 辶 | しんにょう (road) | 近, 週 |

7. たれ **TARE** – Appears at the top and the left of the *kanji*.

| 疒 | やまいだれ (sickness) | 病 |

Japanese Pronunciation

🔊

A. Five Japanese Vowels

/a/ あ is pronounced like *a* in f<u>a</u>ther.　　　　"ah"
/i/ い is pronounced like *i* in mach<u>i</u>ne.　　　"ee"
/u/ う is pronounced like *ue* in S<u>ue</u>.　　　　"oo"
/e/ え is pronounced like *e* in l<u>e</u>dge.　　　"eh"
/o/ お is pronounced like *o* in <u>o</u>bey.　　　"oh"

B. 46 Basic Japanese Syllables

Begin from the top of the right-hand column and read down, then go to the top of the next column on the left.

ん	わ	ら	や	ま	は	な	た	さ	か	あ	
n	wa	ra	ya	ma	ha	na	ta	sa	ka	a	← / a / line
		り		み	ひ	に	ち	し	き	い	
		ri		mi	hi	ni	chi	shi	ki	i	← / i / line
		る	ゆ	む	ふ	ぬ	つ	す	く	う	
		ru	yu	mu	hu	nu	tsu	su	ku	u	← / u / line
		れ		め	へ	ね	て	せ	け	え	
		re		me	he	ne	te	se	ke	e	← / e / line
	を	ろ	よ	も	ほ	の	と	そ	こ	お	
	o	ro	yo	mo	ho	no	to	so	ko	o	← / o / line

(Particle)

C. Other Syllables

ぱ pa	ば ba
ぴ pi	び bi
ぷ pu	ぶ bu
ぺ pe	べ be
ぽ po	ぼ bo

だ da	ざ za	が ga
ぢ ji	じ ji	ぎ gi
づ zu	ず zu	ぐ gu
で de	ぜ ze	げ ge
ど do	ぞ zo	ご go

ぴゃ pya	びゃ bya	じゃ ja	ぎゃ gya	りゃ rya	みゃ mya	ひゃ hya	にゃ nya	ちゃ cha	しゃ sha	きゃ kya
ぴゅ pyu	びゅ byu	じゅ ju	ぎゅ gyu	りゅ ryu	みゅ myu	ひゅ hyu	にゅ nyu	ちゅ chu	しゅ shu	きゅ kyu
ぴょ pyo	びょ byo	じょ jo	ぎょ gyo	りょ ryo	みょ myo	ひょ hyo	にょ nyo	ちょ cho	しょ sho	きょ kyo

D. Equal Stress on Each Syllable

Unlike English, emphasis on syllables tends to be uniform in Japanese. No one syllable should be accented more heavily than any of the other syllables in the word.

1. HI-RO-SHI-MA

Hiroshima

ひろしま

2. O-KI-NA-WA

Okinawa

おきなわ

3. O-SU-SHI

sushi

おすし

4. SA-SHI-MI

raw fish

さしみ

E. Long Vowels

If the same vowel appears twice in succession, it is pronounced as a prolonged sound. It is important to pronounce a long vowel carefully since a long vowel may change a word's meaning.

1a. <u>IE</u> [I–E]
house
いえ

1b. <u>IIE</u> [I–I–E]
no
いいえ

2a. <u>E</u> [E]
picture
え

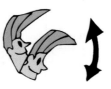

2b. <u>EE</u> [E-E]
yes
ええ

3a. OJ<u>I</u>SAN
[O–JI–SA–N]
uncle
おじさん

3b. OJ<u>II</u>SAN
[O–JI–I–SA–N]
grandfather
おじいさん

4a. OB<u>A</u>SAN
[O–BA–SA–N]
aunt
おばさん

4b. OB<u>AA</u>SAN
[O–BA–A–SA–N]
grandmother
おばあさん

5a. SHU<u>J</u>IN
[SHU–JI–N]
husband
しゅじん

5b. SHU<u>U</u>JIN
[SHU–U–JI–N]
prisoner
しゅうじん

F. /L/ and /R/ Sounds

Japanese /ra/, /ri/, /ru/, /re/, /ro/ sounds are produced so that the initial "r" sounds somewhat like a combination of the English "l" and "r" sounds. Japanese people have difficulty distinguishing English "l" and "r" sounds.

1. <u>R</u>AJIO
radio
ラジオ

2. <u>R</u>EPOOTO
report
レポート

3. <u>R</u>ESUTO<u>R</u>AN
restaurant
レストラン

G. /N/ Sound

This is a nasal sound. It does not occur at the beginning of words, but is found within or at the end of words. It is pronounced by exhaling through the nose. When the /N/ sound comes before the following sounds, it becomes /M/: B, M, P.

1. HO<u>N</u>
book
ほん

2. MIKA<u>N</u>
orange
みかん

3. E<u>N</u>PITSU
pencil
えんぴつ

4. PA<u>N</u>
bread
パン

5. SHI<u>N</u>BU<u>N</u>
newspaper
しんぶん

6. ZUBO<u>N</u>
trousers
ズボン

H. /TSU/ Sound

This is pronounced like "–ts" at the end of the word "cats." It is then lengthened with the /U/ sound. The /TSU/ sound may appear at any position in a word.

1. <u>TSU</u>KI
moon
つき

2. MA<u>TSU</u>
pine tree
まつ

3. KU<u>TSU</u>
shoes
くつ

4. <u>TSU</u>KUE
desk
つくえ

5. MA<u>TSU</u>RI
festival
まつり

6. <u>TSU</u>RI
fishing
つり

I. /FU/ Sound

The English "f" is pronounced by blowing through the upper teeth resting on the lower lip. When pronouncing the Japanese /f/, however, there is no contact between the lip and teeth as one blows out. The Japanese /f/ sounds like a breathy "wh" sound.

1. FUNE
ship
ふね

2. FUJISAN
Mt. Fuji
ふじさん

3. FUE
flute
ふえ

4. TOOFU
tofu
とうふ

5. NAIFU
knife
ナイフ

6. FUYU
winter
ふゆ

J. Double Consonants /っ/

Double consonants such as "kk," "ss," "tt" or "pp" are pronounced with a slight pause between the first and second consonant sounds, like between the words "bat boy" or "pot pie" in English.

1. KOPPU
cup
コップ

2. BATTO
bat
バット

3. ZASSHI
magazines
ざっし

4. GAKKOO
school
がっこう

5. ISSHO
together
いっしょ

6. IPPAI
full
いっぱい

K. Devoiced Vowels

Japanese vowels are usually voiced, but when the vowels /i/ or /u/ occur between two devoiced consonants (/h/, /k/, /p/, /s/, /t/), the vowel is often not pronounced. The final /u/ in *desu* and *masu* is not commonly pronounced.

1. H_ITO

person

ひと

2. K_USURI

medicine

くすり

3. S_USHI

sushi

すし

4. GAK_USEI DES_U.

He is a student.

がくせいです。

5. IKIMAS_U.

I will go.

いきます。

6. OHAYOO GOZAIMAS_U.

Good morning.

おはよう ございます。

L. Pitch

Pitch is important in Japanese pronunciation, as certain syllables in a word must be pronounced with a high or low pitch. The meaning of a word may differ depending on the pitch. See the examples below.

1a. HASHI

bridge

はし　橋

1b. HASHI

chopsticks

はし　箸

2a. HEN

weird

へん　変

2b. HEN

area

へん　辺

3a. $\overline{\text{KA}}$MI
God

かみ　神

3b. KA$\overline{\text{MI}}$
paper

かみ　紙

4a. $\overline{\text{AME}}$
rain

あめ　雨

4b. $\overline{\text{AME}}$
candy

あめ　飴

5a. $\overline{\text{IP}}$PAI
one cupful

いっぱい

5b. IP$\overline{\text{PAI}}$
full

いっぱい

M. Intonation

Intonation is relatively flat in Japanese. For statements, the sentence ending is usually even. Questions without か *ka* end in a rising intonation. (With a か *ka,* the intonation is not raised.)

1a. WAKARIMASU. ⇩

I understand.
わかります。

1b. WAKARIMASU? ⇧

Do you understand?
わかります？

2a. WATASHI. ⇩

Me.
わたし。

2b. WATASHI? ⇧

Me?
わたし？

✓ Can Do!
In this lesson you will learn to

- introduce yourself
- recognize the Japanese sound system
- greet others at different times of the day
- start and end class using Japanese
- count to 100 and give phone numbers
- express agreement and disagreement
- talk about the weather

Online Resources

cheng-tsui.com/
adventuresinjapanese

- Audio
- Vocabulary Lists
- Vocabulary Flashcards
- *Kana* Flashcards
- Activity Worksheets

かいわ　Dialogue

🔊 **READ/LISTEN** What is the girl's name? How do you greet someone in Japanese?

たんご　Vocabulary

1. はじめまして。
Hajimemashite.
How do you do?/
Nice to meet you.

2. わたし
watashi
I (used less formally by anyone)

3. ぼく
boku
I (used informally by males)

---

4. は　　　　　　　　　*wa*　　　　　　[particle marking the topic of the sentence]

5. です　　　　　　　　*desu*　　　　　am, is, are

6. どうぞ　よろしく。　*Doozo yoroshiku.*　Nice to meet you./
It's a pleasure. (*Doozo* means "please."
Yoroshiku means "Please do me a favor.")

ついか　たんご　Additional Vocabulary

1. わたくし　　　　　　*watakushi*　　　I (used formally by anyone)

よみましょう　Language in Context

🔊 **READ/LISTEN/SPEAK** Choose the words you should use to refer to yourself in Japanese.

わたし

I (used less formally by anyone)

ぼく

I (used informally by males)

わたくし

I (used formally by anyone)

The Japanese language has words used only by males and words used only by females. わたし *watashi* is used by anyone, but ぼく *boku* is used only by males. If a female uses ぼく *boku*, she is considered "tomboyish."

ぶんぽう　Grammar

A　Basic Sentences: A is B.

Noun 1 は　　　　　**Noun 2 です。**　　**Noun 1 = Noun 2.**

Noun 1 *wa*　　　　　**Noun 2 *desu*.**

This pattern is used when one equates the first noun to the second.

 MODELS

1. わたしは　　やまもとです。　　　　I am Yamamoto.
   Watashi wa Yamamoto desu.

   (わたし *watashi* may be used by anyone.)

2. ぼくは　　たなか　ケンです。　　　I am Ken Tanaka.
   Boku wa Tanaka Ken desu.

   (ぼく *boku* is used by males only.)

3.★ わたくしは　　スミスです。　　　I am Smith.
   Watakushi wa Sumisu desu.

   (わたくし *watakushi* may be used by anyone in formal situations.)

READ/WRITE The following sentences are scrambled. Write them in the correct order.

1. は　　エミ　　です　　わたし
   wa　　*Emi*　　*desu*　　*watashi*

2. ぼく　　です　　は　　あきお
   boku　　*desu*　　*wa*　　*Akio*

3. です　　は　　わたし　　あおい
   desu　　*wa*　　*watashi*　　*Aoi*

ぶんかノート　Culture Notes

A. How to Bow

When Japanese people greet one another, it is common practice to bow. The Japanese express the degree of respect they have for others by the depth of the bow and its frequency. Hugging and kissing, even among close family and friends, are not commonly seen in Japan. When the Japanese greet foreigners, they may shake hands. When the other person bows, you should also bow. Not acknowledging the other person is considered rude.

When bowing, pay attention that your:

a. Eyes move downward with the bow. Do not attempt to make eye contact during a bow.

b. Feet are positioned together, facing toward the person you are greeting.

c. Hands are placed relaxed but straight alongside your body if you are a male. Females lightly cross their hands at their fingertips in front of their bodies while bowing.

d. Body is not slouched or turned away from the other person.

B. Family Names and Given Names

In Japanese, family names precede given names, which is the opposite from English. This is because in Japan and much of Asia, the family is traditionally considered more important than the individual. In Japan, students are called by their family names at school. If you visit Japan, you should use given names among close friends, and family names in formal situations.

C. Meishi

Japanese business people exchange めいし *meishi* (business cards) when they introduce themselves. めいし *meishi* include information such as one's name, company name, job title, address, telephone number, fax number, e-mail address, etc.

The Japanese handle the めいし *meishi* with respect. It is presented with two hands and given so it faces the other person directly. Upon receiving one, the receiver reads the information on it carefully, and then puts it in a めいしいれ *meishi-ire*, a special case made for holding めいし *meishi*. If the receiver is sitting at a desk or table, the めいし *meishi* may be placed in front of the receiver so he may refer to it in conversation. めいし *meishi* are never placed in back pockets or any other location that would show disrespect to the other person.

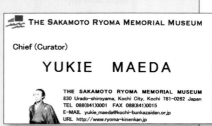

Design your own *meishi*. Japanese high school students don't normally have *meishi*, but they are a great way to introduce yourself to your classmates. Fill out one side in English, and write your name in *hiragana/katakana* (or a Japanese name) on the other side. Make sure you write your name in the correct order! You can add information about your school, class, and contact information. Be creative with your design!

Language Note

Formal Speech and Informal Speech

Certain words in the Japanese language are used in formal situations and others in informal situations. わたくし *watakushi* is used formally in business situations or in public speaking. わたし *watashi* and ぼく *boku* are used in less formal daily situations.

アクティビティー Communicative Activities

Class Work

SPEAK/LISTEN Introduce yourself to your classmates in Japanese. Be sure to bow properly.

たんご Vocabulary

1. おはよう。

Ohayoo.

Good morning.
(Informal)

2. おはよう
ございます。

Ohayoo gozaimasu.

Good morning.
(Formal)

3. こんにちは。

Konnichi wa.

Hello. Hi.

4. さようなら。

Sayoonara.

Good-bye.

5. やまだせんせい

Yamada-sensei

Mr./Mrs./Ms./Dr. Yamada

6. まりさん

Mari-san

Mari

7. はい。

Hai.

Yes.

Hai may be used in response to roll call. It indicates that one is present.

ついか たんご Additional Vocabulary

1. こんばんは。

Konban wa.

Good evening.

Used from dusk through the night. It literally means "tonight is."

2. じゃあね。

Jaa ne.

See you. (Informal)

Informal expression used among friends upon parting. It originally meant "and then."

3. ジョンくん

Jon-kun

Jon. John.

-kun is usually attached to boys' names. It is used instead of *-san* by people of higher status to refer to or address males of lower status.

🔊 **READ/SPEAK** Practice pronouncing the difference between short and long vowel sounds at the beginning and end of *ohayoo*.

おはよう。

Used among friends and family until late morning.
It originally meant "it is early."

おはよう
ございます。

Used formally until late morning. *Gozaimasu*
adds politeness.

READ/SPEAK Should Ken call himself Ken–san in Japanese? Practice using these honorifics with your classmates.

ふじたせんせい。

Sensei is a suffix attached to names of teachers, doctors, and statesmen to show respect. *Sensei* can also be used alone when addressing a person or as a word which means "teacher" or "mentor."

さとうさん。

–san is a suffix attached to names. It is not attached to one's own name or one's own family members' names. *–san* may be used for both males and females. It is attached to both given and family names.

ぶんかノート　Culture Notes

Polite Words

In Japanese there are many words to show politeness and respect for another person. For instance, in the morning you greet your friends with おはよう *ohayoo*, but should greet your teacher with おはようございます *ohayoo gozaimasu*. If you greet your teacher with おはよう *ohayoo*, you show a lack of respect toward your teacher.

せんせい *sensei* itself is a word used to refer to teachers and doctors. By calling your teacher せんせい *sensei*, you show respect to your teacher. When using せんせい *sensei* with a teacher's name, せんせい *sensei* should follow, not precede, the teacher's name, i.e., さいとうせんせい *Saitoo sensei*. Saying "*Sensei Saitoo*" sounds as strange as saying "Smith Ms." in English.

Using ～さん *-san* after a person's first name or last name shows respect. You should never use さん *san* after your own name. When talking about your family members to outsiders, do not use さん *san* after your family members' names.

 Compare Japanese with English or other languages you speak. How do these languages show politeness and respect? What language do you think is more formal? Why?

How would you greet your teacher in Japanese? Your classmates? Your brother or sister? Explain your answers with a classmate and compare your reasoning.

アクティビティー　Communicative Activities

Pair Work

A. SPEAK/LISTEN Say how you would address and greet your teacher:

1. in the morning
2. in the afternoon
3. at night
4. upon leaving

B. SPEAK/LISTEN Say how you would address and greet your friend:

1. in the morning
2. in the afternoon
3. at night
4. upon leaving

Class Work

C. SPEAK/LISTEN Take attendance by calling your classmates' names. Your classmates should respond by saying はい *hai* when their names are called.

たんご　Vocabulary

1. はじめましょう。

Hajimemashoo.

Let's begin.

2. きりつ。*

*Kiritsu.**

Stand.*

3. れい。*

*Rei.**

Bow.*

4. ちゃくせき。*

*Chakuseki.**

Sit.*

5. ～は　（お）やすみ
です。

~ wa (o)yasumi desu.

~ is absent.

6. ～は　ちこく
です。

~ wa chikoku desu.

~ is tardy.

Refers to persons being late to class,
meetings, etc.

7. はやく。

Hayaku.

Hurry!

8. おわりましょう。

Owarimashoo.

Let's finish.

9. これ

kore

this one

* Used at ceremonies or formal situations

10. なに／なん　　*nani / nan*　　what?

Nan is used when the following word is a counter, as in "What page?" *Nan* is also used when the following word begins with a /t/, /d/, or /n/ sound. Otherwise, when it is simply a question word, not involving counting, it is pronounced *nani*.

11. か　　*ka*　?

[Sentence-ending particle indicating a question.]

ついか　たんご　Additional Vocabulary

1. すみません。　おそく　なりました。

Sumimasen. Osoku narimashita.

I am sorry to be late. (Literally: I am sorry. I have become late.)

よみましょう　Language in Context

🔊 **READ/LISTEN/SPEAK** When you are absent, should you say you are "*Oyasumi desu?*" or "*Yasumi desu?*" Say who is absent from class today.

はじめましょう。

Let's begin.

けいこさんは　おやすみです。

The use of お *o* adds politeness. お *o* is not used when referring to your own absence.

これ

Refers to something near the speaker. Used only for things, not for people.

ぶんぽう　Grammar

A Omitting Subjects or Topics

Obvious subjects or topics are omitted in Japanese.

Unlike English sentences which require a subject (i.e., he, she, they, it, we, I, etc.), in Japanese, subjects are frequently omitted, especially when the subject or topic is understood by both the listener and speaker. Such sentences are more natural in Japanese, but also occur in English imperative sentences, like "Sit down," or "Come here."

MODELS

1. Teacher:　ジョンさん。　　　　　　　　"Jon."
　　　　　　　Jon-san.

　　Student:　ちこくです。　　　　　　　　"(He is) tardy."
　　　　　　　Chikoku desu.

READ/WRITE Answer these questions affirmatively and omit the subject.

1. えみこさんは　おやすみですか。
　Emiko-san wa oyasumi desu ka.

2. ベンさんは　ちこくですか。
　Ben-san wa chikoku desu ka.

B Question Particle か

Noun 1 は　なんですか。　　　　　　**What is Noun 1?**
Noun 1 wa　nan desu　ka.

In Japanese, the word order of a question sentence is the same as for statements, except that か *ka* is attached to the end of the sentence.

MODELS

1. Teacher:　これは　なんですか。　　　"What is this?"
　　　　　　　Kore wa nan desu ka.

　　Student:　ひらがなです。　　　　　　"(It is) *hiragana*."
　　　　　　　Hiragana desu.

READ Choose the sentences that are questions from the choices below.

1. (はじめましょう。 　/ 　はじめましょうか。)
   (Hajimemashoo. 　　　　　　Hajimemashoo ka.)

2. (ひらがなですか。 / ひらがなです。)
   (Hiragana desu ka. 　　　　Hiragana desu.)

3. (おわりましょうか。/ おわりましょう。)
   (Owarimashoo ka. 　　　　Owarimashoo.)

ぶんかノート　Culture Notes

Greetings

Greetings are very important in Japanese culture. People greet acquaintances whenever they see each other, even if they are busy. When you greet someone in passing, it is polite to stop in your tracks and acknowledge the other person with a bow and an appropriate greeting. A teenager would be expected to bow politely to an adult but might only nod when greeting a friend or classmate.

To practice these different manners of greeting in your own class, you should greet your teacher with "*Sensei, konnichiwa!*" when entering the classroom. Then greet your classmates as you go to your seat. When class begins, a pre-assigned student should lead the class in a formal greeting to the teacher, complete with a bow. They should also lead a formal departure at the end of class.

 Read the above description of Japanese greetings carefully and compare them to your own culture. How would you greet your friend, a classmate, a teacher, and a friend's parent in your own culture? Write a short paragraph in English explaining your answers.

アクティビティー　Communicative Activities

Class Work

A. SPEAK/LISTEN One student leads the class. Everyone else follows his/her instructions.

- This is the beginning of a *morning* Japanese class. Start the class with the traditional opening.
- This is the beginning of an *afternoon* Japanese class. Start the class with the traditional opening.
- This is the end of a Japanese class. Lead the closing. If a classmate does not stand quickly, tell that student to hurry.

B. SPEAK/LISTEN Take attendance and then report to the teacher who is absent and who is tardy.

Hiragana Pair Work

C. READ/SPEAK Create *hiragana* flash cards by writing each *hiragana* on a square of paper, and its romanization on the back. Then with a partner, practice asking each other what each character is and responding.

たんご　Vocabulary

1. Numbers

1	2	3	4	5
いち	に	さん	し, よん	ご
一	二	三	四	五
ichi	*ni*	*san*	*shi, yon*	*go*
6	7	8	9	10
ろく	しち, なな	はち	く, きゅう	じゅう
六	七	八	九	十
roku	*shichi, nana*	*hachi*	*ku, kyuu*	*juu*

2. すみません。もう　いちど
おねがいします。

Sumimasen. Moo ichido onegaishimasu.

Excuse me. One more time please.
(Please repeat it.)

3. すみません。ゆっくり
おねがいします。

Sumimasen. Yukkuri onegaishimasu.

Excuse me. Slowly, please.

ゆっくり yukkuri means slowly.

4. ちょっと　まって
ください。

Chotto matte kudasai.

Please wait a minute.

5. ありがとう
ございます。

Arigatoo gozaimasu.

Thank you very much.

6. どう
いたしまして。

Doo itashimashite.

You are welcome.

ついか　たんご　Additional Vocabulary

1. でんわばんごう　　　　　　　*denwa bangoo*　　　　　　telephone number

927−6540
（きゅう・にい・なな・の・ろく・ごお・よん・ゼロ）
kyuu　　nii　　nana　　no　　roku　　goo　　yon　　zero

When Japanese people read telephone numbers, they avoid similar sounds and short sounds. し *shi* (four) and しち *shichi* (seven) sound alike. いち *ichi* (one) and しち *shichi* (seven) sound alike. Thus, use よん *yon* for four, なな *nana* for seven and きゅう *kyuu* for nine. The "dash" is pronounced as の *no*. Single character numbers are lengthened to distinguish each number more easily (i.e., に *ni* to にい *nii*, ご *go* to ごお *goo*).

よみましょう　Language in Context

🔊 **SPEAK/READ** Ask a partner to repeat something, then practice pronouncing each of these forms of "Thank you." Which ones should you use with a teacher? With a classmate?

すみません。
もう いちど
おねがいします。

もう *moo* means "more," いちど *ichido* means "one time," *onegaishimasu* is commonly used when you ask a favor of someone.

Depending upon the degree of politeness, parts of "Thank you" may be omitted. Here are expressions of thanks listed from most to least formal.

どうも　ありがとう
ございます。

Doomo arigatoo gozaimasu.

ありがとう
ございます。

Arigatoo gozaimasu.

どうも　ありがとう。

Doomo arigatoo.

ありがとう。

Arigatoo.

どうも。

Doomo.

Set Expressions and Greetings

The Japanese depend heavily on set expressions when greeting each other. One of the most useful expressions in Japanese is すみません *sumimasen*, because it carries so many meanings and can be used in a variety of situations. For example, it may be used to apologize for one's rude, inconsiderate, or thoughtless actions. It may also be used as a way to thank others for going through a lot of trouble to do something for you or give something to you. すみません *sumimasen* may also be used to gain attention, much as English speakers use the expression, "Excuse me. (Are you there?)" or "Excuse me. (I hope you can help me.)"

 Brainstorm a list of situations in which you think saying すみません *sumimasen* would be useful. As a class, compare your list with other students and discuss with the teacher what the most common uses of すみません *sumimasen* might be.

Language Note

Using Polite Expressions

もう　いちど *moo ichido* means "one more time." It is rude to say もう いちど *moo ichido* when making requests to teachers and superiors. Instead, say もう　いちど　おねがいします *moo ichido onegaishimasu* when you would like superiors to repeat something for you.

アクティビティー Communicative Activities

Class Work

A. LISTEN/WRITE Play a game of Bingo with *hiragana*.

On a separate sheet of paper, draw a Bingo chart like the one below. Fill in each block with any *hiragana*. One student randomly reads *hiragana* characters. The other students listen and circle the numbers read until they have Bingo. Say できました *dekimashita* ("I made it") when you have Bingo.

で	き	ま	し	た
		☆		

B. SPEAK/WRITE Write down your classmates' phone numbers in Japanese.

Each student reads his/her own telephone number aloud and others write the numbers down. If you are not able to follow, ask your classmate to repeat his/her number. If the student speaks too quickly, ask the person to speak slowly. Thank the person for repeating his/her number and speaking slowly. In return, the student should say, "You are welcome."

たんご　Vocabulary

🔊 **1.** | **Numbers**

11	じゅういち	20	にじゅう
	juu-ichi		*ni-juu*
12	じゅうに	30	さんじゅう
	juu-ni		*san-juu*
13	じゅうさん	40	よんじゅう
	juu-san		*yon-juu*
14	じゅうし, じゅうよん	50	ごじゅう
	juu-shi, juu-yon		*go-juu*
15	じゅうご	60	ろくじゅう
	juu-go		*roku-juu*
16	じゅうろく	70	しちじゅう, ななじゅう
	juu-roku		*shichi-juu, nana-juu*
17	じゅうしち, じゅうなな	80	はちじゅう
	juu-shichi, juu-nana		*hachi-juu*
18	じゅうはち	90	きゅうじゅう
	juu-hachi		*kyuu-juu*
19	じゅうく, じゅうきゅう	100	ひゃく
	juu-ku, juu-kyuu		*hyaku*

2. それ

sore

that one

Refers to something near the listener.

3. あれ

are

that one over there

Refers to something distant from both speaker and listener.

4. はい、ええ

hai, ee

yes

ええ ee is less formal than はい hai.

5. いいえ

iie

no

6. はい、そうです。*

*Hai, soo desu.**

Yes, it is.*

Expression of agreement. Used as a response.

7. いいえ、そうでは　ありません。*

or **いいえ、そうじゃ　ありません。***

*Iie, soo dewa arimasen.**

or *Iie, soo ja arimasen.**

Expression of disagreement. Used as a response.

そうじゃ　ありません *Soo ja arimasen* is less formal than そうでは　ありません *Soo dewa arimasen*.

* These expressions are only used in response to questions that end with ですか *desu ka.*

ついか　たんご　Additional Vocabulary

Page Numbers

page 1	いちページ	*ichi-peeji*
	いっページ	*ip-peeji*
page 2	にページ	*ni-peeji*
page 3	さんページ	*san-peeji*
page 4	よんページ	*yon-peeji*
page 5	ごページ	*go-peeji*
page 6	ろくページ	*roku-peeji*
page 7	ななページ	*nana-peeji*
page 8	はちページ	*hachi-peeji*
page 9	きゅうページ	*kyuu-peeji*
page 10	じゅっページ	*jup-peeji*
page 11	じゅういちページ	*juu-ichi-peeji*
page 20	にじゅっページ	*ni-jup-peeji*
What page?	なんページ	*nan-peeji?*

よみましょう　Language in Context

SPEAK Point to an object in the room and say the appropriate pronoun, as seen below.

これ

Refers to something
near the speaker.

それ

Refers to something
near the listener.

あれ

Refers to something distant
from both speaker and listener.

A Location Pronouns

これ／それ／あれ は　〜です。　　**This / That / That one over there is ~.**
kore / sore / are wa ~ desu.

これ *kore* refers to something near the speaker. それ *sore* refers to something near the listener. あれ *are* refers to something distant from both speaker and listener. これ *kore*, それ *sore*, あれ *are* cannot be used for people except for people in pictures and photos.

◀))) MODELS ◀

1. Teacher:　これは　なんですか。　　"What is this?"
　　　　　　　Kore wa nan desu ka.

　　Student:　それは　うです。　　"That is U."
　　　　　　　Sore wa u desu.

2. Teacher:　あれは　なんですか。　　"What is that over there?"
　　　　　　　Are wa nan desu ka.

　　Student:　あれは　かです。　　"That is KA."
　　　　　　　Are wa ka desu.

READ Ken is holding a *hiragana* card, Emi is holding a *katakana* card and there is a *kanji* card far away from both Ken and Emi. Choose the correct word in the parentheses.

1. ケン：　（これ ／ それ ／ あれ）は　ひらがなです。
　　Ken:　　　*(Kore　　Sore　　Are)　wa　hiragana desu.*

2. エミ：　（これ ／ それ ／ あれ）は　カタカナです。
　　Emi:　　　*(Kore　　Sore　　Are)　wa　katakana desu.*

3. ケン：　（これ ／ それ ／ あれ）は　かんじです。
　　Ken:　　　*(Kore　　Sore　　Are)　wa　kanji desu.*

B Answering Yes/No Questions

Noun 1 は　　Noun 2 ですか。　Is Noun 1 = Noun 2?

Noun 1 *wa*　　Noun 2 *desu ka.*

When answering a simple yes/no question using the form above, you can respond with the expressions below.

MODELS

1. これは　ひらがなですか。　　　　"Is this *hiragana*?"
   Kore wa hiragana desu ka.

   はい、そうです。　　　　　　　"Yes, it is."
   Hai, soo desu.

   いいえ、そうでは　ありません。　"No, it is not."
   Iie, soo dewa arimasen.

READ Look at the character in the [ ], then choose the correct response to the question.

1. [あ]　これは　ひらがなですか。
   Kore wa hiragana desu ka.

   （はい、そうです。　/　いいえ、そうでは　ありません。）
   　Hai, soo desu.　　　　　　　*Iie, soo dewa arimasen.*

2. [ア]　これは　かんじですか。
   Kore wa kanji desu ka.

   （はい、そうです。　/　いいえ、そうでは　ありません。）
   　Hai, soo desu.　　　　　　　*Iie, soo dewa arimasen.*

ぶんかノート　Culture Notes

Japanese Good Luck and Bad Luck Numbers

In Japanese culture, certain numbers are considered "bad luck" or "good luck," much like the number 13 is considered bad luck in Western culture. The "bad luck" numbers in Japanese are 4 (し *shi*) and 9 (く *ku*). し *shi* can also mean death, while く *ku* suggests suffering. Eight is considered good luck because of the mountain-like shape of the *kanji* character for eight (八). Mountains are regarded with reverence in Japan. Also, the character 八 resembles a fan shape, which is considered lucky because it suggests spreading out, growing, and increasing, as in mounting good fortune.

 Consider your cell phone or home phone number. Based on the information above, do you think you have a "lucky" phone number? Why or why not?

アクティビティー　Communicative Activities

Pair Work

A. SPEAK/LISTEN Count from 1 to 100.

Class Work

B. READ/SPEAK Your teacher will write numbers from 1 to 100 at random on the board. Students will read them aloud.

C. LISTEN/WRITE Play a Bingo game with the numbers 1 to 100.

On a separate sheet of paper, draw a Bingo chart like the one on page 34. Fill in each block with any number you like from 10 to 100. One student randomly reads a number from 1 to 100. The other students circle the number being read until they have Bingo. Say できました *dekimashita* ("I made it") when you have Bingo.

Group Work

D. SPEAK/LISTEN Form groups of three. One student reads page numbers, while the other two race to see who can find the correct page more quickly. Keep track of points on a separate sheet of paper using a chart like the one below. Take turns so that each student will have a chance to be the page caller or a racer.

Name   Points →

◯ = Won   X = Lost

Hiragana Pair Work

E. SPEAK/LISTEN Spread a set of your *hiragana* flashcards (see page 30, Activity C if you haven't made any yet) on your desk, on your partner's desk, and somewhere far from both of you. Ask each other what each card is. Use これ *kore*, それ *sore*, あれ *are* in both questions and answers.

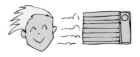

ひょうげん　Expressions

1. あつい
ですねえ。

Atsui desu nee.

It's hot!

2. さむい
ですねえ。

Samui desu nee.

It's cold!

3. すずしい
ですねえ。

Suzushii desu nee.

It's cool (temperature)!

4. そうですねえ。

Soo desu nee.

Yes, it is!

Indicates strong agreement.

5. (お)げんき
ですか。

(O)genki desu ka.

How are you?
(Lit. Are you fine?)

6. はい、げんき
です。

Hai, genki desu.

Yes, I am fine.

7. むしあつい
ですねえ。

Mushiatsui desu nee.

It's hot and humid!

8. いい　(お)てんき
ですねえ。

Ii (o)tenki desu nee.

The weather is nice!

9. あめですねえ。

Ame desu nee.

It's raining (a lot)!

ついか たんご　Additional Vocabulary

1. いいえ、
   ぐあいが　わるいです。　　　　*Iie, guai ga warui desu.*　　No, I feel sick.

2. ねむいです。　　　　　　　*Nemui desu.*　　　　(I) am sleepy.

3. つかれて　います。　　　　*Tsukarete imasu.*　　(I) am tired.

よみましょう　Language in Context

 READ/LISTEN/SPEAK When someone asks how are you, should you say "*Ogenki desu*?" or "*Genki desu*?" Ask a partner how he/she is and respond.

(お)げんきですか。

This expression is used only when one meets a person after not seeing him/her for several days or more.

はい、げんきです。

Notice that the polite prefix "お *o*" is removed here, since the speaker is talking about him/herself.

ぶんぽう　Grammar

A Sentence-Ending Exclamation Particle ねえ

Sentence ＋ ねえ。
　　　　　　　nee

The final particle ねえ *nee* is used to express admiration, surprise, or exclamation.

MODELS

1. あついですねえ。　　　　　It is hot!
   Atsui desu nee.

2. さむいですねえ。　　　　　It is cold!
   Samui desu nee.

3. そうですねえ。　　　　　　It is so! That's right!
   Soo desu nee.

READ Choose the correct Japanese equivalent of the English sentence.

1. It's hot!　（あついですか。　/　あついですねえ。）
(Atsui desu ka.　　　Atsui desu nee.)

2. Is it cold?　（さむいですか。　/　さむいですねえ。）
(Samui desu ka.　　　Samui desu nee.)

ぶんかノート　Culture Notes

Discussing the Weather

A polite conversation in Japan typically starts with a discussion of something neutral. Jumping straight to your point would be considered impolite. The weather is a "safe" common ground from which to start a conversation, similar to how "small talk" in English often concerns the weather.

Another reason is the deep Japanese respect for nature. Japan has historically been very susceptible to the whims of nature, and the Japanese, especially in the past, felt a strong sense of awe and respect for natural phenomena. This "oneness" with nature is reflected even in everyday interactions such as greetings.

Like many nations, Japan was traditionally an agrarian-based society. The earliest settlers adapted from a nomadic lifestyle to one centered around rice cultivation. Because farming and good harvests are dependent on the weather, weather became an important topic of conversation.

 How do you start a conversation when you meet an acquaintance on the street? What kinds of things do you talk about as small talk? How does it compare to how the Japanese begin a conversation?

アクティビティー　Communicative Activities

Pair Work

A. SPEAK/LISTEN In the following scenarios, address the person involved, greet him/her properly, talk about the weather, and ask how he/she is.

1. You enter the Japanese classroom in the morning. Your teacher is there. The room is very cold.

2. You meet your neighbor. It is morning and it is cool.

3. You meet your friend in the afternoon. It is a hot day.

4. You meet your Japanese friend Mari in the morning. It is cold.

5. You have not seen your teacher since the day before the weekend. Ask how he/she is.

B. SPEAK What expression would each of the people pictured below use to describe the weather?

Reading

C. READ/WRITE Write the numeral form of the following Japanese numbers.

1. にじゅう *ni-juu*
2. いち *ichi*
3. じゅうご *juu-go*
4. ろく *roku*
5. ひゃく *hyaku*
6. さん *san*
7. よんじゅうに *yon-juu ni*
8. きゅうじゅうご *kyuu-juu go*
9. なな *nana*
10. じゅうはち *juu-hachi*

Read and Connect

D. READ/SPEAK Be a meteorologist! Use the temperature map of Japan to answer the following.

INTERPRET

1. What do you think the red and blue numbers mean?

2. Can you find the date on this map? What month do you think it is? What day?

DETERMINE

3. Locate Tokyo on the map.

4. Which city is the hottest? Which city is the coldest?

APPLY

5. Describe the weather in the following places to a partner using the expressions you have learned (use the map in the back of the book to help you locate them): Tokyo, Osaka, Sapporo

6. Japan uses the Celsius system to measure temperature. Find out what the high temperature in Tokyo is in Fahrenheit. [Hint: The formula for converting Celsius to Fahrenheit is $F = (C \times 9/5) + 32$]

4月30日　気温　最高 / 最低

なは
那覇
24 / 20

さっぽろ
札幌
10 / 5

あおもり
青森
9 / 6

あきた
秋田
11 / 7

せんだい
仙台
13 / 8

かなざわ
金沢
11 / 8

ながの
長野
11 / 5

まつえ
松江
13 / 8

とうきょう
東京
19 / 14

おおさか
大阪
16 / 11

ひろしま
広島
18 / 10

ふくおか
福岡
18 / 13

かごしま
鹿児島
23 / 13

Review Questions

Ask your partner these questions or say these statements to him/her in Japanese. Your partner answers in Japanese. Check your answers using the audio.

Self Introduction Review page 20

1. How do you do? I am _____ . Nice to meet you. [Bow.]

Greetings Review pages 24 and 41

2. Teacher's name (ex. *Tanaka-sensei*), good morning. [Bow.]

3. Teacher's name (ex. *Tanaka-sensei*), good-bye. [Bow.]

4. How are you?

5. Teacher/ Partner: How are you?

Classroom Expressions Review pages 27, 31, and 36

6. Let's begin. Stand. Bow. Good afternoon. Sit down. [Do it!]

7. Jon, hurry.

8. Mike is tardy. Ben is absent.

9. Let's finish. Stand. Bow. Good-bye. [Do it!]

10. What is this? (Point to something near you.) / What is that? [Point to something near your teacher/ partner.] / What is that over there ? [Point to something distant from both you and your teacher/ partner.]

11. Excuse me. One more time please. [Bow slightly.]

12. Excuse me. Slowly please. [Bow slightly.]

13. Thank you very much (to your teacher). [Bow.]

14. You are welcome.

15. Teacher/ partner: Is this/ that/ that one over there ? (Point to one *hiragana*) [Use three *hiragana* cards.]

Weather Review page 41

16. It's hot!

17. It's cold!

18. It's cool!

Numbers Review pages 31 and 35

19. **READ** 5, 9, 12, 43, 80

20. **READ** 7, 26, 54, 91, 100

21. **READ** 4, 38, 62, 75, 91

Text Chat

You will participate in a simulated exchange of text-chat messages. You should respond as fully and as appropriately as possible.

You will have a conversation with Daisuke Sato, a Japanese high school student, for the first time.

September 5, 10:43 AM

はじめまして。 ぼくは　だいすけ
です。 どうぞ　よろしく。
Hajimemashite.   Boku wa Daisuke desu.
Doozo yoroshiku.

Introduce yourself.

September 5, 10:47 AM

おげんきですか。
Ogenki desu ka.

Respond.

September 5, 10:50 AM

あついですか。
Atsui desu ka.

Respond.

Can Do!
Now I can . . .

- ❑ introduce myself
- ❑ recognize the Japanese sound system
- ❑ greet others at different times of the day
- ❑ start and end class using Japanese
- ❑ report that a classmate is tardy or absent
- ❑ count to 100 and give phone numbers
- ❑ express agreement and disagreement
- ❑ talk about the weather

Where is Japan?
にほんは　どこですか。

RESEARCH Use books, the Internet, or interview a Japanese member of your community to answer the following.

Geography

1. Where is Japan? Find Japan on a world map or on a globe.

2. What does Japan look like? On a separate sheet of paper, draw a simple map of Japan.

3. What is the capital of Japan? Where is the capital of Japan? Mark the capital on the map you drew above.

Compare Choose the correct answer.

4. How big is Japan compared to your state?

   Japan is (bigger than, about the same size as, smaller than) the state I live in now.

5. Which U.S. state is about the same size as Japan?

   California　　New Jersey　　Florida

Determine Choose the correct answer(s).

6. What is the approximate population of Japan?

   100 million　　200 million　　300 million　　400 million　　500 million

7. What is the approximate population of the United States?

   100 million　　200 million　　300 million　　400 million　　500 million

8. What natural disasters are common in Japan?

   typhoons　　earthquakes　　tsunami　　volcanic eruptions　　tornadoes

---

Extend Your Learning
MEDIA LITERACY
Compare newspaper articles about natural disasters in Japan and the U.S. Discuss the similarities and differences in how the disasters are depicted. Consider what kind of pictures are shown, who is interviewed, what questions are asked, and how the response is discussed.

にほんごの　きょうしつ
Japanese Classroom

✓ Can Do!
In this lesson you will learn to

- recognize and respond to classroom expressions in the affirmative and negative
- identify and indicate the location of classroom objects belonging to you or your classmates
- ask how to say something in Japanese
- make requests
- ask someone when their birthday is
- tell someone the time and the date
- read and write *hiragana*

Online Resources

cheng-tsui.com/
adventuresinjapanese

- Audio
- Vocabulary Lists
- Vocabulary Flashcards
- *Kana* Flashcards
- Activity Worksheets

Expressions

1. わかりますか。

Wakarimasu ka.

Do you understand?

2. はい、わかります。

Hai, wakarimasu.

Yes, I understand.

3. いいえ、わかりません。

Iie, wakarimasen.

No, I do not understand.

4. しりません。

Shirimasen.

I do not know.

"I know" is しっています
shitte imasu.

5. みえません。

Miemasen.

I can't see.

6. きこえません。

Kikoemasen.

I can't hear.

7. いいです。

Ii desu.

It is good.

8. だめです。

Dame desu.

That is unacceptable.

9. ええと … ／あのう… ／
そうですねえ …

Eeto . . . / Anoo. . . . / Soo desu nee. . .

Let me see . . . / Well . . .

10. Tree は にほんごで なんと いいますか。

Tree wa Nihongo de nan to iimasu ka.
How do you say "tree" in Japanese?

にほんご *Nihongo* means "Japanese language," で *de* means "means of," なん *nan* means "what," と *to* is a particle used for quotations, いいます *iimasu* means "s... and か *ka* is a sentence ending particle for questions.

Additional Expressions

 1. わすれました。

Wasuremashita.
I forgot (it).

 **2.** なくしました。

Nakushimashita.
I lost (it).

 **3.** おてあらい／トイレへ　いっても　いいですか。

Otearai / toire e itte mo ii desu ka.
May I go to the bathroom?

 4. ロッカーへ　いっても　いいですか。

Rokkaa e itte mo ii desu ka.
May I go to my locker?

 **5.** （お）みずを　のんでも　いいですか。

(O)mizu o nonde mo ii desu ka.
May I get a drink of water? (Lit., "May I drink water?")

 6. えんぴつを　かして　ください。

Enpitsu o kashite kudasai.
Please lend me a pencil.

 7. すみません。しつもんが　あります。

Sumimasen. Shitsumon ga arimasu.
Excuse me. I have a question.

🔊 READ/LISTEN Read ... ntences in Japanese. Say when should you use ええと.

ええと ...

きこえます。

When you need time to think of a response,
use expressions like ええと *eeto* and あのう *anoo*.

ぶんぽう Grammar

A Negative Verb Ending -ません

わかります。 **I understand.**
Wakarimasu.

わかりません。 **I do not understand.**
Wakarimasen.

Japanese verbs consist of two parts, the verb stem and the portion which conjugates. The verb stem (the beginning part of a verb without the -ます *masu*) tells the meaning of the verb. The conjugated portion (the verb ending, i.e., -ます *masu*) tells us the verb tense, whether the verb is affirmative or negative, etc.

The verb -ます *masu* form is an imperfect affirmative form. Imperfect means present and future. It is translated "do, does, will do, going to do." The verb -ません *masen* form is an imperfect negative form. It is translated "do not, does not, will not do."

🔊 MODELS

1. Teacher: みえますか。 Can you see?
   Miemasu ka.

   Student: はい、みえます。 Yes, I can see.
   Hai, miemasu.

2. Student: すみません。せんせい、きこえません。
   Sumimasen. Sensei, kikoemasen.   Excuse me. Teacher, I cannot hear.

3. Teacher: これは　なんですか。
   Kore wa nan desu ka.   What is this?

   Student: しりません。
   Shirimasen.   I do not know.

4. Teacher: わかりますか。
   Wakarimasu ka.   Do you understand?

   Student: いいえ、わかりません。
   Iie, wakarimasen.   No, I do not understand.

READ/WRITE Write an answer to each question in the negative.

1. わかりますか。

   Wakarimasu ka.

2. きこえますか。

   Kikoemasu ka.

ぶんかノート　Culture Notes

Expectations in the Japanese Classroom

Although Japanese society is always changing, classroom behavior tends be more formal in Japan. Some rules that are often enforced include:

1. Students should not eat, drink or chew gum in class.

2. Caps and hats must be removed.

3. The teacher's permission must be asked before any action is taken by the students.

4. Students should remain in their seats throughout class, and need to ask permission before getting up and moving.

 Compare these rules to those in your own classroom. What are the advantages and disadvantages of each system? Drawing from both the Japanese system and that of your school, create a poster of classroom rules and behavior norms for your own class.

アクティビティー Communicative Activities

Pair Work

A. READ/SPEAK Be an optometrist/audiologist! Do the following tests with your partner.

1. **Eye test:** Test your partner using the chart below. Your partner should read each line out loud in Japanese, and tell you when he/she can no longer see the text.

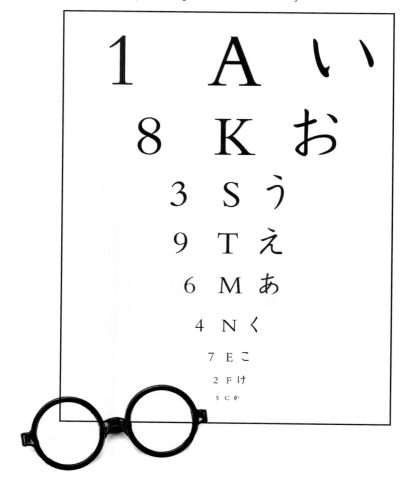

2. **Hearing test:** Use an audio file, and change the volume from low to high and test your partner. Your partner should repeat each line after listening to it, then say when he/she cannot hear the audio. You may also adjust the volume of your own voices to test each other.

B. SPEAK/LISTEN Ask your partner if he/she knows the following words in Japanese. When your partner does not know the answer, he/she will say しりません *shirimasen*.

1. cat

2. You are welcome.

3. May I go to the restroom?

4. teacher

5. telephone number

6. dog

Teacher's directions

🔊 *You are expected to understand and follow the directions your teacher will give you in class.*

1. かいて
ください。

Kaite kudasai.

Please write.

2. よんで
ください。

Yonde kudasai.

Please read.

3. みて
ください。

Mite kudasai.

Please look.

4. きいて
ください。

Kiite kudasai.

Please listen.

5. すわって
ください。

Suwatte kudasai.

Please sit.

6. たって
ください。

Tatte kudasai.

Please stand.

7. だして
ください。

Dashite kudasai.

Please turn in (something).

8. みせて
ください。

Misete kudasai.

Please show me (something).

9. ドアを　あけて
ください。

Doa o akete kudasai.

Please open the door.

Part 2 • Teacher's directions **55**

10. ドアを　しめて
　　ください。

Doa o shimete kudasai.

Please close the door.

11. しずかに　して
　　ください。

Shizuka ni shite kudasai.

Please be quiet.

12. よく
　　できました。

Yoku dekimashita.

Well done.

Additional Expressions

1. でんきを　つけて
　　ください。

Denki o tsukete kudasai.

Please turn on the lights.

2. でんきを　けして
　　ください。

Denki o keshite kudasai.

Please turn off the lights.

3. おおきい　こえで
　　いって　ください。

Ookii koe de itte kudasai.

Please say it in a loud voice.

よみましょう　Language in Context

🔊 **READ/LISTEN** Read these sentences in Japanese. Identify which sentence is a command and which is an acknowledgment.

よく　できました。

ドアを　しめて　ください。

More Expectations in a Japanese Classroom

Traditionally, Japanese schools stressed proper posture in class. While nowadays schools may often be less strict, proper posture while sitting is still considered a mark of a good student, and important for being able to write neatly.

To sit properly:

1. Sit with both feet flat on the floor. (No feet resting on chairs, no crossed legs, etc.)

2. Sit with your back straight, resting only on the seat back. (No slouching, no resting your head on a desk or hands, etc.)

3. Sit facing the teacher. When called to answer a question or when speaking up, you should stand before responding.

 Experiment by trying to sit at your desk in the Japanese style described above for a day. Before trying it, predict what the advantages and disadvantages might be. Then, answer the following questions in a short paragraph describing your experiment to a friend at school.

How comfortable is this position?

How does it affect your work in class?

Does it work better in some classes than in others?

アクティビティー　Communicative Activities

Pair Work

A. SPEAK/LISTEN Play the game Simon Says. Give commands to your partner using expressions you have learned.

Pair Work - Hiragana Speed Reading Contest

B. READ/SPEAK Take out or make a set of *hiragana* flash cards. Show the *hiragana* cards one by one to your partner as your partner reads them aloud. Count how many he/she can read in 20 seconds. Take turns.

たんご Vocabulary

1. えんぴつ	**2. ボールペン**	**3. けしゴム**	**4. かみ**
enpitsu	*boorupen*	*keshigomu*	*kami*
pencil	ballpoint pen	(rubber) eraser	paper

5. ほん 本	**6. きょうかしょ／ テキスト**	**7. じしょ**	**8. ノート**
hon	*kyookasho / tekisuto*	*jisho*	*nooto*
book	textbook	dictionary	notebook

9. (お)かね (お)金	**10. しゃしん**	**11. リュック**	**12. ぼうし**	**13. ごみ**
(o) kane	*shashin*	*ryukku*	*booshi*	*gomi*
money	photo	backpack	cap, hat	trash

ついか たんご Additional Vocabulary

1. かばん	**2. とけい**	**3. かさ**	**4. えんぴつけずり**	**5. ごみばこ**
kaban	*tokei*	*kasa*	*enpitsukezuri*	*gomibako*
bag, briefcase	watch, clock	umbrella	pencil sharpener	wastebasket

READ/LISTEN/SPEAK Read the question and say an answer in Japanese.

これは　なんですか。

おかねです。

Language Note

Japanese Word Order

The Japanese word order in a sentence is topic first, time word or adverb second, and verb last. Particles follow nouns. Correct particle usage is important in order to convey accurate information. Negations occur at the end of sentences. It is therefore difficult for language learners to know whether a sentence is affirmative or negative until the end of the sentence. When forming a question, the word order of the sentence is not changed as it is in English. Rather, the question marker is simply attached at the end of the sentence.

Ex. みえます。 *Miemasu.* (I can see.) みえますか。 *Miemasu ka.* (Can you see?)

Translate a Japanese sentence into English, but keep the Japanese word order. Ask your classmates or a family member if they can understand your sentence. Now try the same with an English sentence into Japanese, keeping the English word order. How important do you think word order is in understanding language? Explain using people's reactions to your sentences as evidence.

アクティビティー Communicative Activities

Pair Work

SPEAK/LISTEN Point to things around you and ask what they are. Use これ *kore*, それ *sore*, and あれ *are* for both questions and answers.

2か4
This book is mine

たんご Vocabulary

1. この + Noun

kono + Noun

this 〜

2. その + Noun

sono + Noun

that 〜

3. あの + Noun

ano + Noun

that 〜 over there

4. あなた

anata

you

Used to address persons of equal or lower status. See Cultural Note.

5. わたしの

watashi-no

mine

6. あなたの

anata-no

yours

よみましょう Language in Context

READ/LISTEN/SPEAK Read this sentence in Japanese. With a partner, point to something and ask whether it is your partner's or a classmate's.

これは　ジョン *Jon* さんのですか。

ぶんぽう　Grammar

A Possessive Particle の

The particle "の" *no* indicates possession. It can change preceding nouns into possessive adjectives (my, your, Alexa's) or possessive pronouns (mine, yours, Noboru's).

MODELS

1. これは　わたしのです。 — This is mine.
   Kore wa watashi-no desu.

2. 「これは　あなたのですか。」 — "Is this yours?"
   Kore wa anata-no desu ka.

   「はい、わたしのです。」 — "Yes, it is mine."
   Hai, watashi-no desu.

3. あれは　けいこさんのです。 — That one over there is Keiko's.
   Are wa Keiko-san-no desu.

READ/WRITE Answer each question affirmatively using the particle の *no*.

1. これは　せんせいの　ほんですか。
   Kore wa sensei-no hon desu ka.

2. あれは　あなたの　かみですか。
   Are wa anata-no kami desu ka.

B This/That—Pre-nominatives

この／その／あの＋ **Noun** は　～です。

kono / sono / ano ＋ *Noun wa ~ desu.*

This is a variation of the Noun 1 = Noun 2 pattern. Demonstrative adjectives such as この *kono*, その *sono*, あの *ano* point to specific nouns: this desk, that chair, etc., depending on their relative position to the speaker. They cannot be used without nouns immediately following them.

MODELS

1. その　えんぴつは　わたしのです。 — That pencil is mine.
   Sono enpitsu wa watashi-no desu.

2. あの　ぼうしは　ぼくのです。 — That cap over there is mine.
   Ano booshi wa boku-no desu.

3. この　おかねは　わたしのです。 — This money is mine.
   Kono okane wa watashi-no desu.

READ Choose the correct pre-nominative for each situation based on the information below.

You have a textbook in your hands, your friend has a photo in her hand, and a backpack far away from both of you belongs to Ken.

1. （この　　その　　あの）　きょうかしょは　わたしのです。
   　(Kono　　Sono　　Ano)　　kyookasho wa watashi-no desu.

2. （この　　その　　あの）　リュックは　ケンさんのです。
   　(Kono　　Sono　　Ano)　　ryukku wa Ken-san-no desu.

3. （この　　その　　あの）　しゃしんは　あなたのです。
   　(Kono　　Sono　　Ano)　　shashin wa anata-no desu.

ぶんかノート　Culture Notes

A. Speaking to People of Higher Status

Japanese makes important distinctions about how to address people of higher status (such as teachers, bosses, and people older than yourself) and people of equal or lower status (such as friends, classmates, or younger siblings). It's important to follow these rules if you want to be polite.

For example, あなた *anata* is used to address persons of equal or lower status. It is rude to use あなた *anata* to refer to your teacher. せんせい *sensei* should be used instead. Try to avoid using あなた *anata* in your conversations. Instead, use the listener's name to avoid being too direct. Whenever possible, avoid using あなた *anata*, especially when it is clear that the subject is "you."

B. Japanese School Supplies-- したじき *shitajiki*

Japanese students go to school well equipped with school supplies. They carry pencils, pens, erasers, notebooks, pencil cases, etc. They also always carry their own supply of tissue. Another necessary item is the したじき *shitajiki*, which is a smooth page-sized solid plastic sheet which is placed under paper so that one can write neatly.

There may be several reasons for using a したじき *shitajiki*. First, Japanese students rarely use loose "sheets of paper." They almost always use notebooks. したじき *shitajiki* provide a solid backing when writing in a notebook. Second, the Japanese traditionally always use both the back and front of a page. By using the したじき *shitajiki*, one can always have a clean sheet (not one which is roughened by pressing heavily on the opposite side of the page).

Language Note

Japanese's Evolving Vocabulary

The Japanese language is constantly undergoing change, as it easily adopts words from other languages. This practice is also true historically, when Chinese words greatly enriched the Japan language. Now, English is a major source from which words are borrowed. For example, the word ちょうめん *choomen*, which is a practice writing tablet, is now called ノート *nooto*. The word "steak" was originally adopted as ビフテキ *bifuteki* (beefsteak), but is now called ステーキ *suteeki*. Gym shoes were called うんどうぐつ *undoogutsu*, but are now called スポーツシューズ *supootsu shuuzu* or スニーカー *suniikaa*.

 English words have also changed over time and been influenced by other languages. What words in English have been borrowed from Japanese? Other languages? Choose any five words and research online or use a dictionary to find out what language they originally came from.

アクティビティー　Communicative Activities

Pair Work

A. SPEAK/LISTEN You and your partner drop your belongings on the floor. Each of you claims your own possessions.

Use この *kono,* その *sono,* あの *ano.*

Class Work

B. SPEAK/LISTEN Lost and Found

Each student loses one item. The lost items are at the Lost & Found corner. One student picks one item which does not belong to him/her and finds the person who lost it by asking questions such as:

「これ／この　〜は　〜さんのですか。」
Kore/kono　〜wa　〜san-no desuka.

If it is yours, say 「はい、そうです。」or 「はい、それは　わたしのです。」.
　　　　　　　　　Hai, soo desu.　　　　*Hai, sore wa watashi-no desu.*

If it is not yours, say 「いいえ、そうでは　ありません。」 or
　　　　　　　　　Iie, soo dewa arimasen.

「いいえ、わたしのでは　ありません。」.
Iie, watashi-no dewa arimasen.

たんご　Vocabulary

1. ここ

koko

here

2. そこ

soko

there

3. あそこ

asoko

over there

4. ティッシュ

tisshu

tissue

5. しゅくだい

shukudai

homework

6. しけん

shiken

exam

7. しょうテスト

shootesuto

quiz

8. ワークシート

waakushiito

worksheet

9. チョコレート

chokoreeto

chocolate

10. あめ or キャンディ

ame or *kyandii*

candy

11. ～を ください。

~ o kudasai.

Please give me ~.

12. はい、 どうぞ。

Hai, doozo.

Here, please. (Here you are.)

13. Counter for flat objects			**14.** Counter for round or unclassified objects		

13. Counter for flat objects			**14.** Counter for round or unclassified objects		
(Paper, plates, CDs, tickets, shirts, tissue, etc.)			(Keys, apples, candies, hamburgers, rings, etc.)		
1	いちまい	*ichimai*	1	ひとつ	*hitotsu*
2	にまい	*nimai*	2	ふたつ	*futatsu*
3	さんまい	*sanmai*	3	みっつ	*mittsu*
4	よんまい	*yonmai*	4	よっつ	*yottsu*
5	ごまい	*gomai*	5	いつつ	*itsutsu*
6	ろくまい	*rokumai*	6	むっつ	*muttsu*
7	ななまい	*nanamai*	7	ななつ	*nanatsu*
8	はちまい	*hachimai*	8	やっつ	*yattsu*
9	きゅうまい	*kyuumai*	9	ここのつ	*kokonotsu*
10	じゅうまい	*juumai*	10	とお *	*too**
?	なんまい	*nanmai*	?	いくつ	*ikutsu*

* Exception: This long "OO" sound is spelled with an お instead of an う.

よみましょう　Language in Context

🔊 **READ/LISTEN/SPEAK** Practice handing your book to a classmate using the expressions and gestures below.

この　ほんを　ください。

はい、どうぞ。

ぶんぽう　Grammar

A　Requests With Counters: ください

Something を (Counter) ください。
　　　　　　o　　　　　*kudasai*

This pattern is used when one requests something. を *o* is a particle which follows the direct object. The counter follows the object being requested. Particles do not follow counters.

MODELS

1. せんせい、ティッシュを　ください。
   Sensei, tisshu o kudasai.　　　　　　　　　　Teacher, please give me some tissue.

2. すみません、ワークシートを　にまい　ください。
   Sumimasen, waakushiito o nimai kudasai.　　　Excuse me, please give me two worksheets.

3. あめを　ひとつ　ください。
   Ame o hitotsu kudasai.　　　　　　　　　　　Please give me one piece of candy.

WRITE Ask your friend to give you the following politely. Write your requests in Japanese.

1. One sheet of paper

2. Two pieces of candy

3. Five sheets of paper

B　Giving Locations of Objects

Something は　ここ／そこ／あそこ　です。
Something *wa*　*koko / soko / asoko*　*desu.*

This is another variation of the Noun 1 = Noun 2 pattern. However, in this usage, Noun 2 is not the same object as Noun 1. Noun 2 indicates the location of Noun 1.

MODELS

1. ティッシュは　あそこです。　　　The tissue is over there.
   Tisshu wa asoko desu.

2. しゅくだいは　ここです。　　　The homework is here.
   Shukudai wa koko desu.

READ Choose the correct location pronoun for each situation based on the information below.

You have an exam in your hand, your friend has a chocolate in her hand, and some homework far away from both of you belongs to Ken.

1. チョコレートは　　（ここ / そこ / あそこ）です。
   Chokoreeto wa (koko soko asoko) desu.

2. しゅくだいは　　（ここ / そこ / あそこ）です。
   Shukudai wa (koko soko asoko) desu.

3. しけんは　（ここ / そこ / あそこ)です。
   Shiken wa (koko soko asoko) desu.

 ありがとう。

 はい、どうぞ。

ぶんかノート　Culture Notes

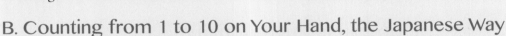

A. Handing over Objects in Japan

When handing something to someone, it is polite to use both hands. It is also polite to receive with both hands. If the relationship between two persons is close, one hand may be used to hand over objects, but things are never thrown to others, as it is considered extremely impolite.

B. Counting from 1 to 10 on Your Hand, the Japanese Way

| 1 | 2 | 3 | 4 | 5 |

| 6 | 7 | 8 | 9 | 10 |

 Is the way of handing over objects in Japanese culture different from your own culture? How would you hand a pencil or book to your teacher, your friend, your younger sibling, or a parent? How would you do this is Japan? Explain your answers.

Language Note

Japanese counters

"Counters" are attached to numbers in Japanese when giving a number of items. This is similar to "a cup of water" or "three loaves of bread" in English. Depending on the item one counts, different counters are used. This concept came from the Chinese language. However, Japanese counters are more complicated than Chinese counters. Some counters are based on the native Japanese counting system: ひとつ *hitotsu*, ふたつ *futatsu*... Some are based on words brought from China: *ichi, ni, san*. The counter changes depending on the kind of things being counted.

Counters based on the native Japanese numbers are ひとつ *hitotsu*, ふたつ *futatsu* which are used for counting things in general, and ひとり *hitori*, ふたり *futari* which are used for counting people.

Examples based on the numbers and counters borrowed from Chinese are:

いっぱい *ippai*, にはい *nihai* (cupfuls, bowlfuls, glassfuls, spoonfuls)

いっぽん *ippon*, にほん *nihon* (long, cylindrical objects)

いちまい *ichimai*, にまい *nimai* (thin, flat objects)

いっぴき *ippiki*, にひき *nihiki* (small animals)

いっさつ *issatsu*, にさつ *nisatsu* (bound items, i.e. books)

いっさい *issai*, にさい *nisai* (age)

いちだい *ichidai*, にだい *nidai* (mechanically operated things)

アクティビティー　Communicative Activities

Pair Work

A. SPEAK/LISTEN You want the following things from your partner. Ask your partner for the things you want and your partner will hand them properly to you. You thank him/her and he/she responds, "You are welcome."

1. one sheet of paper

2. two sheets of tissue

3. three sheets of worksheets

4. one piece of candy

5. two pieces of chocolate

6. five cookies

7. (something of your choice)

Class Work

B. SPEAK/LISTEN Your teacher has some candy or fruit (フルーツ *furuutsu*). Ask your teacher for them. Be humble. The teacher will give you them only if your request is correct. As the teacher asks each student, ask for one more than the previous student, using the correct counter. Then count them in Japanese while you are receiving them. Don't forget to thank your teacher and bow slightly.

たんご Vocabulary

🔊 1.

	Months of the year			
1	いちがつ	一月	*ichi-gatsu*	January
2	にがつ	二月	*ni-gatsu*	February
3	さんがつ	三月	*san-gatsu*	March
4	しがつ *	四月	*shi-gatsu**	April
5	ごがつ	五月	*go-gatsu*	May
6	ろくがつ	六月	*roku-gatsu*	June
7	しちがつ	七月	*shichi-gatsu*	July
8	はちがつ	八月	*hachi-gatsu*	August
9	くがつ *	九月	*ku-gatsu**	September
10	じゅうがつ	十月	*juu-gatsu*	October
11	じゅういちがつ	十一月	*juuichi-gatsu*	November
12	じゅうにがつ	十二月	*juuni-gatsu*	December
?	なんがつ	何月	*nan-gatsu?*	what month?

* For these months, always use しがつ *shigatsu* and くがつ *kugatsu*, never よんがつ *yongatsu* or
きゅうがつ *kyuugatsu*.

にがつ

しがつ

はちがつ

じゅういちがつ

2. Days of the month*

ついたち *tsuitachi* 1 日	じゅういちにち *juuichinichi* 11 日	にじゅういちにち *nijuuichinichi* 21 日
ふつか *futsuka* 2 日	じゅうににち *juuninichi* 12 日	にじゅうににち *nijuuninichi* 22 日
みっか *mikka* 3 日	じゅうさんにち *juusannichi* 13 日	にじゅうさんにち *nijuusannichi* 23 日
よっか *yokka* 4 日	じゅうよっか *juuyokka* 14 日	にじゅうよっか *nijuuyokka* 24 日
いつか *itsuka* 5 日	じゅうごにち *juugonichi* 15 日	にじゅうごにち *nijuugonichi* 25 日
むいか *muika* 6 日	じゅうろくにち *juurokunichi* 16 日	にじゅうろくにち *nijuurokunichi* 26 日
なのか *nanoka* 7 日	じゅうしちにち *juushichinichi* 17 日	にじゅうしちにち *nijuushichinichi* 27 日
ようか *yooka* 8 日	じゅうはちにち *juuhachinichi* 18 日	にじゅうはちにち *nijuuhachinichi* 28 日
ここのか *kokonoka* 9 日	じゅうくにち *juukunichi* 19 日	にじゅうくにち *nijuukunichi* 29 日
とおか *tooka* 10 日	はつか *hatsuka* 20 日	さんじゅうにち *sanjuunichi* 30 日
		さんじゅういちにち *sanjuuichinichi* 31 日

* The days with blue backgrounds have irregular pronunciations.

3. なんにち？

何日

nan-nichi?

What day?

4. きょう

kyoo

today

5. いつ

itsu

when?

6. （お）たんじょうび

(o)tanjoobi

birthday

お *o* is a polite prefix.

7. （お）たんじょうび
おめでとう（ございます）。

(o)tanjoobi omedetoo (gozaimasu)

Happy Birthday!

おめでとう *omedetoo* means "Congratulations."
ございます *gozaimasu* makes the greeting more formal.

よみましょう Language in Context

🔊 **READ/LISTEN/SPEAK** Read these sentences in Japanese. Ask your classmates when their birthdays are, and say "Happy Birthday" in Japanese to the person whose birthday is the closest to today's date.

おたんじょうびは　いつですか。　　おたんじょうび　おめでとう。

ぶんかノート　Culture Notes

A. Let's Sing the Happy Birthday Song in Japanese ♪♪♪ ♪♪♪

Search for the lyrics to the Happy Birthday song in Japanese online. Then sing the song in your class.

ひな dolls for Girls' Day

B. Japanese Holidays and Festivals

1月1日*	おしょうがつ	*Oshoogatsu*	New Year's Day*
3月3日	ひなまつり	*Hina Matsuri*	Girls' Day
5月5日*	こどものひ	*Kodomo no Hi*	Children's Day*
7月7日	たなばた	*Tanabata*	Star Festival
11月3日*	ぶんかのひ	*Bunka no Hi*	Culture Day*
11月15日	しちごさん	*Shichigosan*	Festival Day for 3, 5 and 7 Year Old Children

* = national holiday

A boy and girl dressed up for しちごさん

Carp Streamers on こどものひ

C. Japanese Proverb 「みっかぼうず」

みっか *mikka* means "three days" and ぼうず *boozu* means "a monk." This phrase is used to describe someone who does not persevere or someone who is not a steady, reliable worker.

Research one of the Japanese holidays shown above online, and prepare a presentation to share with your class. Be sure to mention any rituals or traditions, special foods, or gifts involved in celebrating the holiday, as well as when and why it was first celebrated.

アクティビティー　Communicative Activities

Class Work

A. SPEAK/LISTEN As a class, take turns giving your birthdates in Japanese. Write down your classmates' names and birthdates on a separate sheet of paper using a chart like the one below. Choose one student to read the correct answers so that everyone can check their answers.

Ex. 「わたしの　たんじょうびは　～がつ　～にちです。」
Watashi-no　tanjoobi wa　~gatsu　~nichi desu.

なまえ *namae*	たんじょうび *tanjoobi*

Pair Work

B. SPEAK/LISTEN Ask your partner for the dates of the following days.

Ex. 「きょうは　なんがつ　なんにちですか。」
Kyoo wa nan-gatsu nan-nichi desu ka.

「きょうは　いちがつ　とおかです。」
Kyoo wa ichi-gatsu tooka desu.

1. Today
2. Christmas (クリスマス *Kurisumasu*)
3. Valentine's Day (バレンタインデー *Barentaindee*)
4. Independence Day (どくりつきねんび *Dokuritsu Kinen Bi*)
5. New Year's Day (おしょうがつ *Oshoogatsu*)
6. Girls' Day (ひなまつり *Hina Matsuri*)
7. Culture Day (ぶんかのひ *Bunka no Hi*)
8. Festival Day for 3, 5 and 7 Year Old Children (しちごさん *Shichi-Go-San*)

2か7
What day of the week is it? What time is it?

たんご Vocabulary

A. Days of the week

1. にちようび	日曜日	*nichiyoobi*	Sunday
2. げつようび	月曜日	*getsuyoobi*	Monday
3. かようび	火曜日	*kayoobi*	Tuesday
4. すいようび	水曜日	*suiyoobi*	Wednesday
5. もくようび	木曜日	*mokuyoobi*	Thursday
6. きんようび	金曜日	*kinyoobi*	Friday
7. どようび	土曜日	*doyoobi*	Saturday
8. なんようび	何曜日	*nanyoobi*	What day of the week?

B. Time of Day—Hours

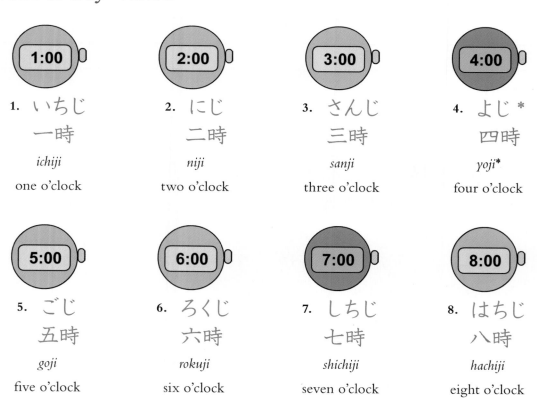

1. いちじ 一時 *ichiji* one o'clock
2. にじ 二時 *niji* two o'clock
3. さんじ 三時 *sanji* three o'clock
4. よじ * 四時 *yoji** four o'clock
5. ごじ 五時 *goji* five o'clock
6. ろくじ 六時 *rokuji* six o'clock
7. しちじ 七時 *shichiji* seven o'clock
8. はちじ 八時 *hachiji* eight o'clock

9. くじ *
　九時

*kuji**

nine o'clock

10. じゅうじ
　十時

juuji

ten o'clock

11. じゅういちじ
　十一時

juuichiji

eleven o'clock

12. じゅうにじ
　十二時

juuniji

twelve o'clock

* しじ *shiji* and きゅうじ *kyuuji* are never used.

---

13. なんじ　　何時　　　*nanji*　　　　　　　　　　　what time?

C. Others

1. くじはん

kuji han

half past 9:00

2. くじごろ

kuji goro

about 9:00

3. くじはんごろ

kuji hangoro

about half past 9:00

4. いま　　　　　　　*ima*　　　　　　　　　　　now

よみましょう　Language in Context

🔊 **READ/LISTEN/SPEAK** Read these sentences in Japanese, then ask a classmate what time it is.

なんじですか。

さんじはんです。

A. Kanji (Chinese characters) for Days of the Week

Below are the original meanings of the words for the days of the week and the *kanji* for each of them. As noted in the Introduction, some Chinese characters (*kanji*) depict a pictorial image of the words they represent. The illustrations below show how the *kanji* used in the days of the week were derived.

→ 日	sun, day	Sunday	→ 月	moon, month	Monday
→ 火	fire	Tuesday	→ 水	water	Wednesday
→ 木	tree	Thursday	→ 金	gold	Friday
→ 土	soil	Saturday		

B. Writing Dates in Japanese

When writing dates in Japanese, start with the largest unit, which is the year, followed by the character for year (年) *nen*, the month (月) *gatsu*, the date (日) *nichi* and day of the week (曜日) *yoobi*. Since you are just beginning to write Japanese, you may write the dates in *hiragana*, following your teacher's instructions.

Ex.　2016 年〔ねん〕　3月〔がつ〕　10日〔とおか〕
木曜日〔もくようび〕

NOTE: When reading years in Japanese, begin the year with せん *sen* "thousand" or にせん *nisen* "two thousand."

Research online the origins of the names of the week in English and in Japanese, then compare them. Are their origins similar in anyway? Different? What do they represent? Write a short paragraph summarizing your findings.

アクティビティー　Communicative Activities

Pair Work

A. SPEAK/LISTEN Ask your partner what day of the week it is. Alternate asking and answering, changing the day of the week each time until you have gone through all the days.

「きょうは　なんようびですか。」

Kyoo wa nan-yoobi desu ka.

「きょうは　～ようびです。」

Kyoo wa ～yoobi desu.

B. SPEAK/LISTEN Ask your partner what time it is now. Your partner answers using one of the choices below. Take turns.

Ex. Question:　いま　なんじですか。

Ima nanji desu ka.

Answer: ～じです。	*～ji desu.*	"It is ~ o'clock."
～じはんです。	*～ji han desu.*	"It is half past ~ o'clock."
～じごろです。	*～ji goro desu.*	"It is about ~ o'clock."
～じはんごろです。	*～ji han goro desu.*	"It is about half past ~ o'clock."

1. 1:00
2. 2:02
3. 7:30
4. 8:32
5. 9:00

6. 12:03
7. 2:58
8. 3:01
9. 4:30
10. 5:00

Writing

C. WRITE Write the following dates in Japanese.

1. Wednesday, January 6
2. Tuesday, September 13
3. Sunday, August 8

4. Friday, April 23
5. Saturday, December 30
6. Monday, February 29

Review Questions

Say these expressions or ask your partner these questions in Japanese. Your partner answers in Japanese. Check your answers using the audio.

Classroom Expressions Review pages 50, 55, and 64

1. Do you understand?
2. Yes, I understand.
3. No, I do not understand.
4. I do not know.
5. I cannot see.
6. I cannot hear.
7. How do you say "dog" in Japanese?
8. It is good.
9. It is unacceptable.
10. Here, please. [Hand something to another person.]
11. The tissues are over there. [Point.]
12. The homework is here. [Point.]

Requests Review page 64

13. Please give me one sheet of paper.
14. Please give me one piece of candy.

Personal Belongings Review pages 58 an 60

15. Is this yours? [Point.] [Do not use あなた to refer to your teacher!]
16. Is this money yours? [Point.] [Do not use あなた to refer to your teacher!]
17. That one over there is mine. [Point.]
18. That pencil (near the teacher/ partner) is mine.

Date & Time Review pages 69 and 74

19. What is the date today?
20. When is your birthday?
21. What day of the week is it today?
22. What time is it now?

Text Chat

You will participate in a simulated exchange of text–chat messages. You should respond as fully and as appropriately as possible. You will have a conversation with Kaito Tanaka, a Japanese high school student.

September, 18, 05:12 PM

はじめまして。　たなか　かいと
です。　どうぞ　よろしく。

*Hajimemashite.　Tanaka Kaito desu.
Doozo yoroshiku.*

> Introduce yourself.

September, 18, 05:19 PM

おたんじょうびは　いつですか。

Otanjoobi wa itsu desu ka.

> Respond.

September, 18, 05:22 PM

ここは　いま　すいようびです。
いちじです。

Koko wa ima suiyoobi desu.　Ichi-ji desu.

> Give the time and date where you are.

Can Do!
Now I can . . .

- [ ] respond to questions in the affirmative and the negative
- [ ] identify objects in the classroom that belong to me or my classmates
- [ ] ask how to say words in Japanese
- [ ] indicate the location of objects in the classroom

- [ ] make requests
- [ ] tell the time and date
- [ ] ask someone their birthday
- [ ] read and write *hiragana*

Origami Balloon
おりがみ　ふうせん

おりがみ *origami* means "folding paper." おり *ori* is from the verb おります *orimasu* which means "to fold." がみ *gami* is from the word かみ *kami* which means "paper." Origami is a Japanese traditional craft which both adults and children enjoy. First start with simple shapes like balloons, and soon you will have fun folding origami animals, flowers, toys, and more!

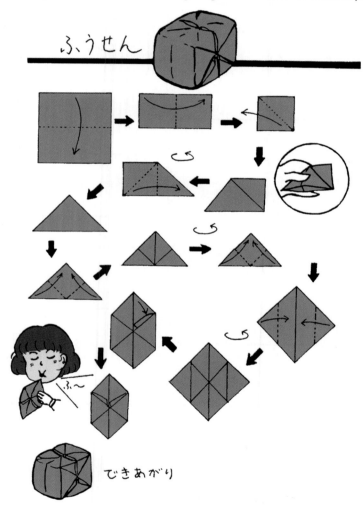

アクティビティー　Communicative Activities

1. Count in Japanese how many times you can bounce an origami balloon in the air.

2. Count in Japanese how many times you can bounce an origami balloon back and forth with your partner.

3か
Sanka

かぞく
Family

✓ Can Do!
In this lesson you will learn to

- say your age, name of school, grade
- introduce your family members (number of people, age, grade, job, nationality)
- ask about someone else's family (name, age, job)
- introduce a friend (name, age, grade, school)

Online Resources

cheng-tsui.com/adventuresinjapanese

- Audio
- Vocabulary Lists
- Vocabulary Flashcards
- *Kana* and *Kanji* Flashcards
- Activity Worksheets

Kanji
used in this lesson

In this lesson, you will learn some of the *kanji* for numbers and dates.

	Kanji	Meaning	Readings	Examples	
1.	一	one	*ichi*	<ruby>一<rt>いち</rt></ruby>まい	one (flat object)
			hito	<ruby>一<rt>ひと</rt></ruby>つ	one (general counter)
			*	<ruby>一日<rt>ついたち</rt></ruby>	1st day of the month
2.	二	two	*ni*	<ruby>二<rt>に</rt></ruby>まい	two (flat objects)
			futa	<ruby>二<rt>ふた</rt></ruby>つ	two (general counter)
			*	<ruby>二日<rt>ふつか</rt></ruby>	2nd day of the month
3.	三	three	*san*	<ruby>三<rt>さん</rt></ruby>まい	three (flat objects)
			mi(k/t)	<ruby>三<rt>みっ</rt></ruby>つ	three (general counter)
				<ruby>三日<rt>みっか</rt></ruby>	3rd day of the month
4.	四	four	*yon*	<ruby>四<rt>よん</rt></ruby>まい	four (flat objects)
			yo(k/t)	<ruby>四<rt>よっ</rt></ruby>つ	four (general counter)
				<ruby>四日<rt>よっか</rt></ruby>	4th day of the month
			shi	<ruby>四<rt>し</rt></ruby>がつ	April
5.	五	five	*go*	<ruby>五<rt>ご</rt></ruby>まい	five (flat objects)
			itsu	<ruby>五<rt>いっ</rt></ruby>つ	five (general counter)
				<ruby>五日<rt>いつか</rt></ruby>	5th day of the month
6.	日	sun, day	*ni*	<ruby>日<rt>に</rt></ruby>ほん	Japan
			nichi	なん<ruby>日<rt>にち</rt></ruby>	What day of the month?
			hi	<ruby>日<rt>ひ</rt></ruby>づけ	date
			bi	<ruby>日<rt>にち</rt></ruby>よう<ruby>日<rt>び</rt></ruby>	Sunday
			ka	<ruby>二日<rt>ふつか</rt></ruby>	2nd day of the month

WORKBOOK page 213

* Indicates irregular readings of the *kanji*

おはなし　Story

🔊 **READ/LISTEN** How many people are in the writer's family? What is his/her father's name?

これは　私_{わたし}の　かぞくの
しゃしんです。

かぞくは　六人_{ろくにん}です。

これは　父_{ちち}です。

父_{ちち}の　名前_{なまえ}は　ジャック^{Jakku}です。

父_{ちち}は　45さいです。

たんご　Vocabulary

🔊

| 1. ちち
父
chichi
(my) father | 2. はは
母
haha
(my) mother | 3. あに
ani
(my) older brother | 4. あね
ane
(my) older sister | 5. おとうと
otooto
(my) younger brother | 6. いもうと
imooto
(my) younger sister |

7. かぞく	8. きょうだい	9. なまえ 名前	10. だれ
kazoku	*kyoodai*	*namae*	*dare*
(my) family	(my) sibling(s)	name	who?

Counters

Note that the words in red are irregular.

11. People				12. Ages		
1	ひとり	一人	*hitori*	いっさい	一歳	*is-sai*
2	ふたり	二人	*futari*	にさい	二歳	*ni-sai*
3	さんにん	三人	*san-nin*	さんさい	三歳	*san-sai*
4	よにん	四人	*yo-nin**	よんさい	四歳	*yon-sai*
5	ごにん	五人	*go-nin*	ごさい	五歳	*go-sai*
6	ろくにん	六人	*roku-nin*	ろくさい	六歳	*roku-sai*
7	なな／ しちにん	七人	*nana/* *shichi-nin*	ななさい	七歳	*nana-sai*
8	はちにん	八人	*hachi-nin*	はっさい	八歳	*has-sai*
9	きゅうにん	九人	*kyuu-nin*	きゅうさい	九歳	*kyuu-sai***
10	じゅうにん	十人	*juu-nin*	じゅっさい	十歳	*jus-sai*
11	じゅういちにん	十一人	*juuichi-nin*	じゅういっさい	十一歳	*juuis-sai*
20	、 、 、			はたち	二十歳	*hatachi*
?	なんにん	何人	*nan-nin?*	なんさい／ （お）いくつ	何歳	*nan-sai?/* *(o)ikutsu?*

* Do not use しにん *shinin* for four people. しにん *shinin* means "a dead person."

** Do not use くさい *kusai* for nine years old. くさい *kusai* means "is smelly."

13. そうですか。

Soo desu ka.

Is that so?

14. ほんとうですか。

Hontoo desu ka.

Is that true?/Really?

15. の

no

A possessive and descriptive particle.

ついか　たんご　Additional Vocabulary

1.	いぬ　　　　犬	*inu*	dog
2.	ねこ	*neko*	cat
3.	どなた	*donata*	who? (polite form of だれ *dare*)
4.	ペット	*petto*	a pet
5.	ぎりの〜	*giri no ~*	~ in-law (family member)
6.	うえの〜	*ue no ~*	older (of two) ~
7.	したの〜	*shita no ~*	younger (of two) ~
8.	そふ	*sofu*	(my) grandfather
9.	そぼ	*sobo*	(my) grandmother

よみましょう　Language in Context

◀))) READ/LISTEN Read these sentences in Japanese. Compare the use of の.

そうですか。

Used often by a listener to respond to new information, usually with a nod.

これは わたしの ほんです。

の is possessive in this sentence.

これは にほんごの ほんです。

の is descriptive in this sentence.

ぶんぽう　Grammar

A Possessive and Descriptive Particle の

NOUN 1 の NOUN 2

NOUN 1 *no* NOUN 2

The particle の *no* used here indicates possession or description. This の *no* appears between two nouns. The first noun modifies the second.

◀))) MODELS

1. あにの　なまえは　マイクです。
   Ani no namae wa Maiku desu.　　My older brother's name is Mike.

2. これは　にほんごの　ほんです。
   Kore wa Nihongo no hon desu.　　This is a Japanese language book.

3. ぎりの　ははは　４０さいです。
   Giri no haha wa yonjus-sai desu.　　His mother–in–law is 40 years old.

4. これは　わたしの　かぞくの　しゃしんです。
   Kore wa watashi no kazoku no shashin desu.　　This is my family's photo.

READ/WRITE Write either the particle の or は in the ( ) based on the information below. Write X if no particle is required.

My name is Mayumi. This is my family's photo. There are three people in my family.

1. わたし（ 1 ）　なまえ（ 2 ）　まゆみです。
   Watashi　　　　*namae*　　　　*Mayumi desu.*

2. これ（ 3 ）　かぞく（ 4 ）　しゃしん（ 5 ）　です。
   Kore　　　*kazoku*　　　*shashin*　　　*desu.*

3. わたし（ 6 ）　かぞく（ 7 ）　さんにんです。
   Watashi　　　*kazoku*　　　*sannin desu*

ぶんかノート　Culture Notes

"In-group" versus "Out-group"

Languages reflect the structure, values, and attitudes of their societies. One of the primary social forces that affects the Japanese language is "in-group" vs. "out-group." Japanese people are constantly making distinctions between those people who are associated with themselves and those who are not, and this affects how they speak to others. Generally, when speaking to or about someone from your "out-group," you must use more polite language.

Members of the "in-group" may vary according to the circumstances. The "in-group" may be yourself, your family, your friends, your school, your company, or even your own country. The set of family terms which you are learning in this lesson is an example of how the language is used to make a distinction between one's own family (in-group) and another's family (out-group).

Based on the above, determine who is the "in-group" and who is the "out-group" in each of these situations.

1) You and your parents

2) Your family and a neighbor

3) You and your teacher

4) A worker and his/her boss

5) A boss and a customer/client

6) A Japanese person and an American stranger

Language Note

Japanese Aizuchi

そうですか。 "*Soo desu ka?*" is an example of *aizuchi*, or expressions which Japanese use frequently in conversations to indicate to the listener that they are listening to the speaker. Other words such as はい *hai*, ええ *ee*, or うん *un* are also used as *aizuchi*. The use of *aizuchi* is similar to the English use of "uh huh," but they are used much more frequently in Japanese, particulary when speaking over the phone. Aizuchi can be used both in formal and informal situations.

アクティビティー　Communicative Activities

Pair Work

A. SPEAK/LISTEN Bring a photo or drawing of a TV family to class. Present it to the class in Japanese.

Ex. これは　わたしの　かぞくの　しゃしんです。

　　Kore wa watashi-no kazoku-no shashin desu.

1. Describe what kind of photo or drawing it is.

2. Describe how many people there are in the family.

3. Describe each family member, including pets.

4. Give each family member's name and age.

Family Photos

B. WRITE

1. Bring a photo of your family to class or draw a picture of them on a separate sheet of paper. Using the lesson vocabulary, label each of the individuals in the image in Japanese by their position in the family.

2. Describe how this family photo from Japan is different from or similar to family photos you're used to seeing. Explain possible reasons for those differences and similarities.

Class Work - Song

🔊 **C. SPEAK** Let's sing two counting songs to the tune of "Ten Little Children."

1. ひとつ　ふたつ　みっつの　ハンバーガー

Hitotsu futatsu mittsu no hanbaagaa [1, 2, 3 hamburgers]

よっつ　いつつ　むっつの　ハンバーガー

Yottsu itsutsu muttsu no hanbaagaa [4, 5, 6 hamburgers]

ななつ　やっつ　ここのつの　ハンバーガー

Nanatsu yattsu kokonotsu no hanbaagaa [7, 8, 9 hamburgers]

とおの　ハンバーガー

Too no hanbaagaa [10 hamburgers]

むしゃ　むしゃ　むしゃ　むしゃ
ハンバーガーは　おいしい

Musha musha musha musha hanbaagaa wa oishii [Munch, munch, munch, munch. Hamburgers taste good.]

むしゃ　むしゃ　むしゃ　むしゃ　ハンバーガーは　おいしい

Musha musha musha musha hanbaagaa wa oishii

むしゃ　むしゃ　むしゃ　むしゃ　ハンバーガーは　おいしい

Musha musha musha musha hanbaagaa wa oishii

ハンバーガーは　おいしいね

Hanbaagaa wa oishii ne

2. ひとり　ふたり　さんにんの　こども

Hitori futari sannin no kodomo [1, 2, 3 children]

よにん　ごにん　ろくにんの　こども

Yonin gonin rokunin no kodomo [4, 5, 6 children]

しちにん　はちにん　きゅうにんの　こども

Shichinin hachinin kyuunin no kodomo [7, 8, 9 children]

じゅうにんの　こども

Juunin no kodomo [10 children]

わいわい　がやがや　こどもは　たのしい

Waiwai gayagaya kodomo wa tanoshii [(Sound of children playing) Children have fun.]

わいわい　がやがや　こどもは　たのしい

Waiwai gayagaya kodomo wa tanoshii

わいわい　がやがや　こどもは　たのしい

Waiwai gayagaya kodomo wa tanoshii

こどもは　たのしいね

Kodomo wa tanoshii ne

WORKBOOK page 5

かいわ　Dialogue

🔊 **READ/LISTEN** How many people are in Ken's family? How old is his sister?

ごかぞくは　何人ですか。

五人です。　父と　母と
あねと　いもうとと　ぼくです。

そうですか。
おねえさんの
名前は
何ですか。

ジーナです。

おねえさんは
何さいですか。

17さいです。

たんご　Vocabulary

🔊

1. おとうさん
   お父さん

   otoosan

   (someone's) father

2. おかあさん
   お母さん

   okaasan

   (someone's) mother

3. おじいさん

   ojiisan

   grandfather,
   elderly man

4. おばあさん

   obaasan

   grandmother,
   elderly woman

5. おにいさん

oniisan

(someone's) older brother

6. おねえさん

oneesan

(someone's) older sister

7. おとうとさん

otootosan

(someone's) younger brother

8. いもうとさん

imootosan

(someone's) younger sister

9. と

to

and

10. ごかぞく*

gokazoku

(someone's) family

11. おなまえ*

onamae

(someone's) name

* [ご and お are polite prefixes for nouns.]

12. そして　　　　*soshite*　　　　And (used only at the beginning of a sentence)

ついか　たんご　Additional Vocabulary

1. おじさん

ojisan

(someone's) uncle
(middle-aged) man

2. おばさん

obasan

(someone's) aunt
(middle-aged) woman

3. いとこ

itoko

(own) cousin

よみましょう　Language in Context

🔊 **READ/LISTEN** Read these sentences in Japanese. Say what words you should use to refer to your own mother or to someone else's.

わたしの　ははです。　　　　おかあさん、おはよう。

Use はは or ちち when talking about your parents with others. Use おかあさん or おとうさん
when talking to your parents or when talking about someone else's parents.

ぶんぽう　Grammar

A　Noun Connector Particle と

Noun 1 と Noun 2　　**Noun 1 and Noun 2**

Noun 1 to Noun 2

The particle と *to* conjoins two or more nouns. It is translated as "and." It cannot ever be used to conjoin anything but nouns. It is not replaceable by commas, as is common in English when a string of nouns are listed together.

◀))) MODELS

1. ベンさんと　エミさんは　おやすみです。
   Ben-san to Emi-san wa oyasumi desu.　　Ben and Emi are absent.

2. かぞくは　ちちと　ははと　わたしです。
   Kazoku wa chichi to haha to watashi desu.　　My family is my father, my mother and me.

READ/WRITE Write one of the particles と, の, or は in the ( ) based on the information below. Write X if no particle is required.

My family consists of my mother, myself, and my younger sister. My grandfather and grandmother are 65 years old. This is a photo of my dog and cat.

1. かぞく（ 1 ）　　はは（ 2 ）　　わたし（ 3 ）　　いもうとです。
   Kazoku　　　　*haha*　　　　*watashi*　　　　*imooto desu*

2. わたし（ 4 ）　　おじいさん（ 5 ）　　おばあさん（ 6 ）
   Watashi　　　　*ojiisan*　　　　*obaasan*

   ６５さいです。
   rokujuu-go-sai desu

3. これ（ 7 ）　　わたし（ 8 ）　　いぬ（ 9 ）
   Kore　　　*watashi*　　　*inu*

   ねこ（ 10 ）　　しゃしんです。
   neko　　　　*shashin desu*

B　Abbreviated Questions

〜は？　　　　**How about ~?**
~wa?

When the predicate of a question is understood by both the listener and speaker, it is common to use this abbreviated form. This is used more frequently in speaking than in writing. It is usually accompanied by a rise in pitch, similarly to questions in English.

1. あなたは？　　　How about you?
   Anata wa?

2. おなまえは？　　What is your/his/her name?
   Onamae wa?

3. おねえさんは？　How about your older sister?
   Oneesan wa?

4. しゅくだいは？　How about (your) homework?
   Shukudai wa?

5. これは？　　　　How about this?
   Kore wa?

SPEAK How do you say about the following in an abbreviated form? Pay attention to your pitch.

1. How about me?

2. How about your little sister?

3. How about that one over there?

C Sentence Connector そして

Sentence 1 。 そして、 **Sentence 2。**　　　　**Sentence 1. And Sentence 2.**
Soshite

そして *soshite*, which means "and," is only used at the beginning of sentences. However, since beginning a sentence with "And" is not common in English, English translations sometimes combine the two sentences into one.

1. ちちは　43さいです。　そして、ははは　38さいです。
   Chichi wa yonjuusan-sai desu. Soshite, haha wa sanjuu-has-sai desu.
   My father is 43. And my mother is 38 years old.

2. あねの　なまえは　まゆみです。　そして、18さいです。
   Ane no namae wa Mayumi desu. Soshite, juuhas-sai desu.
   My older sister's name is Mayumi. And she is 18 years old.

READ/WRITE Rewrite the sentences below using your own personal information. Write the correct sentence connector in place of the ( ) based on the information below.

My name is __. And I am __ years old. My mother's name is __. And my father's name is __.

1. わたしの　なまえは　_1_です。（ 2 ）_3_です。
   Watashi-no namae wa   desu.   desu.

2. ははの　なまえは　_4_です。（ 5 ）ちちの　なまえは　_6_です。
   Haha-no namae wa   desu.   chichi-no namae wa   desu.

ぶんかノート　Culture Notes

Addressing Family Members in Japanese

When talking to someone else about a family member, the terms ちち *chichi* and はは *haha*, etc., are used. However, when the Japanese address family members directly, おとうさん *otoosan* or パパ *papa* is used for father, おかあさん *okaasan* or ママ *mama* for mother, おにいさん *oniisan* for older brothers, and おねえさん *oneesan* for older sisters. Younger brothers and sisters are addressed by given names. さん *san* is not used when addressing or referring to siblings by name.

The Japanese do not use given names for family members older than themselves. Even spouses rarely use their given names when addressing one another. When children are smaller, they tend to use ちゃん *chan* instead of さん *san* to address others, i.e., おとうちゃん *otoochan* instead of おとうさん *otoosan*, おねえちゃん *oneechan* instead of おねえさん *oneesan*. パパ *papa* and ママ *mama* are also generally used by children.

 Watch an episode of a Japanese children's cartoon in Japanese online. What do the family members call each other? Count the number of times you hear *-san* and *-chan*. Which characters use these terms the most? Explain the reasons characters may use these different forms.

アクティビティー　Communicative Activities

Pair Work

SPEAK/WRITE Ask about your partner's family and draw a family tree. Find out how many people are in the family, what their relationships are, and their names and ages.

Q. 「ごかぞくは　なんにんですか。」
Gokazoku wa nan-nin desu ka.

A. 「〜にんです。」
~ nin desu.

Q. 「ごかぞくは　だれですか。」
Gokazoku wa dare desu ka.

A. 「ちちと　ははと　〜と　〜です。」
Chichi to haha to ~ to ~ desu.

Q. 「おとうさんの　おなまえは　なんですか。」
Otoosan-no onamae wa nan desu ka.

A. 「ちちの　なまえは　〜です。」
Chichi-no namae wa ~ desu.

Q. 「おとうさんは　なんさいですか。」
Otoosan wa nan-sai desu ka.

A. 「ちちは　〜さいです。」
Chichi wa ~ sai desu.

WORKBOOK　page 7

かいわ　Dialogue

 READ/LISTEN　What grade is Ken in? What grade is Emi in?

エミ：　お名前は？

ケン：　ケンです。

エミ：　ケンさんは　高校生ですか。

ケン：　いいえ、ぼくは　高校生

　　　　では　ありません。中学生です。

エミ：　何年生ですか。

ケン：　三年生です。

エミ：　そうですか。私も　中学三年生です。

たんご　Vocabulary

1. がっこう
   学校
   gakkoo
   school

2. せいと
   生徒
   seito
   elementary, intermediate,
   or high school student

3. がくせい
   学生
   gakusei
   college student

4. ちゅうがく
   中学
   chuugaku
   intermediate school
   (U.S. middle school or Jr. high)

5. こうこう 高校 *kookoo* high school	6. ちゅうがくせい 中学生 *chuugakusei* intermediate school student	7. こうこうせい 高校生 *kookoosei* high school student

8.	ちゅうがく　いちねんせい	*chuugaku ichinensei*	7th grader
9.	ちゅうがく　にねんせい	*chuugaku ninensei*	8th grader
10.	ちゅうがく　さんねんせい	*chuugaku sannensei*	9th grader, freshman
11.	こうこう　いちねんせい	*kookoo ichinensei*	10th grader, sophomore
12.	こうこう　にねんせい	*kookoo ninensei*	11th grader, junior
13.	こうこう　さんねんせい	*kookoo sannensei*	12th grader, senior
14.	なんねんせい	*nannensei?*	what grade?
15.	～も	*mo*	too, also

ついか　たんご　Additional Vocabulary

1.	だいがく	*daigaku*	college, university
2.	だいがくせい	*daigakusei*	college student
3.	しょうがっこう	*shoogakkoo*	elementary school
4.	しょうがくせい	*shoogakusei*	elementary school student
5.	ようちえん	*yoochien*	kindergarten
6.	ほいくえん	*hoikuen*	preschool

よみましょう　Language in Context

🔊 **READ/LISTEN** Read these sentences in Japanese. Say what grade you are in.

ぼくは　ちゅうがくせいです。

あねは　こうこうせいです。

ぶんぽう　Grammar

A Basic Negative Sentence: A is not B.

Noun 1 は **Noun 2** では　ありません／じゃ　ありません。
Noun 1 ≠ Noun 2

Noun 1 *wa* Noun 2 *dewa arimasen/ja arimasen.*

This pattern is the negative counterpart of NOUN 1 は *wa* NOUN 2 です *desu.* では
ありません *dewa arimasen* is more polite and formal than じゃ　ありません *ja arimasen.*

🔊 MODELS

1. わたしは　こうこうせいでは　ありません。
   Watashi wa kookoosei dewa arimasen.
   I am not a high school student.

2. ジョンさんは　おやすみでは　ありません。
   Jon-san wa oyasumi dewa arimasen.
   Jon is not absent.

3. ははは　５０さいじゃ　ありません。
   Haha wa gojussai ja arimasen.
   My mother is not 50 years old.

READ/WRITE Answer each question negatively.

1. がくせいですか。 （いいえ）
   Gakusei desu ka.　　　　　*(Iie)*

2. 18さいですか。 （いいえ）
   Juuhas-sai desu ka.　　　　*(Iie)*

3. おかあさんですか。（いいえ）
   Okaasan desu ka.　　　　*(Iie)*

B Inclusive Particle も ───────

Noun 1 も **Noun 2** です。	**Noun 1 is also Noun 2. /**
Noun 1 *mo* Noun 2 *desu.*	**Noun 1 is Noun 2 too.**
Noun 1 も **Noun 2** では ありません。	**Noun 1 is not Noun 2, either.**
Noun 1 *mo* Noun 2 *dewa arimasen.*	

も *mo* is used immediately after the noun to which the meaning of "also" applies. *Mo* is translated as "also" in affirmative sentences and "either" or "neither ~ nor" in negative sentences. も *mo* replaces particles を *o*, が *ga*, は *wa*.

◀)) MODELS ▷

1. ゆみさんは　14さいです。　わたしも　14さいです。
   Yumi-san wa juuyon-sai desu. Watashi mo *juuyon-sai* desu.
   Yumi is 14. I am 14, too.

2. わたしは　ちゅうがくせいでは　ありません。
   Watashi wa chuugakusei dewa arimasen.

   あにも　ちゅうがくせいでは　ありません。
   Ani mo *chuugakusei* dewa arimasen.
   I am not an intermediate school student. My older brother is not an intermediate school student, either.

3. ちちも　ははも　40さいです。
   Chichi mo *haha* mo *yonjus-sai* desu.
   Both my father and mother are 40 years old.

4. わたしも　あにも　ちゅうがくせいじゃ　ありません。
   Watashi mo *ani* mo *chuugakusei* ja arimasen.
   Neither I nor my older brother is an intermediate school student.

> **Noun 1** も **Noun 2** も **Noun 3** です。   **Both Noun 1 and Noun 2 are**
>
> *Noun 1 mo Noun 2 mo Noun 3 desu.*   **Noun 3.**
>
> **Noun 1** も **Noun 2** も **Noun 3**
>
> では　ありません。／じゃ　ありません
>
> Noun 1 *mo* Noun 2 *mo* Noun 3 *dewa arimasen / ja arimasen.*
>
> Neither Noun 1 nor Noun 2 are Noun 3.

READ/WRITE Write the correct particle in the ( ) based on the information below.

Ken is 15. Emi is 15, too. Ken is not 16. Emi is not 16, either. Both Ken and Emi are 15.

1. ケンさん（ 1 ）　　15さいです。エミさん（ 2 ）　　15さいです。
   Ken-san   *juugo-sai desu.*   *Emi-san*   *juugo-sai desu.*

2. ケンさん（ 3 ）　　16さいでは　ありません。
   Ken-san   *juuroku-sai dewa arimasen.*

   エミさん（ 4 ）　　16さいでは　　ありません。
   Emi-san   *juuroku-sai dewa*   *arimasen.*

3. ケンさん（ 5 ）　　エミさん（ 6 ）　　15さいです。
   Ken-san   *Emi-san*   *juugo-sai desu.*

ぶんかノート　Culture Notes

The Structure of the Japanese School System

These days, an increasing number of Japanese children attend preschool and almost all children attend kindergarten. Japanese students attend elementary school for six years, intermediate school for three years, and high school for another three years, in a 6–3–3 system. In most places in the U.S., schools typically have a 5–3–4 system with five years of elementary school, three years of middle school, and four years of high school. College in Japan typically lasts four years, similar to the U.S.

Research the Japanese school system online. Answer at least three of the following questions.

- What is the number of compulsory years for schooling?
- How many months do students attend school?
- How long is a typical school day?
- How many students are usually in a classroom?
- What subjects are studied in elementary and middle schools?
- What types of high schools may students attend?

Language Note

あなた *anata* ≠ You

あなた *anata* is used to address persons of equal or lower status.

It's better to avoid the use of あなた *anata*, especially when it is clear that the subject is "you," because you don't want to unintentionally speak down to someone.

アクティビティー　Communicative Activities

Class Work

A. SPEAK/WRITE Ask your classmates for their full names and grades. On a separate sheet of paper, draw a seating chart with the names and the grades of each student in English. Later your teacher will ask you the grade level of each student. Answer in Japanese.

Ex. おなまえは？　　　なんねんせいですか。

　　Onamae wa?　　　*Nan-nensei desu ka.*

Pair Work

B. SPEAK/LISTEN Ask your partner the following questions about your classmates. Your partner answers based on the information from the previous activity.

1. ～さんは　こうこうせいですか。

　　~san wa kookoosei desu ka.

2. ～さんは　なんねんせいですか。

　　~san wa nan-nensei desu ka.

WORKBOOK　page 9

かいわ　Dialogue

READ/LISTEN What is the girl's name? What grade is she in?

お名前は？

中村明子です。

何人ですか。

学校は　どこですか。

日本人です。

京王高校です。

何年生ですか。

高校　一年生です。

Introducing Others

READ/SPEAK Practice introducing one of your classmates.

こちらは　なかむら　あきこさんです。

Kochira wa Nakamura Akiko-san desu.

なかむらさんは　にほんじんです。

Nakamura san wa nihonjin desu.

にほんの　こうこう　いちねんせいです。

Nihon no kookoo ichi-nensei desu.

1. どこ

doko

where?

2. こちら

kochira

this one

Polite form of これ
and may be used to refer to a person.

3. にほん
日本

Nihon

Japan

4. にほんじん
日本人

Nihon-jin

Japanese citizen

5. アメリカ

Amerika

U.S.A.

6. アメリカじん
アメリカ人

Amerika-jin

U.S. citizen

7. なにじん
何人

Nani-jin?

What nationality?

8. ちゅうごく
中ごく

Chuugoku

China

9. かんこく

Kankoku

South Korea

10. フランス

Furansu

France

11. スペイン

Supein

Spain

12. インド

Indo

India

13. ブラジル

Burajiru

Brazil

ついか　たんご　Additional Vocabulary

1. ロシア　　　　　*Roshia*　　　Russia
2. イギリス　　　　*Igirisu*　　　England
3. ドイツ　　　　　*Doitsu*　　　Germany
4. メキシコ　　　　*Mekishiko*　　Mexico
5. フィリピン　　　*Firipin*　　　Philippines
6. ナイジェリア　　*Naijeria*　　　Nigeria
7. にっけいじん　　*Nikkeijin*　　ethnically Japanese, but a citizen of another country, i.e., Japanese American

ぶんかノート　　Culture Notes

Japanese Nationality versus Ethnicity

Different terms are used for someone whose nationality is Japanese and for someone whose ethnicity is Japanese. にほんじん *Nihonjin* is a person who is a Japanese citizen. A person who is ethnically Japanese, but a citizen of a country other than Japan (i.e., America, Brazil, etc.) is にっけいじん *Nikkeijin*. Japanese Americans are にっけいアメリカじん *Nikkei Amerikajin*. Chinese Americans are ちゅうごくけいアメリカじん *Chuugokukei Amerikajin* and Korean Americans are かんこくけいアメリカじん *Kankokukei Amerikajin*.

 Choose a country with a Japanese immigrant population (U.S., U.K., Canada, Brazil, Peru, etc.) and research the *Nikkeijin* living there. How have they integrated into the society of that country and impacted it in turn? How have the *Nikkeijin* adapted to the culture of the country they live in? Prepare a presentation for your class describing the history, culture, and impact of the *Nikkeijin* in your chosen country.

にっけいじん　　Japanese Immigrants	
	Country
History	
Culture	
Impact	

Class Work

A. SPEAK/LISTEN Ask your partner for his/her name, age, grade, and nationality. Then introduce him/her to the class.

Ex. Q: おなまえは？
Onamae wa?

A: （あきこ）です。
(Akiko)   desu.

Q: なんねんせいですか。
Nan-nensei desu ka.

A: （こうこう　いちねんせい）です。
(Kookoo ichinensei) desu.

Q: なにじんですか。
Nani-jin desu ka.

A: ～じんです。
~jin desu.

Q: なんさいですか。
Nan-sai desu ka.

A: ～さいです。
~sai desu.

Speak and Connect

B. SPEAK/LISTEN Be a statistician! Form a group of 4-5 and ask each group member their nationality or a family member's. Write each person's nationality on a separate sheet of paper in a chart like the one below. One student from each group will report to the class. Tally the total number of students belonging to each nationality in the class. The teacher will ask you questions about the results you received.

Ex. 「～さんは、　なにじんですか。」
~san wa nani-jin desu ka.

Ex. 「～じんです。」
~ jin desu.

なまえ *namae*	Nationality

WORKBOOK page 11

かいわ　Dialogue

🔊 **READ/LISTEN** What is Ken's father's job? What did Ken's mother do before?

お父さんの　おしごとは　何ですか。

いしゃです。

どこの　びょういんの　おいしゃさんですか。

Kaizaa
カイザー
びょういんです。

そうですか。
お母さんは？

母は　今
しゅふです。
そして、まえ
先生でした。

たんご　Vocabulary

🔊

1. (お) しごと*

(o) shigoto

job

2. いしゃ**

*isha***

medical doctor

3. おいしゃさん

oishasan

medical doctor
Polite form of *isha*.

4. びょういん

byooin

hospital

* Use *oshigoto* when referring to someone else's job or occupation. Use *shigoto* when speaking about oneself or one's own family.

** When addressing a medical doctor, one uses the doctor's last name, followed by *sensei*, i.e., *Oda-Sensei*. *Isha* is not used.

5. べんごし

bengoshi

lawyer

6. かいしゃいん

kaishain

company employee

7. しゅふ

shufu

housewife

8. エンジニア

enjinia

engineer

9. けいかん

keikan

police officer

10. しょうぼうし

shoobooshi

firefighter

11. ウェイター／
ウェイトレス

weitaa/weitoresu

waiter /waitress

12. シェフ

shefu

chef, cook

---

13. まえ   *mae*   before

ついか　たんご　**Additional Vocabulary**

1. こうむいん	*koomuin*	government worker
2. かいけいし	*kaikeishi*	accountant
3. ひしょ	*hisho*	secretary
4. パイロット	*pairotto*	pilot
5. フライトアテンダント	*furaitoatendanto*	flight attendant
6. ふどうさんや	*fudoosanya*	real estate salesperson
7. しゃちょう	*shachoo*	company president
8. かんごし	*kangoshi*	nurse
9. びようし	*biyooshi*	hair stylist
10. やくざいし	*yakuzaishi*	pharmacist

🔊 **READ/LISTEN/SPEAK** Read these sentences in Japanese. Say how you would greet a doctor.

こんにちは。もりぐちせんせい。　こちらは　けいかんです。

ぶんぽう Grammar

A Basic Past Tense Sentences: A was B

Noun 1 は Noun 2 でした。 **N1 was/were N2.**
　　Noun 1 *wa* Noun 2 *deshita.*

Noun 1 は Noun 2 では／じゃ　ありませんでした。
　　Noun 1 *wa* Noun 2 *dewa/ja arimasendeshita.* **N1 was not/were not N2.**

This pattern is a variation of the "N1 は *wa* N2 です *desu.*" pattern. These new patterns are used when one expresses a statement in the past and the negative past form.

🔊 MODELS

1. ちちは　まえ　かいしゃいんでした。
   Chichi wa mae kaishain deshita.
   My father was a company employee before.

2. ははは　まえ　せんせいでした。
   Haha wa mae sensei deshita.
   My mother was a teacher before.

3. わたしは　まえ　この　がっこうの　せいとでは
   ありませんでした。
   Watashi wa mae kono gakkoo no seito dewa arimasendeshita.
   I was not a student of this school before.

READ/WRITE Answer each question negatively.

1. きょうは　いつかですか。　　　　　　　　（いいえ）
   Kyoo wa itsuka desu ka.　　　　　　　　　*(Iie)*

2. おばあさんは　まえ　せんせいでしたか。（いいえ）
   Obaasan wa mae sensei deshita ka.　　　　　*(Iie)*

3. おじいさんは　まえ　シェフでしたか。　　（いいえ）
   Ojiisan wa mae shefu deshita ka.　　　　　　*(Iie)*

ぶんかノート　Culture Notes

Describing Occupations

The Japanese tend to be very general about describing their occupations to others. Often, Japanese children know very little about the specifics of their parents' jobs, except for the name of the workplace. Even spouses are sometimes not clear about the exact responsibilities of their spouses' jobs.

What jobs or industries do you think employ the most people in Japan? Make predictions based on what you already know, then research the question online. Compare the results to your predictions. Explain why you made the predictions you did, and why they may be similar to or different from your actual findings.

アクティビティー　Communicative Activities

Pair Work

A. SPEAK/LISTEN Ask your partner about his/her family, what his/her parents do and what grade his/her siblings are in. Ask where his/her family members work or study.

Ex. 「おとうさんの　おしごとは　なんですか。」
Otoosan-no oshigoto wa nani desu ka.

"What is your father's occupation?"

「おしごとは　どこですか。」
Oshigoto wa doko desu ka.

"Where does he work?" (Literally, "Where is his work?")

「おねえさんは　なんねんせいですか。」

Oneesan wa nan-nensei desu ka.

"What grade is your older sister?"

「おねえさんの　がっこうは　どこですか。」

Oneesan-no gakkoo wa doko desu ka.

"What (=Where) is your older sister's school?"

Family	Job or Grade	Place of work or school

B. SPEAK/LISTEN Introduce your partner and his/her family to the class.

　　Ex. 「〜さんの　おとうさんは　(Workplace)　の　(Occupation) です。」

　　　~san-no otoosan wa (workplace)-*no* (occupation)*desu.*

Reading

C. READ/WRITE Read the following e-mail from a Japanese student. Answer the questions below in English or Japanese, depending on your teacher's directions.

はじめまして。

わたしは　おかだ　ゆきです。　15さいです。　こうこう
いち
一ねんせいです。　かぞくは　ちちと　ははと　いもうとです。

　　　　　　　　　　　resutoran　　　*shefu*
ちちは　とうきょう レストランの　シェフです。

ははは、　けいかんです。　いもうとは　ちゅうがく
に
二ねんせいです。

どうぞ　よろしく。

UNDERSTAND

1. What is the writer's name?

2. How many people are in the writer's family?

3. What are the writer's parents' jobs?

4. What grade is the writer's sister in?

Review Questions

Ask your partner these questions in Japanese. Your partner answers in Japanese. Check your answers using the audio.

Introducing Yourself and Your Family Review pages 83–84 and 90–91

1. What is your name?

2. How old are you?

3. When is your birthday?

4. How many people are there in your family?

5. Who is in your family?

6. How old is/are your sibling(s)?

7. How old is your father/mother?

8. When is your father's/mother's/sibling's birthday?

School Year Review pages 95–96

9. What school do you go to?

10. What grade are you in?

11. What grade is/are your sibling(s) in?

Nationality Review pages 101–102

12. What nationality are you?

13. What nationality is your mother/father?

Jobs Review pages 105–106

14. What is your father's job?

15. What is your mother's job?

Text Chat

You will participate in a simulated exchange of text–chat messages. You should respond as fully and as appropriately as possible.

You will have a conversation with Shuuichi Yamamoto, a Japanese high school student, about family.

October 3, 04:45 PM

はじめまして。　やまもと　しゅういち
です。　どうぞ　よろしく。

Hajimemashite. Yamamoto Shuuichi desu. Doozo yoroshiku.

Respond.

October 3, 04:53 PM

ぼくは　こうこう　一ねんせいです。
そして、16さいです。

Boku wa kookoo ichinensei desu. Soshite, juuroku-sai desu.

Respond similarly.

October 3, 05:02 PM

ぼくの　かぞくは　三にんです。
ははと　あにと　ぼくです。

Boku no kazoku wa san-nin desu. Haha to ani to boku desu.

Describe your family.

Can Do!

Now I can . . .

- ☐ introduce myself (name, age, grade, birthday)

- ☐ introduce my family members (relationship, name, age, grade, birthday, job, nationality)

- ☐ ask about someone's family members (name, age, grade, birthday, job, nationality)

- ☐ introduce a new friend (name, age, school, grade)

Family
かぞく

RESEARCH Use books, the Internet, or interview a Japanese member of your community to answer the following.

List

1. Write down the members of your household (e.g., mom, dad, older brother, step sister, grandmother, other adult, etc.) in Japanese.

Determine

2. What members of the family usually live under one roof in the U.S.?

3. What members of the family usually live under one roof in Japan?

4. How long do children usually live with their parents in the U.S.?

5. How long do children usually live with their parents in Japan?

Describe

6. What were some duties and responsibilities of traditional gender roles in Japan?

7. What were some duties and responsibilities of traditional gender roles in your country?

8. Describe at least two ways that traditional gender roles have changed in contemporary Japan.

9. Describe at least two ways that traditional gender roles have changed in your own country's contemporary society.

Identify

10. In traditional Japanese culture, the eldest son usually received certain benefits, but he also undertook certain responsibilities. Name one of these benefits and one of these responsibilities of eldest sons in Japan.

Extend Your Learning
TECHNOLOGY LITERACY
Collaborate in an e-pal exchange with students in Japan. Discuss questions 2–5 with them. Then create a presentation in table format showing how your perceptions about living situations of families in each country were similar to or differed from those of the Japanese students. Include a paragraph that summarizes your findings.

Story 3-1   page 83

これは　わたしの　かぞくの　しゃしんです。
かぞくは　ろくにんです。
これは　ちちです。
ちちの　なまえは　ジャックです。
ちちは　４５さいです。

Kore wa watashi no kazoku no shashin desu.
Kazoku wa rokunin desu.
Kore wa chichi desu.
Chichi no namae wa Jakku desu.
Chichi wa yonjuugo-sai desu.

Dialogue 3-2   page 90

エミ：　ごかぞくは　なんにんですか。
ケン：　ごにんです。ちちと　ははと　あねと　いもうとと　ぼくです。
エミ：　そうですか。おねえさんの　おなまえは　なんですか。
ケン：　ジーナです。
エミ：　おねえさんは　なんさいですか。
ケン：　１７さいです。

Emi: Gokazoku wa nan-nin desu ka.
Ken: Go-nin desu. Chichi to haha to ane to imooto to boku desu.
Emi: Soo desu ka. Oneesan no onamae wa nan desu ka.
Ken: Jiina desu.
Emi: Oneesan wa nan-sai desu ka.
Ken: Juunana-sai desu.

Dialogue 3-3   page 95

エミ：　おなまえは？
ケン：　ケンです。
エミ：　ケンさんは　こうこうせいですか。
ケン：　いいえ、ぼくは　こうこうせいでは　ありません。
　　　　ちゅうがくせいです。

エミ：　なんねんせいですか。

ケン：　さんねんせいです。

エミ：　そうですか。わたしも　ちゅうがく　さんねんせいです。

Emi: Onamae wa?
Ken: Ken desu.
Emi: Ken-san wa kookoosei desu ka.
Ken: Iie, boku wa kookoosei dewa arimasen. Chuugakusei desu.
Emi: Nan-nensei desu ka?
Ken: Sannensei desu.
Emi: Soo desu ka. Watashi mo chuugaku sannensei desu.

Dialogue 3-4   page 101

ケン：　おなまえは？

なかむら：　なかむら　あきこです。

ケン：　なにじんですか。がっこうは　どこですか。

なかむら：　にほんじんです。けいおうこうこうです。

ケン：　なんねんせいですか。

なかむら：　こうこう　いちねんせいです。

Ken: Onamae wa?
Nakamura: Nakamura Akiko desu.
Ken: Nani-jin desu ka. Gakkoo wa doko desu ka.
Nakamura: Nihonjin desu. Keioo Kookoo desu.
Ken: Nan-nensei desu ka.
Nakamura: Kookoo ichi-nensei desu.

Dialogue 3-5   page 105

エミ：　おとうさんの　おしごとは　なんですか。

ケン：　いしゃです。

エミ：　どこの　びょういんの　おいしゃさんですか。

ケン：　カイザーびょういんです。

エミ：　そうですか。おかあさんは？

ケン：　ははは　いま　しゅふです。そして、まえ　せんせいでした。

Emi: Otoosan no oshigoto wa nan desu ka.
Ken: Isha desu.
Emi: Doko no byooin no oishasan desu ka.
Ken: Kaizaa-Byooin desu.
Emi: Soo desu ka. Okaasan wa?
Ken: Haha wa ima shufu desu. Soshite, mae sensei deshita.

まいにち
Everyday Life

✓ Can Do!
In this lesson you will learn to

- ask what languages someone speaks
- say where you do an activity
- discuss what you do every day
- discuss what you did in the past
- discuss food and meals
- describe doing an action with someone

Online
Resources

cheng-tsui.com/
adventuresinjapanese

- Audio
- Vocabulary Lists
- Vocabulary Flashcards
- *Kana* and *Kanji* Flashcards
- Activity Worksheets

Kanji
used in this lesson

In this lesson, you will learn more *kanji* for numbers and dates.

	Kanji	Meaning	Readings	Examples		
7.	六	six	*roku*	ろく 六	six	
			mu(t/k)	むっ 六つ	six (general things)	
			*	むいか 六日	6th day (of month)	
8.	七	seven	*shichi*	しち 七	seven	
			nana	なな 七つ	seven (general things)	
			*	なのか 七日	7th day (of month)	
9.	八	eight	*hachi*	はち 八	eight	
			ya(t/k)	やっ 八つ	eight (general things)	
			*	ようか 八日	8th day (of month)	
10.	九	nine	*kyuu*	きゅう 九	nine	
			kokono	ここの 九つ	nine (general things)	
			ku	くがつ 九月	September	
11.	十	ten	*juu*	じゅう 十	ten	
			too	とお 十	ten (general objects)	
				とおか 十日	10th day (of month)	
12.	月	moon, month	*gatsu*	いちがつ 一月	January	
			getsu	げつようび 月曜日	Monday	

WORKBOOK page 217

* Indicates irregular readings of the *kanji*

Recognition Kanji

ashita

明日

tomorrow

かいわ　Dialogue

🔊 READ/LISTEN What language does Ken's mother speak? Does Ken speak the language at home?

READ Find these sentence patterns in the dialogue.

1. | Person | は | Place | で | | Language | を | はなします。|

wa *de* *o* *hanashimasu.*

2. | Sentence 1 | 。 | でも、| | Sentence 2 | [Sentence 1. However, Sentence 2.]

demo

たんご　Vocabulary

1. はなします [はなす]	2. にほんご 日本語	3. えいご えい語	4. うち	5. ともだち
hanashimasu [hanasu]	*Nihongo*	*Eigo*	*uchi*	*tomodachi*
to speak, talk	Japanese	English	house	friend

6. ちゅうごくご	中ごく語	*Chuugokugo*	Chinese language
7. かんこくご	かんこく語	*Kankokugo*	Korean language
8. スペインご	スペイン語	*Supeingo*	Spanish language
9. フランスご	フランス語	*Furansugo*	French language
10. アラビアご	アラビア語	*Arabiago*	Arabic language
11. タイご	タイ語	*Taigo*	Thai language
12. なにご	何語	*nanigo*	what language
13. (Place +) で		(Place +) *de*	at, in (a place)
14. よく		*yoku*	well, often
15. すこし		*sukoshi*	a little
16. ちょっと		*chotto*	a little; a tad

(More colloquial usage than すこし *sukoshi*.)

ついか　たんご　Additional Vocabulary

1. ドイツご	ドイツ語	*Doitsugo*	German language
2. ポルトガルご	ポルトガル語	*Porutogarugo*	Portuguese language
3. ラテンご	ラテン語	*Ratengo*	Latin language
4. ロシアご	ロシア語	*Roshiago*	Russian language

よみましょう　Language in Context

🔊 **READ/LISTEN/SPEAK** Read these sentences in Japanese. Say what languages you speak.

うちで　ちゅうごくごを
はなします。

こちらは　ともだちの
みどりさんです。

ぶんぽう　Grammar

A Particles

Direct Object Particle を

Object ＋ を (Object particle)
　　　　　　o

The particle を *o* immediately follows the direct object of a sentence.

 MODELS

1. ははは　日ほんごを　はなします。　　My mother speaks Japanese.
Haha wa Nihongo o hanashimasu.

2. わたしは　ちゅうごくごを　はなしません。
Watashi wa Chuugokugo o hanashimasen.　　　　　I do not speak Chinese.

3. すみません。　かみを　ください。
Sumimasen. Kami o kudasai.　　　　　Excuse me. Please give me some paper.

Location Particle で

Place ＋ で ＋ Action verb。   at, in
de

The particle で *de* immediately follows the place word where the action of the sentence occurs.

◀)) MODELS

1. わたしは　うちで　日ほんごを　はなします。
   Watashi wa uchi de Nihongo o hanashimasu.
   I speak Japanese at home.

2. ぼくは　がっこうで　えいごを　はなします。
   Boku wa gakkoo de Eigo o hanashimasu.
   I speak English at school.

READ/WRITE Write either the particle で or を in the ( ).

1. せんせいは　にほんご（ 1 ）　はなします。　わたしは
   うち（ 2 ）　えいご（ 3 ）　はなします。　わたしは
   がっこう（ 4 ）　にほんご（ 5 ）　はなします。

B Adverbs

よく　　　　　*yoku*　　　well, often

すこし　　　　*sukoshi*　　a little

ちょっと　　　*chotto*　　　a little; a tad (More colloquial usage than すこし *sukoshi*.)

Adverbs describe verbs. In Japanese sentences, adverbs generally come somewhere after the topic of the sentence and before the verb. No particles follow adverbs.

◀)) MODELS

1. おばあさんは　日ほんごを　よく　はなします。
   Obaasan wa Nihongo o yoku hanashimasu.　　My grandmother speaks Japanese well.

2. あねは　すこし　スペインごを　はなします。
   Ane wa sukoshi Supeingo o hanashimasu.　　My older sister speaks a little Spanish.

3. よく　みえます。
   Yoku miemasu.　　　　I can see well.

READ Choose the correct adverb from the options in the ( ) based on the context.

1. せんせいは　にほんごを　（よく / すこし）　はなします。

2. わたしは　にほんごを　（よく / ちょっと）　はなします。

3. わたしは　えいごを　（よく / すこし）　はなします。

C Sentence Connector でも

Sentence 1。 でも 、 **Sentence 2**。　[**Sentence 1. However, Sentence 2.**]
Demo

でも *demo* which means "however" is only used at the beginning of sentences.

MODELS

1. これは　わたしのです。　でも、それは　あなたのです。
   Kore wa watashino desu.　Demo, sore wa anatano desu.
   This is mine. However, that is yours.

2. ははは　日ほんごを　はなします。　でも、ちちは
   はなしません。
   Haha wa Nihongo o hanashimasu.　Demo, chichi wa hanashimasen.
   My mother speaks Japanese. However, my father does not speak it.

READ Choose the correct conjunction from the options in the ( ).

1. わたしは　にほんごを　よく
   はなしません。（そして / でも）、えいごを
   よく　はなします。

2. ともだちは　ちゅうごくじんです。（そして /
   でも）、ちゅうごくごを　よく　はなします。

3. ゆみさんは　16さいです。（そして / でも）、
   わたしも　16さいです。

D Answering Yes/No Questions Without です

When a question ends with a verb, the answer should also be answered with the same verb.
そうです *soo desu* and そうでは　ありません *soo dewa arimasen* are incorrect responses.

 MODELS

Ex. Verb question:	日ほんごを　はなしますか。	
	Nihongo o hanashimasu ka.	Do you speak Japanese?
Affirmative answer:	はい、はなします。	Yes, I do.
	Hai, hanashimasu.	
Negative answer:	いいえ、はなしません。	No, I don't.
	Iie, hanashimasen.	

READ Choose the correct response to each question from the options in the ( ).

1. 「にほんごを　はなしますか。」

   「はい、（はなします　そうです）。」

2. 「タイ *Tai* ごを　はなしますか。」

   「いいえ、（はなしません。　そうでは　ありません。）」

ぶんかノート　Culture Notes

Speaking Respectfully

The *masu* form is a formal usage of verbs and is safe and respectful to use with any Japanese person. However, among close relatives or friends, plain forms are used instead of *masu* forms. Plain forms are not used with teachers, older non-family members, or strangers, as it would be considered rude. Correct usage of plain dictionary forms and polite *masu* forms is important, as it demonstrates politeness and respect.

Which form should you use to address each of the following people? Explain.

- Your best friend
- Your math teacher
- An older neighbor
- A parent
- A server in a restaurant

Language Note

Verb Masu Form and the Dictionary Form

In this text you see another verb form in [ ] after the *masu* form. This is called the *dictionary form* since it is the form used to look up verbs in the Japanese dictionary. The dictionary form is also called the imperfect affirmative *plain form*. Using plain forms does not change the meaning of the sentence, but its use is less formal.

のみます　← *masu* form
［のむ］　← Dictionary or plain form

アクティビティー　Communicative Activities

Pair Work

A. SPEAK/LISTEN/WRITE Ask your partner what language each of these people speak at home, school, or work (しごと *shigoto*). Your partner will answer appropriately, then also respond with another language the person speaks using でも *demo*. Write your answers in Japanese on a separate sheet of paper using a chart like the one below.

Ex. Question: 〜さんは　うちで　なにごを　はなしますか。
~san wa uchi de nanigo o hanashimasu ka.

Answer: 〜さんは　（うちで）　えいごを　はなします。
~ san wa (uchi de) Eigo o hanashimasu.

でも、がっこうで　日ほんごを　はなします。
Demo, gakkoo de Nihongo o hanashimasu.

Name	Languages Spoken	Home	School/Work
1. Sonja	German, studying in U.K.		
2. Cindy	U.S. studying in Saudi Arabia		
3. Your friend's father	Japanese, working in U.S.		
4. Your friend's mother	Chinese, working in U.S.		
5. Ivan	Russian, studying in Japan		

Reading

B. READ/WRITE Read the passage below and answer the questions. Write your answers in Japanese using complete sentences.

私の　母は　うちで　日本語を　はなします。でも、

ベンさんの　お母さんは　うちで　フランス語を　はなします。

UNDERSTAND

1. Does the author's mother speak French?

2. What language does Ben's mother speak at home?

APPLY

3. What languages do you speak at home?

4. What languages do you speak at school?

WORKBOOK page 19

4か2
what do you eat?

かいわ　Dialogue

🔊 **READ/LISTEN** What does Ken's family eat every day? What do they drink?

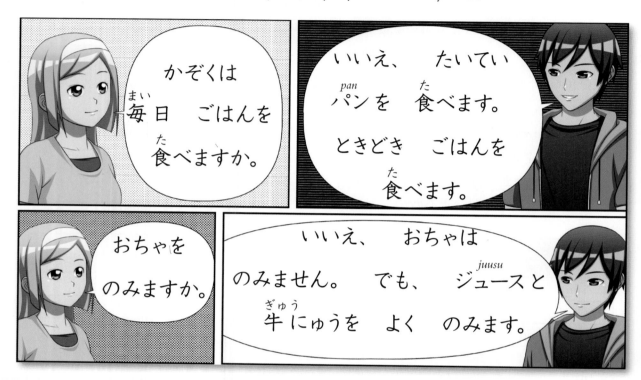

ぶんけい　Sentence Patterns

READ Find these sentence patterns in the dialogue.

1. Person は adverb ✕ food を　たべます。
2. Person は adverb ✕ drink を　のみます。

Adverbs	
まいにち　every day *mainichi*	いつも　always *itsumo*
たいてい　usually *taitei*	よく　　often, well *yoku*
ときどき　sometimes *tokidoki*	

たんご Vocabulary

1. たべます
[たべる]
食べます

tabemasu [taberu]

to eat

2. のみます
[のむ]

nomimasu [nomu]

to drink

3. ごはん

gohan

cooked rice

4. パン

pan

bread

5. (お)みず

(お)水

(o) mizu

water

6. ジュース

juusu

juice

7. ぎゅうにゅう, ミルク
牛にゅう

gyuunyuu, miruku

(cow's) milk

8. コーラ

koora

cola

9. おちゃ

ocha

tea

10. コーヒー

koohii

coffee

11. まいにち　毎日

mainichi

every day

12. ときどき　　　　　*tokidoki*　　　　sometimes

13. たいてい　　　　　*taitei*　　　　usually

14. いつも　　　　　　*itsumo*　　　　always

ついか たんご　Additional Vocabulary

1. トースト　　　　　*toosuto*　　　　toast
2. シリアル　　　　　*shiriaru*　　　　cereal
3. ホットケーキ　　　*hotto keeki*　　　pancakes
4. たまご　　　　　　*tamago*　　　　egg
5. ベーコン　　　　　*beekon*　　　　bacon
6. サラダ　　　　　　*sarada*　　　　salad
7. くだもの　　　　　*kudamono*　　　fruit (native Japanese term)
8. フルーツ　　　　　*furuutsu*　　　fruit
9. こうちゃ　　　　　*koocha*　　　　black tea
10. けっして + Neg.　*kesshite+Neg.*　never

よみましょう　Language in Context

🔊 **READ/LISTEN/SPEAK**　Read these sentences in Japanese. Say what you eat everyday. Say one thing you drink sometimes.

いつも　おちゃを　のみます。

ときどき　ごはんを　食べます。

ぶんぽう　Grammar

A Emphatic Particle は in Contrastive Sentences

Object ＋ は ＋ Negative predicate 。
　　　　　wa

When the content of a sentence suggests a contrast, the object particle を *o* may be replaced by the particle は *wa*.

◀))) MODELS

1. わたしは　日ほんごを　はなします。
　　でも、　ちゅうごくごは　はなしません。

　　Watashi wa Nihongo o hanashimasu. Demo, Chuugokugo wa hanashimasen.
　　I speak Japanese. But I do not speak Chinese.

2. わたしは　おちゃを　のみません。
　　でも、　コーヒーは　のみます。

　　Watashi wa ocha o nomimasen. Demo, koohii wa nomimasu.
　　I don't drink tea. But I do drink coffee.

READ Choose the correct particle from the options in the ( ).

1. ぼくは　おみずを　のみます。でも、　おちゃ（を / は）
のみません。

2. ぼくは　にほんご（を / は）　すこし　はなします。
でも、　ちゅうごくご（を / は）　はなしません。

ぶんかノート　Culture Notes

What Do Japanese Eat for breakfast?

Japanese traditionally have rice at all three meals. Recently, dietary habits have changed and more families, especially younger ones, have Western-style breakfasts. While cereals are becoming a more common sight, they are still not part of a typical Western breakfast in Japan.

right A Western-style breakfast in Japan with buttered toast, eggs and/or meat: a vegetable salad is often included, particularly at hotels or restaurants

left A traditional Japanese breakfast with rice, miso soup, pickled vegetables, and sometimes grilled fish or a raw egg

What do you usually eat for breakfast? After researching online, create a chart comparing common breakfast foods in Japan, the United States, and another country of your choosing.

アクティビティー　Communicative Activities

Pair Work

A. SPEAK/LISTEN/WRITE Ask your partner if he/she eats or drinks any of the vocabulary items from pages 125–126 every day. Write your partner's answers in Japanese on a separate sheet of paper using a chart like the one below.

Your partner will respond using ときどき *tokidoki* "sometimes," たいてい *taitei* "usually," いつも *itsumo* "always," or they will respond negatively.

> まい日　ごはんを
> たべますか。
> *Mainichi gohan o tabemasu ka.*

> ときどき　ごはんを
> たべます。
> *Tokidoki gohan o tabemasu.*

Food or Beverage	ときどき, たいてい, いつも
1. rice	
2. water	

B. SPEAK/LISTEN/WRITE Find out what your partner's family members often eat and drink at home.

> おとうさんは　うちで
> なにを　よく　たべますか。
> *Otoosan wa uchi de nani o yoku tabemasu ka.*

> ちちは　〜を　よく
> たべます。
> *Chichi wa ~o yoku tabemasu.*

Family Member	Food	Drink

WORKBOOK page 21

かいわ　Dialogue

🔊 **READ/LISTEN** What did Ken eat this morning? What did he eat for lunch?

Ken
ケン: きのう　七時に　ばんごはんを

食べました。

Emi
エミ: ばんごはんに　何を　食べましたか。

Ken　*Kareeraisu*
ケン: カレーライスを　食べました。

Emi きょう
エミ: 今日　あさごはんに

なに　た
何を　食べましたか。

Ken なに　た
ケン: 何も　食べませんでした。　でも、

piza た
おひるごはんに　ピザを　食べました。

ぶんけい　Sentence Patterns

READ Find these sentence patterns in the dialogue.

Person は　general time × meal に
wa　　　　　　　　　　*ni*

food を　たべました。
o　　*tabemashita*

なにも　たべませんでした。
nanimo　　*tabemasendeshita*

1. きのう	2. きょう 今日	3. あした 明日	4. あさ
kinoo	*kyoo*	*ashita*	*asa*
yesterday	today	tomorrow	morning

5. (お)ひる	6. ばん	7. よる	8. ゆうがた
(o) hiru	*ban*	*yoru*	*yuugata*
daytime	evening, night	night	late afternoon, early evening

9. あさごはん	10. (お)ひる (ごはん)	11. ばんごはん
asagohan	*(o)hiru(gohan)*	*bangohan*
breakfast	lunch	dinner, supper

12. なにも + Neg.　　　　*nani mo + Neg.*　　　　(not) anything, nothing

ついか　たんご　Additional Vocabulary

1.	(お) べんとう	*(o)bentoo*	box lunch
2.	おむすび / おにぎり	*omusubi / onigiri*	rice ball
3.	ラーメン	*raamen*	Chinese noodles in hot soup
4.	うどん	*udon*	thick white noodles
5.	ピザ	*piza*	pizza
6.	ホットドッグ	*hottodoggu*	hot dog
7.	ハンバーガー	*hanbaagaa*	hamburger
8.	ステーキ	*suteeki*	steak
9.	さかな	*sakana*	fish
10.	スパゲッティ	*supagetti*	spaghetti
11.	(お)すし	*(o)sushi*	sushi
12.	てんぷら	*tenpura*	tempura
13.	カレーライス	*kareeraisu*	curry rice

よみましょう　Language in Context

))) READ/LISTEN/SPEAK Read these sentences in Japanese. Do you know what *bento* is? *Unagi*?

たいてい　べんとうを　食べます。

今日　ひるごはんに
うなぎを　食べました。

A Time Words

General Time Words without Particles

There are two types of time words in Japanese: general time and specific time. General time words are not attached to a number, nor do they suggest any degree of specificity. Words such as きょう *kyoo* "today," あさ *asa* "morning," きのう *kinoo* "yesterday," etc., are in this category. General time words do not take any particles unless they are the topic of a sentence.

◀))) MODELS ▷

1. わたしは　きのう　あさごはんを　たべませんでした。
   Watashi wa kinoo asagohan o tabemasendeshita.
   I did not eat breakfast yesterday.

2. きのうの　ばん　日ほんごを　はなしました。
   Kinoo no ban nihongo o hanashimashita.
   I spoke Japanese last night.

Specific Time Particle に　　Specific time ＋ に on, at

The second type of time words in Japanese are specific time words. General time words such as きょう *kyoo* "today," いま *ima* "now," まいにち *mainichi* "every day," etc., are not followed by the particle に. Specific time words, such as 一じ *ichiji* "one o'clock," 日よう日 *nichiyoobi* "Sunday," 一月 *ichigatsu* "January" are followed by the particle に *ni*.

◀))) MODELS ▷

1. わたしは　しちじに　ばんごはんを　たべました。
   Watashiwa shichiji ni bangohan o tabemashita.　　　I ate dinner at 7 o'clock.

2. 日よう日に　あさごはんを　たべません。
   Nichiyoobi ni asagohan o tabemasen.　　　I do not eat breakfast on Sunday.

READ Choose the correct particle from the options in the ( ). X means no particle is required.

1. あさ（に / X）　ジュース *juusu* を　のみます。

2. どようび（に / X）　レストラン *resutoran* で　たべました。

3. まいにち（に / X）　にほんごを　はなします。

4. きのう（に / X）　ハじ（に / X）　ばんごはんを　たべました。

B Occasion/Meal Particle に ─────

あさごはん／ひるごはん／ばんごはん＋に   for breakfast/lunch/dinner

Asagohan / hirugohan / bangohan + ni

The particle に *ni* in this situation indicates a specific occasion. NOTE: Particles such as に, で, から and others serve many functions in Japanese grammar. For example, this に *ni* is different from the specific time ＋ に *ni* form from Grammar Note A in meaning and usage.

MODELS ▶

1. 「おひるごはんに　なにを　たべますか。」
   Ohirugohan ni nani o tabemasu ka.   "What are you going to eat for lunch?"

   「ピザを　たべます。」
   Piza o tabemasu.   "I will eat pizza."

2. きのう　ばんごはんに　おすしを　たべました。
   Kinoo bangohan ni osushi o tabemashita.   I ate sushi for dinner yesterday.

READ Choose the correct particle from the options in the ( ). X means no particle is required.

1. 「あさごはん (を / に)　なにを　たべますか。」

   「パン *pan* (を / に)　たべます。」

2. わたしは　きのう　ばんごはん (を / に)　たべませんでした。

3. わたしは　まいにち　あさごはん (を / に)　シリアル *shiriaru*
   (を / に)　たべます。

C Past Tense Verb Endings -ました and ませんでした ─────

Verb-ました   **did, have done [completed and affirmative form of verb]**
Verb-*mashita*

Verb-ませんでした **did not, have not done [completed and negative form of verb]**
Verb-*masendeshita*

MODELS ▶

1. 「あさごはんを　たべましたか。」   "Did you eat breakfast?"
   Asagohan o tabemashita ka.

   「いいえ、たべませんでした。」   "No, I did not eat."
   Iie, tabemasendeshita.

2. ちちは　きょう　コーヒーを　のみませんでした。
   Chichi wa kyoo koohii o nomimasendeshita.   My father did not drink coffee today.

READ Choose the correct verb endings from the options in the ( ) based on the information below.

Yesterday I didn't eat lunch, but I ate dinner. Today I did not eat breakfast, but I will eat lunch.

1. わたしは　きのう　おひるごはんを　（たべません /
たべませんでした）。でも、きのう　ばんごはんを
（たべます / たべました）。きょう　あさごはんを
（たべません / たべませんでした）。でも、きょう
おひるごはんを　（たべます / たべました）。

D　Didn't ~ Anything

なにも＋ **Negative predicate。** **(not) anything, nothing**

Nanimo + Negative predicate.

なにも *nanimo* used with a negative predicate means "nothing" or "not anything."

MODELS

1. 「あさ　なにを　たべましたか。」
   Asa nani o tabemashita ka.　　　　　"What did you eat in the morning?"

   「なにも　たべませんでした。」　"I did not eat anything."
   Nani mo tabemasendeshita.

2. 「なにを　のみますか。」　　　　"What will you drink?"
   Nani o nomimasu ka.

   「なにも　のみません。」　　　　"I won't drink anything."
   Nani mo nomimasen.

READ/WRITE Answer the questions using なにも and the proper verb form.

1. きょう　あさごはんに　なにを　のみましたか。

2. おひるごはんに　たいてい　なにを　たべますか。

3. ばんごはんに　たいてい　なにを　のみますか。

Lunch and Dinner in Japan

Lunch and dinner in Japan are extremely varied. They may be traditional, i.e., rice, miso soup, pickled vegetables and fish, or they may be a dish from any country in the world. Japanese meals have begun to take on a more Western appearance in recent years, with fewer vegetables and more beef and chicken. Likewise, "Western foods" as we know them (spaghetti, pizza, etc.) can also reflect a Japanese influence.

Yakitori, skewered grilled chicken

Many Chinese foods, like ramen noodles, have become a popular part of Japanese lunch and dinner menus, although they too have been altered significantly to suit the tastes of the Japanese.

Yakizakana, grilled fish

Using the Internet, look up a common Western food (like pizza, hamburgers, or spaghetti) and find out how their taste and appearance differ in Japan.

Use a graphic organizer like the one below to keep track of the similarities and differences. Make a digital presentation and share your findings with the class.

Japanese style spaghetti with squid and *shiso* leaves

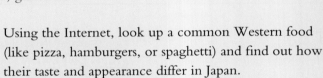

West
Tomato Sauce
Meatballs

Japan
Crab or Fish
Green vegetables
Clear sauce/broth

Spaghetti noodles
Savory taste
Sometimes spicy

Pair Work

A. SPEAK/LISTEN/WRITE Ask your partner what he/she ate yesterday and today.
Write your answers in Japanese on a separate sheet of paper in a chart like the one below.

Ex. Question: きのう　ばんごはんに　なにを　たべましたか。
Kinoo bangohan ni nani o tabemashita ka.

そして、なにを　のみましたか。
Soshite, nani o nomimashita ka.

Answer:
〜と　〜を　たべました。　そして、〜を　のみました。
~ to　　~ o　　tabemashita.　Soshite,　~ o　　nomimashita.

Yesterday's Dinner	Today's Breakfast	Today's Lunch

Reading

B. UNDERSTAND

1. What meal is this menu for?

2. How much does ramen cost?

3. How much do *soba* noodles cost?

IDENTIFY

4. Which *kanji* do you think means "meal" based on the context?

5. Which menu item is the "grilled fish set meal"?

APPLY

6. Which menu item would you like to order? Explain your answer in English.

WORKBOOK page 23

おひるごはん
メニュー

とんかつ定食	¥980
焼き魚定食	¥880
ハンバーグ定食	¥750
ラーメン	¥680
カレーライス	¥500
やきそば	¥450

かいわ Dialogue

🔊 **READ/LISTEN** Where does Emi usually eat lunch? Who does she eat with?

どこで おひるごはんを 食べますか。

たいてい カフェテリア*kafeteria*で 食べます。

だれと 食べますか。

ともだちと いっしょに 食べます。

ぶんけい Sentence Patterns

READ Find these sentence patterns in the dialogue.

Person は general time ✕ place で person と (いっしょに) thing を action verb 。
wa *de* *to* *(issho ni)* *o*

1. としょかん

toshokan

library

**2. カフェテリア/
しょくどう**

*kafeteria/
shokudoo*

cafeteria

3. ばいてん

baiten

snack bar, kiosk

Found in most Japanese
schools, *baiten* sell snacks as
well as school supplies.

**4. Person + と
（いっしょに）**

*Person +
to (issho ni)*

(together) with person

5. しんぶん

shinbun

newspaper

6. ざっし

zasshi

magazine

7. おんがく

ongaku

music

**8. よみます
[よむ]**

*yomimasu
[yomu]*

to read

**9. ききます
[きく]**

kikimasu [kiku]

to listen, hear

**10. します
[する]**

shimasu [suru]

to do

**11. べんきょう（を）　します
[べんきょう（を）　する]**

*benkyoo (o) shimasu
[benkyoo (o) suru]*

to study

ついか　たんご　Additional Vocabulary

1. CD（シーディー）　　　　　*shiidii*　　　　　　　CD

よみましょう　Language in Context

🔊 **READ/LISTEN/WRITE**　What did you read in the library?

としょかんで　　　　　　　ざっし　　　　　　　　しんぶん
ほんを　よみました。

ぶんぽう　Grammar

Ⓐ　"With" Particle　と（いっしょに）

Person ＋ と（いっしょに）**(together) with ~**

Person　＋　*to*　　*(issho ni)*

The particle と *to* follows a noun which names the person with whom an action is being done.

Often いっしょに *issho ni* "together with" appears after と *to*.

🔊 MODELS

1. 「だれと　おひるごはんを　たべますか。」
   Dare to ohirugohan o tabemasu ka.　　　　　"With whom do you eat lunch?"

   「ともだちと　いっしょに　たべます。」
   Tomodachi to issho ni tabemasu.　　　　　"I eat with my friend."

2. ベンさんと　いっしょに　しゅくだいを　しました。
   Ben-san to issho ni shukudai o shimashita.　　　I did my homework with Ben.

READ/WRITE Answer the questions using いっしょに and the suggestions provided in the ( ).

1. たいてい　だれと　あさごはんを　たべますか。(はは)

2. だれと　にほんごの　しゅくだいを　しましたか。(ともだち)

3. だれと　おんがくを　ききましたか。(ケン*Ken*さん)

B Nominal Verbs

Noun ＋ (を)　します **verbs.**
(o)　　　　shimasu

There are many verbs in this group. One such verb is べんきょう(を)　します *benkyoo (o) shimasu* "to study." べんきょう *benkyoo* itself is a noun and します *shimasu* is the verb "to do." べんきょう(を)　します *benkyoo (o) shimasu* literally means "to do studies."

◀)) MODELS

1. 「としょかんで　べんきょう(を)　しました。」
   Toshokan de benkyoo (o) shimashita.   "I studied at the library."

   「なにを　べんきょうしましたか。」
   Nani o benkyooshimashita ka.   "What did you study?"

Most Japanese sentences do not contain two を *o* particles. When there is something to study, を *o* follows the main direct object and is eliminated after べんきょう *benkyoo.*

◀)) MODELS

2. わたしは　日ほんごを　べんきょうします。
   Watashi wa Nihongo o benkyooshimasu.   I study Japanese.

To avoid having two を *o* (two direct objects), use の *no* after what was originally the first direct object.

◀)) MODELS

3. としょかんで　日ほんごの　べんきょうを　しました。
   Toshokan de Nihongo no benkyoo o shimasu.   I did (my) Japanese studies at the library.

Now compare:

a. 日ほんごを　べんきょうします。
   Nihongo o benkyoo shimasu.   I will study Japanese.

b. 日ほんごの　べんきょうを　します。
   Nihongo no benkyoo o shimasu.   I will do my Japanese studies.

READ Choose the correct particle from the options in the ( ). X means no particle is required.

1. わたしは　にほんご（を / の / X）　べんきょうします。

2. まいにち　にほんご（を / の / X）　べんきょうを　します。

3. きのう　としょかんで　べんきょう（を / の）　しました。

ぶんかノート　Culture Notes

Typical Japanese High School Student's School Day

Schools in Japan usually start at 8:30 in the morning. Most Japanese students commute to school by bus, train, subway, bike, etc. Commuting by car is not common, especially as high school students are below the legal driving age in Japan. The vast majority of schools require students to wear uniforms (せいふく *seifuku*), and some schools may also have strict regulations regarding hair styles and length.

The curriculum is set by the federal government of Japan and students do not choose their own subjects. For example, English is a required foreign language and is taught beginning in the 7th grade. Recently, English is being introduced at even earlier grades.

Classes in Japan are usually as large as 40 students. Students in one homeroom often take all the same courses together. Because of this, all students in a given course are in the same grade. Mixed classes of students from different grade levels are not common. Even a one grade level difference can affect the relationships between students in a Japanese school, since younger students are expected to treat older students with respect. Upperclassmen are called せんぱい *senpai* and underclassmen are called こうはい *koohai*.

After school, students may attend different kinds of sports and cultural clubs of their own choice. In Japan, school athletics do not have seasons; students play one sport all year long. Because clubs often meet daily, it is very rare to be a member of more than one club. Students from all grade levels interact in these clubs, and therefore the relationship between せんぱい *senpai* and こうはい *koohai* is very important in them.

Research online the different kinds of after-school clubs common in Japan. What club would you join if you lived in Japan? Write a paragraph explaining your reasons.

Pair Work

A. SPEAK/LISTEN/WRITE Ask where and with whom your partner does the following things on a daily basis. Write your partner's answers in Japanese on a separate sheet of paper, using a chart like the one below.

Ex. Eating breakfast.

Question 1: どこで　あさごはんを　たべますか。
Doko de asagohan o tabemasuka.

Question 2: だれと　（いっしょに）　あさごはんを　たべますか。
Dare to (issho ni) asagohan o tabemasu ka.

Activity	Where?	With whom?★
1. Eating lunch		
2. Eating dinner		
3. Studying		
4. Doing homework		

Activity	Where?	With whom?★
5. Talking to friends		
6. Listening to music		
7. Reading books		
8. Reading newspaper		

* 一人（ひとり）で　alone

Reading

B. READ/WRITE Read the e-mail from a Japanese student below and answer the questions. Write your answers in Japanese using complete sentences.

私は　今日の　あさ　父と　いっしょに　しんぶんを　よみました。　あさごはんに　パンを　食べました。

十二時に　カフェテリアで　おひるごはんを　食べました。

UNDERSTAND

1. What did the author do with his/her father this morning?

2. When did the author eat lunch today?

APPLY

3. What did you eat for breakfast this morning? Did you eat with anyone?

4. When and where do you usually eat lunch?

WORKBOOK page 25

かいわ　Dialogue

🔊 **READ/LISTEN** What did Ken do last night?

きのうの　ばん　うちで
何を　しましたか。

Terebi
テレビを　見ました。
そして、　ともだちと
でんわで　はなしました。
でも、　しゅくだいを
しませんでした。

だめですねえ。

ぶんけい　Sentence Patterns

READ Find these sentence patterns in the dialogue.

Person は *wa* 　　general time ✕ 　place で *de* 　　thing を *o* action verb 。

　　　　　　　　　　　　　　person と(いっしょに) *to (issho ni)*

　　　　　　　　　　　　　　tool で *de*

たんご　Vocabulary

1. みます
[みる]
見ます

mimasu [miru]

to watch, look, see

2. かきます
[かく]

kakimasu [kaku]

to write, draw

3. タイプ(を)します
[タイプ(を)する]

taipu (o) shimasu [taipu (o) suru]

to type

4. テレビ

terebi

TV

5. レポート

repooto

report, paper

6. てがみ
手がみ

tegami

letter

7. ラジオ

rajio

radio

8. でんわ

denwa

telephone

9. パソコン

pasokon

personal computer

10. コンピューター

konpyuutaa

computer

11. ケータイ

keetai

cellular phone

12. スマートフォン/
スマホ

sumaatofon/sumaho

smartphone

13. tool + で

de

by means of, with, on, in

14. DVD (ディーブイディー)

diibuiidii

DVD

ついか　たんご　Additional Vocabulary

1.	ニュース	*nyuusu*	news
2.	アニメ	*anime*	cartoons
3.	テレビゲーム	*terebi geemu*	video game
4.	まんが	*manga*	comics
5.	ビデオ	*bideo*	video
6.	メール(を)します	*meeru (o) shimasu*	to email; to text
7.	インターネット	*intaanetto*	Internet
8.	どうが	*dooga*	Internet video / motion picture

よみましょう　Language in Context

🔊 **READ/LISTEN/SPEAK** Read these sentences in Japanese. Say something you did at home yesterday. Say something you do everyday.

きのう　パソコンで
どうがを　みました。

まいにち　スマホで
メールを　します。

ぶんぽう　Grammar

A Means and Method Particle で

Means, Tool ＋ で by, with, on, in (means, tool, vehicle)

で *de* follows a noun that is the means by which an action occurs, i.e., tool, utensil, vehicle, language.

 MODELS

1. ともだちと　でんわで　よく　はなします。
   Tomodachi to denwa de yoku hanashimasu.　　　I talk to my friend on the telephone a lot.

2. コンピューターで　えいごの　レポートを　タイプしました。
   Konpyuutaa de Eigo no repooto o taipushimashita.　　I typed my English paper by computer.

3. しけんを　えんぴつで　かきます。
   Shiken o enpitsu de kakimasu.　　　I will write the exam in pencil.

READ/WRITE Answer the questions using で.

1. にほんごの　しゅくだいを　なにで　かきますか。

2. ケータイ *keetai* で　なにを　しますか。

3. コンピューター *konpyuutaa* で　なにを　しますか。

4. まいにち　でんわで　ともだちと　はなしますか。

ぶんかノート　Culture Notes

Cram School

In addition to school clubs, many Japanese students go to じゅく *juku* "cram school" after their regular classes. Attendance rates at cram schools are close to 60% in high school as students prepare for college entrance exams. Cram schools provide students with extra help in the academic subjects needed for their exams. Families provide students with many forms of moral support. For example, Japanese students are typically not expected to do chores around the home. When they're not studying, most students enjoy watching TV, reading comics, playing video games at home, or staying later at school to participate in clubs.

 Write a tweet in response to the statement
"… Japanese students are typically not expected to do chores around the home."

Pair Work

A. SPEAK/LISTEN Ask your partner what he/she did last night at home.

> きのうの　ばん　うちで
> なにを　しましたか。
> *Kinoo no ban uchi de nani o shimashita ka.*

B. SPEAK/LISTEN/WRITE Ask your partner whether he/she often does the following. Write はい or いいえ on a separate sheet of paper, using a chart like the one below.

Ex. watch TV

> よく　テレビを　みますか。
> *Yoku terebi o mimasu ka.*

1. Watch videos		**4.** Type on the computer	
2. Listen to the radio		**5.** Read the newspaper	
3. Text on the phone		**6.** Write letters	

C. SPEAK/LISTEN Ask your partner how he/she does the following.

Ex. write papers

> なにで　レポートを
> かきますか。
> *Nanide repooto o kakimasuka.*

1. Type papers (reports)	
2. Talk to friends from home	

Speak and Connect

D. SPEAK/LISTEN/WRITE Be a sociologist! With your partner, gather responses to the questions in Activity B from the students in your class. Predict what, if any, gender differences you expect to find. Then create a double bar graph displaying the number of male and female students who do each activity. Compare your predictions to your results. Were your predictions accurate? Explain.

WORKBOOK page 27

Review Questions

🔊 Ask your partner these questions in Japanese. Your partner answers in Japanese. Check your answers using the audio.

Home Review pages 117–118

1. Do you speak Japanese at home?

2. What language do you speak at home?

Food Review pages 124, 129, 137, and 143

3. Does your family eat rice everyday?

4. What do you usually drink?

5. What did you eat for dinner yesterday?

6. Did you eat breakfast today?

7. Where do you usually eat lunch?

8. With whom do you eat lunch?

Leisure Review pages 124, 137, and 143

9. Do you read the newspaper everyday?

10. Do you listen to music at the cafeteria?

11. What do you do at the library? [List at least two activities.]

12. Where do you talk with your friends?

13. Did you watch TV last night?

14. Do you talk to your friends on the phone everyday?

School Review page 143

15. Do you type your English papers on the computer?

16. Did you do yesterday's Japanese homework?

Text Chat

You will participate in a simulated exchange of text-chat messages. You should respond as fully and as appropriately as possible.

You will have a conversation with Mariko Yamamoto, a Japanese high school student, about a meal.

October 12, 01:29 PM

きのう　ばんごはんに
なにを　たべましたか。

Describe specific examples.

October 12, 01:34 PM

どこで　おひるごはんを
たべますか。

Give more than one location.

October 12, 01:55 PM

だいたい　なにを
のみますか。

Respond.

Can Do!
Now I can . . .

- ☐ ask what languages someone speaks
- ☐ say where I do an activity
- ☐ discuss what I do every day
- ☐ discuss what I did in the past
- ☐ discuss food and meals
- ☐ describe doing an action with someone

Making *(O)musubi*
(お)むすび Rice balls

Rice balls, a favorite food of the Japanese, are called *omusubi* or *onigiri*. They are delicious, portable, and fun to make! Rice balls are most often triangular in shape, though in Japan they may also be oblong shaped. The rice is often seasoned with salt or other flavorings. This not only adds flavor, but helps to preserve the rice. Inside the rice ball, you usually place pickled plums, flavored strips of kelp, or dried bonito flakes. Then "wrap" the rice ball with *nori* (seaweed) for extra flavoring and also to prevent the rice from sticking to other foods. The *nori* also prevents the rice from sticking to your hands as you eat the rice ball. Try this recipe and enjoy your *omusubi!* Take a photo of yourself and the *omusubi* and show it to your teacher, or bring your creation to class if your teacher asks!

Ingredients: 2 cups uncooked rice (glutinous rice or sushi rice)
Umeboshi (pickled plum)
Salt
Strips of *nori* (seasoned dry seaweed)

1. You will need a rice cooker and uncooked glutinous rice. Place 2 cups of rice in the inner pot of the rice cooker. If you don't have a rice cooker, you may use a heavy 2-quart pot. Two cups of uncooked rice will make about 4 rice balls.

2. Briskly wash the rice in cold water. Rinse several times until water loses most of its cloudiness. Drain out water.

3. Pour cold water into the rice pot until the line marked "2" on the side of the pot. If you don't have a rice cooker, follow the directions on the rice packaging.

4. Cook rice.

5. After the button of the rice cooker "pops," let stand for 5–10 minutes. Using a wet rice paddle, mix the rice. Cover and let stand a few minutes.

6. Sprinkle salt on your clean, moistened hands. Scoop about a 1/4 of the hot cooked rice on the palm of your hands. Place an *umeboshi* in the center of the rice. Be careful! The rice is hot!

7. Using both hands, form your rice ball into a triangular shape. Use your hands as a mold and gently apply pressure as you shape the rice ball.

8. Apply a wide strip of nori around the rice ball. Wrap the nori firmly around the rice ball.

9. Ready to eat — hot or cold!

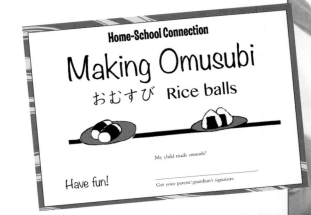

Home-School Connection

Making Omusubi
おむすび Rice balls

My child made *omusubi!*

Have fun! Get your parent/guardian's signature.

Dialogue
Review

Dialogue 4-1   page 117

エミ：　おとうさんと　おかあさんは　にほんごを　はなしますか。

ケン：　ちちは　にほんごを　はなしません。でも、はははは
　　　　にほんごを よく　はなします。

エミ：　ケンさんは　うちで　にほんごを　はなしますか。

ケン：　いいえ。

Emi: Otoosan to okaasan wa Nihongo o hanashimasu ka.
Ken: Chichi wa Nihongo o hanashimasen. Demo, haha wa Nihongo o yoku hanashimasu.
Emi: Ken-san wa uchi de Nihongo o hanashimasu ka.
Ken: Iie.

Dialogue 4-2   page 124

エミ：　かぞくは　まいにち　ごはんを　たべますか。

ケン：　いいえ、たいてい　パンを　たべます。ときどき
　　　　ごはんを　たべます。

エミ：　おちゃを　のみますか。

ケン：　いいえ、おちゃは　のみません。でも、ジュースと
　　　　ぎゅうにゅうを　よく　のみます。

Emi: Kazoku wa mainichi gohan o tabemasu ka.
Ken: Iie, taitei pan o tabemasu. Tokidoki gohan o tabemasu.
Emi: Ocha o nomimasu ka.
Ken: Iie, ocha wa nomimasen. Demo, juusu to gyuunyuu o yoku nomimasu.

Dialogue 4-3   page 129

ケン：　きのう　しちじに　ばんごはんを　たべました。

エミ：　ばんごはんに　なにを　たべましたか。

ケン：　カレーライスを　たべました。

エミ：　きょう　あさごはんに　なにを　たべましたか。

ケン：　なにも　たべませんでした。

Ken: Kinoo shichiji ni bangohan o tabemashita.
Emi: Bangohan ni nani o tabemashita ka.
Ken: Kareeraisu o tabemashita.
Emi: Kyoo asagohan ni nani o tabemashita ka.
Ken: Nani mo tabemasendeshita.

Dialogue 4-4   page 137

ケン：　どこで　おひるごはんを　たべますか。

エミ：　たいてい　カフェテリアで　たべます。

ケン：　だれと　たべますか。

エミ：　ともだちと　いっしょに　たべます。

Ken: Doko de ohirugohan o tabemasu ka.
Emi: Taitei kafeteria de tabemasu.
Ken: Dare to tabemasu ka.
Emi: Tomodachi to issho ni tabemasu.

Dialogue 4-5   page 143

エミ：　きのうの　ばん　うちで　なにを　しましたか。

ケン：　テレビを　みました。そして、ともだちと　でんわで
　　　　　はなしました。でも、しゅくだいを　しませんでした。

エミ：　だめですねえ。

Emi: Kinoo no ban uchi de nani o shimashita ka.
Ken: Terebi o mimashita. Soshite, tomodachi to denwa de hanashimashita.
　　　　Demo, shukudai o shimasendeshita.
Emi: Dame desu nee.

おまけ *Omake* means "bonus" or "extra" in Japanese. In *Adventures in Japanese,* there are many more Project Corners not found in the textbook. You can find these *Omake* Project Corners on the companion website at **cheng-tsui.com/adventuresinjapanese.**

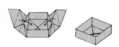

Origami Box

Instructions on how to make an origami box or はこ *hako.*

Song – Rain

Lyrics and music for the Japanese song あめふり *Amefuri.*

Japanese Tongue Twisters

Fun tongue twisters to improve your Japanese pronunciation and speaking skills.

Gomokunarabe

Instructions on how to play the Japanese game of Go（ごもくならべ *Gomoku narabe*）, along with a printable gameboard and pieces, so you can start to play right away.

Rolling Musubi

A classic Japanese folktale（おむすびころりん *Omusubi Kororin*） in traditional Japanese storybook form (read from right to left) and illustrated.

しゅみ
Hobbies

Can Do!
In this lesson you will learn to

- share your hobbies
- communicate your likes and dislikes (food, sports, colors)
- communicate your strengths and weaknesses
- express the degree of your likes, dislikes, strengths and weaknesses

Online Resources

cheng-tsui.com/
adventuresinjapanese

- Audio
- Vocabulary Lists
- Vocabulary Flashcards
- *Kana* and *Kanji* Flashcards
- Activity Worksheets

In this lesson, you will learn the *kanji* for the days of the week.

	Kanji	Meaning	Readings	Examples	
13.	火	fire	か ひ	か よ う び 火曜日 ひ 火	Tuesday fire
14.	水	water	すい みず	す い よ う び 水曜日 みず お水	Wednesday water
15.	木	tree	もく き	も く よ う び 木曜日 き 木	Thursday tree
16.	金	gold	きん かね	き ん よ う び 金曜日 かね お金	Friday money
17.	土	soil	ど つち	ど よ う び 土曜日 つち 土	Saturday soil
18.	本	origin, book	ほん ぽん もと	ほん 本 に ほん 日本 に っ ぽん 日本 や ま もと 山本	book Japan Japan Yamamoto (surname)

The base of a tree is its origin. Books are made from felled trees. The trunk of the tree is long and cylindrical.

WORKBOOK page 221

Recognition Kanji

よ う
曜

day of the week

かいわ Dialogue

🔊 **READ/LISTEN** What are Ken's hobbies? What are Emi's hobbies?

READ Find these sentence patterns in the dialogue.

1. Person の　しゅみ は　　　　　hobby です。　　　　[Person's hobby is ~.]

2. W-Question:　しゅみは　なんですか。

   W-Answer:　（わたしの　しゅみは）　〜です。

3. Yes/No Question:　しゅみは　スポーツ *supootsu* ですか。

   Yes Answer:　はい、そうです。 or はい、スポーツ *supootsu* です。

   No Answer:　いいえ、そうでは／じゃ　ありません。

   or いいえ、スポーツ *supootsu* では／じゃ　ありません。

   or いいえ、your hobby です。

たんご　Vocabulary

1. しゅみ

   hobby

2. スポーツ

   supootsu

   sports

3. ダンス

   dansu

   dance, dancing

4. うた

   song, singing

5. えいが

   movies

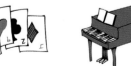

6. テレビ
   ゲーム

   terebi geemu

   video game

7. トランプ

   toranpu

   (playing) cards

8. ピアノ

   piano

   piano

9. ギター

   gitaa

   guitar

10. ジョギング

    jogingu

    jogging

11. すいえい 水えい	**12.** どくしょ	**13.** え	**14.** そうですねえ ...
swimming	reading	painting, drawing	Let me see . . .

Used when one is trying to think of
an answer.

ついか　たんご　Additional Vocabulary

1.	バイオリン	*baiorin*	violin
2.	さいほう		sewing
3.	おしゃべり		chatting, talking
4.	かいもの		shopping
5.	りょこう		traveling
6.	ブログ	*burogu*	blog
7.	サーフィン	*saafin*	surfing
8.	スケートボード	*sukeetoboodo*	skateboarding
9.	りょうり		cooking
10.	ポップ	*poppu*	pop (music)
11.	ロック	*rokku*	rock (music)
12.	ジャズ	*jazu*	jazz (music)
13.	クラシック	*kurashikku*	classical (music)
14.	ヒップホップ	*hippu hoppu*	hip hop (music)
15.	ネットサーフィン(を　します)	*nettosaafin*	to surf the net

🔊 **READ/LISTEN/SPEAK** Read these sentences in Japanese. Say what you watch on TV.

テレビで　サッカーを
みます。

そうですねえ…

Used when one is trying to think of an answer

ぶんかノート　Culture Notes

けんどう uniforms and swords

Sports in Japan

Many sports popular in the West are also popular in Japan, especially baseball and soccer. Basketball is becoming increasingly popular as well. Football, however, has nowhere near the following it has in the U.S. Golf is immensely popular among many adults, but the high cost restricts many from golfing often.

The most popular traditional sport of the Japanese, すもう, also has a strong following, especially among adult Japanese. けんどう, a uniquely Japanese form of fencing with bamboo swords, is also popular.

Research online to identify other traditional Japanese sports or contemporary sports that are popular in Japan. Prepare a brief summary of at least two of these sports and describe a famous athlete, team, or school. Include images in your summaries.

アクティビティー Communicative Activities

Pair Work

A. SPEAK/LISTEN/WRITE Ask what hobbies your partner and his/her family members have. Write your partner's family members and their hobbies on a separate sheet of paper in a chart like the one below.

Ex. 「（〜さんの）　しゅみは　なんですか。」

　　「（〜の　しゅみは）　〜です。」

かぞく	しゅみ

Reading

B. READ/WRITE Read the following e-mail from a Japanese student. Answer the questions below in Japanese using complete sentences.

私の　名前は　ひとみです。私の　かぞくは　三人です。
父と　あにと　私です。私の　しゅみは　ギター（gitaa）と　うたと
どくしょです。あにの　しゅみは　すいえいと　スポーツ（supootsu）です。
父の　しゅみは　えいがと　どくしょです。

UNDERSTAND

1. How many people are in Hitomi's family?

2. What are Hitomi's hobbies?

3. What are her father's hobbies?

APPLY

4. What are your hobbies?

5. Write an e-mail replying to Hitomi explaining how many people are in your family and what their hobbies are.

WORKBOOK page 31

5か2
What do you like?

かいわ　Dialogue

🔊 **READ/LISTEN** Does Ken like sushi? What food does Ken like?

ぶんけい　Sentence Patterns

READ Find this sentence pattern in the dialogue.

Person は Noun が

どんな + Noun が

	Like/Dislike	Verb	（か）。
	すき	です。	
	だいすき	では／じゃ ありません。	
	きらい	でした。	
	だいきらい	では／じゃ ありませんでした。	

たんご　Vocabulary

1. すき
[な Adj.]
好き

like

2. だいすき
[な Adj.]
大好き

like very much, love

3. きらい
[な Adj.]

dislike

4. だいきらい
[な Adj.]
大きらい

dislike a lot, hate

---

5. どんな〜

what kind of ~?

6. もの

(tangible) things

7. たべもの
食べもの

food

8. のみもの

beverage

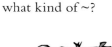

9. （お）すし

sushi

10. さしみ

raw fish, *sashimi*

11. てんぷら
天ぷら

tempura

ついか　たんご　Additional Vocabulary

1. やさい	vegetable	**7.** りんご			apple
2. くだもの	fruit	**8.** トマト	*tomato*	tomato
3. ほうれんそう	spinach	**9.** オレンジ	*orenji*	orange
4. にんじん	carrot	**10.** メロン	*meron*	melon
5. いちご	strawberry	**11.** アイスクリーム	*aisukuriimu*	ice cream
6. すいか	watermelon	**12.** ケーキ	*keeki*	cake

🔊 **READ/LISTEN** Read these sentences in Japanese. Say whether you like or dislike sushi.

おすしが　好きです。　　　おすしが　きらいです。

ぶんぽう　Grammar

Ⓐ　な Adjectives

A word which modifies a noun is called an adjective. There are two kinds of adjectives in Japanese: い adjectives and な adjectives. い adjectives are mostly original Japanese adjectives such as あつい "hot," さむい "cold," etc. な adjectives are mostly of Chinese origin, such as すき "like," きらい "dislike," etc.

How can you tell whether an adjective is an い adjective or a な adjective? Most い adjectives end with -*ai*, -*ii*, -*ui*, or -*oi*, while most of な adjectives do not have these endings, with a few exceptions such as きらい. If you memorize those exceptions, you will not have any problems.

When used with です, adjectives in Japanese can be conjugated depending on tense and whether the sentence is affirmative or negative. な adjectives conjugate like nouns, while い adjectives have different rules. い adjective conjugation will be introduced in the next lesson.

な **adjective conjugation:**

すきです。	(I) like (it).
すきでは／じゃ　ありません。	(I) do not like (it).
すきでした。	(I) liked (it).
すきでは／じゃ　ありませんでした。	(I) did not like (it).

READ/WRITE Complete the sentences using the choices below based on the information given.

です　　では　ありません　　でした　　では　ありませんでした

I didn't like sushi before, but I like it now. I used to like milk, but I don't like it any more.

わたしは　まえ　おすしは　すき__1__。でも、　いま
おすしが　すき　__2__。わたしは　まえ　ぎゅうにゅうが
すき　__3__。でも、　いま　ぎゅうにゅうは　すき　__4__。

B Basic Sentence Structure: A Likes B. ─────────

Noun 1 は　Noun 2 が	すき	です。	**N1 likes N2.**
	だいすき	です。	**N1 likes N2 very much./ N1 loves N2.**
	きらい	です。	**N1 dislikes N2.**
	だいきらい	です。	**N1 dislikes N2 very much./ N1 hates N2.**

N1 tells us who is being discussed, while N2 tells us what is under discussion. All four words used in the examples above as predicates are な adjectives, even though some end in *-ai*.

1. わたしは　どくしょが　すきです。　　　I like reading (books).

2. おとうとは　テレビゲーム *terebi geemu* が　だいすきです。
My younger brother loves video games.

3. おばあさんは　テレビ *terebi* が　きらいです。
My grandmother dislikes TV.

4. ちちは　えいがが　だいきらいです。　　My father hates movies.

READ/WRITE Complete the sentences using the choices below based on the information given.

| すき | きらい | だいすき | だいきらい |

I like tempura. And I like sashimi very much. I dislike playing cards.
And I hate video games.

わたしは　てんぷらが　__1__　です。　そして、さしみが　__2__　です。

わたしは　トランプ *toranpu* が　__3__　です。

そして、テレビゲーム *terebi geemu* が　__4__　です。

C Question Word どんな

どんな ＋ **Noun** ？　　　**What kind/sort of ~ ?**

どんな must always be followed by a noun, which is usually a category, i.e., food, sports, people, hobbies, etc.

◀))) MODELS

1. 「どんな　たべものが　すきですか。」
   "What kind of food do you like?"

   「ちゅうごくの　たべものが　すきです。」　"I like Chinese food."

2. 「どんな　スポーツ *supootsu* が　すきですか。」
   "What kind of sports do you like?"

   「フットボール *futtobooru* が　すきです。」　"I like football."

READ/WRITE Complete the following questions by choosing an appropriate noun to be inserted in the ( ) based on the responses given.

1. 「どんな　（ 1 ）が　すきですか。」「おちゃが　すきです。」

2. 「どんな　（ 2 ）が　すきですか。」
   「てんぷらが　だいすきです。」

3. 「どんな　（ 3 ）が　すきですか。」
   「すいえいが　すきです。」

A. Seasonal Foods and Drinks in Japan

In addition to popular year-round foods, Japan has many special seasonal dishes. For example, cold dishes, such as *somen* noodles or cold *soba* noodles are eaten only during the summer. Shaved ice and fruits such as watermelon, cherries, and peaches are popular during the summer. Cold drinks, (fruit juices, iced tea and iced coffee) are consumed in far greater quantities during the summer. Even meals at home will vary according to the season, and are often also presented in different serving dishes according to the season. The importance of these dishes is connected to Japan's agrarian past and the significance Shintoism places on nature.

ざるそば, a summer dish of cold buckwheat noodles topped with shredded *nori* seaweed

おでん, a winter dish made of boiled eggs, fishcakes, *daikon* radishes, and other vegetables in a light soy broth

B. "Sukiyaki" Song

「うえを　むいて　あるこう」 is a beautiful, classic Japanese song sung by the famous male singer さかもと きゅう. The song title means "Let's walk with our chins up." The song was popular not only in Japan, but also in the U.S., where it became (as of yet) the only Japanese song to top U.S. music charts. Because Americans could not understand the Japanese lyrics, it was re-named "Sukiyaki" in the U.S., after a popular Japanese dish. The song, however, makes no mention of food!

Research food and drinks that are popular during the winter in Japan. Then, using your findings and the information above, create one shopping list for a summer picnic and one for a winter celebration planned for friends. Use either Japanese or English.

アクティビティー　Communicative Activities

Pair Work

A. SPEAK/LISTEN Ask your partner if he/she likes foods from the following countries or not. Create a chart like the one below on a separate sheet of paper and mark the correct columns.

Ex.　Question:　日本の　たべものが　すきですか。

Yes Answer:　はい、すきです。

No Answer:　いいえ、すきでは　ありません／すきじゃ
ありません。

or いいえ、きらいです。

	だいすき	すき	きらい	だいきらい
日本				
ちゅうごく				
かんこく				
インド　*Indo*				
タイ　*Tai*				
アメリカ　*Amerika*				
メキシコ　*Mekishiko*				
イタリア　*Itaria*				
フランス　*Furansu*				

B. SPEAK/LISTEN/WRITE Ask what kind of foods and drinks your partner likes or dislikes. Write his/her answers on a separate sheet of paper in a chart like the one below.

Ex. Question:　どんな　たべものが　すきですか。

Answer:　おすしと　てんぷらが　すきです。

もの	すき	きらい
たべもの		
のみもの		

WORKBOOK page 33

かいわ　Dialogue

🔊 **READ/LISTEN** What is Ken good at? What sport does Emi like?

Ken
ケンさんは　何_{なに}が　とくい
ですか。

ぼくは　やきゅうが
とくいです。エミさんは？
Emi

私_{わたし}は　バレーボール*bareebooru*が
好_すきですが、上手_{じょうず}
では　ありません。

ぶんけい　Sentence Patterns

READ Find these sentence patterns in the dialogue.

1. Person は thing (intangible) が Adjective　です（か）。

どんな　こと
｛ じょうず
　 へた
　 とくい
　 にがて ｝
｛ では　ありません（か）。or
　 じゃ　ありません（か）。
　 でした（か）。
　 では　ありませんでした（か）。or
　 じゃ　ありませんでした（か）。｝

2. Sentence 1 ＋が、Sentence 2。　[Sentence 1, but Sentence 2.]

たんご　Vocabulary

1. じょうず
[な Adj.]
上手
skillful,
be good at

Refers to someone else. Never used to refer to oneself, except in the negative, as it would sound boastful.

2. へた
[な Adj.]
下手
unskillful,
be poor at

3. とくい
[な Adj.]

be strong in,
can do well

May be used to refer to oneself.

4. にがて
[な Adj.]
にが手
be weak in,
don't do well with

Used to refer to oneself. It also can be used for persons, food, etc., to which one reacts negatively.

5. こと

thing (intangible)
⇔もの thing (tangible)

6. フットボール

futtobooru
football

7. やきゅう

baseball

8. バスケット
（ボール）

basuketto (booru)
basketball

---

9. バレー（ボール）

baree (booru)
volleyball

10. サッカー

sakkaa
soccer

11. テニス

tenisu
tennis

12. ゴルフ

gorufu
golf

13.　Sentence 1 ＋が、Sentence 2。　Sentence 1, but Sentence 2.

　　= Sentence 1。でも、Sentence 2。　Sentence 1. But/However, Sentence 2.

ついか　たんご　Additional Vocabulary

1. ボーリング　　　*booringu*　　　bowling

2. スキー　　　　　*sukii*　　　　　skiing

3. スケート　　　　*sukeeto*　　　　skating

4. りくじょう　　　　　　　　　　track

5. きかいたいそう　　　　　　　　gymnastics

よみましょう　Language in Context

🔊 **READ/LISTEN** Read these sentences in Japanese. When should you use へた and じょうず?

ぼくは
フットボールが
すきですが、へたです。

へた can be used to describe your own skill or talent.
This is a way of expressing humility.

クリスさんは
フットボールが
じょうずです。

じょうず is only used to refer to others' abilities,
never to your own, unless you are using
a negative form. Using it to describe yourself
sounds boastful.

A · Contrasting Conjunction が

Sentence 1 ＋ が、Sentence 2。　　　　**Sentence 1, but Sentence 2.**

= Sentence 1。でも、Sentence 2。　　　Sentence 1. But / However, Sentence 2.

Unlike the previous pattern of S1。でも、S2。, this pattern combines the two contrasting sentences with が.

MODELS

1. わたしは　サッカー *sakkaa* が　すきですが、じょうずでは
   ありません。

   I like soccer, but I am not skillful.

2. ちちは　ゴルフ *gorufu* が　じょうずですが、ははは
   へたです。

   My father is good at golf, but my mother is poor at it.

3. おとうとは　テレビゲーム *terebi geemu* が　だいすきですが、
   わたしは　きらいです。

   My younger brother likes video games very much, but I dislike them.

READ/WRITE Rewrite the following sentence pairs as one sentence using が.

1. わたしは　うたが　すきです。でも、じょうずでは
   ありません。

2. ぼくは　テニス *tenisu* が　へたです。でも、すきです。

3. あねは　ダンス *dansu* が　とくいです。でも、わたしは
   ダンス *dansu* が　にがてです。

Modesty in Japanese Culture

Modesty and humility are important in Japanese culture. In Japan, praising yourself, your family, or other members of your "in-group" can be considered rude and boastful. This is why you should avoid using terms like じょうず to describe yourself or your "in-group."

Instead of praising yourself or your family, it would be considered appropriate in Japanese culture to make yourself or your family members appear as less than they actually are. This applies not only to persons in your in-group, but also to belongings, works, or acts of those persons. A Japanese person might still compliment a family member or another of their "in-group," but not in front of an outsider.

For example, if you give a Japanese person a gift, you would say that it is insignificant, even if you took great care in making it or spent a lot money on it. Likewise, if someone praises your Japanese, it would be considered more polite to disagree than to thank them for the compliment.

 Consider the following situations. Based on the above, explain whether they would be considered rude or polite by a Japanese speaker

1. Your friend compliments you on a new shirt.

2. You tell a classmate that your Japanese is very good.

3. You tell a friend's mother that her cooking is very good.

4. You tell a friend that your father's cooking is very good.

5. You tell a friend that your brother is good at soccer.

6. You tell a classmate that you are not very good at tennis.

アクティビティー　Communicative Activities

Pair Work

A. SPEAK/LISTEN/WRITE Ask your partner what kind of activities each of his/her family member likes and whether they are skillful at them or not. On a separate sheet of paper, create a chart like the one below. Write family members in the first column, what they like in the second, and check either Not じょうず or へた in the last two columns. Keep in mind the importance of modesty in Japan when describing your family members' skills.

Ex. Question 1: おとうさんは　どんな　ことが　すきですか。

Answer 1: ちちは　ゴルフ *gorufu* が　すきです。

Question 2: おとうさんは　ゴルフ *gorufu* が　じょうずですか。

Answer 2: いいえ、じょうずでは　ありません。

かぞく	すき	Not じょうず (Check mark.)	へた (Check mark.)

Reading

B. READ/WRITE Read the following e-mail from a Japanese student. Answer the questions below in Japanese using complete sentences.

> こんにちは。
>
> ぼくは　あべ　じろうです。ぼくは　スポーツ *supootsu* が　好きですが、上手では　ありません。ぼくは　どくしょが　大好きです。
>
> そして、おんがくも　大好きです。ギター *gitaa* が　とくいです。
>
> でも、カラオケ *karaoke* は　にがてです。

UNDERSTAND

1. What does Jiro like very much?

2. What does Jiro say he can do well?

3. What does Jiro say he cannot do well?

APPLY

4. Write an e-mail in Japanese replying to Jiro explaining what you like and dislike and what you are good at/not good at, etc.

WORKBOOK page 35

かいわ　Dialogue

READ/LISTEN Does Ken say his Japanese is good or bad? Doe Emi agree with him?

日本語が　とても
上手ですねえ。

いいえ、ぜんぜん
上手では　ありません。
とても　下手です。

いいえ。
上手
ですよ。

ぶんけい　Sentence Patterns

READ Find this sentence pattern in the dialogue.

Person は noun (activity) が Adverb　　　　　　　Affirmative/Negative Predicate

とても　　　　　　　　　　じょうずです。
すこし or ちょっと
まあまあ
あまり　　　　　　　じょうずでは　ありません。*
ぜんぜん　　　　or　じょうずじゃ　ありません。*

* では is more formal than じゃ and may be replaced by じゃ in less formal situations.

たんご　Vocabulary

1. **とても** ＋ Affirmative predicate.   very ~

2. **まあまあ** ＋ Affirmative predicate with a positive meaning.   so-so ~

3. **あまり** ＋ Negative predicate.   not very ~

4. **ぜんぜん** ＋ Negative predicate.   not ~ at all

ついか　たんご　Additional Vocabulary

1. **そんな　ことは　ありません。**   Far from it!

よみましょう　Language in Context

🔊 **READ/LISTEN** Read these sentences in Japanese. Tell a partner how well he/she speaks Japanese. You partner should respond appropriately.

日本ごが　とても
じょうずですねえ。

そんな　ことは　ありません。

すみません。　ぼくは
えいごが　あまり　じょうず
では　ありません。

A Emphatic Adverbs

とても ～	+ Affirmative predicate。	very ～
すこし／ちょっと ～	+ Affirmative predicate。	a little ～ （すこし is more formal.）
まあまあ ～	+ Affirmative predicate with a positive meaning/ です	so-so ～
あまり ～	+ Negative predicate。	not very ～
ぜんぜん ～	+ Negative predicate。	not ～ at all

🔊 MODELS

1. おばあさんは　日本ごが　とても　じょうずですね。
   Your grandmother is very good at speaking Japanese, isn't she?

2. ははは　日本ごが　あまり　じょうずでは　ありません。
   My mother is not very good at speaking Japanese.

3. 「すいえいが　じょうずですか。」　　"Are you good at swimming?"
   「まあまあです。」　　"I'm so-so (at it)."

4. ぼくは　バスケット *basuketto* が　ちょっと　にがてです。
   I am a little weak at basketball. (I cannot do it well and I do not like it so much.)

5. ぼくは　テニス *tenisu* が　だいすきですが、ぜんぜん
   じょうずでは　ありません。
   I love tennis but I am not good at it at all.

READ/WRITE Complete the Japanese sentences using the choices below based on the information.

| とても | すこし／ちょっと | まあまあ | あまり | ぜんぜん |

My mother is very good at golfing, but my father is not very good at it. My grandmother is so-so at karaoke, but my grandfather is not good at it at all. I am not very good at baseball, but I love it.

ははは　ゴルフ *gorufu* が　__1__　じょうずですが、ちちは
__2__　じょうずでは　ありません。おばあさんは
カラオケ *karaoke* が　__3__　じょうずですが、おじいさんは
__4__　じょうずでは　ありません。わたしは　やきゅうが
__5__　じょうずでは　ありませんが、だいすきです。

ぶんかノート　Culture Notes

Karaoke

カラオケ *karaoke* is a fun form of musical entertainment
that originated in Japan. カラ *kara* means "empty" and
オケ *oke* is a short form of オーケストラ *ookesutora*
which means "orchestra." Literally, it means "empty
orchestra." In karaoke, you sing along to pre-recorded
instrumental versions of songs, allowing you to become
the singer. Karaoke is now popular in other countries
and people have adapted it to fit their own music.

 Using a webcam or other camera, record yourself singing karaoke. You may want to
build your confidence by singing a song in English first before trying a song in Japanese.
Share it with your teacher and classmates. Or set up a karaoke competition with other
Japanese language classes in your community and share your videos.

Language Note

そんな　ことは　ありません

This expression means "Far from it." When Japanese people praise your
Japanese even though it is still inadequate, this is the appropriate response to
give. In general, Japanese people value modesty and it is considered impolite
to simply accept compliments from others.

アクティビティー　Communicative Activities

Pair Work

SPEAK/LISTEN Compliment your partner on at least three things. Your partner will respond by giving
a modest reply. Switch roles.

Ex. 「日本ごが　とても　じょうずですねえ。」

　　「いいえ、ぜんぜん　じょうずでは　ありません。」

or 　「いいえ、そんな　ことは　ありません。」

WORKBOOK　page 37

かいわ Dialogue

🔊 **READ/LISTEN** What colors does Emi like? What colors does Ken like?

ぶんけい Sentence Patterns

READ Find these sentence patterns in the dialogue.

1. Person は Color が Adjective Verb (?)
   なにいろ すき です（か）。
   きらい

2. Person の Noun は Color です（か）。
   なにいろ

1. いろ

color

2. なにいろ
何いろ

What color?

3. あか

red

4. しろ
白

white

5. くろ

black

6. あお

blue

7. きいろ

yellow

8. ちゃいろ

brown
(Lit. "tea color")

9. みどり

green

10. むらさき

purple

---

11. ピンク

pinku
pink

12. オレンジ
（いろ）

orenji (iro)
orange (color)

13. グレー

guree
grey

14. きんいろ
金いろ

gold (color)

15. ぎんいろ

silver (color)

ついか たんご Additional Vocabulary

These words are original Japanese color words, but recently Japanese people prefer to use newer words borrowed from English instead, especially when describing modern or Western items.

1. ももいろ   pink color (peach color)

2. だいだいいろ   orange color (tangerine orange color)

3. はいいろ   grey color (ash color)

4. ねずみいろ   grey color (mouse color)

🔊 **READ/LISTEN** Read these sentences in Japanese. Can you recognize the *kanji* in these sentences?

なにいろが　好きですか。

かつみさんは　ピンクが
大好きです。

ぶんかノート　Culture Notes

A. Colors in Japanese Culture

Certain colors have significance in Japanese culture. Red and white are used for happy occasions such as weddings, engagements, baby births, etc. Black is used for funerals. Purple is a noble color and is used by the imperial family. If you have a chance to meet the Imperial Family, avoid wearing purple as it is a color reserved for them! Green has a clean, new and fresh image and therefore is used often to create a positive image. For example, グリーンしゃ *guriin-sha* is the executive car of trains. The ticket window where you can purchase reserved train tickets tickets is called みどりのまどぐち.

B. The Japanese Flag

The Japanese flag is called ひのまる which literally means "circle of the sun."

The ancient Chinese referred to Japan as a "place where the sun rises" because of its relative geographical location. Since Japan is east of China, the sun appeared to rise from the direction of Japan. The name "*Nihon*" literally means "origin of the sun."

あか

しろ
白

C. A Japanese Proverb 「十にんといろ」

十にん is a counter for ten people. といろ is an
abbreviated form of とおいろ which means ten colors.
「十にんといろ」 literally means "Ten people, ten colors." a
people, many tastes."

 Design and create a birthday card for a Japanese friend or classmate. Look back at Lesson
2–6 for expressions you can use. Use the information above to choose which colors you
will use in your design, and explain your choices in a separate paragraph.

Language Note

The Many Meanings of あお

あお is translated as "blue," but traditionally also meant green. This meaning
is still used in some cases today. The green color of traffic lights is considered
あお in Japanese. New young leaves and fresh green grass are not described as
みどり, but as あお. Also, as with "green" in English, young inexperienced
people are sometimes referred to as being あおい (the adjective form of あお),
because of their youth and lack of experience.

アクティビティー Communicative Activities

Pair Work

A. SPEAK/LISTEN/WRITE Ask for the colors of your partner's belongings and write down the answers.

Ex. 「～さんの　うちは　なにいろですか。」
「（わたしの　うちは）　しろです。」

Things	いろ
1. House	
2. Bag	
3. Cap or hat	
4. School colors	
5. Sports uniform (ユニフォーム *yunifoomu*)	
6. Eraser	
7. Car (くるま)	
8. Dog or cat color*	

* いません。 I do not have (a pet).

Speak and Connect

B. SPEAK/LISTEN Be a statistician! Let's find out what color is the most popular and the least popular in your class. Divide into groups and ask your classmates within your group to raise their hands as each of you takes turns asking about each color. Tally the results on a separate sheet of paper using a chart like the one below, then calculate the percentage of the class that likes each color. Then report the results to the entire class.

Ex. 「だれが　あかが　すきですか。」

いろ	すき	%	きらい	いろ	すき	%	きらい
1. あか				8. むらさき			
2. しろ				9. ピンク *pinku*			
3. くろ				10. オレンジ *orenji*			
4. あお				11. グレー *guree*			
5. きいろ				12. きんいろ			
6. ちゃいろ				13. ぎんいろ			
7. みどり							

Reading

C. READ/WRITE Read the following e-mail from a Japanese student. Answer the questions below in Japanese using complete sentences.

私の　名前は　だいすけです。　あかと　あおと　くろが　好きです。
白と　みどりが　きらいです。　私の　ねこは　くろです。　私は
アニメ（*anime*）が　好きです。　ともだちの　けんじさんも　アニメ（*anime*）が
好きです。　ときどき　けんじさんと　いっしょに　アニメ（*anime*）を　みます。

UNDERSTAND

1. What colors does Daisuke dislike?

2. What color is Daisuke's cat?

3. What do Daisuke and his friend Kenji do together?

APPLY

4. What colors do you like?

5. Write a short e-mail replying to Daisuke. Tell him what colors you like, what hobbies you have, and what activities you are strong in.

WORKBOOK page 39

Review Questions

Ask your partner these questions in Japanese. Your partner answers in Japanese. Check your answers using the audio.

Hobbies & Occupations Review pages 160 and 105-06

1. What is your hobby?

2. What is your father's job?

3. What is your mother's job?

Likes & Dislikes Review pages 162 and 178

4. Do you like sushi?

5. What kind of foods do you like?

6. What kind of drinks do you like?

7. Do you like golf?

8. What color(s) do you like?

9. What color(s) do you dislike?

Skills Review pages 164 and 169

10. What are you good at?

11. Are you good/skillful at baseball?

12. You are very good/skillful at speaking Japanese! [Respond to the compliment.]

13. Is your mother/father good/skillful at golf? [Respond appropriately to someone outside your family.]

Text Chat

You will participate in a simulated exchange of text–chat messages. You should respond as fully and as appropriately as possible.

You will have a conversation with Sadao Yamanaka, a Japanese high school student, about hobbies and sports.

November 1, 11:03 AM

しゅみは　なんですか。

Give more than one example.

November 1, 11:09 AM

そうですか。
どんな　ス *supootsu* ポ ーツが
とくいですか。

Respond and give your opinion of your abilities.

November 1, 11:14 AM

日本ごが　じょうずですねえ。

Respond appropriately.

Can Do!
Now I can . . .

☐ ask a friend what his/her hobbies are

☐ ask a friend what he/she likes and dislikes
(food, drinks, activities, colors)

☐ discuss strengths and weaknesses

☐ describe objects using color

Education and School

RESEARCH Use books, the Internet, or interview a Japanese member of your community to answer the following.

Determine

1. What is the average cost of one year of public high school education in your country?

2. What is the average cost of one year of public high school education in Japan?

3. What is the average cost of one year of private high school education in the your country?

4. What is the average cost of one year of private high school education in Japan?

Compare

5. Roughly what percentage of students in your city or state attend private schools?

6. Roughly what percentage of students in Japan attend private schools?

7. What days of the week do you go to school? What time does your school begin and end?

8. What days of the week do Japanese students go to school? At what time does school begin and end in Japan?

Apply

9. Many Japanese students spend time outside of school at *juku*, or "cram schools." Would you like to go to a *juku* if you lived in Japan? Explain.

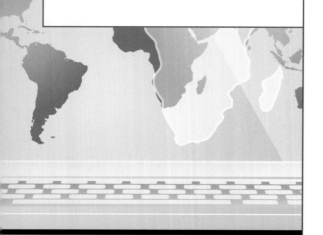

Extend Your Learning
JUSTIFY
As a class, use your research from the questions above to discuss the social values reflected in the education systems of the United States and Japan. Consider things like the importance of education and of specific subjects, the relationship between the individual and society, the role of the state, and the role of family. Your teacher will assign you a side in the debate. One team will argue for adopting the Japanese education system in the United States and the other team will argue against it.

✓ Can Do!
In this lesson you will learn to

- identify body parts in Japanese
- describe physical characteristics of yourself and others
- describe your own personality and those of others

Online Resources

cheng-tsui.com/
adventuresinjapanese

- Audio
- Vocabulary Lists
- Vocabulary Flashcards
- *Kana* and *Kanji* Flashcards
- Activity Worksheets

Kanji
used in this lesson

In this lesson, you will learn *kanji* for parts of the body and for mother and father.

	Kanji	Meaning	Readings		Examples		
19.	口	mouth	くち	くち 口	mouth		
			ぐち	みずぐち 水口	Mizuguchi (last name)		
20.	目	eye	め	め 目	eye		
			もく	もく 目ひょう	objective, target, goal		
21.	耳	ear	みみ	みみ 耳	ear		
22.	手	hand	て *	て 手 じょうず 上手	hand skillful		
23.	父	father	ちち	ちち 父	one's own father		
			とう	とう お父さん	someone else's father		

A Japanese father with upright shoulders sits cross-legged.

	Kanji	Meaning	Readings		Examples		
24.	母	mother	はは	はは 母	one's own mother		
			かあ	かあ お母さん	someone else's mother		

A mother caresses her baby with her two arms as she feeds it.

WORKBOOK　page 225

* Indicates irregular readings of the *kanji*

かいわ　Dialogue

🔊 **READ/LISTEN** Is Emi's father tall? Is Emi's mother tall?

お父さんは　せが高いですか。

でも、母は　せが　ひくいです。

はい、父は　ちょっと　せが　高いです。

READ Find these sentence structures in the dialogue.

Person は　　せ(い)が　Adverb　　　　　Adj.　　　　です。

とても　　　　たかい
すこし or ちょっと　ひくい
まあまあ

たんご   Vocabulary

🔊 "Japanese Sumo Wrestler"*

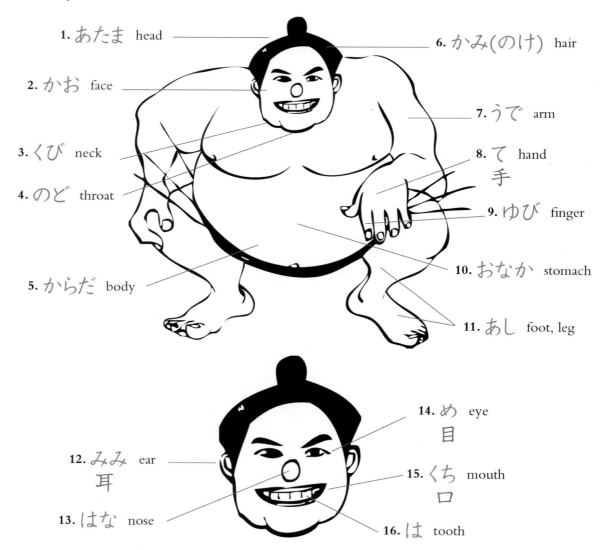

1. あたま head

2. かお face

3. くび neck

4. のど throat

5. からだ body

6. かみ(のけ) hair

7. うで arm

8. て hand
   手

9. ゆび finger

10. おなか stomach

11. あし foot, leg

12. みみ ear
    耳

13. はな nose

14. め eye
    目

15. くち mouth
    口

16. は tooth

17. せ（い）	**18.** こころ	**19.** こえ	**20.** たかい	**21.** ひくい
height	heart, spirit	voice	is tall	is short (height), low

* See Cultural Note on page 208 of Lesson 6-4 for more about sumo wrestlers.

ついか　たんご　Additional Vocabulary

1. せなか	back	**9.** あご	chin
2. かた	shoulder	**10.** むね	chest
3. ひざ	knee	**11.** おしり	backside; buttocks
4. ひじ	elbow	**12.** ほね	bone
5. まゆげ	eyebrow	**13.** きんにく	muscle
6. まつげ	eyelash	**14.** こし	waist; hips
7. くちびる	lip	**15.** ひげ	beard; mustache
8. ほお	cheek	**16.** あしの　ゆび	toe

よみましょう　Language in Context

🔊 **READ/LISTEN** Read these sentences in Japanese.

ハリーさんは　せが
たかいです。
でも、リリーさんは
せが　ひくいです。

ぶんぽう　Grammar

A Describing Physical Characteristics

Noun 1 (person) ＋は　Noun 2 (attribute) ＋が　(adjective) です。

Literally, this construction is translated "As for N1, N2 is . . .," and is a sentence of description. This is commonly used to describe a person's physical characteristics. "As for so and so, his/her height is tall," etc.

The particle が is considered a subject marker. The topic particle は is often used to replace が. When this occurs, the noun preceding は becomes the topic of the sentence.

N1 の N2 は 〜 です。　has a slightly different meaning. Compare:

わたしは　せが　たかいです。　　As for me, I'm tall. (The topic is I.)

わたしの　せは　たかいです。　　My height is tall. (The topic is height.)

◀)) MODELS ▷

1. わたしは　すこし　せが　ひくいです。 I am a little short.
2. あには　せが　とても　たかいです。　My older brother is very tall.

READ/WRITE Complete the sentences based on the information given below. Write the correct particle in each ( ) and choose the correct adverb from the options in each 〔 〕.

My older brother is very tall, my younger brother is a little tall, but I am very short. My friend's sister is very tall, but my friend is a little short.

あに（ 1 ）　　せ（ 2 ）　〔とても／すこし〕　たかいです。
おとうと（ 3 ）　せ（ 4 ）　〔とても／すこし〕　たかいです。
わたし（ 5 ）　　せ（ 6 ）　〔とても／すこし〕　ひくいです。
ともだち（ 7 ）　あね（ 8 ）　せ（ 9 ）　〔とても／すこし〕
たかいですが、わたし（ 10 ）　ともだち（ 11 ）　せ（ 12 ）
〔とても／すこし〕　ひくいです。

ぶんかノート　Culture Notes

🔊 Expressions with the Body

There are many figurative expressions in the Japanese language that refer to body parts. Many also appear in proverbs. Here are some simple and common expressions. Some are similar to English.

1. あたまが　いいです。   is smart

2. あたまが　わるいです。   is unintelligent

3. はなが　たかいです。   has a long (tall) nose/ is proud, boastful

4. こころが　ひろいです。   is open-minded/generous

5. こころが　せまいです。   is narrow-minded

6. みみが　はやいです。   quick to pick up on gossip

7. くびに　なります。   to be fired

8. かおが　ひろいです。   is well-known

 Translate the above Japanese phrases using parts of the body into English, being as literal as you can. Compare these literal translations with similar phrases in English. Is the meaning always the same in both languages? Which expressions differ? Which are the most similar?

Language Note

Singular/Plural Nouns

Unlike English where most nouns have a singular and plural form (i.e., boy/boys; woman/women), in Japanese, singular and plural forms are almost non-existent. One must use contextual cues to decide whether a noun is singular or plural. For example, は may mean one tooth or several.

Pair Work

A. SPEAK/LISTEN As you name parts of the body, your partner points to the corresponding parts of his/her body. Take turns.

B. SPEAK/LISTEN/WRITE Ask whether your partner's family members are tall or short. On a separate sheet of paper, create a chart like the one below, write the family members' names in the first column, then check the appropriate box.

Ex. A さん： ごかぞくは　なんにんですか。

B さん： 四にんです。

A さん： だれですか。

B さん： ちちと　ははと　あねと　わたしです。

A さん： そうですか。　おとうさんは　せが　たかいですか。

B さん： いいえ、ちちは　せが　すこし　ひくいです。

A さん： そうですか。

かぞく	とても たかい	すこし たかい	まあまあ	すこし ひくい	とても ひくい

Class Game

C. SPEAK/LISTEN This game is played somewhat like "Simon Says." One student leader stands in front of the class as the others face him/her. The leader begins by pointing to his/her nose three times, saying はな each time. After the third はな, he/she chooses another body part, e.g., くち. At this point, the leader may either point correctly to his/her mouth or point incorrectly to another body part. Even if the leader points to a body part other than his/her mouth, the rest of the class must point to their mouths. If they follow the leader's incorrect action, they are "out" and must sit down. The last student standing is the winner and becomes the next leader.

WORKBOOK page 43

かいわ Dialogue

🔊 **READ/LISTEN** Is Ken's sister tall? Is her hair long or short?

ぶんけい Sentence Patterns

READ Find these sentence structures in the dialogue.

1. Person は Attribute が Adverb Adj.(-い) です。

        とても

        すこし or ちょっと

        まあまあ

        あまり   い Adj.(-く) ないです。

        ぜんぜん   い Adj.(-く) ありません。

2. Question: 〜さんは めが いいですか。

   Yes answer: はい、いいです。

   No answer: いいえ、よく ないです。

        or いいえ、よく ありません。

1. いい , よい
[い Adj.]

good

Use よい in conjugations.

2. わるい
[い Adj.]

bad

3. おおきい
[い Adj.]
大きい

big

4. ちいさい
[い Adj.]
小さい

small

5. ながい [い Adj.]

long

6. みじかい [い Adj.]

short (not for height)

よみましょう　Language in Context

READ/LISTEN/SPEAK Read these sentences in Japanese. Describe someone in your class who is smart, has good hearing, or has good eyesight.

父は　目が　わるい
ですが、耳が　いいです。

みつこさんは　あたまが
いいです。

A い Adjective Conjugation

い adjectives are the second type of adjective in Japanese, besides な adjectives. They are usually native Japanese terms, rather than Chinese. Most end in –*ai*, –*ii*, –*ui*, or –*oi*. When used with です, they conjugate differently from な adjectives, as seen below.

な adjectives were introduced in Lesson 5-2. Most of them do not end in –*ai*, –*ii*, –*ui*, or –*oi*, although there are some exceptions that you must remember, such as きらい "dislike" and とくい "be strong in." な adjectives conjugate like nouns when used with です. See pages 164–65 to review.

い **adjective conjugation:**

せが　たかいです。	(I) am tall.
せが　たかく　ないです。／ たかく　ありません。	(I) am not tall.
せが　たかかったです。	(I) was tall.
せが　たかく　なかったです。／ たかく　ありませんでした。	(I) was not tall.

いい **"good" conjugates from the** よい **form:**

いいです。	(It) is good.
よく　ないです。／よく　ありません。	(It) is not good.
よかったです。	(It) was good.
よく　なかったです。／ よく　ありませんでした。	(It) was not good.

◀))) MODELS

1. わたしは　せが　あまり　たかく　ないです。
   I am not very tall.

2. やまださんは　とても　あたまが　いいです。
   Mr. Yamada is very smart.

3. おばあさんは　めも　みみも　よく　ないです。
   My grandmother's eyesight and hearing are bad.

READ/WRITE Answer the questions about Ken's mother based on the information below. Use complete sentences.

His mother is short. Her eyesight is not very good now, but was very good before.

1. お母さんは　せが　たかいですか。

2. お母さんは　いま　目が　いいですか。

3. お母さんは　まえ　目が　よかったですか。

B Expressions using body part words

◀))) MODELS

1. あたまが　いいです。　　　is smart

2. あたまが　わるいです。　　is unintelligent

3. かおが　いいです。　　　　is good looking

4. かおが　わるいです。　　　is homely

5. めが　いいです。　　　　　has good eyesight

6. めが　わるいです。　　　　has bad eyesight

7. みみが　いいです。　　　　has good hearing

8. みみが　わるいです。　　　has bad hearing

9. せが　たかいです。　　　　is tall (height)

10. せが　ひくいです。　　　　is short (height)

11. はなが　たかいです。　　　has a long (tall) nose, prideful

12. はなが　ひくいです。　　　has a short (flat) nose

13. こえが　おおきいです。　　has a loud voice

14. こえが　ちいさいです。　　has a soft voice

15. こころが　いいです。　　　is good natured

READ Choose the correct word from the options in the ( ) to describe Emi's father based on the information below.

Her father is handsome and very tall, but he has a very loud voice.

お父さんは　かおが　（いい / わるい）です。お父さんは
せが　（たかい / ひくい）です。お父さんは　こえが
とても（おおきい / ちいさい）です。

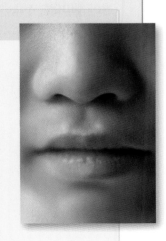

ぶんかノート　Culture Notes

Changing Styles and Conceptions of Beauty in Japan

From its medieval period until the Meiji Restoration of the 19th century, Japan had a conception of beauty distinct from that of the West and even many parts of Asia. During that period, women, particularly those of the upper classes, wore white face powder, grew their hair long and straight, and painted false eyebrows high on their foreheads after shaving or plucking their natural eyebrows.

When they married, these women would blacken their teeth in a custom called はぐる (literally, "teeth black") in order to indicate their new status. Occasionally, these styles were also adopted by upper-class men.

Today, most of these practices have disappeared, and Japan's modern conception of beauty is largely similar to those of other Asian and Western countries. Some of these old styles are still reflected in traditional cultural items like ひな dolls, combined with more modern styles.

 Look at a picture of George Washington, Thomas Jefferson, John Adams, or another famous figure of the American Revolution. How have styles in the U.S. or your own country changed since then? Compare these changes to those in Japan as described above. Think of at least two examples of how these older styles are still seen today.

Language Notes

A. はなが　たかい
The Japanese describe a nose as being tall たかい or low ひくい, not long or flat as in English. How far one's nose protrudes out from one's face determines whether one's nose is たかい or ひくい. A good translation of はなが　たかい would be to have a big or long nose. Conversely, はなが　ひくい would be a small or flat nose.

B. スマート and "smart"
When Japanese people say 「あなたは　スマート *sumaato* ですねえ。」, it does not mean "You are intelligent." It means "You are slim/stylish." It is similar to the English use of "smart" in the sentence "She is a smart dresser!" In addition, スマート *sumaato* in Japanese implies slenderness.

アクティビティー Communicative Activities

Pair Work

SPEAK/LISTEN/WRITE Ask your partner about his/her family members' characteristics or ask them to describe the family pictured below.

On a separate sheet of paper, create a chart like the one below. Write the names (titles) of each of your partner's family members in the blocks in the top row and fill in the blocks below each with the correct description for each person *in Japanese*. Use adverbs in your descriptions.

Ex. 「おとうさんは　せが　たかいですか。」
　　「はい、すこし　たかいです。」

Name			
1. Height			
2. Intelligence			
3. Eyes			
4. Voice			
5. Hair			
6. Hands			
7. Legs (long/short)			
8. Heart			

WORKBOOK　page 45

おはなし　Story

🔊 **READ/LISTEN** What color are the writer's father's eyes? What color are the writer's?

<ruby>父<rt>ちち</rt></ruby>の　<ruby>目<rt>め</rt></ruby>は　あおいですが、　<ruby>母<rt>はは</rt></ruby>の　<ruby>目<rt>め</rt></ruby>は　ちゃいろいです。
ぼくの　<ruby>目<rt>め</rt></ruby>も　ちゃいろいです。

たんご　Vocabulary

🔊

1. あかい

[い Adj.]

red

2. しろい

[い Adj.]

白い

white

3. くろい

[い Adj.]

black

4. あおい

[い Adj.]

blue

5. きいろい　[い Adj.]

yellow

6. ちゃいろい　[い Adj.]

brown

ついか　たんご　Additional Vocabulary

1. きんぱつ [Noun]   blonde (hair)

2. まっすぐ [な Adj.]   straight

3. カール _kaaru_ して　います [Verb]   is curly

よみましょう　Language in Context

 READ/LISTEN/SPEAK Read these sentences in Japanese. Describe what color your eyes are.

いもうとさんは　目が
あおいです。

けんじさんは　目が
ちゃいろいです。

ぶんぽう　Grammar

A　Colors ─────────────────────────

All colors have a noun form, but basic colors also have an い adjective form. Generally, when a color immediately precedes a noun and is its descriptor, the い adjective form is used rather than the noun form. However, when conjoining more than two colors with と, the noun forms of the color must be used.

MODELS

1. ぼくの　ぼうしは　あかです。 My cap is a red color.

2. ぼくの　ぼうしは　あかいです。 My cap is red.

3. ぼくの　ぼうしは　あかと　しろです。 My cap is red and white.

Negative form:

MODELS

4. ぼくの　ぼうしは　あかでは　ありません。 My cap is not a red color.

5. ぼくの　ぼうしは　あかく　ないです。 My cap is not red.

　　　　　　or　あかく　ありません。

6. ぼくの　ぼうしは　あかと　しろでは　ありません。

My cap is not red and white.

READ/WRITE Answer the questions about Ken using complete sentences.

Ken's eyes are brown and his hair is brown. His backpack is black and white.

1. ケン _Ken_ さんの　目は　あおですか。

2. ケン _Ken_ さんの　かみの　けは　くろいですか。

3. ケン _Ken_ さんの　リュック _ryukku_ は　あかと　しろですか。

ぶんかノート　Culture Notes

"Grey Hair" and "White Hair" in Japan

When getting older in America, people are often concerned about their hair turning "grey." However, the Japanese describe the same phenomenon as "having white hair" or "white hair appearing."

Search online for photos of the Imperial Family of Japan, particularly the older members. Notice that they allow their hair to grow "white" naturally. Because the Imperial Family must represent the beliefs of the Shinto religion, which espouses nature worship, they will not dye their hair because it is unnatural to do so. However, other Japanese people may still dye their hair.

Consider the connotations of the terms "white hair" and "gray hair" and write a paragraph comparing them. When would you use each term to describe someone's hair? How do you think each term affects the way someone thinks about aging?

アクティビティー Communicative Activities

Pair Work

A. SPEAK/LISTEN/WRITE Ask your partner about the eye color and hair color of each member of his/her family or their friends.

Write the names of your partner's family members or friends in the first column and the correct colors in the second and third columns.

Ex. Question: おとうさんは　めが　なにいろですか。

or おとうさんの　めは　なにいろですか。

Answer: （ちちは　めが）　ちゃいろいです。

or （ちちの　めは）　ちゃいろいです。

かぞく／ともだち	めの　いろ	かみの　いろ

Class Work

B. SPEAK/LISTEN Game: 10 Questions

Gather pictures of ten famous people. One student volunteer chooses one of the 10 people and tells only the teacher which person he/she has chosen. The rest of the class asks the student volunteer no more than 10 Yes/No questions as they try to guess which person was chosen. The student volunteer must give a Yes/No answer to every question asked.

Connect

C. SPEAK/WRITE Be a mathematician! Count the number of people in your class with different hair color and eye color, and calculate the percentage of each in the whole class. Then create pie charts for eye color and hair color based on the percentages. Label these charts in Japanese.

WORKBOOK page 47

おはなし　Story

 READ/LISTEN How old is the writer's grandfather? What adjectives does he use to describe him?

おじいさん

ぼくの　おじいさんは　六十五さいです。

とても　わかいです。　ちょっと

やせて　います が、　とても　げんきです。
futtobooru
フットボールが　大好きです。
まい　　　　　*terebi*　　　*み*
そして、　毎ばん　テレビを　見ます。

そして、　とても　やさしいです。

たんご　Vocabulary

1. ふとって　います
[Verb]

is fat, heavy

2. やせて　います
[Verb]

is thin

3. わかい
[い Adj.]

young, energetic (used for young adults or older, not children)

4. としを　とって
います [Verb]

is old (age)

5. きびしい
[い Adj.]

strict

6. やさしい
[い Adj.]

nice, kind

7. Question 1. (それとも) Question 2.　　　　Question 1, or Question 2.

8.
Adjective and Verb-phrase Conjugation		
	Affirmative	**Negative**
fat	ふとって　います	ふとって　いません
thin	やせて　います	やせて　いません
young	わかいです	わかく　ないです or わかく　ありません
old (age)	としを　とって　います	としを　とって　いません
strict	きびしいです	きびしく　ないです or きびしく　ありません
nice, kind	やさしいです	やさしく　ないです or やさしく　ありません

ついか　たんご　Additional Vocabulary

1. めがねを　かけて　います。　　　　is wearing glasses

2. しにました。　　　　died, passed away

よみましょう　Language in Context

🔊 **READ/LISTEN/WRITE** Read these sentences in Japanese. Describe someone.

つじさんは　としを
とって　います。

カプールせんせいは　やさしいです。

ぶんぽう　Grammar

A Sentence Connector それとも

Question 1。 (それとも、)　**Question 2。**　**Question 1?, or Question 2?**

それとも means "or" and is used at the beginning of a new sentence. It is used to link two sentences when the alternatives given are verbs, い adjectives or な adjectives. それとも may also be omitted in these cases. When the two alternatives are nouns, a different form that will be introduced in a later lesson is used.

 MODELS

1. おとうさんは　ふとって　いますか。(それとも、)
   やせて　いますか。

   Is your father fat? Or is he thin?

2. せんせいは　きびしいですか。(それとも、) やさしいですか。

   Is your teacher strict? Or is he/she nice?

3. ジュース *juusu* を　のみますか。ミルク *miruku* を　のみますか。

   Do you drink juice? Or do you drink milk?

4. おすしが　すきですか。きらいですか。

   Do you like sushi? Or do you dislike sushi?

READ/WRITE For each of the following sentences, write a second sentence using それとも and the antonym (opposite) of the adjective in the first sentence.

1. お母さんは　やさしいですか。　(それとも…)

2. お父さんは　ふとって　いますか。　(それとも…)

3. おばあさんは　としを　とって　いますか。　(それとも…)

ぶんかノート   Culture Notes

Why Are すもうとり So Heavy?

すもうとり are sumo wrestlers and are famous for their large size, which helps them hold their ground and push opponents out of the ring in a sumo match. A large すもうとり can weigh as much as 600 pounds. They wake up early in the morning to practice すもう. Young すもうとり, because of their low rank, must do all of the menial work, such as cleanup and cooking. This includes preparing ちゃんこなべ, which is a stew consisting of huge quantities of meat and vegetables. すもうとり may eat as many as eight to ten huge bowls of this a day. It is no wonder that they gain so much weight! When すもうとり retire, most lose weight and try to maintain a normal lifestyle at a reasonable weight.

You can also use the recipe
to make your own
ちゃんこなべ.

 Look online to find a recipe for ちゃんこなべ. What ingredients might help すもうとり gain weight? Describe the possible positive and negative effects of ちゃんこなべ on health.

アクティビティー   Communicative Activities

Pair Work

A. SPEAK/LISTEN Ask the following questions. Use the cues to think of a specific person's name to substitute in the parenthesis. If your response is no, answer in the negative form. Take turns.

1. (Sumo wrestler) は　やせて　いますか。

2. (Famous person) は　ふとって　いますか。

3. (Teacher) は　わかいですか。

4. (President) は　としを　とって　いますか。

5. (Father or mother or teacher) は　きびしいですか。

6. (Friend, teacher) は　やさしいですか。

7. (Student, father, teacher) は　せ(い)が　たかいですか。

8. (Student, mother) は　めが　あおいですか。

9. (Famous Person) は　おおきいですか。

10. (Student) は　かみが　ながいですか。

11. (Partner) は　あたまが　いいですか。

B. SPEAK/LISTEN/WRITE Ask your partner about his/her parents and grandparents. On a separate sheet of paper, create a chart like the one below. In the blanks, write your partner's responses in Japanese.

Ex. 「おとうさんは　やせて　いますか。　ふとって　いますか。」

「ちちは　すこし　やせて　います。」

とくちょう	おとうさん	おかあさん	おじいさん	おばあさん
1. Heavy or thin				
2. Strict or nice				
3. Young or old				
4. Tall or short				
5. Hair color				
6. Eyesight				

Reading

C. READ/WRITE Read the following e-mail from a Japanese friend. Answer the questions below in Japanese using complete sentences.

私の　おばあさんは　七十さいです。　とても　年を　とって
いますが、とても　げんきです。　せが　ひくいです。
そして、ふとって　います。　おすしが　大好きです。

UNDERSTAND

1. How old is the writer's grandmother?

2. Is the grandmother short or tall?

APPLY

3. Write a response e-mail describing one of your family members.

6か5
Little sister is cute

かいわ　Dialogue

🔊 READ/LISTEN Is Ken's sister quiet or noisy?

いもうとさんは
かわいいですね。
うるさいですか。

いもうと？
いもうとは　いつも
うるさいですよ。
そして、じゃまです。

たんご　Vocabulary

🔊

1. きれい [な Adj.]　　　　　　　　**2.** きたない [い Adj.]

pretty　　　　　clean　　　neat, nice　　　dirty　　　　messy

3. かわいい
[い Adj.]

cute

4. しずか
[な Adj.]

quiet

Not used to describe
someone's personality.

5. うるさい
[い Adj.]

noisy, annoying

6. じゃま
[な Adj.]

a hindrance, a
nuisance, in the way

7. いいですね。

It is good, isn't it?

ね is used when the speaker seeks agreement or
confirmation.

8. いいですよ。

It is good, you know.

よ expresses emphasis or exclamation.

9.

Adjective Conjugation

Vocabulary	Affirmative	Negative
pretty, clean, neat	きれいです	きれいでは　ないです or きれいでは　ありません
dirty, messy	きたないです	きたなく　ないです or きたなく　ありません
cute	かわいいです	かわいく　ないです or かわいく　ありません
quiet	しずかです	しずかでは　ないです or しずかでは　ありません
noisy	うるさいです	うるさく　ないです or うるさく　ありません
hindrance	じゃまです	じゃまでは　ないです or じゃまでは　ありません

* じゃ may replace では in any context. じゃ is less formal.

ついか　たんご　Additional Vocabulary

1. ハンサム　　*hansamu*　　handsome

2. びじん　　　　　　　　　　a beauty; beautiful woman

よみましょう　Language in Context

🔊 **READ/LISTEN/SPEAK** Read these sentences in Japanese and compare the use of the sentence ending particles. Ask a partner if he/she thinks something is good and respond.

いいですね。

The sentence ending particle ね is used when the speaker wishes to seek agreement or confirmation from the listener

いいですよ。

The sentence ending particle よ expresses emphasis or exclamation

ぶんぽう　Grammar

A Sentence Ending Particles ─────

Sentence ＋ か。

Sentence ＋ね。

Sentence ＋よ。

Sentence ＋ねえ。

You've now learned several sentence ending particles. か indicates that the sentence is a question. ね is used when the speaker wants agreement from the listener. よ expresses emphasis. ねえ expresses exclamation and surprise. Do not confuse their usages!

Compare:

あついですか。	Is it hot?
あついですね。	It is hot, isn't it?
あついですよ。	It is hot, you know.
あついですねえ。	It is so hot!

◀)) MODELS ▶

1. 「うるさいですよ。」 "You are noisy, you know. (Be quiet.)"
   「すみません。」 "I am sorry."

2. 「かわいいですねえ。」 "She is so cute!"
   「そうですねえ!」 "Yes, she is!"

3. 「あたまが いいですね。」 "You are smart, aren't you?"
   「いいえ、よく ないですよ。」 "No, I am not smart, you know."

READ Choose the correct sentence ending particle from the options in the ( ) based on the information given.

1. A Japanese person was very impressed by your Japanese.

   日本じん： 日本ごが 上手です（か / ね / よ / ねえ）。

2. Your Japanese friend wants your agreement to his/her opinion.

   ともだち： この 本は いいです（か / ね / よ / ねえ）。

3. A Japanese teacher complains about your noisy electric guitar.

   せんせい： ギター*gitaa*は うるさいです（か / ね / よ / ねえ）。

4. A friend wants to ask you a question.

   ともだち： おすしが すきです（か / ね / よ / ねえ）。

B Adjective Conjugation Review ─────────

There are two types of adjectives in Japanese: い adjectives and な adjectives. Both describe nouns, but are conjugated differently. Adjectives which end in *-ai*, *-ii*, *-ui* or *-oi* are usually い adjectives, and the adjectives without these endings are usually な adjectives. Two な adjectives that are exceptions are きらい "dislike" and とくい "strong in/good at." The conjugations are as follows.

	い adjectives	な adjectives
affirmative	おおきいです	しずかです
	is big	is quiet
negative	おおきく　ないです or おおきく　ありません	しずかでは　ありません or しずかじゃ　ありません
	is not big	is not quiet
additional adjectives	たかい　　しろい ひくい　　わかい いい, よい　きびしい わるい　　やさしい おおきい　きたない ちいさい　かわいい ながい　　うるさい あかい　　　　etc.	すき　　　　じゃま きらい *　　　　etc. じょうず へた とくい * にがて きれい * しずか

* Exceptions

READ/WRITE Answer the questions negatively in complete sentences.

1. おねえさんは　せが　たかいですか。
2. おねえさんは　日本ごが　上手ですか。
3. おねえさんは　きれいですか。

ぶんかノート　Culture Notes

Kawaii Culture in Japan

Kawaii means cute, but it plays a much larger role in Japanese culture than cuteness does in the U.S. Many popular characters in *anime* and *manga* (Japanese comics) have *kawaii* features, such as large eyes or cute costumes. Sometimes, artists draw small, cute, childish versions of characters with larger eyes and heads called "*chibi*" (which can also describe a small child or person).

In addition to *anime* and *manga*, *kawaii* is increasingly an influence on major Japanese brands, industry, and fashion. Many popular *kawaii* brands have become major Japanese exports and can be seen around the world. Several businesses and official institutions in Japan have even adopted *kawaii* mascots to represent them, including Japan Post and the NHK (Japan's public broadcasting service).

Based on the Culture Note, create a *kawaii* mascot for your school. Draw your mascot and write a short paragraph explaining how it represents the school.

アクティビティー　Communicative Activities

Pair Work

A. SPEAK/LISTEN Ask the following questions using the cues in the parentheses as topics for your sentences. If the answer is "no," use the negative form. Take turns.

1. (Partner's hands, partner's mother, partner's *hiragana*) は　きれいですか。

2. (Partner's room へや, partner's *hiragana*) は　きたないですか。

3. (Classmate) は　かわいいですか。

4. (Library) は　しずかですか。

5. (Father, mother) は　うるさいですか。

6. (Partner's sibling) は　じゃまですか。

B. SPEAK/LISTEN/WRITE Ask your partner if his/her friends have the characteristics below.

Write your partner's responses down in Japanese. Use the correct い adjective or な adjective affirmative or negative form. Take turns.

Ex.　A:　ともだちは　だれですか。

　　　B:　～さんです。

　　　A:　～さんは　やさしいですか。

　　　B:　いいえ、ぜんぜん
　　　　　やさしく　ありません。

　　　A:　そうですか。

1. cute
2. nuisance
3. old
4. intelligent
5. big
6. long-haired
7. tall

Class Work

C. SPEAK/LISTEN 10 Questions – Teacher to Students

The teacher has one student in mind. Ask your teacher 10 Yes/No questions to find out which student the teacher has in mind. Second, play this game with a partner. Finally, have one student volunteer to stand in front of the class as classmates ask the volunteer questions. Guess which classmate the student volunteer is thinking about. (Add. vocab.: おとこ male, おんな female.)

WORKBOOK page 51

Review Questions

Ask your partner these questions in Japanese. Your partner answers in Japanese. Check your answers using the audio.

Characteristics   Review pages 190, 195–96, 205, 210

1. Is your mother/father tall?

2. You are very smart! [Respond to the compliment.]

3. Is your father/mother's hair long?

4. Are your eyes bad?

5. Does your father have a large belly?

6. Is your grandmother thin?

7. Is your Japanese teacher young?

8. Is your English teacher old?

9. Is your father nice?

10. Is your mother strict?

11. You are noisy! [Respond to the comment.]

12. Are your hands clean?

13. Is your *hiragana* (writing) messy?

Descriptives   Review page 210

14. Is the library quiet?

15. That student over there is pretty, isn't she?

16. Am I in your way?

Colors   Review page 201

17. Are your eyes blue?

18. What color is your shirt (*shatsu*)?

19. Are your school colors white and blue?

20. What color is your mother's hair?

Text Chat

You will participate in a simulated exchange of text–chat messages. You should respond as fully and as appropriately as possible.

You will have a conversation with Setsuko Hara, a Japanese high school student, about appearances and hobbies.

December 29, 02:56 PM

かみのけは　なにいろですか。
ながいですか。

Describe specific examples.

December 29, 02:58 PM

ちゃいろい　目が　すきですか。
それとも、あおい　目が　すきですか。

Give your preference.

December 29, 03:01 PM

わたしの　しゅみは　*supootsu*
スポーツですが、
すもうは　きらいです。しゅみは
なんですか。

Give two examples.

Can Do!
Now I can . . .

- [ ] ask a friend about his/her physical characteristics (size, height, color, personality, etc.)

- [ ] describe my own physical appearance (size, height, eye and hair color, personality, etc.)

- [ ] describe my own personality or someone else's

Zoo-san Song
ぞうさん Elephants

ぞうさん　まど　みちお作詞 / 團　伊玖磨作曲

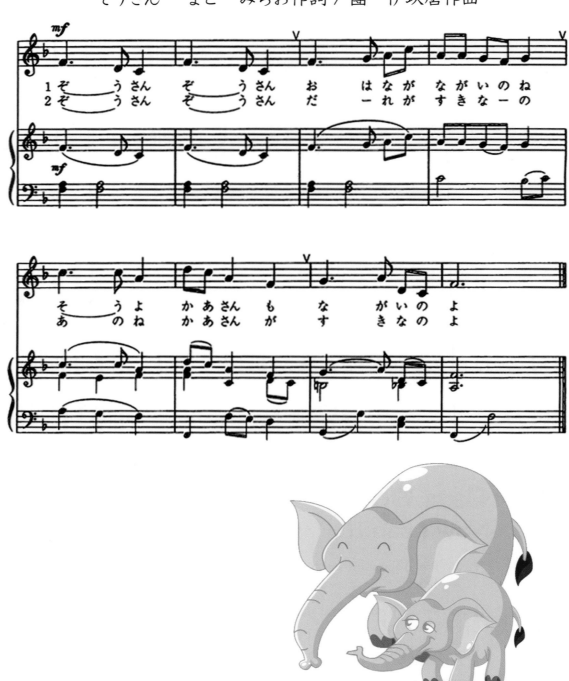

土曜日
Saturday

 Can Do!
In this lesson you will learn to

- tell someone the time in hours and minutes
- describe your daily schedule
- tell how you commute to and from school
- invite someone to do an activity
- suggest doing a certain activity
- negotiate day and/or time of an activity
- accept/decline an invitation
- give details of a trip you have taken

Online
Resources

cheng-tsui.com/
adventuresinjapanese

- Audio
- Vocabulary Lists
- Vocabulary Flashcards
- *Kana* and *Kanji* Flashcards
- Activity Worksheets

Kanji
used in this lesson

In this lesson, you will learn *kanji* used for traveling.

	Kanji	Meaning	Readings	Examples	
25.	分	minute	わ	分かりません。	I do not understand.
			ふん	二分 (にふん)	two minutes
			ぷん	六分 (ろっぷん)	six minutes
26.	行	go	い(く) こう	行きます りょ行します (こう)	go travel
27.	来	come	き(ます)	来ます (き)	come
28.	車	vehicle	くるま しゃ	車 (くるま) じどう車 (しゃ) じてん車 (しゃ)	car car bicycle
29.	山	mountain	やま さん	山 (やま) 山本さん (やまもと) ふじ山 (さん)	mountain Mr./Ms. Yamamoto Mt. Fuji (can also use ふじやま)
30.	川	river	かわ	川 (かわ) 川口さん (かわぐち) 川手さん (かわて)	river Mr./Ms. Kawaguchi Mr./Ms. Kawate

WORKBOOK page 229

かいわ Dialogue

READ What does Ken want to do on Saturday? What does Emi suggest?

この　土曜日に
えいがを
見ませんか。

何時（なんじ）ですか。

6時（じ）15分（ふん）
ですよ。

はい、
いっしょに
見（み）ましょう。

たんご Vocabulary

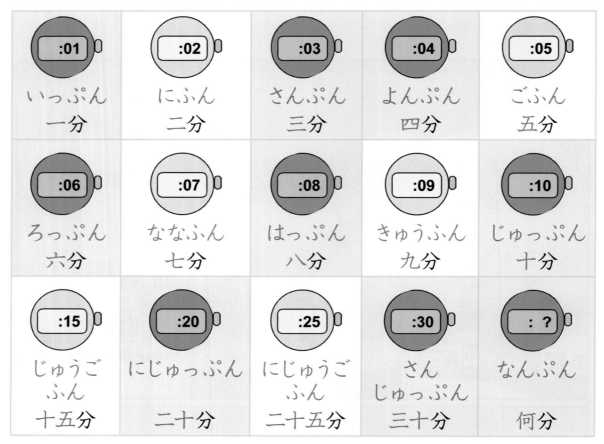

1. Minutes*

:01 いっぷん 一分	:02 にふん 二分	:03 さんぷん 三分	:04 よんぷん 四分	:05 ごふん 五分
:06 ろっぷん 六分	:07 ななふん 七分	:08 はっぷん 八分	:09 きゅうふん 九分	:10 じゅっぷん 十分
:15 じゅうごふん 十五分	:20 にじゅっぷん 二十分	:25 にじゅうごふん 二十五分	:30 さんじゅっぷん 三十分	: ? なんぷん 何分

* The minutes with blue backgrounds have irregular pronunciations

2. くじまえ
   九時まえ

   before 9:00

3. くじすぎ
   九時すぎ

   after 9:00

4. くじ　ごふんまえ
   九時五分まえ

   five minutes before 9:00

ごろ "about," すぎ "past/after," and まえ "before" appear between the specific time word and the particle に.

5. はやい	6. おそい	7. こんばん	8. こんばんは。
[いAdj.]	[いAdj.]		
早い		今ばん	
early	late	tonight	Good evening.

9. ごぜん	a.m.	[Ex. ごぜん1じ "1:00 a.m."]
10. ごご	p.m.	[Ex. ごご1じ "1:00 p.m."]

ついか たんご Additional Vocabulary

1. いいえ、けっこうです。 　　　　　　　No, thank you.

2. ざんねんですが... 　　　　　　　Unfortunately . . .

When you decline an invitation politely, you may use this (#2) as a preface. This by itself can be a complete sentence. Japanese prefer not to give clear explanations, so this is particularly convenient to use when declining an invitation. No specific "excuse" needs to follow.

よみましょう　Language in Context

🔊 **READ/LISTEN/SPEAK** Read these sentences in Japanese. Suggest an activity to a partner.

6時15分の　えいがを
みましょう。

こんばん　おすしを
たべませんか。

ぶんぽう　Grammar

A   Suggestion Verb Ending –ましょう

Verb–ましょう。   **Let's do ～. [Suggestion]**

When –ましょう is attached to a verb stem (portion of the verb remaining after removing –ます), the verb means "Let's do . . ." and is used when one makes a suggestion to others.

◀))) MODELS ▷

1. おひるごはんを　たべましょう。   Let's eat lunch!

2. えいがを　みましょう。   Let's watch a movie!

3. お水を　のみましょう。   Let's drink water!

READ/WRITE Suggest your friend do the following actions by changing the verb ending to the –*mashoo* form.

1. 日本ごを　はなします。

2. おひるごはんを　たべます。

3. アニメ *anime* を　みます。

B   Invitation Verb Ending –ませんか

Verb–ませんか。   **Won't you do ～?/ Would you like to do ～? [Invitation]**

The negative –ません form plus か may have two interpretations. It may simply be a negative question. Often, however, it is used as an invitation to the listener to do something.

◀))) MODELS ▷

1. 「この　ざっしを　よみませんか。」
   "Won't you read this magazine?"

   「どうも　ありがとう。」
   "Thank you very much."

2. 「ジュース *juusu* を　のみませんか。」
   "Won't you drink some juice?"

   「いいえ、けっこうです。」
   "No, thank you."

READ/WRITE Invite your friend to do the following actions by changing the verb ending to *–masen ka.*

1. この　おんがくを　ききますか。

2. いっしょに　ダンス *dansu* を　しますか。

3. この　ペン *pen* で　かきますか。

ぶんかノート　Culture Notes

A. Punctuality in Japan

In Japan, it is important to be on time, particularly in the cities. Everything runs precisely on schedule – buses, trains, TV programming, etc. It is impolite to be late for appointments. In fact, many Japanese people plan to arrive at meetings early. If you are going to be late, you must call ahead to give notification, even if it is only a few minutes, and apologize as soon as you get there. Simple apologies are more acceptable than giving excuses.

B. 24-Hour Time versus 12-Hour Time

For most public transportation systems in Japan (planes, trains, subways, buses, etc.), time schedules are given in 24-hour time, also called military time, to avoid confusion. For example, a plane arriving at 8:00 a.m. would be listed as arriving at 08:00, but a plane arriving at 8:00 p.m. would be listed as a 20:00 arrival. However, in daily conversation, 12-hour time is more commonly used.

24-hour time at a train station

 Imagine that you and a colleague are running late for a meeting with a superior (older person) in Japan. Based on the information above, what should you say to your superior when you arrive? Write a short statement predicting how he/she might react if you said that your bus was late and that another person you were waiting for did not show up.

アクティビティー   Communicative Activities

Class Work

A. SPEAK/LISTEN The class wants to set up a standard curfew time for students. Some students suggest a time. Everyone has two flash cards: an おそい card and a はやい card. When a student suggests a curfew time, the other students raise their cards and express their opinions. Try to make responsible decisions.

1. Curfew time on Monday, Tuesday, Wednesday, Thursday: _____

2. Curfew time on Friday and Saturday: _____

Pair Work

B. SPEAK/LISTEN/WRITE Ask your partner what time he/she eats breakfast, lunch, and dinner every day. Fill in the blanks. Write your answers in Japanese on a separate sheet of paper, using a chart like the one below.

	あさごはん	おひるごはん	ばんごはん
Time			

C. SPEAK/LISTEN/WRITE You want to invite your friend to the following activities. Decide on an agreeable day and time. Write your answers in Japanese on a separate sheet of paper, using a chart like the one below.

Activity	Day of the week	Time★
1. Eating lunch together at the cafeteria		
2. Playing tennis together		
3. Watching a movie together		

★ 土曜日の　一時 one o'clock on Saturday

D. SPEAK/LISTEN/WRITE You want to do some activities together with your friend. Invite him/her to do each of the activities below. Decide which day of the week is convenient for both of you. Write your schedule in Japanese on a separate sheet of paper, using a chart like the one below.

Ex.　Question:　〜曜日に　いっしょに　おひるごはんを
　　　　　　　　たべませんか。

　　　Yes Answer:　いいですよ。いっしょに　たべましょう。

　　　No Answer:　いいえ、ざんねんですが、〜曜日はちょっと
　　　　　　　　、、、〜曜日に　たべませんか。

1. Eating lunch at the snack bar together.

2. Talking in the cafeteria together.

3. Doing Japanese homework together.

4. Listening to music together.

5. Watching a movie together.

Our schedule:

Sun	Mon	Tue	Wed	Thu	Fri	Sat

WORKBOOK　page 57

7か2
What time do you go home?

かいわ　Dialogue

🔊 **READ/LISTEN** What time does Emi go home?

何時に　うちへ　かえりますか。
(なんじ)

４時ごろに　かえります。
(じ)

じゃ、いっしょに　かえりましょう。
それから、こんばん　でんわで
はなしましょう。

ぶんけい　Sentence Patterns

READ Find this sentence pattern in the dialogue.

Person は　Specific time に　　　　Place へ／に　Direction verb 。
　　　　～じ（ごろ）に　　　　　　　"to"
　　　　　　　　　　　　　　　　　　　　いきます go
　　　　　　　　　　　　　　　　　　　　きます come
　　　　　　　　　　　　　　　　　　　　かえります return
　　　　　　　　　　　　　　　　　　　　　　　　（to a place）

たんご　Vocabulary

1. いきます [いく]
行きます　[行く]

to go

2. きます [くる]
来ます　[来る]

to come

3. かえります [かえる]

to return (place),
to go/come home

4. おきます [おきる]

to wake up, get up

5. ねます [ねる]

to sleep, go to bed

6. かいしゃ

company

7. Place ＋ へ／に ＋ Direction verb 。　　　　to (place)

8. Activity ＋ に ＋ Direction verb 。　　　　to, for (activity)

9. Sentence 1 。それから、　Sentence 2 。　　Sentence 1. And then Sentence 2.

よみましょう　Language in Context

READ/LISTEN/WRITE Read these sentences in Japanese. Write when you get up and what you do after that.

お父さんは　なん時に
かいしゃへ　行きますか。

7時に　おきます。それから、
あさごはんを　たべます。

A Direction Verbs

🔊 MODELS

Direction verbs are verbs which indicate direction or motion. There are three basic direction verbs:

いきます	行きます	"go" (Implies motion away from speaker's location.)
きます	来ます	"come" (Implies motion toward speaker's location.)
かえります		"return (to a place)"

READ Choose the correct direction verb based on the information given.

1. がっこうへ　（行きます　来ます　かえります）。[You are at home.]

2. がっこうへ　（行きます　来ます　かえります）。[You are at school.]

3. うちへ　（行きます　来ます　かえります）。　[You are at school.]

B Particles

Directional Particles へ／に

Place ＋ へ／に ＋ Direction verb （いきます／きます／かえります）。
(go/come/return) to

Verbs used in this construction indicate direction or motion to the place of destination. The particles へ and に immediately follow the place of destination.

🔊 MODELS

1. ぼくは　きょう　7時はんに　がっこうへ　来ました。
   I came to school at 7:30 today.

2. 父は　10時ごろ　うちに　かえりました。
   My father came home about 10:00.

3. ともだちは　日曜日に　うちへ　来ました。
   My friend came to my house on Sunday.

Event Directional Particle に

Activity ＋ に ＋ Direction verb 。　　　　**to, for**

Shopping, movies, dancing, lunch, parties, classes, etc., are some examples of activities.

Activities or events are followed by the particle に (not へ) when used with direction verbs.

MODELS

1. 土曜日の　7時はんに　えいがに　行きました。
   I went to a movie at 7:30 on Saturday.

2. この　金曜日に　ともだちと　ダンス *dansu* に　行きます。
   I will go dancing with my friend this Friday.

3. 父は　日曜日に　ゴルフ *gorufu* に　行きます。
   My father goes golfing on Sundays.

READ/WRITE Write へ or に in each of the ( ). Both choices are possible for some of the sentences.

1. 土曜日に　えいが（　）　行きました。

2. きのう　六時ごろに　うち（　）　かえりました。

3. ともだちは　日曜日の　パーティー *paatii*（　）　来ます。

C Sentence Connector それから

MODELS

Sentence 1。それから、Sentence 2。　　　Sentence 1. And then Sentence 2.

1. あさ　6時に　おきました。それから、あさごはんを
   たべました。
   I got up at 6:00 in the morning. And then, I ate breakfast.

2. あには　8時すぎに　うちへ　かえりました。
   それから、えいがに　行きました。
   My older brother came home after 8 o'clock. And then, he went to a movie.

3. わたしは　としょかんへ　行きました。
   それから、日本ごを　べんきょうしました。
   I went to the library. And then, I studied Japanese.

READ Choose the correct sentence connectors from the options in the ( ) based on the information given below.

At about four I came back home. Then I watched TV. And I ate dinner. And then I did my homework. And I listened to music. Then I went to bed.

四時ごろに　うちへ　かえりました。　（それから、　そして、）
テレビ *terebi* を　みました。　（それから、そして、）　ばんごはんを
たべました。　（それから、　そして、）　しゅくだいを　しました。
（それから、　そして、）　おんがくを　ききました。　（それから、
そして、）　ねました。

ぶんかノート　Culture Notes

Commuting in Japan

Japanese people who live in urban areas do not usually commute by car. Public transportation such as buses, electric trains, and subways is common. In big cities such as Tokyo, Osaka, etc., the railway is most convenient because of its efficiency and dependability. You can almost set a clock by the arrival and departure of trains. Once you get on, you can study, sleep, listen to music, text, e-mail, etc., but talking on the phone is considered rude, and most passengers keep their phones on silent. However, rush hour, which generally runs from 6:30 – 8:30 a.m. in Tokyo, can be a harrowing experience for those not used to massive crowds. Public transportation does not run all night long. If you are out late and miss the last bus or train, you may have to catch a taxi home.

 Using Google Maps, get directions from Shinjuku station to Harajuku station in Tokyo. Calculate the time it would take to travel between stations by public transportation, by car, and by walking. Write your answers in Japanese.

Language Note

Use of いきます and きます

The Japanese usages of いきます and きます are slightly different from their usage in English. In Japanese, いきます is used to indicate motion away from the speaker's location, or a location associated with the speaker. きます is used to indicate motion toward the speaker, or toward a location associated with the speaker. When your friend invites you to a party at his house, he would say 「パーティー *paatii* に　きませんか。」. What would your response be? Would it be 「はい、きます。」 or 「はい、いきます。」? Because your friend's house is not associated with you, the correct answer is 「はい、いきます。」.

アクティビティー　Communicative Activities

Pair Work

A. SPEAK/LISTEN/WRITE Ask your partner for the times he does the following activities on a normal school day. Write your partner's answers in Japanese on a separate sheet of paper, using a chart like the one below. Take turns.

Ex. Question: あさ　なん時に　おきますか。

Answer: 〜時に　おきます。

Activity	Time
1. Get up in the morning	
2. Eat breakfast	
3. Come to school	
4. Go to the library	
5. Eat lunch	
6. Return home	
7. Eat dinner	
8. Go to bed	

B. SPEAK/LISTEN/WRITE Ask your partner what he/she did last Saturday and what time he/she did each activity. On a separate sheet of paper, create a schedule of your partner's activities, using the one below as a model. Start from early morning and end at bedtime.

_____ さん [partner's name] の　土曜日

[Time]　　　[Things he/she did.]

_____ に　おきました。

_____ に

_____ に

_____ に

Additional activities:

それから、_____ に　ねました。

WORKBOOK page 59

7か3
I come to school by bus

かいわ　Dialogue

🔊 **READ/LISTEN** How does Emi come to school? How does Ken usually come to school?

何で　学校へ　来ますか。

バスで　来ます。
ケンさんは？

たいてい　じてん車で　来ます。

ぶんけい　Sentence Patterns

READ Find these sentence patterns in the dialogue.

1. Person は　　Specific time に　　Place へ／に "to"　　Direction verb 。
　　　～じ(ごろ) に　　Transportation で "by"

2. Subject / だれ が　　～ます(か)。

たんご　Vocabulary

1. くるま,
   じどうしゃ

   車、じどう車

   car, vehicle

2. バス

   basu

   bus

3. タクシー

   takushii

   taxi

4. じてんしゃ

   じてん車

   bicycle

5. ちかてつ

   subway

6. でんしゃ

   でん車

   electric train

7. ひこうき

   ひ行き

   airplane

8. ふね

   boat, ship

9. あるいて
   いきます

   [あるいて　いく]

   あるいて　行きます

   to go by walking

10. あるいて
    きます

    [あるいて　くる]

    あるいて　来ます

    to come by walking

11. あるいて
    かえります

    [あるいて　かえる]

    あるいて　かえります

    to return by walking

12. Transportation mode ＋で　　　　by (transportation mode)

13. Subject/だれ＋が　　〜ます(か)。　　[Subject particle]

ついか　たんご　Additional Vocabulary

1. しんかんせん

bullet train

よみましょう　Language in Context

🔊 **READ/LISTEN/SPEAK** Read these sentences in Japanese. Say how you go or come to school.

ともだちと　いっしょに
あるいて　かえります。

じてん車で　がっこうへ
行きます。

ぶんぽう　Grammar

A Transportation Mode Particle で —————————

Transportation mode ＋で　by (transportation mode)

The particle で immediately follows the noun which is the mode of transportation, means, or tool by which an action occurs.

🔊 MODELS

1. わたしは　バス basu で　がっこうへ　来ます。
   I come to school by bus.

2. 母は　車で　かいしゃに　行きます。
   My mother goes to her company by car.

3. おじいさんと　おばあさんは　きのう　ひこうきで
   日本へ　行きました。
   My grandfather and grandmother went to Japan by airplane yesterday.

READ/WRITE Write the correct particle in each ( ).

1. 「なに (1)　　がっこう (2)　　行きますか。」
「あるいて　　行きます。」

2. 山川さんは　　八時ごろに　　車 (3)　　　がっこう (4)
行きます。

3. 父は　　ちかてつ (5)　　　かいしゃ (6)　　　行きます。

B　**Subject Particle** が

Subject/ だれ＋が

が marks the subject of a sentence when the information expressed by the subject is introduced for the first time. When the subject is presented as the topic (that is, the information has already been introduced), however, the topic marker は replaces が.

◀)) MODELS ▷

1. だれが　　バス *basu* で　　がっこうへ　　来ますか。
Who comes to school by bus?

2. だれが　　車で　　来ますか。　　　Who comes by car?

READ/WRITE Choose the correct particle in the ( ). Then answer the questions on a separate sheet of paper

1. だれ (は / が)　　じてん車で　　がっこうへ　　来ますか。

2. なに (は / が)　　すきですか。

3. だれ (は / が)　　あるいて
来ますか。

わたし (は / が)
あるいて　　来ます。

ぶんかノート　Culture Notes

A. What is a しんかんせん?

The しんかんせん, literally translated as the "new trunk line" but more commonly known as the bullet train, stretches from northern Honshu to Kyushu in the south, and also connects eastern and western Japan. Soon, the しんかんせん is expected to span almost the entire length of the island chain, extending from Hakodate in Hokkaido to Kagoshima at the southernmost tip of Kyushu. It is the fastest means of ground transportation in Japan, traveling at a speed of about 200 mph, though faster speeds have been measured. It's commonly used for long distance travel and business trips.

B. Japanese Cars Drive on the Left Side of the Road

Unlike cars in the U.S., Japanese cars drive in the left lanes of the highway. The steering wheels in Japanese cars are also located on the right side. Other countries that drive on the left side of the road include the U.K., India, Australia, and South Africa.

C. Japanese Taxis

In Japan, taxis are quite common in big cities, so they are easy to find. When a taxi turns on a red sign in its window, that means it is available. Raising your hand signals the driver to stop. Wait until the driver opens the door remotely. Do not stand close to the door – you may be hit! Tipping taxi drivers in Japan is not common.

If you're not confident about your Japanese language skills, it's a good idea to carry the business card of your destination (or the correct address), and show it to the taxi driver when you enter the taxi. Your taxi driver may not speak English well.

Research the Japanese and U.S. train systems online and answer these questions.

	Japan	USA
How fast does the fastest train go?		
What is the longest train route?		
Approximately how many people travel by train each year?		

アクティビティー　Communicative Activities

Pair Work

A. SPEAK/LISTEN/WRITE Ask your partner how each member of his/her family comes or goes to school or work and what time each leaves home. Write your answers in Japanese on a separate sheet of paper, using a chart like the one below.

Ex. Question 1: お父さんは　なにで　しごとに　行きますか。

Answer 1: 父は　車で　行きます。

Question 2: お父さんは　なん時に　しごとに　行きますか。

Answer 2: 父は　〜時に　行きます。

Family member	Transportation	Departure time

B. SPEAK/WRITE You want to go to the following places with your partner. Suggest a means of transportation to your partner or ask him/her to suggest one, as shown in the example below. Write your answers in Japanese on a separate sheet of paper, using a chart like the one below.

Ex. 　A: えいがに　行きませんか。　B: はい、行きましょう。

　A: なにで　行きますか。　　B: 車で　行きましょう。

Destination	Transportation	Destination	Transportation
1. Japan		**4.** Airport（くうこう）	
2. [Another state]		**5.** Library	
3. Alaska (*Arasuka*)		**6.** Movie	

Class Work

C. SPEAK/LISTEN Ask all of your classmates how they come to school. Tally their responses on a separate sheet of paper, using a chart like the one below.

Ex. 　「だれが　バス *basu* で　がっこうへ　来ますか。」

バス *basu*	車	じてん車	あるいて	ちかてつ

WORKBOOK　page 61

かいわ   Dialogue

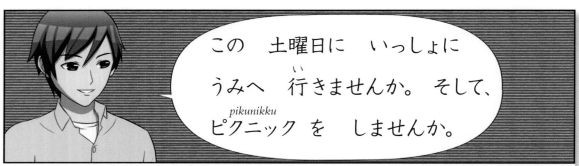

🔊 **READ/LISTEN** Where does Ken suggest going this Saturday? What does he suggest doing there?

この　土曜日に　いっしょに

うみへ　行きませんか。　そして、

pikunikku

ピクニック を　しませんか。

いいですねえ。　うみで、

pikunikku

ピクニック を　しましょう。

たんご   Vocabulary

1. うみ

beach, ocean, sea

2. やま
山

mountain

3. かわ
川

river

4. りょこう
りょ行

trip, traveling

5. デパート

depaato

department store

6. レストラン

resutoran

restaurant

7. かいもの

shopping

8. しょくじ

meal, dining

9. パーティー

paatii

party

10. ピクニック

pikunikku

picnic

11. キャンプ

kyanpu

camping

12. いそがしい

[い Adj.]

busy

---

13. どこへも ＋ Neg. of direction verb 。　　　do not go/return anywhere

ついか　たんご　**Additional Vocabulary**

1. きっさてん		coffee shop
2. ショッピングセンター	*shoppingu sentaa*	shopping center
3. コンサート	*konsaato*	concert
4. デート	*deeto*	dating
5. ハイキング	*haikingu*	hiking
6. ひま [な Adj.]		free (time), have nothing to do

よみましょう　Language in Context

🔊 **READ/LISTEN/WRITE** Read these sentences in Japanese. Write down what you will do on Saturday.

デパートで　かいものを　します。

レストランで　しょくじを　します。

ぶんぽう　Grammar

A　Nominal Verbs

Noun ＋ (を) ＋します Verbs

This object particle を is optional when used in this context.

Noun form:

べんきょう　studying

タイプ *taipu*　typing

でんわ　a telephone

りょこう　a trip, travel, traveling

かいもの　shopping

しょくじ　a meal, dining

Verb form:

べんきょう(を)　します　to study

タイプ(を)　します　to type

でんわ(を)　します　to make a phone call

りょこう(を)　します　to take a trip, to travel

かいもの(を)　します　to shop

しょくじ(を)　します　to have a meal, to dine

If the sentence already has a direct object, this を should be omitted.

◀)) MODELS

1. うちで　べんきょう(を)　しました。
   I studied at home.

2. うちで　日本ごを　べんきょう　しました。
   I studied Japanese at home.

3. じゃ、明日　でんわ(を)　します。
   Well then, I will call you tomorrow.

4. 日本へ　りょこう(を)　しましょう。
   Let's travel to Japan.

5. きのう　かいもの(を)　しました。
   I shopped yesterday.

6. きのう　しゅくだいを　タイプ *taipu* しました。
   I typed (my) homework yesterday.

7. レストラン *resutoran* で　しょくじを　しましょう。
   Let's have a meal at a restaurant.

READ Choose the correct particle from the options in the ( ). X means no particle is required.

1. 日本ご（を ／ の ／ X）　べんきょうを　します。

2. 日本ごを　べんきょう（を ／ の ／ X）　します。

3. レポート（を ／ の ／ X）　タイプ（を ／ の ／ X）　しました。

B Alternate Translations of します

します is a common verb, and can be translated in many ways besides "to do."

スポーツ *supootsu* を　します	to play sports
テレビゲーム *terebi geemu* を　します	to play video games
パーティー *paatii* を　します	to have a party
ピクニック *pikunikku* を　します	to have a picnic
キャンプ *kyanpu* を　します	to camp, to go camping
デート *deeto* を　します	to have a date, to date, to go out on a date

◀ MODELS

1. 父は　ゴルフ *gorufu* が　だいすきです。そして、
日曜日に　いつも　ゴルフ *gorufu* を　します。

My father loves golf. And he always plays golf on Sundays.

2. やまへ　行きましょう。そして、キャンプ *kyanpu* を
しましょう。

Let's go to the mountains. And let's go camping.

READ Choose the correct English equivalents for します
from the options in the ( ).

1. テニス *tenisu* を　します。　　(have　play)

2. ピクニック *pikunikku* を　します。　(have　play)

3. キャンプ *kyanpu* を　しましょう。　(go　do)

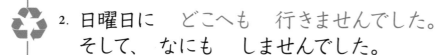

C どこへも - Anywhere/nowhere

どこへも＋ Negative form of direction verb 。 do not go/ return anywhere.

MODELS

1. 「金曜日の　ばん　どこへ　行きましたか。」
   "Where did you go on Friday night?"

   「どこへも　行きませんでした。」
   "I did not go anywhere."

2. 日曜日に　どこへも　行きませんでした。
   そして、　なにも　しませんでした。

   I did not go anywhere on Sunday. And I did not do anything.

READ/WRITE Write an appropriate negative response to each question using なにも or どこへも.

1. 土曜日の　ばん　どこへ　行きますか。

2. なにを　しますか。

3. きのうの　ばん　どこへ
   行きましたか。

ぶんかノート　Culture Notes

Japanese Weekends

Until several years ago, most Japanese people only had one-day weekends. Adults worked six days a week and children went to school Monday through Saturday. In 1998, changes in Japan's education policy allowed most schools to take two-day weekends, although some alternated between one-day and two-day weekends.

Recently, this has become a topic of debate, as Japan's Education Board has increased the number of class hours per week, pressuring more schools to hold classes on Saturday. A gap between private schools, many of which kept Saturday classes, and public schools has emerged. More schools are now holding Saturday classes when needed, or holding guest lectures, review sessions, and other lower stress events on Saturdays.

In their free time, young people may stay home and watch television, read, or play computer games. They often also go shopping or play sports. Most businesses have also changed to a two-day weekend resulting in an increase in free time for adults as well, although employees may work overtime on Saturday or weekday evenings.

 How do you think the shift from a one-day to a two-day weekend has affected family life in Japan? How might it affect your own family if you went to school six days a week? Explain your responses to each question in a paragraph.

アクティビティー　Communicative Activities

Pair Work

A. SPEAK/WRITE Invite your friend to do the following activities with you and decide where and when you want to do them. Write your answers in Japanese on a separate sheet of paper, using a chart like the one below.

Ex. A: いっしょに　かいものを　しませんか。

B: はい。どこで　かいものを　しますか。

A: (Shopping place)で　かいものを　しましょう。

B: はい。いつ　かいものを　しますか。

A: ～曜日の　～時ごろに　かいものを　しましょう。

B: はい、いいですね。

Activities	Where?	When? ～曜日　～じ
1. Shopping		
2. Dining		
3. Party		
4. Picnic		
5. Tennis		
6. Movies		

WORKBOOK　page 63

かいわ　Dialogue

🔊 READ/LISTEN　When was Emi in Los Angeles? What did she like there?

Emi
エミ: 10日から　15日まで
　　　Rosanzerusu
　　　ロサンゼルスに　行きました。
Ken
ケン: どうでしたか。

Emi
エミ: あつかったです。　でも、
　　　　　び
　　　はな火は　きれいでしたよ。
Ken　　やす
ケン: お休みを　たのしみに　して　います。

たんご　Vocabulary

🔊

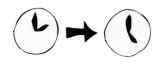

1. (お)やすみ
(お) 休み

day off, vacation

2. はなび
はな火

fireworks

3. ～から～まで

from ~ to ~

4. どうですか。

How is it?

5. （〜を）　たのしみに　して　います。

I am looking forward to (something).

6. ハワイ	*Hawai*	Hawaii
7. ロサンゼルス	*Rosanzerusu*	Los Angeles
8. グランドキャニオン	*Gurandokyanion*	Grand Canyon
9. サンフランシスコ	*Sanfuranshisuko*	San Francisco
10. ニューヨーク	*Nyuuyooku*	New York
11. ボストン	*Bosuton*	Boston
12. フロリダ	*Furorida*	Florida

ついか　たんご　Additional Vocabulary

1. いかがですか。	How is it? [Polite equiv. of どうですか。]
2. とうきょう	Tokyo
3. おおさか	Osaka
4. きょうと	Kyoto
5. ひろしま	Hiroshima
6. ほっかいどう	Hokkaido
7. きゅうしゅう	Kyushu

とうきょう

🔊 **READ/LISTEN/WRITE** Read these sentences in Japanese. Explain where and when you want to travel.

5日から　8日まで　きょうとへ
行きました。

日本りょこうを　たのしみに　して
います。

ぶんぽう　Grammar

A "From" and "To" Prepositions から and まで

Noun 1 から   Noun 2 まで   From N1 to N2

N1 and N2 may represent times or places.

🔊 MODELS

1. 父は　土曜日に　ボストン *Bosuton* から　シカゴ *Shikago* まで
行きます。

   My father will go from Boston to Chicago on Saturday.

2. わたしの　びじゅつの　クラス *kurasu* は　1時はんから　です。

   My art class is from 1:30.

3. わたしは　10時から　11時まで　えいごの　じゅぎょうが
あります。

   I have (my) English class from 10:00 to 11:00.

READ Choose the correct particles from the options in the ( ).

1. 「いつ　べんきょうを　しましたか。」

   「きのう　三時 (から / まで)　五時 (から / まで)
   しました。」

2. 「きのう　よく　ねましたか。」

   「はい、あさ　十時 (から / まで)　ねました。」

3. 「日本ごの　クラス *kurasu* は　いつですか。」

   「九時はん (から / まで) です。」

ハワイ

ぶんかノート　Culture Notes

Popular Travel Destinations in Japan

Over 15 million Japanese people travel abroad every year. Foreign travel destinations gain and lose popularity depending on Japan's political and economic relationships with other countries. Generally, however, the U. S. steadily ranks as a favorite among Japanese travelers. Within the U.S., Hawaii is the most frequently visited, followed by the West Coast, then the East Coast. Japanese tourists also frequent Western Europe, but in recent years, Eastern Europe has also become a popular destination due to lower costs. Taiwan, Thailand, Philippines, and South Korea are popular Asian countries that Japanese people choose to visit.

Japanese people also travel extensively within their own country. Popular domestic destinations include Kyoto, Tokyo, Nara, Hiroshima, Okinawa, and Hokkaido.

 Research one of the above travel destinations popular in Japan online and provide examples of the following.

	Examples
Major tourist attractions	
Special local foods	
Other attractions nearby	
Climate/weather	

アクティビティー　Communicative Activities

Pair Work

A. SPEAK/LISTEN Ask your partner the following questions. Your partner answers based on fact. Take turns.

1. まい日　なん時から　なん時まで　ねますか。

2. なん曜日から　なん曜日まで　がっこうへ　行きますか。

3. 日本ごの　クラス *kurasu* は、　なん時から　なん時まで　ですか。

4. きのう　なん時から　なん時まで　べんきょうを　しましたか。

5. きのう　なん時から　なん時まで　テレビ *terebi* を　みましたか。

6. おやすみは　なん日から　ですか。

B. SPEAK/LISTEN Your partner has planned a trip. Ask the following questions in Japanese and your partner answers based on the plan. Take turns.

1. おやすみに　どこで　りょ行　しますか。

2. いつから　いつまで　行きますか。

3. 車で　りょ行　しますか。

4. なにを　たのしみに　して　いますか。

C. SPEAK/LISTEN Ask the following questions in Japanese to your partner. Your partner answers based on a trip he/she has taken in the past. Take turns.

1. まえ　どこで　りょ行　しましたか。

2. いつから　いつまで　行きましたか。

3. だれと　りょこうを　しましたか。

4. なにを　たのしみに　して　いますか。

5. かいものを　しましたか。

Reading

D. READ/WRITE You have received a letter from your pen-pal Daisuke. Read the letter and answer the questions in Japanese.

(Your name)さん　おげんきですか。11月15日から　11月20日まで
^{*Amerika*}
アメリカで　りょ行を　しました。^{*Rosanzerusu*}ロサンゼルスに
^{*i*}
行きました。あつかったですよ！　^{*Rosanzerusu*}ロサンゼルスで　^{*resutoran*}レストランと
うみに　行きました。^{*kuruma*}車で　^{*Hariuddo*}ハリウッドへ　^{*i*}行きました。
^{*Rosanzerusu*}ロサンゼルスが　^{*daisu*}大好きです。(X)さん　日本へ　^{*ki*}来ませんか。

どうぞ　おげんきで。
^{やまもとだいすけ}
山本大輔

UNDERSTAND

1. When did Daisuke take a trip to America?

2. What did Daisuke do in Los Angeles?

3. What did Daisuke like?

APPLY

4. Write a response to Daisuke, telling him about a trip you recently took or a trip you plan to take. Include when you took the trip, where you went, activities that you did, and how you traveled.

 Reading-- Review

E. READ/WRITE Read the following questions and respond based on fact. Using what you have learned from previous lessons, write your answers in Japanese on a separate sheet of paper.

1. クラス *kurasu* で　日本ごを　よく　はなしましたか。

2. きのうの　クラス *kurasu* で　うるさかったですか。

3. 日本ごの　しゅくだいを　いつも　しましたか。

4. きょうかしょを　ときどき　わすれましたか。

5. まい日　日本ごを　べんきょうしましたか。

WORKBOOK page 65

Lesson 7
Review

Review Questions

🔊 Ask your partner these questions in Japanese. Your partner answers in Japanese. Check your answers using the audio.

Time & Schedules Review pages 221 and 228–29

1. What time is it now?

2. When is the Japanese exam?

3. What time does Japanese class (クラス *kurasu*) end?

4. What time did you get up this morning?

5. What time did you come to school today?

6. About what time will you go home today?

7. What time did you go to sleep last night? Was it early?

8. What time do you usually go to bed?

9. What time does your father go to work?

10. What time do you usually eat lunch?

Suggestions & Invitations Review pages 224 and 240

11. Let's eat lunch together at 12:00.

12. Would you like to go to a movie with me on Saturday? [Answer: Decline politely.]

13. Would you like to go to the beach on Saturday? And let's have a picnic. [Answer: Decline politely.]

14. Would you like to go to a restaurant tonight? And let's have a meal together. [Answer: Accept politely.]

Modes of Transportation Review page 234

15. How do you come to school?

16. Do you walk to school?

17. How do you go to Japan?

Activities & Travel Review pages 240 and 246

18. What did you do on Saturday?

19. Where did you go on Sunday?

20. Where does your mother usually shop?

21. Are you busy now?

22. Where have you traveled before?

23. What do you do at the beach?

24. What are you looking forward to?

Text Chat

You will participate in a simulated exchange of text-chat messages. You should respond as fully and as appropriately as possible.

You will have a conversation with Yumi Yamakawa, an exchange student from Japan at your school, about this Saturday's plans.

January 23, 03:46 PM

あさ　たいてい
なん時に　おきますか。

Respond.

January 23, 03:52 PM

この　土曜日に
なにを　しますか。

Give two activities.

January 23, 03:58 PM

土曜日に　いっしょに
えいがに　行きませんか。

Accept and ask what time the movie is.

Can Do!
Now I can . . .

- ☐ tell time using hours and minutes
- ☐ talk about my daily schedule
- ☐ tell others how I commute to school
- ☐ suggest an activity to do
- ☐ invite someone to do an activity with me
- ☐ accept or decline an invitation
- ☐ talk about a trip I took

New Year's
おしょうがつ

RESEARCH Use books, the Internet, or interview a Japanese member of your community to answer the following.

Determine

1. What holdiays are commonly celebrated during the winter in the U.S.?

2. What holidays are commonly celebrated during the winter in Japan?

3. What ceremonies or rituals are undertaken during New Year's (*Oshoogatsu*) in Japan?

4. What religions do these New Year's ceremonies or rituals in Japan originate from?

Compare

5. How is Christmas celebrated in the U.S.?

6. How is Christmas celebrated in Japan?

7. How is the New Year celebrated in your hometown?

8. How is the New Year celebrated in Japan?

Apply

9. How might you combine Japanese traditions and those of your own country to celebrate the New Year? Write a short essay describing a New Year's celebration combining elements from Japan and your own country. Explain why you chose the traditions you selected.

Extend Your Learning
COMMUNICATION
Many of the Japanese people visit temples and shrines on *Oshoogatsu*. Find out why by researching one of the most commonly practiced religions in Japan and present the information to your class using a slideshow. You should consider the central beliefs and practices of the religion, its origin and history in Japan, and any rituals associated with *Oshoogatsu*. Your teacher may also ask you to include a short introduction and conclusion in Japanese.

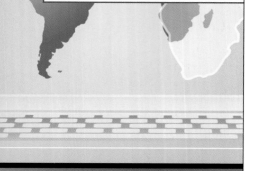

学校
School

✓ Can Do!
In this lesson you will learn to

- ask where certain objects or people are
- describe where certain objects or people are
- describe your school
- describe your house
- describe your room

Online Resources

cheng-tsui.com/
adventuresinjapanese

- Audio
- Vocabulary Lists
- Vocabulary Flashcards
- *Kana* or *Kanji* Flashcards
- Activity Worksheets

In this lesson, you will learn some *kanji* associated with people.

	Kanji	Meaning	Readings	Examples	
31.	人	person	ひと にん じん *	ひと あの 人 さんにん 三人 にほんじん 日本人 ひとり 一人	that person three people Japanese (person/ people) one (person)
32.	子	child	こ	こ 子ども	child
33.	女	female	おんな	おんな　　ひと 女 の 人 おんな　　こ 女 の 子	woman, lady girl
34.	好	like	す(き)	す 好き	like
35.	田	rice field	た だ	たぐち 田口さん やまだ 山田さん かねだ 金田さん ほんだ 本田さん	Mr./Ms. Taguchi Mr./Ms. Yamada Mr./Ms. Kaneda Mr./Ms. Honda
36.	男	male	おとこ	おとこ　　　ひと 男 の 人 おとこ　　こ 男 の 子	man boy

女 ＋ 子 ＝ 好
Woman   child

Everyone likes girls (female children).

田 ＋
rice field

an arm (power)
A man is the source of strength in a ricefield.

Recognition Kanji

わたし
私
I, me

🔊 **READ/LISTEN**　Where is Jon? What has he done wrong?

READ Find these sentence patterns in the dialogue.

1. Topic (Animate) は Place に います。 [(Animate object) is at a place.]

2. Topic (Inanimate) は Place に あります。 [(Inanimate object) is at a place.]

  You have learned two other particles which are used after place words. The type of verb one uses determines the particle after the place word. Let's clarify their usage.

Place で Action verb 。 (Ex. たべます eat, よみます read, はなします talk, etc.)

Place へ／に Direction verb 。 (Ex. 行きます go, 来ます come, かえります return home)

Place に Existence verb 。 (Ex. います exist–animate, あります exist–inanimate)

たんご Vocabulary

1. います [いる]
there is, are (animate objects)
Verb of existence.

2. あります [ある]
there is, are (inanimate objects)
Verb of existence.

3. そと
outside

4. ドア *doa* , と
door

5. まど
window

6. つくえ
desk

7. いす
chair

8. えんぴつけずり

pencil sharpener

9. ごみばこ

trash can

10. いぬ
犬

dog

11. ねこ

cat

---

12. Location に ＋ Existence verb。 　　　　　in, at

13. また 　　　　　again

ついか　たんご　Additional Vocabulary

1. いらっしゃいます 　　　　　there is, are (animate objects)
　　　　　[polite equivalent of います]

2. こくばん 　　　　　blackboard

3. こくばんけし 　　　　　blackboard eraser

4. ホワイトボード　*howaitoboodo* 　　white board

5. クーラー　*kuuraa* 　　　　　air conditioner

6. でんき 　　　　　electricity, lights

7. スイッチ　*suitchi* 　　　　　(light) switch

よみましょう　Language in Context

🔊 **READ/LISTEN/WRITE** Read these sentences in Japanese. Name something that is here and something that is outside.

きょうかしょは　ここに　あります。　　ねこは　そとに　います。

ぶんぽう　Grammar

A Existence Verbs ——————

Topic (Animate) は＋ **Location** に ＋ います。

Topic (Inanimate) は＋ **Location** に ＋ あります。

います and あります are both existence verbs. います is used when the object being discussed is animate, while あります is used when it is inanimate. The particle に follows the place word where the object exists.

There are some exceptions to these rules. For example, with vehicles like cars that people operate, the verb います should be used when the topic is a car with a driver in it, but the verb あります should be used when the topic is an empty car.

◀))) MODELS ▷

1. 「えんぴつけずりは　どこに　ありますか。」
   "Where is the pencil sharpener?"

   「あそこに　ありますよ。」
   "It is over there, you know."

2. 「ぼくの　きょうかしょは　ここに　あります。」
   "My textbook is here."

3. 「ジョン *Jon* くんは　どこに　いましたか。」
   "Where was Jon?"

   「ジョン *Jon* さんは　そとに　いました。」
   "Jon was outside."

READ Choose the correct existence verb from the options in the ( ).

1. いすは　あそこに　（あります／います）。

2. ねこは　どこに　（あります／います）か。

3. 私の　ともだちは　あそこに　（あります／います）。

B Using です in Place of Existence Verbs

Topic (Animate) は＋ Location に ＋ います。＝
Topic (Animate) は＋ Location です。

Topic (Inanimate) は＋ Location に ＋ あります。＝
Topic (Inanimate) は＋ Location です。

You may replace に います／あります with です. The meaning of the sentence does not change.

MODELS

1. 「ごみばこは　どこですか。」   "Where is the trash can?"

   「あそこです。」   "It is over there."

2. 「ジョン *Jon* さんは　どこですか。」   "Where is Jon?"

   「ジョン *Jon* さんは　そとです。」   "Jon is outside."

READ/WRITE Rewrite the sentences using です.

1. 「いぬは　どこに　いますか。」　「そとに　いますよ。」

2. 「えんぴつけずりは　どこに　ありますか。」
   「あそこに　あります。」

ぶんかノート　Culture Notes

A. Japanese Classrooms

Most Japanese high school classrooms accommodate 40 students.
Desks are situated in rows with narrow aisles facing the front of the classroom where the teacher stands. The front of the room or the area around the teacher's lectern may even be elevated so the teacher can easily see to the back of the classroom.

When students arrive at school, they change into "school shoes," and their walking shoes are left in shoe lockers near the entrance.

In Japan, students remain in one classroom while teachers shift from one class to another. Students are responsible for cleaning their own classrooms, hallways, and bathrooms. Chores include sweeping, mopping, and cleaning boards.

B. Japanese Conversational Strategy

When Japanese people are asked where someone is or where something is located, they often answer by first repeating the name of the thing in the form of a question before telling where it is.

「すみません。　あきさんは
どこに　いますか。」

「あきさんですか。　あきさんは
あそこに　います。」

 Read the above text explaining and modeling conversational strategy closely. With a partner, practice conversing in Japanese with the topics below, following the above models. One person should ask about the person/object, and the other should respond by first repeating the information in the form of a question, then giving its location.

1. A window

2. The teacher's desk

3. A classmate

4. A teacher

5. A classmate's notebook

アクティビティー　Communicative Activities

Pair Work

A. SPEAK/WRITE Ask your partner where the following things are located. Write down his/her answers on a separate sheet of paper.

1. Pencil sharpener

2. Trash can

3. (Box of) tissues

4. Teacher's desk

5. (A student in class)

6. Teacher

B. SPEAK/LISTEN Draw the house, car, and library shown in the images below on a separate sheet of paper. Draw each of them twice. Select items from the list below and draw them in the first set of locations.

Do not show your picture to your partner. Ask your partner where his/her objects are located, then recreate your partner's picture in the second block of drawings. After you have both completed this exercise, compare your pictures with your partner's and check that you have communicated accurately with one another.

Things to draw: **dog, cat, book, old man, homework, soccer ball, money, lunch** or any object you would like.

WORKBOOK page 69

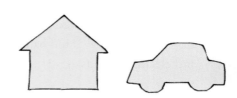
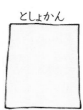

としょかん

かいわ　Dialogue

 READ/LISTEN How does Ken describe the pool? What is the name of the woman he sees?

エミ：　あそこに　プールが　あります。

　　　行きましょうか。

ケン：　はい、　行きましょう。

　　　大きいですねえ。

あそこに　かわいい　女の子が

いますよ。

エミ：　あれは　ケリーさんです。

ぶんけい　Sentence Patterns

READ Find these sentence patterns in the dialogue.

1. Place に Topic (Animate) が　います。　　[There is (animate object) at a place.]

2. Place に Topic (Inanimate) が　あります。　[There is (inanimate object) at a place.]

3. Verb - ましょうか。　　　　　Shall we do ~ ? [polite suggestion]

Note the difference between these two similar sentence patterns.

Topic (Animate) は Place に　います。　The (animate object) is at a place.
　　　　　　　　　　　　　　　　[The emphasis is on the **place**.]

Place に Topic (Animate) が　います。　There is (animate object) at a place.
　　　　　　　　　　　　　　　　[The emphasis is on **what** exists.]

たんご　Vocabulary

1. おとこ 男 male	2. おんな 女 female	3. ひと 人 person	4. こども 子ども child

5. おとこのひと 男の人 man	6. おんなのひと 女の人 woman, lady	7. おとこのこ 男の子 boy	8. おんなのこ 女の子 girl

9. トイレ, (お)てあらい
toire
toilet, bathroom, restroom

10. プール
puuru
pool

11. 〜 かた
person

Polite form of ひと. Must be
preceded by a word such as
この or あの.

ついか　たんご　Additional Vocabulary

1. どなた　　　　　　　　　　　　　　　who? [polite equiv. of だれ]
2. たいいくかん　　　　　　　　　　　　gym
3. ちゅうしゃじょう　　　　　　　　　　parking lot
4. チャペル　　　　　　*chaperu*　　　chapel
5. うんどうじょう　　　　　　　　　　　athletic field
6. きょうぎじょう　　　　　　　　　　　track field
7. コンピュータールーム　*konpyuuta ruumu*　computer room
8. ランゲージラボ　　　*rangeeji rabo*　language lab
9. テニスコート　　　　*tenisu kooto*　tennis court
10. こうちょうせんせい　　　　　　　　school principal

よみましょう　Language in Context

🔊 **READ/LISTEN** Read these sentences in Japanese. When should you use かた instead of ひと? Explain your answer in English.

この　かたは
こうちょうせんせいです。

あそこに　プールが　あります。

A Verbs of Existence and Subject Particle が

Topic (Animate) は　**Location** に　います。

Topic (Inanimate) は　**Location** に　あります。

Vs.

Location に　**Subject (Animate)** が　います。

Location に　**Subject (Inanimate)** が　あります。

In Japanese, emphasis often depends on the location of a word in a sentence and the particle that follows it. います and あります are often used with place words followed by the particle に. When the topic of the sentence, followed by は is followed by the place word and に, the new information being shared is the location of the noun.

MODELS

1. いぬは　あそこに　います。

   The dog is over there. [The emphasis is on the place of existence.]

When the place word followed by に appears first in the sentence, the new information being shared is not the place, but the noun. Because it is the new piece of information, it is followed by the particle が, which emphasizes its importance. In this sentence construction, the English translation is usually, "There is a (noun) at (location)."

MODELS

2. あそこに　いぬが　います。

   There is a dog over there. [The emphasis lies on what exists.]

MODELS

Compare:

3. プール _puuru_ は　あそこに　あります。

   The pool is over there.

4. あそこに　プール _puuru_ が　あります。

   There is a pool over there.

READ Choose the correct particle from the options in the ( ).

1. 母 (は　が)　うちに　います。

2. あそこに　ねこ (は　が)　いますよ。

3. あそこに　トイレ _toire_ (は　が)　あります。

B Polite Suggestions Verb- ましょうか

Verb - ましょうか。   Shall we do 〜 ? [Polite suggestion]

This form of verb is used to politely suggest doing something together with others.

Compare:

1. 行きましょうか。   Shall we go? [Suggestion to others]

2. 行きましょう。   Let's go. [Own suggested decision]

3. 行きませんか。   Would you like to go? [Invitation]

MODELS

1. 「いま　おひるごはんを　たべましょうか。」
   Shall we eat lunch now?

   「はい、たべましょう。」
   Yes, let's eat.

2. 「土曜日に　うみへ　行きましょうか。」
   Shall we go to the beach on Saturday?

   「ええ、行きましょう。」
   Yes, let's go.

READ Choose the correct verb ending from the options in the ( ) based on the prompt.

1. いま　しゅくだいを　（しましょう　しません）か。 [Suggestion]

2. 「土曜日に　えいがに　（行きましょう　行きません）か。」

   [Invitation]

   「はい、（行きましょう　行きません）。」

男子トイレ →
女子トイレ →

ぶんかノート　Culture Notes

A. 男 and 女

In order to use a public restroom in Japan, it is important to know these *kanji*. Which door should you choose to enter?

B. ぶしゅ (Radicals) in Kanji

Most of the *kanji* you learned earlier in this volume were simple *kanji* made up of one part. These kinds of *kanji* are usually called pictographs if they represent actual objects, or ideographs if they represent abstract concepts. Examples of pictographs include 日 and 山, and ideographs include 一 and 中.

You are now beginning to see more complex *kanji* made up of two or more parts. These parts are called ぶしゅ or radicals. Some radicals help give a clue to the character's meaning, while others may hint at the sound of the character. Examples of these *kanji* include 時, 分, and 男. Instead of memorizing every character individually, you will find it easier to learn *kanji* if you memorize them by breaking them down into familiar parts like radicals. For more information, review the introductory section on *kanji* on page 9.

 Look at the *kanji* below and find the radicals based on *kanji* you have already learned. White a short sentence explaining what you think each character may mean.

1. 横
2. 銀
3. 間
4. 期
5. 昨
6. 崎

Language Notes

A. トイレ versus (お)てあらい

There are many Japanese words used to refer to toilets, bathrooms, and restrooms, much like in English. The て of (お)てあらい means "hands" and あらい is a stem form of あらいます, which means "to wash." So (お)てあらい means "a place to wash hands." This is a polite expression and it is quite commonly used in Japan, especially by women.

トイレ *toire* comes from English and is most often used by young Japanese, especially young men. お attached to トイレ *toire* adds politeness to the word, and is more often used by women. Other euphemistic terms, such as WC (water closet, from British English) and けしょうしつ "powder room" are also used.

B. かれ and かのじょ

かれ means "he, him" and かのじょ means "she, her." Originally, these terms were not part of the Japanese language. They developed as a result of Western influence. Today, these words are more commonly used by young people to mean "boyfriend" and "girlfriend." わたしの　かれ means "my boyfriend" and ぼくの　かのじょ means "my girlfriend."

アクティビティー　Communicative Activities

Pair Work

A. SPEAK/WRITE You are taking a Japanese guest to the following places on your school campus. Explain where they are. Your guest gives his/her impressions of each place. Write your answers and the guest's in Japanese on a separate sheet of paper, using a chart like the one below.

Ex. 　せいと：　あそこに　プール *puuru* が　あります。
　　　　　　　行きましょうか。

　　　日本人：　はい、行きましょう。

　　　せいと：　プール *puuru* は　ここです。

　　　日本人：　わあ、おおきいですねえ。

Place	Location	Guest's Impression
1. Pool		
2. Gym		
3. Cafeteria		
4. Library		

B. SPEAK/LISTEN/WRITE You are visiting your friend's school and see the following people on campus. Ask who they are. Write your answers in Japanese on a separate sheet of paper, using a chart like the one below.

Ex. Visitor: 　すみません、あの　女の子は　だれですか。

　　Host: 　あの　女の子ですか。あの子は　〜さんです。

　　Visitor: 　そうですか。（かわいいですねえ。）

People	Who?
1. Girl	
2. Boy	
3. Lady	
4. Distinguished man	

WORKBOOK page 71

8か3
There are many flowers

かいわ　Dialogue

🔊 **READ/LISTEN** How does Emi describe the flowers? How many fish are in the pond?

あそこに　はなが　たくさん
ありますねえ。　きれいですねえ。

いけに　さかなが　一ぴき　いますよ。

ぶんけい　Sentence Patterns

READ Find these sentence patterns in the dialogue.

1. Place に　Subject が　Counter X　います／あります 。
2. Place に　Counter の　Subject が　います／あります 。

たんご　Vocabulary

Measure Words			
large mechanized goods	birds	small animals	long cylindrical objects
1.	2.	3.	4. 
1　いちだい	いちわ	いっぴき	いっぽん　一本
2　にだい	にわ	にひき	にほん　二本
3　さんだい	さんわ	さんびき	さんぼん　三本
4　よんだい	よんわ	よんひき	よんほん　四本
5　ごだい	ごわ	ごひき	ごほん　五本
6　ろくだい	ろくわ	ろっぴき	ろっぽん　六本
7　ななだい	ななわ	ななひき	ななほん　七本
8　はちだい	はちわ	はっぴき	はっぽん　八本
9　きゅうだい	きゅうわ	きゅうひき	きゅうほん　九本
10　じゅうだい	じゅうわ	じゅっぴき	じゅっぽん　十本
11　じゅういち　だい	じゅう　いちわ	じゅう　いっぴき	じゅう　いっぽん　十一本
?　なんだい	なんわ	なんびき	なんぼん　何本

5. き　木

tree

6. はな

flower

7. いけ

pond

8. さかな

fish

9. とり

bird

10. たくさん

a lot, many

11. すこし

a few, a little

🔊 **READ/LISTEN** Read these sentences in Japanese. Note whether the subject or the counter is emphasized in each sentence.

人が　たくさん　いますねえ！

うちに　いぬが　いっぴき　います。

ぶんぽう　Grammar

A Emphasizing Counters

Place に　Subject (Animate object) が　Counter　います。

Place に　Subject (Inanimate object) が　Counter　あります。

When a counter or quantity is included in this structure, it generally follows the subject. This puts more emphasis on the number rather than the subject. Particles do not follow counters or quantity words.

🔊 **MODELS**

1. あそこに　おおきい　木が　一本　あります。
   There is ONE big tree over there.

2. そとに　ねこが　二ひき　います。
   There are TWO cats outside.

3. うちに　車が　二だい　あります。
   There are TWO cars at home.

4. ここに　はなが　たくさん　あります。
   There are LOTS of flowers here.

READ/WRITE Using the prompts given, respond with the correct counter given in the ( ), then choose the correct existence verb.

1. いけに　さかなが　（ many ）　（あります　います）ねえ。

2. あの　木に　とりが　（ two ）　（あります　います）よ。

3. ここに　えんぴつが　（ one ）　（あります　います）。

B Emphasizing Subjects

Place に　**Counter** の　**Subject** が　います／あります。

When a counter describes the subject, it precedes the subject. This puts more emphasis on the subject rather than the number. In this case, the particle の follows the counter.

MODELS

1. あそこに　おおきい　一本の　木が　あります。
   There is a big TREE over there.

2. そとに　二ひきの　ねこが　います。
   There are two CATS outside.

3. うちに　二だいの　車が　あります。
   There are two CARS at home.

4. ここに　たくさんの　はなが　あります。
   There are lots of FLOWERS here.

READ Choose the correct particle from the options in the ( ). X means no particle is required.

1. うちに　二だい（の　X）テレビ _terebi_ が　あります。

2. うちに　いぬが　二ひき（の　X）います。

3. ここに　たくさん（の　X）子どもが　います。

ぶんかノート　Culture Notes

Four Seasons in Japan

In Japan, people's lives are strongly influenced by four distinct seasons, although the seasons vary in intensity between Okinawa in the south and Hokkaido in the north. Their importance in Japanese culture can be tied to the effects of seasonal weather on Japan's traditional agrarian society, and to their role in Shintoism. Spring months are March, April, and May. Summer months are June, July, and August. Autumn months are September, October, and November. Winter months are December, January, and February. The rainy season called つゆ, which affects most of Japan, is in June and July.

あき Fall

なつ Summer

ふゆ Winter

はる Spring

Japanese people often associate annually recurring events with the natural events of the season. For example, April, which marks the beginning of the school year, is commonly associated with the cherry blossom (さくら) season.

What natural events or seasonal changes do you associate with the start of the school year? What about the end of the school year? Write a short paragraph in English to a Japanese friend detailing and explaining your answers.

アクティビティー　Communicative Activities

Pair Work

A. SPEAK/LISTEN Draw two copies each of the three drawings below on a separate sheet of paper. Then draw one or more of each of the items listed below the picture in the first set of drawings. Example: you may choose to draw 3 trees, 5 flowers, and 2 fish.

Do not show your drawings to your partner. After you and your partner have finished your drawings, ask your partner how many of each item are in his/her picture. Ask where they are located and draw them in the second set of drawings. Compare your pictures and your partner's to see whether you successfully communicated the number and location of the objects.

Q: 山に　木が　二本　ありますか。

A: いいえ、　山に　木が　五本　あります。

Q: そうですか。　五本ですね。　　A: はい。

1. tree, fish, men　　**2.** fish, boat, people　　**3.** dog, boy, TV

Reading

B. READ/WRITE Read the following e-mail from a Japanese student describing the area around his/her school. Answer the questions below in Japanese using complete sentences.

> 今 私は 学校に います。　あそこに 木が あります。
>
> そして、　木に 白い とりが たくさん います。　あかい
>
> はなも たくさん あります。　とても きれいですよ。　そとに、
>
> いけが あります。　いけは あまり 大きくありませんが、
>
> 大きい さかなが 五ひき います。　今 私と ともだちは
>
> おひるごはんに カフェテリア*kafeteria*へ 行きます。

UNDERSTAND

1. What is in the tree?

2. What color are the flowers?

3. How many fish are there in the pond?

APPLY

4. What is there a lot of in the room you are in?

5. A Japanese friend is coming to visit your school. Write a short letter describing your school and what your friend may see there.

8か4
The office is in that building

かいわ Dialogue

🔊 **READ/LISTEN** Where is the school office? How does Emi describe the painting?

たんご Vocabulary

🔊

1. たてもの

building

2. じむしょ

office

3. きょうしつ

classroom

4. ロッカー
rokkaa

locker

5. あたらしい
[い `Adj.]
new

6. ふるい
[い `Adj.]
old (not for
person's/animal's age)

7. うつくしい
[い `Adj.]
beautiful

8. ゆうめい
[な Adj.]
famous

Negative forms

5. あたらしく　ないです — is not new

6. ふるく　ないです — is not old

7. うつくしく　ないです — is not beautiful

8. ゆうめいでは　ありません — is not famous

ついか　たんご　Additional Vocabulary

1. けんきゅうしつ — research room, teacher's office

2. こうてい, キャンパス　*kyanpasu* — campus

3. しばふ — lawn

よみましょう　Language in Context

🔊 **READ/LISTEN/SPEAK** Read these sentences in Japanese. Ask a partner whether your school is old or new and respond.

この　たてものは　ふるいです。

スカイツリーは
ゆうめいです。

ぶんかノート　Culture Notes

Summer uniforms

A. School Uniforms

A majority of students in both private (しりつ) and public (こうりつ) schools in Japan wear school uniforms. Traditionally, school uniforms have been conservative in style and color, often navy, black, or gray. More recently, however, some schools have invited famous fashion designers to create their uniforms, so they are more appealing to students.

Dress codes are often still rather strict – no makeup, jewelry, or permed hair. Hair style and length are also relatively restricted. Boys' uniforms often also include caps with the school insignia attached to the front of the cap. Students all own at least 2 types of uniforms: a summer uniform and a heavier winter uniform. Students are required to switch from summer to winter uniforms in October and from winter to summer uniforms in June.

B. A Japanese Proverb 「かえるのこはかえる」

「かえるのこはかえる」 means "A frog's child is a frog." A child resembles his/her parents and will act like his/her parents. A child has the same kind of ability as his/her parents. Therefore, parents should not expect more of their child than they themselves could achieve. This is similar to the English expression: "The apple doesn't fall very far from the tree."

Ask your teacher to help you write to or videoconference with an English class at a Japanese high school. Ask them to send you pictures of their school uniforms. Share a copy of your dress code with them and send them pictures of the kinds of clothes you wear to school every day.

アクティビティー　Communicative Activities

Pair Work

A. SPEAK/LISTEN Ask your partner where the following people are and what kind of persons they are.

Ex.　Question 1:　お母さん は　いま　どこに　いますか。

　　　Question 2:　お母さん は　どんな　人ですか。

Person	Where?	What kind of person?
1. Mother		
2. Father		
3. Friend		
4. (A famous or beautiful person)		

Reading

B. READ/WRITE You and your partner are visiting a college campus. Based on the list of buildings below, write down what building each place is in, and give your impressions of the building based on what it looks like in the images below.

ステート *suteeto* 大学 State University			
ベイカーホール **Baker Hall**	スミスホール **Smith Hall**	なかとみホール **Nakatomi Hall**	だいがくセンター **University Center**
日本語 英語 フランス語	科学 数学 生徒の ロッカー	プール 女トイレ 男トイレ	学校の　じむしょ けんきゅうしつ カフェテリア

Place	Where?	Impressions
1. Japanese classroom		
2. English classroom		
3. Lockers		
4. School office		
5. Men's or women's restroom		
6. Cafeteria		

WORKBOOK page 75

8か5
My room is small

かいわ　Dialogue

🔊 **READ/LISTEN** Is Ken's house near or far? Is it big?

Ken
ケンさんの　うちは　ちかいですか。

いいえ、　ちょっと　とおいです。

うちは　ひろいですか。

すこし　ひろいです。　でも、　ぼくの
へやは　せまいです。

たんご　Vocabulary

🔊

1. にわ	2. ガレージ	3. へや	4. ベッド
	gareeji		*beddo*
garden, yard	garage (at one's residence)	room	bed

5. ねずみ
mouse

6. ぶた
pig

7. ひろい
[いＡdj.]
wide, spacious

8. せまい
[いＡdj.]
narrow, small (room)

9. ちかい
[いＡdj.]
near, close

10. とおい
[いＡdj.]
far

ついか　たんご　Additional Vocabulary

1. ポスター　*posutaa*　poster
2. 本ばこ　bookcase
3. かべ　wall
4. ゆか　floor

5. カーペット　*kaapetto*　carpet
6. てんじょう　ceiling
7. スピーカー　*supiikaa*　speaker (for sound)
8. ごきぶり　cockroach

よみましょう　Language in Context

🔊 **READ/LISTEN** Read these sentences in Japanese. Is your room big or small?

この　うちに　ガレージは　ありません。　へやは　すこし　せまいです。

ブーブー

ぶんかノート　Culture Notes

A. Japanese Animal Sounds

What sounds do Japanese animals make? Every culture perceives the sounds of animal cries somewhat differently. Here are a few examples of animal sounds in Japanese. Do you notice any patterns?

いぬ	ワンワン *wanwan*
ねこ	ニャーニャー *nyaanyaa*
うし [cow]	モー *moo*
うま [horse]	ヒヒーン *hihiin*
ぶた	ブーブー *buubuu*
ねずみ	チューチュー *chuuchuu*
(ちいさい) とり	ピーピー *piipii*
ライオン *raion* [lion]	ガオー *gaoo*
さる [monkey]	キャッキャ *kyakkya*
にわとり [chicken/rooster]	コケコッコー *kokekokko*

B. A Japanese Proverb 「ねこに　こばん」

ねこ is a cat. こばん is a gold coin used during the Tokugawa period. 「ねこに　こばん」means "To give a gold coin to a cat." It is used when someone receives something and cannot appreciate its value. This is similar to the English expression, "To cast pearls before swine."

C. A Japanese Proverb 「さるも　木から　おちる」

さる is a monkey. も means "even." 木 is a tree. から means "from." おちる means "to fall." 「さるも　木から　おちる」means "Even a monkey falls from a tree." This proverb means that even skillful people sometimes make mistakes.

 Read the explanations of the two proverbs carefully. Choose one, and write a short narrative describing a situation from your own life (or imagine a situation) that reflects the proverb's meaning in order to explain the proverb to a friend from your own country.

Pair Work

A. SPEAK/LISTEN Draw two copies each of the three drawings below on a separate sheet of paper. Then draw several of the items listed below each image in the first set of drawings.

Do not show your drawings to your partner. After you and your partner have finished your drawings, ask your partner where each item is located and draw them in the second set of drawings. Compare your pictures and your partner's to see whether you successfully communicated the location of the objects.

1. 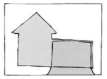   **2.**   **3.**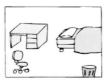

car	tree	mouse
mouse	flower	cat
TV	dog	book
woman	fish	girl
trash can	boy	pencil

B. SPEAK/LISTEN/WRITE Interview your partner and ask about his/her house. Write down your partner's answers in Japanese on a separate sheet of paper.

1. Big or small?

2. Have a yard or not?

3. New or old?

4. What color?

5. How many cars?

C. SPEAK/LISTEN/WRITE Interview your partner. Ask about his/her room. Write down your partner's answers in Japanese on a separate sheet of paper.

1. Have a bed?

2. Have a desk and a chair?

3. Have a T.V.?

4. Have a computer?

5. Have a telephone?

6. Spacious or not?

7. Messy or clean?

8. What color?

WORKBOOK page 77

Lesson 8
Review

Review Questions

Ask your partner these questions in Japanese. Your partner answers in Japanese.
Check your answers using the audio.

School Campus Review pages 258, 263, 276, and 278

1. Where is the school office?

2. Where is the men's / women's restroom?

3. How many students are there at your school?

4. Is your school new?

5. Is your school well known (famous)?

6. Who is that (distinguished looking) man over there?
   [Answer: my English teacher]

7. Are there many fish in the school pond?

8. Shall we go to the pool together?

9. Is your school's football team [チーム] well known (famous)?

Japanese Class Review pages 258 and 263

10. Is your Japanese classroom clean?

11. Where is your Japanese teacher?

12. Where is the pencil sharpener?

13. What is over there? [Point to something distant.]

14. Who is that girl over there? [Answer: my friend]

15. How many male students are there in your Japanese class?
    And how many female students?

Your Home Review pages 280–81

16. Where is your house?

17. Is your house close?

18. How many cars are there at your house?

19. Do you have a yard at your house?

20. Is your yard pretty (beautiful)?

21. Is your house big?

22. What time do you return home every day?

23. Is your room spacious?

24. What is there in your room? (Name several things.)

25. What color is your room?

Text Chat

You will participate in a simulated exchange of text–chat messages. You should respond as fully and as appropriately as possible.

You will have a conversation with Taro Yamada, a Japanese high school student, about your school.

2月11日　03:35 PM

> どんな　がっこうですか。

Give your opinion.

2月11日　03:40 PM

> 日本ごの　きょうしつに　せいとが　たくさん　いますか。

Respond with the number.

2月11日　03:45 PM

> きょうしつに　なにが　ありますか。

Give at least two examples.

Can Do!
Now I can . . .

- ☐ ask and reply to someone about the location of certain objects or people
- ☐ describe my school
- ☐ describe my house
- ☐ describe my room

Game - *Karuta*
かるた

The game of *karuta* is a favorite activity of Japanese children and adults. The word *karuta* is derived from the word "card." *Karuta* is played in groups. There must be at least three people: the reader and two other players. The other players may compete individually or in groups. The object of the game is to be the first to touch and grab the card which matches the proverb or poem called out by the reader. As the game proceeds, one accumulates as many cards as one can, and the winner is the one who has the most cards at the end of the game.

During the New Year's season, adults play ひゃくにんいっしゅ *Hyaku-nin Isshu*, which is based on similar rules. In this game, however, players must be quick to match the second half of a classical poem with the first half of the poem which is read by the reader. National tournaments pitting skilled competitors are part of the New Year's celebrations in Japan.

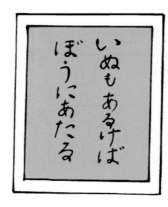

Reader's card   Playing card

Karuta, played by children, features famous Japanese proverbs. The card held by the reader has the entire proverb, while the playing card depicts the proverb with illustrations.

In the example cards shown above, the reader would read the proverb "いぬも　あるけば ぼうに　あたる." The contestants would listen for the first sound of the proverb, "い", then search quickly for the card marked "い" from all of the cards which are randomly laid on the floor. The first person to lay his hands on the correct card takes it and keeps it. If one grabs the wrong card, one must return that card to the floor.

> **Literal meaning:** When a dog walks, it, too, will stumble on a stick.
> **Interpretation:** "Every dog has his day." or "A flying crow always catches something."
> People may use proverbs in different contexts appropriate to their needs.

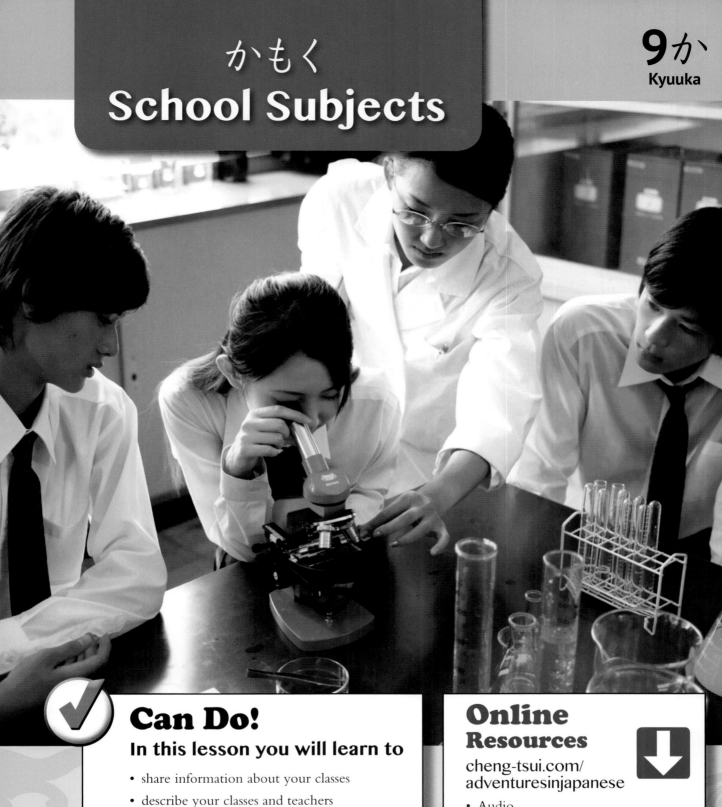

かもく
School Subjects

Can Do!
In this lesson you will learn to

- share information about your classes
- describe your classes and teachers
- communicate reasons why you are happy or sad
- name what tangible objects you want
- communicate about what activities you do after school

Online Resources

cheng-tsui.com/adventuresinjapanese

- Audio
- Vocabulary Lists
- Vocabulary Flashcards
- *Kana* and *Kanji* Flashcards
- Activity Worksheets

Kanji
used in this lesson

In this lesson, you will learn *kanji* commonly used in school.

	Kanji	Meaning	Readings		Examples	
37.	先	first, previous	せん	せんせい 先生	teacher	
				せん 先しゅう	last week	
38.	生	be born, person	せい	せんせい 先生	teacher	
				せいと 生徒	pre-college student	
						Sprouts point upward from layers of earth.
39.	今	now	いま	いま 今、一時です。	It's 1 o'clock now.	
				いまだ 今田さん	Mr./Ms. Imada	
				いまがわ 今川さん	Mr./Ms. Imagawa	
			こん	こん 今しゅう	this week	Now, three people are deciding whether to come or go.
			*	きょう 今日	today	
40.	毎	every	まい	まいにち 毎日	every day	
				まい 毎しゅう	every week	
41.	年	year	とし	ことし 今年	this year	
				まいとし 毎年	every year	
			ねん	まいねん 毎年	every year	Once a year, people cut the rice that was born from the earth.
				らいねん 来年	next year	
42.	休	rest, absent	やす(み) (お)休み	やす (お)休み	holiday, day off	

WORKBOOK   page 237

* Indicates irregular readings of the *kanji*

Recognition Kanji	Recognition Kanji
せいと **生徒** student (pre-college)	らい **来** next (week, month, year)

かいわ   Dialogue

 READ/LISTEN What classes does Ken have? When is his lunch break?

今日　何の
じゅぎょうが
ありますか。

すう学と
か学と
えい語と
日本語と
たいいくが
あります。

おひるの
休み時かんは
いつですか。

11時はんから
12時はんまで
です。

READ　Find this sentence pattern in the dialogue.

Person は　(time X)　　　　　subject が time/place から time/place まで　あります。

私は　きょう　えいごのじゅぎょうが　　　1時から　　　2時まで　あります。

[I will have my English class from 1 o'clock to 2 o'clock today.]

たんご　Vocabulary

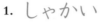

1. しゃかい　　2. かがく　　3. すうがく　　4. えいご　　5. がいこくご
　　　　　　　　か学　　　すう学　　　えい語　　　がいこく語

social studies　　science　　math　　English　　foreign language

6. びじゅつ　　7. たいいく　　8. ホームルーム　　9. やすみじかん
　　　　　　　　　　　　　　　　　　　　　　　　　休み時かん

art　　physical education　　homeroom　　a break

10. かもく　　　11. じゅぎょう, クラス　　12. あります
　　か目

subject(s)　　class, instruction　　to have

ついか たんご　Additional Vocabulary

1. ～を　とっています　　　　is taking ～
2. れきし　　　　　　　　　　history
3. アメリカし　　　　　　　　U.S. history
4. アジアし　　　　　　　　　Asian history
5. ヨーロッパし　　　　　　　European history
6. けいざい　　　　　　　　　economics
7. せいぶつ　　　　　　　　　biology
8. ぶつり　　　　　　　　　　physics
9. かがく　　　　　　　　　　chemistry
10. だいすう　　　　　　　　algebra
11. きか　　　　　　　　　　geometry
12. びぶんせきぶん　　　　　calculus
13. じしゅう　　　　　　　　study hall

よみましょう　Language in Context

🔊 **READ/LISTEN/SPEAK** Read these sentences in Japanese. Ask a partner when he/she has class and respond to your partner's question.

2時から　3時まで　すうがくの
クラスが　あります。

しゃかいの　クラスが
だい好きです。

ぶんぽう　Grammar

A Using あります as "to have"

Subject が　あります **"have"**

An additional meaning of あります is "have." は may replace が in negative sentences.

MODELS

1. 「明日　しけんが　あります。」　　　"I have an exam tomorrow."

2. 「今日　しゅくだいが　ありますか。」
   "Do we have homework today?"

   「いいえ、ありませんよ。」　　　"No, we do not."

3. 「今日　たいいくの　じゅぎょうは　ありませんでした。」
   "We did not have P.E. class today."

READ/WRITE Answer the questions affirmatively or negatively as indicated.

1. 「今日　しゅくだいが　ありますか。」（はい）

2. 「明日　日本ごの　じゅぎょうが　ありますか。」（いいえ）

3. 「きのう　しけんが　ありましたか。」（いいえ）

ぶんかノート　Culture Notes

The Homeroom Teacher in Japanese Schools

The roles of the homeroom teacher and homeroom classes in a Japanese school are much more encompassing than in most American schools. There is a homeroom meeting every morning. Students have classes together with their homeroom classmates in the same classroom throughout most of the day. Subject teachers move from classroom to classroom, with the exception of P.E. and music. Homeroom students eat lunch together and clean their room and other places in the school together after school.

The relationship between students and their homeroom teacher is very close. The homeroom teacher takes care of the same homeroom students from entrance to graduation and becomes their personal, academic and college counselor. Elementary (and sometimes even higher level) school homeroom teachers often visit parents of their students at home, too. The relationship of the homeroom student and his/her teacher generally lasts a lifetime. Students often invite their homeroom teachers to their weddings and keep in regular contact with them. Class reunions are usually organized around homeroom classes and include the teacher as well.

 Read the culture note carefully and make create a Venn diagram like the one below comparing homeroom teachers in Japan and at your own school. When finished, consider the duties in the "In Japan" group. Pick three and explain what other people at your school might fulfill these duties and how in a short paragraph. You may want to consider teachers, principals, counselors, coaches, and even parents.

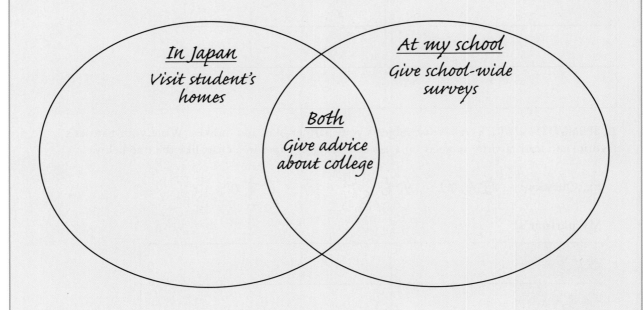

In Japan
Visit student's homes

At my school
Give school-wide surveys

Both
Give advice about college

Pair Work

A. SPEAK/LISTEN/WRITE Ask your partner what classes he/she has today and from what time to what time each class is and when his/her lunch break is. Write your partner's schedule on a separate sheet of paper in a chart like the one below.

Ex. Question 1: 今日　なんの　じゅぎょうが　ありますか
　　　　　　　　or ありましたか。

Question 2: Subject は　なん時から　なん時まで　ありますか
　　　　　　　　or ありましたか。

Question 3: おひるの　休み時かんは　いつですか。

My partner's schedule for today:

Class	Time
	〜
	〜
	〜
	〜
	〜

B. SPEAK/LISTEN/WRITE Ask what subjects your partner likes and dislikes. Write your partner's favorite and least favorite subjects on a separate sheet of paper in a chart like the one below.

Ex. Question: なんの　かもくが　好きですか。

My partner's:

好き	
きらい	

WORKBOOK　page 81

かいわ　Dialogue

 READ/LISTEN Who is Ken's teacher? How is his class?

エミ：　つぎの　じゅぎょうは　何^{なん}ですか。

ケン：　か学^{がく}です。

エミ：　先生^{せんせい}は　だれですか。

ケン：　スミス先生^{せんせい}です。

エミ：　どんな　先生^{せんせい}ですか。

ケン：　ちょっと　きびしいですが、　とても
　　　　いいです。

エミ：　じゅぎょうは　どうですか。

ケン：　おもしろいですが、　ちょっと
　　　　むずかしいです。

たんご　Vocabulary

1. つぎ

next

2. むずかしい [い Adj.]

difficult

3. やさしい [いAdj.]

easy

4. たのしい [いAdj.]　　**5.** おもしろい [いAdj.]　　**6.** つまらない [いAdj.]

fun, enjoyable　　　　　　　interesting　　　　　　boring, uninteresting

ついか　たんご　Additional Vocabulary

1. いじわる [なAdj.]　　　　　　　mean

2. こわい [いAdj.]　　　　　　　scary

3. へん [なAdj.]　　　　　　　　weird, strange

4. おかしい [いAdj.]　　　　　　funny (humorous), weird

5. いかがですか。　　　　　　How is it? [Polite equiv. of どうですか。]

よみましょう　Language in Context

🔊 **READ/LISTEN/SPEAK** Read these sentences in Japanese. Tell a classmate what activity you think is fun or interesting.

　この　ざっしは　おもしろいです。　　　　ダンスは　たのしいです。

ぶんかノート　Culture Notes

Foreign Language Education in Japanese Schools

English is a required course from 5th grade through 12th grade in Japan, though some elementary schools also introduce it at earlier levels. English has become one of the most commonly selected subjects on Japan's college entrance exams, despite the high difficulty of the test. English language education in Japan is highly grammar oriented, and emphasizes mainly reading and writing. Many students can read difficult materials in English, but cannot speak or comprehend spoken English well. Some students attend private English conversation schools (えいかいわがっこう) to improve their English speaking skills.

English class in Japan

Although English is overwhelmingly the most commonly taught foreign language in Japan, other languages are offered in schools, particularly at the college level. These include popular European languages like German, French, and Spanish as well as the Asian languages of Japan's closest neighbors, Chinese and Korean.

Online, research what the three most commonly spoken foreign languages are in your country, then what the three most commonly taught languages are in Japan. Are they the same? Make inferences as to why the two lists may be similar or different.

アクティビティー　Communicative Activities

Pair Work

A. SPEAK/LISTEN/WRITE Ask your partner about his/her next class (つぎの　クラス). If Japanese is your last class of the day, ask about your partner's previous class (まえの　クラス). Write down your partner's answers on a separate sheet of paper.

1. What is your next class?

2. Where is the classroom?

3. Who is the teacher?

4. How is the teacher?

5. How is the class?

B. SPEAK/LISTEN/WRITE Ask about the classes your partner will have/has had today. Write down your partner's responses on a separate sheet of paper using a chart like the one below.

Ex. 「今日　なんの　クラスが　ありますか or ありましたか。」

「(Subject) は　なん時から　なん時まで　ありますか or ありましたか。」

「(Subject) の　きょうしつは　どこですか or どこでしたか。」

「(Subject) の　先生は　だれですか or だれでしたか。」

「(Teacher's name) 先生は　どうですか or どうでしたか。」

「(Subject) の　じゅぎょうは　どうですか or どうでしたか。」

Subject	Time	Classroom	(Who?) Teacher (How?)	Class (How?)

Reading

C. READ/WRITE Read the following e-mail from a Japanese pen-pal named Yuki. Answer the questions below in Japanese using complete sentences.

私は　すう学が　好きでしたが、今年　すう学が
好きでは　ありません。とても　むずかしいです。先生も
とても　きびしいです。そして、よく　分かりません。

UNDERSTAND

1. Did Yuki like math before?

2. Does Yuki like math now?

3. What is Yuki's math teacher like?

APPLY

4. Send an e-mail replying to Yuki. Describe one of your classes and the teacher of that class.

WORKBOOK page 83

かいわ　Dialogue

🔊 **READ/LISTEN** Why is Emi happy? What class had a test?

今日_{きょう}　私は　とても　うれしいです。

なぜですか。

おとといの　しゃかいの　しけんの
せいせきが　良_よかったからです。

良_よかったですねえ。

ぶんけい　Sentence Patterns

READ Find these sentence patterns in the dialogue.

1. い adjective –かったです　　　　　　　　　　[was ~]

2. い adjective –く　なかったです or
　　　　　　　　–く　ありませんでした　　　　[was not ~]

3. Sentence 1 (Reason) から、 Sentence 2 (Result)。　[Sentence 1, so Sentence 2.]

4. Sentence 1 (Reason) からです。　　　　　　[It is because Sentence 1.]

たんご　Vocabulary

1. なぜ／どうして

Why?

Although both are used frequently,
どうして is more often used colloquially.

2. せいせき

grade

3. ひどい [いAdj.]

terrible

4. うれしい
[いAdj.]

glad, happy

5. かなしい
[いAdj.]

sad

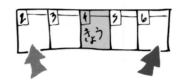

6. おととい

the day before
yesterday

7. あさって

the day after
tomorrow

---

8. いいです
ねえ。

How nice!

Used when one
receives good news of
something which will
soon occur.

9. よかった
ですねえ。

How nice!

Expression of happiness
or support about a past
event.

10. ざんねん
ですねえ。

How disappointing!,
Too bad!

Expression of
disappointment about
something which won't
happen.

11. ざんねん
でしたねえ。

How disappointing!

Expression of disappointment
about an unfortunate past event.

---

12. Sentence 1 (Reason)＋から、　Sentence 2 (Result)。

Sentence 1 (Reason), so Sentence 2 (Result).

ついか　たんご　Additional Vocabulary

1.	がっかりです。	I am disappointed.
2.	こうへい [なAdj.]	is fair
3.	ふこうへい [なAdj.]	is unfair

よみましょう　Language in Context

 READ/LISTEN/SPEAK Read these sentences in Japanese. Congratulate a classmate for something.

せいせきが　よかったから、
うれしいです。

よかったですねえ！

ぶんぽう　Grammar

A Causation Sentence Connector から

Sentence 1 (Reason) ＋ から、Sentence 2 (Result)。

= Sentence 1 (Reason), so Sentence 2 (Result).

The conjunction から, which even in this construction more literally means "from," follows a reason or cause. However, in this context から is best translated as "so," or more literally "from the reason of." The reason must appear first in this sentence structure. The second portion expresses a result or consequence, and may be omitted if it is understood. For example, as a response to a "why" question, only the reason is required in the response, so the second portion of the sentence is often dropped.

When the first portion (reason) of the sentence ends with an い Adjective, the です before から is often omitted. However, if a noun or な adjective precedes です in the first part of the sentence, the です must not be dropped.

1. 「日本ごは　おもしろい (です) から、好きです。」
   "Japanese is interesting, so I like it."

2. 「しけんは　明日ですから、今ばん　べんきょうします。」
   "I have an exam tomorrow, so I'll study tonight."

3. 「なぜ　せいせきが　わるかったですか。」
   "Why was your grade bad?"

   「べんきょうしませんでしたから。」
   "It is because I did not study."

READ Choose the correct word from the options in the ( ) based on the context of the sentence.

1. しけんが　よかったから、(うれしい　かなしい) です。

2. しゅくだいが　たくさん　ありますから、(うれしい　かなしい) です。

3. せいせきが　ひどかったから、(うれしい　かなしい) です。

B Review: い Adjective Conjugation

うれしいです。	is happy
うれしく　ないです。／うれしく　ありません。	is not happy
うれしかったです。	was happy
うれしく　なかったです。／うれしく　ありませんでした。	was not happy

♻ いい "good" conjugates from its よい form.

いいです。	is good
よく　ないです。／よく　ありません。	is not good
よかったです。	was good
よく　なかったです。／よく　ありませんでした。	was not good

1. きのうの　しけんは　むずかしかったです。
   Yesterday's exam was difficult.

2. えいがは　とても　おもしろかったです。
   The movie was very interesting.

3. その　先生は　ぜんぜん　きびしくなかったです。
   That teacher was not strict at all.

READ/WRITE Correctly conjugate the い Adjective in the ( ) based on the context of the sentence.

1. きのうの　えいがは　（おもしろい）。

2. 私の　せいせきが　（いい）から、うれしいです。

3. 私の　今の　えいごの　先生は　ぜんぜん　（やさしい）。

ぶんかノート　Culture Notes

University Admissions in Japan

College admission in Japan is mainly determined by the results of an entrance exam held early during the final year of high school. Recently, the Japanese government has recommended that other criteria be considered for college admission, but very few colleges have made changes in their admission policies, and they still depend mainly on exam scores. Because the test is so critical to admission, students often attend じゅく, or cram schools, to prepare for college entrance exams.

The University of Tokyo, Japan's most prestigious school

Competition is often incredibly stiff, especially among applicants for top-tier universities. As a result, some students are not admitted to the schools they apply for. Such students are called ろうにん. Originally, this term referred to samurai (feudal warriors) without masters. The student who is not successful, like the masterless samurai, belongs to no school. ろうにん will return to schools called よびこう to prepare for another round of entrance exams the following year. Some students may remain ろうにん for several years.

In recent years, the formerly fierce competition to enter universities has become less intense, particularly at schools that are not top ranked. The competition, however, may have trickled down to the junior high and elementary school levels. Many parents want their young children in the best elementary and intermediate schools so that they can advance to top universities by the time they are ready for college.

 Research the College Entrance Exam in Japan online. List the topics and types of questions the exam covers, and compare them to the college entrance examinations used in the U.S. or your own country. Then, write a short essay explaining whether you would rather apply to college in Japan or in your own country. Justify your response with evidence from your research.

アクティビティー Communicative Activities

Pair Work

A. WRITE/SPEAK Copy the following sentences on separate pieces of paper. Fold all the papers separately and put them on the desk or in a cap. Randomly pick one and say うれしいです or かなしいです depending on the message on your paper. Your partner will ask なぜですか. Explain the reason in Japanese. Take turns.

Ex. Student A: 　私は　　うれしいです。

　　Student B: 　なぜ　　うれしいですか。

　　Student A: 　日本ごの　　しけんが　ᴀでしたから、うれしいです。

　　　　　　　or 日本ごの　　しけんが　ᴀでしたからです。

Ex. My Japanese exam grade was good.

1. My math exam grade was an F.

2. My friend does not like me now.

3. My dog died. (died = しにました)

4. I lost lots of money. (lost = なくしました)

5. Tomorrow is Saturday.

6. I have no homework today.

Class Work

B. SPEAK/LISTEN Every student states whether he/she feels happy or sad. After each statement, a classmate will ask for a reason. Each student responds. Who can give the best reason?

WORKBOOK page 85

かいわ　Dialogue

🔊 **READ/LISTEN** Why is Ken busy? What is on Friday? What does Ken want?

ぶんけい　Sentence Patterns

READ Find these sentence patterns in the dialogue.

1. Person は Something が ほしい／ほしくない です。　[Person wants/ does not want something.]

2. Person/Thing は／が おおい／すくない です。　[There are many/few 〜.]

1. せんしゅう
先しゅう
last week

2. こんしゅう
今しゅう
this week

3. らいしゅう
来しゅう
next week

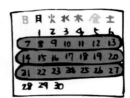

4. まいしゅう
毎しゅう
every week

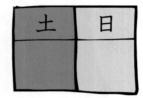

5. しゅうまつ
weekend

6. おおい [いAdj.]
are many, much

7. すくない [いAdj.]
are few, little

Although these are adjectives, they are not used before nouns.

Neg. form: おおくないです　　　Neg. form: すくなくないです

8. (something) が
ほしい [いAdj.]
want (something)

Neg. form: ほしくないです

9. たいへん [なAdj.]*
大へん*
hard, difficult*

Neg. form:
たいへんではありません.

10. それに
Moreover, Besides

* たいへん is used in situations which are physically or psychologically challenging. むずかしい is generally used to describe situations that are academically challenging or difficult.

ついか　たんご　Additional Vocabulary

1. ストレス　　　　　　　　　stress

🔊 **READ/LISTEN/WRITE** Read these sentences in Japanese. Write down something you want and something you don't want.

しゅくだいが　おおいです。

あたらしい　ケータイが　ほしいです。

ぶんぽう　Grammar

A Verb ほしい "To Want" Something

Noun が　　ほしい(ん)です。	**want ～**
Noun が/は ほしくない(ん)です。/ほしくありません。	**do not want ～**
Noun が　　ほしかった(ん)です。	**wanted ～**
Noun が/は ほしくなかった(ん)です。/ほしくありませんでした。	**did not want ～**

ほしいです is used when one expresses a desire for **something**. The particle が generally follows the object that the subject of the sentence wants. は often replaces が when ほしい is in a negative form. ほしい is conjugated as an い adjective. Do not use this pattern when you ask a person of higher status what he/she wants. It is considered too direct and rude. ん is often used at the end of the verb when the speaker wants to explain a situation.

Note: When one wants **to do** something, the -TAI form is used and will be introduced in Lesson 10-2.

1. 「なにを　のみますか。」　　　　　　"What will you have (to drink)?"

　「今　お水が　ほしいです。」　　　　"I want water now."

2. 「コーヒーは　ほしくないです。　ジュースを　ください。」

　　　　　　　　　　　　　"I don't want coffee. Please give me some juice."

3. 「はやく　休みが　ほしいです。」　　"I want a vacation soon."

READ/WRITE Choose the correct particle from the options in the ( ) and write the correct form of ほしいです in the blank based on the information below.

Last week I wanted a car, but now I don't want one. I want a good friend now.

先しゅう　車（を　が）　__1__　。　でも、今　車（は　が）

　__2__　。　私は　今　いい　ともだち（を　が）　__3__　。

B Adjectives of Quantity おおい and すくない

Subject が＋　おおいです。　　　　There are many / much 〜.

Subject が＋　すくないです。　　　There are few / little 〜.

Both おおい and すくない are い adjectives. However they are not used before nouns.

MODELS

1. すうがくは　しゅくだいが　とても　おおいです。
   There is a lot of homework in math.

2. この　クラスに　男の　生徒は　すくないですね。
   There are few male students in this class, aren't there?

READ Choose the correct word from the options in the ( ) so that the meaning does not change.

1. しけんが　たくさん　あります。＝しけんは
   （おおい　すくない）です。

2. すこしの　男の　生徒が　います。＝男の　生徒は
   （おおい　すくない）です。

3. 日本ごの　しゅくだいが　（おおい　すくない）から、
   たいへんです。

ぶんかノート　Culture Notes

Sports in Japanese Schools

In Japan, students belong to one sports team and play that sport all year long. There are no seasonal sports in high school. The most popular high school sport is baseball, but other popular sports include soccer, basketball, volleyball, tennis, swimming, and Japanese martial arts, most of which have both male and female teams.

The relationship among the team players is very important. In sports teams, an age difference of even a year among its players is significant. Younger students call the older students せんぱい and the older students call the younger students こうはい. こうはい are expected to arrive at games early and practice earlier than せんぱい. They must prepare the equipment for practice, greet せんぱい with respect and clean up after practice. This kind of vertical relationship also often exists in Japanese companies and work environments.

せんぱい　　　こうはい

 Read the description of the relationship between junior and senior teammates in Japan. Imagine if these relationships were applied to a high school sports team in the U.S. Choose a sport you are familiar with, and write a short letter to a non-Japanese school coach describing what the possible duties of a こうはい and a せんぱい participating in that sport might be.

アクティビティー　Communicative Activities

Pair Work

A. SPEAK/LISTEN Ask your partner about the courses he/she is taking. Ask what subjects he/she is taking, what kind of teachers he/she has, how the courses are, whether there is lots of homework, whether his/her grade is good, and what grade he/she wants. Write your partner's answers on a separate sheet of paper using a chart like the one below

Ex.　「なんの　かもくを　とっています (is taking) か。」

　　　「先生は　どうですか。」

　　　「じゅぎょうは　どうですか。」

　　　「しゅくだいは　おおいですか。」

「せいせきは　どうですか。」

「どんな　せいせきが　ほしいですか。」

My partner's courses:

Subject	Teacher (How?)	Class (How?)	Homework (Lots?)	Grade (How?)	Grade (Wish?)

B. SPEAK/LISTEN On a separate sheet of paper, create two calendars like the one below. Fill in the first calendar with the various exams below. Then ask your partner for his/her schedule of exams and papers and fill in the second calendar with the information you receive. When both of you finish, compare answers to see whether you communicated successfully or not.

Ex.　Question:　日本ごの　しけんは　いつですか。

　　　Answer:　〜しゅうの　〜曜日です。

1. 日本ごの　しけん　2. えいごの　レポート　3. しゃかいの　レポート

4. かがくの　しけん　5. すうがくの　しけん　6. たいいくの　しけん

	Sunday	Monday	Tuesday	Wednesday	Thursday	Friday	Saturday
Last week							
This week							
Next week							

WORKBOOK page 87

かいわ　Dialogue

🔊 **READ/LISTEN** What is Emi doing after school? What is she looking forward to?

ほうかご　何^{なに}を　しますか。

しゅくだいや　バンドの
れんしゅうなど　あります。
来年^{らいねん}　バンドと　りょ行します。
たのしみに　して　います。

たんご　Vocabulary

1. ほうかご	2. きょねん	3. ことし	4. らいねん	5. まいとし／まいねん
		今年	来年	毎年
after school	last year	this year	next year	every year

6. バンド	7. れんしゅう	8. うたいます [うたう]	9. およぎます [およぐ]
band	practice	to sing	to swim

10. あそびます
[あそぶ]

to play, amuse

Not used with sports or musical
instruments.

11. ゲームを
します[する]

to play a game

12. Noun 1 や Noun 2
（など）

Noun 1 and Noun 2, etc.

ついか　たんご　Additional Vocabulary

1. オーケストラ　　orchestra

2. バレー　　ballet

3. コーラス　　chorus, choir

4. チアーリーディング　　cheerleading

5. ボランティア　　volunteering

6. アルバイト　　part-time job

よみましょう　Language in Context

🔊 **READ/LISTEN/WRITE** Read these sentences in Japanese. Describe what you do after school.

ほうかご、　やきゅうの　れんしゅうが
あります。

えんぴつや　ノートなど
あります。

A Listing Nouns with や

Noun 1 や (Noun 2 や) Noun 3 など

や is used to conjoin two or more nouns. It means "and" but suggests the inclusion of other similar items besides those named. Therefore, the word など "etc." is often used in the same sentence. など may replace particles after the final noun or be added before the existing particle.

 Noun 1 と Noun 2

と "and" is also used to conjoin nouns. However, と is exhaustive, and suggests the inclusion of only those nouns mentioned.

Compare:

ピザや　ホットドッグを　たべました。 I ate pizza, hotdogs (and more).

ピザと　ホットドッグを　たべました。 I ate pizza and hotdogs.

MODELS

1. ほうかご　バレーや　バンドの　れんしゅうなど(が)
   あります。

   I have ballet and band practice and so on after school.

2. としょかんで　しんぶんや　ざっしなど(を)　よみました。

   I read newspapers, magazines, and the like at the library.

3. 父は　火曜日に　おおさかや　きょうとなど(へ)
   りょ行しました。

   My father traveled to Osaka, Kyoto, etc., on Tuesday.

READ/WRITE In each ( ), choose from the particles を, へ, や, and など based on the information.

Emi ate pizza and salad. Ken ate sushi, pizza, etc. Ken wants to travel to Japan and Italy and some other countries to try the food in those countries.

エミさんは　ピザ（ 1 ）　サラダ（ 2 ）　たべました。

ケンさんは　すし（ 3 ）　ピザ（ 4 ）（ 5 ）　たべました。

ケンさんは　日本（ 6 ）　イタリア（ 7 ）（ 8 ）　りょ行を
したいです。

ぶんかノート　Culture Notes

After-School Activities in Japan

Popular after-school activities for high school students include participation in club activities and attendance at cram schools (じゅく). Sports clubs, such as tennis, swimming, soccer, baseball, basketball, volleyball, track, じゅうどう, and けんどう (Japanese fencing) are common. Sports clubs play the chosen sport throughout the year and serve as their school's athletic teams. Other popular clubs include choir, orchestra, foreign language, art, science, acting and dance, and traditional cultural arts (such as tea ceremony and calligraphy) clubs. Students commit to one club and spend many after-school hours, weekends, and vacation time with other club members.

バレーボールの　れんしゅう

 Read the above note carefully. Compare the description of school clubs in Japan with clubs at your own school. Write your answers in a chart like the one below.

	Clubs in Japan	Clubs at your school
Club themes		
Time commitment		
Number of clubs students participate in		

アクティビティー　Communicative Activities

Pair Work

A. SPEAK/LISTEN Ask your partner what he/she does after school and your partner will answer using －や －など. Take turns. Choose your answers from the list of activities below or add your own.

Q: ほうかごに　なにを　しますか。

A: ほうかごに　〜や　〜など（を）　します。

1. ゲーム
2. べんきょう
3. しゅくだい
4. スポーツ
5. クラブ

6. ダンスの　れんしゅう
7. ピアノの　れんしゅう
8. バンドの　れんしゅう
9. チアーリーディング (cheerleading)
10. **Your own**

B. SPEAK/LISTEN Ask your partner the following questions. Your partner will answer based on fact. Take turns.

1. ほうかごは　いそがしいですか。

2. ほうかごに　なにを　しますか。

3. ほうかごに　がっこうで　しゅくだいを　しますか。

4. ほうかごに　ともだちと　あそびますか。

5. ほうかごに　およぎますか。

6. ほうかごに　ともだちと　はなしますか。

7. ほうかごは　たのしいですか。

Reading

C. READ/WRITE Read the following questions and write your responses in Japanese on a separate sheet of paper.

1. おたんじょう日は、　なん年　なん月　なん日ですか。

2. 毎年　たんじょうパーティーを　しますか。

3. きょ年　どこで　パーティーを　しましたか。

4. 今年　どこで　パーティーを　しますか。

5. 来年　たんじょう日に　なにを　しますか。

6. たんじょう日に　いつも　うたを　うたいますか。

WORKBOOK　page 89

Review Questions

Ask your partner these questions or say these statements in Japanese. Your partner answers in Japanese. Check your answers using the audio.

Classes   Review pages 290, 295, 299, and 305

1. What classes are you taking this year?

2. What subjects do you have today?

3. What is your next class?

4. Who is your math teacher? How is that teacher?

5. What kind of teacher is your English teacher?

6. How is your social studies teacher?

7. Where is your science classroom? Is it nearby?

8. Is your Japanese grade good?

9. Is there a lot of homework this week?

10. Do you want a new cell phone?

11. What do you do after school?

Reasons   Review pages 299 and 305

12. Why are you happy/sad?

13. I am sad because my exam yesterday was terrible.

14. I am happy because my exam the day before yesterday was very good.

15. Why are you so busy? [Give two reasons.]

Wants and Needs   Review pages 307 and 311

16. What (thing) do you want now?

17. What do you eat at the school cafeteria?

18. What are you looking forward to now?

After-school Activities Review page 311

19. What activity did you do after school last year?

20. What activity are you doing after school this year?

21. What activity will you do after school next year?

Text Chat

You will participate in a simulated exchange of text–chat messages. You should respond as fully and as appropriately as possible.

You will have a conversation with Daiki Yasui, a Japanese high school student in Japan, about your school.

3月22日　04:23 PM

がっこうは　たのしいですか。

Respond and justify your opinion.

3月22日　04:28 PM

今日　なんの　じゅぎょうが ありますか。

Give at least two examples.

3月22日　04:35 PM

ほうかごに　なにを　しますか。

Give some examples.

Can Do!
Now I can . . .

- ☐ share my class schedule
- ☐ describe my classes and teachers
- ☐ discuss my grades
- ☐ tell others why I am feeling happy or sad
- ☐ share information about things I want
- ☐ converse about after school activities

Japanese Holidays
にほんの　しゅくじつ

RESEARCH Use books, the Internet, or interview a Japanese member of your community to answer the following.

Determine

1. Name four Japanese national holidays.

2. Name two national holidays in your country, and one local or regional holiday or celebration.

3. The Japanese celebrate a series of holidays that have become known as "Golden Week." What holidays fall during this week and when is "Golden Week" celebrated?

4. The traditional Japanese calendar revolves around the emperor. Eras are named after the emperor currently in power. What is the name of the present era? In what year did it start? What year is it now, according to the traditional Japanese calendar?

Describe

5. How is Valentine's Day celebrated in America?

6. In Japan, a holiday called "White Day" comes a month after Valentine's Day. What is the difference between Valentine's Day and White Day in Japan?

Extend Your Learning
CREATIVITY, INNOVATION, AND COLLABORATION
In a group of 3–5 students, choose a Japanese holiday, research it, and plan a way to celebrate it in class. Consider how the classroom should be decorated, what activities can be done, what food should be prepared, what kind of clothing might be worn, and any Japanese expressions that may be associated with the holiday. Your teacher may ask you to share this information with your class as you "host" a celebration of the holiday.

おげんきですか
How are you?

Can Do!
In this lesson you will learn to

- ask about a friend's health
- communicate that you are not well
- ask a friend what he/she wants to do
- talk about activities you want to do and do not want to do
- ask about a sports event
- describe sports events and teams

Online Resources

cheng-tsui.com/
adventuresinjapanese

- Audio
- Vocabulary Lists
- Vocabulary Flashcards
- *Kana* and *Kanji* Flashcards
- Activity Worksheets

Kanji
used in this lesson

In this lesson, you will learn the *kanji* for size and different levels of school.

	Kanji	Meaning	Readings	Examples	

43. 大 big

おお
(きい)

おお　　ひと
大きい人　　　a big person

おおやま
大山さん　　　Mr./Ms. Oyama

だい

だい
大好き　　　like very much

44. 小 small

ちい
(さい)

ちい　　ひと
小さい人　　　a small person

しょう

しょうがっこう
小学校　　　elementary school

45. 中 inside, middle

なか

なかもと
中本さん　　　Mr./Ms. Nakamoto

なかぐち
中口さん　　　Mr./Ms. Nakaguchi

ちゅう

ちゅうがくせい
中学生　　　intermediate school student

ちゅうごく
中国　　　China

46. 早 early (time)

はや(い)

はや
早い　　　early

はやかわ
早川さん　　　Mr./Ms. Hayakawa

日 ＋ 十 ＝ 早
sun　　10

On Sundays, 10 o'clock is early.

47. 学 study

がく

だいがく
大学　　　college, university

しょうがくせい
小学生　　　elementary school student

がっ

がっこう
学校　　　school

Children study under the school roof, which displays the school emblem.

48. 校 school

こう

がっこう
学校　　　school

ちゅうがっこう
中学校　　　intermediate school

In the wooden school house, six students sit with their legs crossed.

WORKBOOK page 241

Recognition Kanji

こうこう
高校
high school

かいわ   Dialogue

READ/LISTEN What happened to Emi? How is she feeling?

たんご　Vocabulary

1. どう
   しましたか。

What happened?

2. びょうき

illness, sickness

びょうきです means
"I am sick."

3. かぜ

a cold

4. ねつ

fever

5. いたい
   [いAdj.]

painful, sore

6. だいじょうぶ
   [なAdj.]

大じょうぶ

all right

7. しにます
   [しぬ]

to die

8. かわいそうに。

How pitiful.

Expresses sympathy for someone/
something of a lower status.

ついか　たんご　Additional Vocabulary

1. (お)きのどくに。 　　　　　I'm sorry. [Formal expression of sympathy]

2. かぜを　ひきました。 　　　I caught a cold.

3. ねんざしました。 　　　　　I sprained (something).

4. ほねを　おりました。 　　　(I) fractured my bone.

🔊 **READ/LISTEN/SPEAK**　Read these sentences in Japanese. Say that you have either a cold or a high fever.

かぜです。

When they catch colds, the Japanese wear masks to prevent spreading germs. かぜです means "I have a cold."

私は　ねつが　あります。

ねつが　あります。 means "I have a fever."
ねつが　たかいです。 means "I have a high fever."

ぶんかノート　Culture Notes

くすりや

Japanese Medical Care

When Japanese people catch colds, they generally go to pharmacies (くすりや) to get medicine. For more serious conditions, Japan has a universal health care system that provides health care at an affordable cost for its citizens. All citizens are required to have health insurance, but there is no punishment for not doing so (besides having to pay in full for health care). Most health insurance is provided by employers, but National Health Insurance is available through local governments for the self-employed, students, and others not covered by employers. Depending on age and income, patients are expected to pay between 10–30% of medical fees. However, the government strictly regulates medical fees to keep costs at a minimum.

Most hospitals and clinics do not operate on an appointment system. Therefore, when the Japanese go to a hospital or a clinic, they have to wait their turn. Physical examinations for students are all done at school, where students are visited by doctors and receive medical exams and immunization shots.

Research the average life expectancy in Japan and in your own country online. Which country's is higher? Brainstorm a list of possible reasons why there may be a difference.

アクティビティー　Communicative Activities

Pair Work

A. SPEAK/LISTEN Your partner has a problem. Ask what happened. Your partner explains the problem, using a situation from the list below. You express your concern. Switch roles and continue until you have completed all the situations.

Ex.　　Person A: ～さん、どう　しましたか。　　Person B: かぜです。

　　　　Person A: だいじょうぶですか。

　　　　Person B: はい、だいじょうぶです。

　　　　Person A: おだいじに。

1. You have a cold.
2. You have a stomachache.
3. You have a sore throat.
4. You have a headache.
5. You have a slight fever.
6. Your eyes hurt.
7. Your dog died.
8. Your grandmother is very sick.

Reading

B. READ/WRITE Read the following e-mail from a Japanese student named Shinji. Answer the questions below in Japanese using complete sentences.

> おげんきですか。
>
> 先しゅう　私は　びょうきでしたから、学校（がっこう）を　三日
> 休みました。ねつが　たかかったです。そして、あたまが
> いたかったです。でも、今日は　すこし　大じょうぶに　なりました。
> 明日　学校（がっこう）へ　行きます。

UNDERSTAND

1. When did Shinji get sick?
2. What were some of Shinji's symptoms?
3. When is Shinji going back to school?

APPLY

4. Write an e-mail response to Shinji expressing your sympathy and describing a sickness you once had.

WORKBOOK page 93

かいわ　Dialogue

🔊 **READ/LISTEN** Why does Ken want to go home early?

今日 早く
うちへ
かえりたい
です。

なぜ
ですか。

すこし
ねつが
あります。

ぶんけい　Sentence Patterns

READ Find these sentence patterns in the dialogue

Person は Object を/が Verb (Stem form)* ＋ たい(ん)です。　[want to do ~]

Person は Object を/が Verb (Stem form)* ＋ たく　ない(ん)です。 [do not want to do ~]

* The verb stem is the portion of the verb preceding -ます。

1. やすみます
[やすむ]
休みます

2. (がっこうを) やす
みます[やすむ]
(学校を)休みます
[休む]

3. くすり (を
のみます) [のむ]

to rest

to be absent (from school)

(to take) medicine

4. ゆうべ
今うべ

5. けさ
今さ

6. こんばん
今ばん

7. ねむい
[いAdj.]

last night

this morning

tonight

sleepy

Neg. form: ねむくないです

8. つかれて　います/ つかれました

9. はやく
[Adverb]
早く

10. おそく
[Adverb]

is tired　　　　　got tired

early

late

Neg. form: つかれて　いません

はやい is an adjective. It describes nouns.
はやく is an adverb which usually describes verbs.
"I'll return home early." is 「はやく　かえります。」and
"It is early." is 「はやいです。」

ついか　たんご　Additional Vocabulary

1. ほけんしつ　　　　infirmary

2. アスピリン　　　　aspirin

よみましょう　Language in Context

🔊 **READ/LISTEN/SPEAK** Read these sentences in Japanese. Why do the Japanese use the verb
のみます with medicine? Say something you want to do.

くすりを　のみたいです。

Ancient Japanese medicines were in liquid or powder
form. They literally "drank" their medicine.

つかれて　いますから、
早く　ねたいです。

ぶんぽう　Grammar

A Verb たい Form

Verb (Stem form) ＋たい(ん)です	**want to do ～**
Verb (Stem form) ＋たく　ない(ん)です／ 　　たく　ありません	**do not want to do ～**
Verb (Stem form) ＋たかった(ん)です	**wanted to do ～**
Verb (Stem form) ＋たく　なかった(ん)です／ 　　たく　ありませんでした	**did not want to do ～**

This structure is used when one wants **to do** a certain action. When one wants **something**,
the ほしい structure is used.

たい conjugates as an い adj. In a ‑たい sentence that includes a direct object, the direct
object may be followed with either を or が. By using が, one emphasizes a high desire to do
the activity. When the verb has a negative ending, を or が may be replaced with は. ん is
often added when a speaker is explaining to a listener what the speaker wants to do.

Warning! Do not use this pattern when asking a person of higher status what he/she wants to do. It is considered impolite and too direct.

◀))) MODELS ▷

1. 「今　テレビを (or が)　みたいです。」
"I want to watch TV now."

2. 「早く　おひるごはんを (or が)　たべたいです。」
"I want to eat lunch early."

3. 「おちゃを　のみますか。」
"Will you drink tea?"

「すみません。おちゃは　のみたく　ありません。
お水が (or を)　のみたいです。」

"Sorry. I do not want to drink tea. I want to drink some water."

4. 「ゆうべ　フットボールを (or が)　みたかったんですが、
いそがしかったんです。」

"I wanted to watch football last night, but I was busy."

READ/WRITE Rewrite the sentences below using the correct form of the verbs in the ( ) based on the information below.

Today I didn't want to come to school, and I want to go home early. I do not want to do my homework.

1. 私は　今日　学校へ　　（来ます）。

2. 今日　早く　（かえります）。

3. そして、　しゅくだい（を　は）　　（します）。

ぶんかノート　Culture Notes

A. Polite Requests in Japanese

Japanese people tend to avoid directness in language and behavior, particularly when speaking to people of higher status or outside one's "in-group." As in English, Japanese uses more polite styles of speech when addressing these people, but these forms of speech are much more commonly used in Japan and are important to master.

For example, you might ask a friend, "You want coffee?" but when speaking to a boss, customer, or teacher, you would say, "Would you like some coffee?" Likewise, the polite form of "What do you want to drink?" in Japanese should not be 「なにが　のみたいですか。」, but 「おのみものは なにが　いいでしょうか。」.

Japanese is full of similar structures that express messages in indirect ways. The expectation is to be sensitive to others' needs by being observant, not by asking others directly.

B. A Japanese Proverb 「ばかに　つける　くすりは　ない」

ばか means "fool." つける means "to apply." くすり means "medicine." ない means "does not exist." 「ばかに　つける　くすりは ない」 means "There is no cure for foolishness."

 Read the explanation of the proverb above. Explain the proverb's meaning to a friend by writing a short narrative describing a situation from your own life that reflects the proverb.

アクティビティー　Communicative Activities

Pair Work

A. SPEAK/LISTEN You want to do the following. Your partner asks you why and you give reasons.

Ex.　Person A:　アスピリンを／が　のみたいです。

　　　　　B:　なぜですか。　A:　あたまが　いたいからです。

1. I want to take some aspirin (アスピリン).
2. I want to rest a while.
3. I want to go to the hospital.
4. I want to return home early.
5. I do not want to eat anything.
6. I want to be absent tomorrow.
7. I want to sleep.
8. I do not want to take medicine.

B. SPEAK/LISTEN Tell what you wanted to do. Your partner asks you why. You give a reason.

Ex.　Person A:　きのう　〜さんと　はなしたかったです。

　　　　　B:　なぜですか。　A:　パーティーが　ありますから。

1. I wanted to talk to you yesterday.
2. I wanted to return home early yesterday.
3. I wanted to go to bed early last night.
4. I did not want to get up early this morning.
5. I did not want to eat anything this morning.
6. I wanted to come to school early.

WORKBOOK　page 95

かいわ　Dialogue

🔊 **READ/LISTEN**　Did Emi's team win the volleyball game?

> きのうの
> バレーボールの
> しあいは
> どうでしたか。

> 私たちは
> まけました。
> とても　つよい
> チームでしたよ。

> それは
> ざんねんで
> したねえ。

ぶんけい　Sentence Patterns

READ　Find this sentence pattern in the dialogue.

い Adjective　X　Noun

Ex. 大きい　ぼうし　a big cap

たんご　Vocabulary

1. しあい

(sports) game

2. わたしたち
　 私たち

we

たち is a suffix for animate plurals.

3. ぼくたち

we [used by males]

4. チーム

team

5. かちます
　 [かつ]

to win

6. まけます
　 [まける]

to lose

7. つよい
　 [いAdj.]

strong

8. よわい
　 [いAdj.]

weak

よみましょう　Language in Context

READ/LISTEN Read these sentences in Japanese. How do the different verbs change the meaning of each sentence? Explain in English.

私たちは　じゅうどうの
しあいが　あります。

しあいが　あります means to "have a game or match."

じゅうどうの　しあいを
します。

しあいを　します means to
"play/participate in a game or match."

ぶんぽう　Grammar

A　い Adjectives Modifying Nouns ─────

い Adjective ＋ Noun

🔊 MODELS ▷

When an い adjective appears before a noun, no particle follows the い adjective.

1. つよい　チームでした。 (They) were a strong team.

2. とても　おもしろい　えいがです。 It is a very interesting movie.

3. 私は　あかい　はなが　好きです。 I like red flowers.

READ/WRITE Choose the correct particle for each ( ) from among が, の, と, and を. Write X when no particle is required.

1. おいしい（ 1 ）　おすし（ 2 or 3 ）　たべたいです。

2. ケンさん（ 4 ）　エミさんは　いい（ 5 ）　ともだちです。

3. 私たち（ 6 ）　チームは　とても　つよい（ 7 ）　チームです。

ぶんかノート　Culture Notes

A. じゃんけんぽん Game

Rock-paper-scissors is a popular hand game throughout the world, often used to determine who goes first or gets to make a decision in many situations. You have probably played it yourself, but did you know it originated in Asia? A version of the game was first noted in 16th-century China, but had likely already existed for a long time. The game came to Japan around the same time, and eventually became known there as じゃんけんぽん.

In the early 20th century, increased contact between Japan and the West brought the game to many new countries. At first it was known as a "Japanese" game, but in many places its origin has now been forgotten. To play the Japanese version, simply use the expressions below while "counting off" with your hands instead of "rock, paper, scissors." Throw out your hand signal as you say the last syllable.

グー　　チョキ　　パー
rock　　scissors　　paper

「じゃん けん ぽん」to start a game　　　　「あいこでしょ」to break a tie between the same "hands"

B. すもう

Sumo wrestling is the most popular of the Japanese traditional sports. It is the official national sport of Japan, and is several centuries old. Many of its traditions are deeply entwined with Shintoism, including the traditional purification of the ring with salt before a match. Names of すもうとり (sumo wrestlers) often end with words drawn from やま (mountain), うみ (ocean), はな (flower), etc.

In sumo wrestling, two すもうとり compete in a ring called a どひょう. Unlike Greco–Roman wrestling, the goal is not to pin or knock-out the opponent, but to push them out of the ring or force them to touch the ground. すもうとり may slap, push, or grab each other's まわし (belt), but may not kick or punch their opponent. Tournaments are held six times a year in different parts of Japan.

 Research a famous すもうとり and prepare a brief report on him. Consider what country he came from, the length of his career, and what he did/is doing after retirement, if applicable.

アクティビティー Communicative Activities

Pair Work

SPEAK/LISTEN Play a *jan-ken-pon* game with your partner five times and report who won most of the games. Be sure to use the correct phrases for starting a game and breaking ties.

Ex.　「〜さんが　かちました。」

Group Work

Hold a すもう tournament in a small group by cutting out paper すもうとり. Name your すもうとり and color their まわし (belt). Report who won or lost each match to your teacher.

 You can find the patterns and directions for making the wrestlers and the ring at the companion website: **cheng-tsui.com/adventuresinjapanese**

WORKBOOK page 87

かいわ　Dialogue

🔊 **READ/LISTEN** What is Ken going to do during spring break?

> はる休みに　とても　大^{だい}じな
> しあいが　あります。

> がんばって　ください。

> はい、　がんばります。

ぶんけい　Sentence Patterns

READ Find this sentence pattern in the dialogue.

な Adjective + な + Noun

Ex. きれい な　ぼうし a pretty hat

たんご　Vocabulary

1. はる

spring

2. なつ

summer

3. あき

autumn, fall

4. ふゆ

winter

5. せんげつ
先月

last month

6. こんげつ
今月

this month

7. らいげつ
来月

next month

8. まいつき
毎月

every month

9. だいじ [なAdj.]
大じ

important

10. がんばって。

Good luck! / Do your best.

11. がんばります。

I will do my best.

ついか　たんご　Additional Vocabulary

1. トーナメント　　　　tournament

🔊 **READ/LISTEN/SPEAK** Read these sentences in Japanese. Ask a partner when his/her favorite sport starts practice and respond.

来月から　やきゅうの
れんしゅうを　します。

がんばって！

ぶんぽう Grammar

A な Adjectives Modifying Nouns

な **Adjective** + な + **Noun**

When な adjectives modify nouns, な appears between the な adjective and the noun.

🔊 MODELS

1. 明日　だいじな　しあいが　あります。
   There is an important game tomorrow.

2. 「好きな　スポーツは　なんですか。」 "What is your favorite sport?"

   「ゴルフが　好きです。」 "I like golfing."

3. きれいな　人ですねえ。 She is a pretty lady!

READ Choose the correct particle from the options in the ( ). X means no particle is required.

1. 田中先生は　きれい（の / な / Ｘ）　先生ですが、とても
   きびしい（の / な / Ｘ）　先生です。

2. ケンさんは　私（の／な／X）　大じ（の／な／X）
ともだちです。

3. 私たち（の／な／X）　チームは　いい（の／な／X）
チームですが、今日は　ひどい（の／な／X）　しあいでした。

B　Review of な Adjectives

げんき	fine	下手	unskilled	じゃま	hindrance
だめ	no good	とくい	strong at	ゆうめい	famous
好き	like	にが手	weak at	たいへん	hard
きらい	dislike	きれい	pretty	だいじょうぶ	all right
上手	skillful	しずか	quiet	だいじ	important

ぶんかノート　Culture Notes

はる休みの
さくら

はる休み, なつ休み, and ふゆ休み in Japan

In Japan, はる休み (spring vacation) is from around the 20th of March to the 10th of April and is generally the most relaxing vacation for Japanese students and parents. It is the vacation which marks the end of one school year and the beginning of the next, so there is no homework and no pressure from school.

なつ休み (summer vacation) is much shorter than summer vacation in the U.S. It is from around the 20th of July to the end of August, and homework is assigned during the vacation. ふゆ休み (winter vacation) is from about the 20th of December to the 10th of January. Christmas is not a national holiday in Japan, but おしょうがつ (New Year's) January 1st, 2nd, and 3rd is a time for family celebration, much like Christmas is in the West.

Carefully read the description of Japanese school holidays above. Do you prefer your own country's school holiday schedule or Japan's? Write a short essay comparing the two systems and justify your opinion with examples.

アクティビティー　Communicative Activities

Pair Work

A. SPEAK/LISTEN/WRITE Interview your partner on his/her likes and dislikes. Write your partner's responses on a separate sheet of paper.

> Ex. Question:　好きな　たべものは　なんですか。
>
> 　　Answer:　〜です。

1. 好きな　たべもの　　　　＿＿＿＿＿
2. きらいな　たべもの　　　＿＿＿＿＿
3. 好きな　車　　　　　　　＿＿＿＿＿
4. 好きな　本　　　　　　　＿＿＿＿＿
5. 上手な　スポーツ　　　　＿＿＿＿＿
6. 下手な　スポーツ　　　　＿＿＿＿＿

B. SPEAK/LISTEN Ask your partner about the people below. Your partner will answer with descriptions based on the pictures below. You may use the cues below or make up your own descriptions.

> Ex. Question:　〜さんは　どんな　人ですか。
>
> 　Answer:　〜さんは　い Adj. 人です。　or
>
> 　　　　　　〜さんは　な Adj.　な　人です。

| ベン | だいすけ | ジェイン | ゆか | Someone else |
| うるさい | しずか | きれい | かわいい | |

C. WRITE/LISTEN/SPEAK Divide the dates below between you and your partner. Randomly select dates for each of your events from the calendar below and write them down without telling your partner. After you have chosen your dates, ask your partner what date each of his/her events is on and write down the answers. When finished, check your answers by comparing them to your partner's original dates.

Ex. 「やきゅうの　しあいは　いつですか。」

1. today
2. vacation (spring)
3. piano concert
4. birthday party
5. important basketball game

6. good movie
7. Japanese exam
8. dog's death
9. basketball game
10. prom (プロム)

Make Your Own Calendar

Last Month

日	月	火	水	木	金	土
		1	2	3	4	
5	6	7	8	9	10	11
12	13	14	15	16	17	18
19	20	21	22	23	24	25
26	27	28	29	30		

This Month

日	月	火	水	木	金	土
					1	2
3	4	5	6	7	8	9
10	11	12	13	14	15	16
17	18	19	20	21	22	23
24	25	26	27	28	29	30
31						

Next Month

日	月	火	水	木	金	土
		1	2	3	4	5
6	7	8	9	10	11	12
13	14	15	16	17	18	19
20	21	22	23	24	25	26
27	28	29	30			

WORKBOOK page 99

10か5
Shall we meet at my house?

かいわ　Dialogue

🔊 **READ/LISTEN** What does Ken want to do? What does Emi suggest doing afterwards?

ケン：　明日　ここの　大学（だいがく）と　ステート
　　　　大学（だいがく）の　バレーボールの　しあいが
　　　　あります。いっしょに
　　　　行きませんか。

エミ：　どこで　ありますか。

ケン：　大学（だいがく）で　あります。

エミ：　じゃ、5時に　私の　うちで
　　　　あいましょうか。

ケン：　ええ。そして、しあいの　あとで
　　　　えいがに　行きましょう。

ぶんけい　Sentence Patterns

READ Find this sentence pattern in the dialogue.

Activity　は　　Place　で　あります 。　[There is an activity at ~.]

たんご　Vocabulary

1. だいがく
大学

college, university

2. だいがくせい
大学生

college student

3. 〜のまえに

before 〜

4. 〜のあとで

after 〜

5. (Place で) あいます
[あう]

to meet (at a place)

6. れんしゅう(を)
します [する]

to practice

7. はしります
[はしる]

to run

よみましょう　Language in Context

🔊 **READ/LISTEN/SPEAK** Read these sentences in Japanese. Say when and where the tennis match will be.

全国高校テニス大会
場所：東京大学
日時：3月5日（土曜日）
13:00 – 15:00

しあいの　まえに
れんしゅうを　します。

しあいは　大学で　あります。

ぶんぽう Grammar

A Using Location Particle で with Existence Verbs

Place ＋ で **Activity/Event** ＋ が あります。

When an activity or event occurs at a place, the particle で (not に) is used after the place word.

MODELS

1. 「今日 しあいは どこで ありますか。」
   "Where is the game today?"

   「マッキンレー高校で あります。」
   "It will be at McKinley High School."

2. 金曜日の ダンスは カフェテリアで あります。
   Friday's dance will be at the cafeteria.

READ/WRITE Write the correct particle for each ( ) choosing from among の, へ, に and で.

1. 今日（ 1 ） バレーボール（ 2 ） しあいは ぼくたち（ 3 ）
   学校（ 4 ） あります。

2. ピクニックは この 土曜日（ 5 ） こうえん（ 6 ）
   あります。 こうえん（ 7 or 8 ） いっしょに 行きましょう。

ぶんかノート Culture Notes

High School and College Sports in Japan

In Japan, high school sports are very popular spectator events, comparable to the popularity of college sports in the U.S. Baseball and soccer are generally the most popular. There are two national baseball tournaments a year, one in March and one in August. Many Japanese people watch these games on TV and cheer for their home teams. Except for major tournaments, people are not charged admission to attend high school or college games.

Koshien Baseball Stadium near Kobe, home of Japan's national high school baseball tournaments

 Online, research the winners of the last five national high school baseball tournaments in Japan. Locate the cities or prefectures the teams are from and circle them on a map of Japan.

アクティビティー　Communicative Activities

Pair Work

A. SPEAK/LISTEN/WRITE You want to do the following activities with your partner. Ask your partner when and where the event will start, and decide on where and when to meet. Write your answers on a separate sheet of paper using a chart like the one below.

Ex. Question 1: えいがは　どこで　ありますか。

Question 2: えいがは　いつですか。

Question 3: どこで　あいましょうか。

Question 4: なん時に　あいましょうか。

	Place	Time	Place to meet	Time to meet
1. movie				
2. concert （コンサート）				
3. college basketball game				
4. dancing （ダンス）				
5. running				
6. tennis practice				

Reading

B. READ/WRITE Read the advertisement for a sports match in Japan at right and answer the questions in Japanese.

UNDERSTAND

1. What sport is being advertised?

2. What level will the players be? (Middle school, high school, college, professional プロ)

3. What date and day of the week will the match be held?

4. What time will the match be held?

CREATE

5. Create a similar advertisement in Japanese for a sporting event at your own school. Be sure to include details.

WORKBOOK page 101

Lesson 10
Review

Review Questions

Ask your partner these questions or say these statements in Japanese. Your partner answers in Japanese. Check your answers using the audio.

Health   Review pages 322 and 326

1. Are you sick now?

2. My dog died last week. [Respond to the comment.]

3. I have a slight stomachache. [Respond to the comment.]

4. I have a slight fever. [Respond to the comment.]

5. I have a cold. [Respond to the comment.]

6. Do you want to rest now?

7. I just took some medicine now. [Respond to the comment.]

8. Did you go to bed late last night? What time did you go to bed?

9. Did you get up early this morning? What time did you get up?

10. Are you tired now?

Sports & Tournaments   Review pages 330, 332, and 340

11. Is our school baseball team strong?

12. [Play じゃんけんぽん.] Who won?

13. Where will the (university name) and (university name) baseball game be?

14. Let's go to a [basketball] game tonight. Where shall we meet?

15. Do you practice baseball everyday?

The Weekend   Review pages 335 and 340

16. What do you want to do this weekend?

17. I have an important exam tomorrow. [Respond to the comment.]

18. Let's go to a movie this weekend. Where shall we meet?

Spring Break Review page 335

19. When is spring vacation?

20. What do you want to do during spring vacation?

21. What did you do during the winter vacation?

Text Chat

You will participate in a simulated exchange of text-chat messages. You should respond as fully and as appropriately as possible.

You will have a conversation with Aiko, a Japanese high school student, about her health.

4月17日　11:43 AM

こんにちは。今日　学校を
休みました。

Ask a question.

4月17日　11:48 AM

ねつが　あります。そして、あたまが
いたいです。

Show sympathy.

4月17日　11:54 AM

でも、明日　大じな　サッカーの
しあいが　あります。

Give encouragement.

Can Do!
Now I can . . .

- [ ] ask someone about their health
- [ ] express why I am not feeling well
- [ ] talk about activities I want to do
- [ ] describe a sports event
- [ ] describe a sports team

Origami Cranes
おりづる

Origami Cranes, or おりづる, are one of the most popular origami shapes.
In traditional Japanese culture, cranes (つる) were thought to live up to 1000 years,
and represented longevity. せんばづる (a thousand cranes) is a tradition of folding
a thousand paper cranes for good luck and well-being. In Japan, the せんばづる is
offered to a sick person as a get-well token.

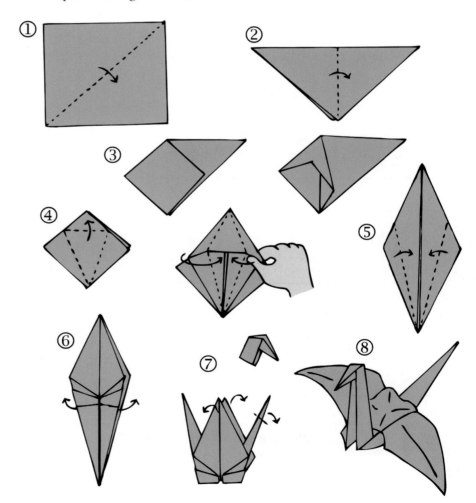

For more detailed directions, visit the companion website at
cheng-tsui.com/adventuresinjapanese

ショッピング
Shopping

Can Do!
In this lesson you will learn to

- make requests
- ask for permission
- count Japanese currency
- suggest items to purchase
- ask about prices in Japanese yen

Online Resources

cheng-tsui.com/
adventuresinjapanese

- Audio
- Vocabulary Lists
- Vocabulary Flashcards
- *Kana* and *Kanji* Flashcards
- Activity Worksheets

Kanji
used in this lesson

In this lesson, you will learn *kanji* used for money and large numbers.

	Kanji	Meaning	Readings	Examples		
49.	白	white	しろ	しろ　いぬ 白い犬	a white dog	The sun's white rays are pointing up.
50.	百	hundred	ひゃく	ひゃくにん 百　人	100 people	One white coin is a 100.
			びゃく	さんびゃく 三　百	300	
			ぴゃく	ろっぴゃく 六　百	600	
				はっぴゃく 八　百	800	
51.	千	1,000	せん	せん 千	1,000	An army of a thousand soldiers is marching.
				はっせん 八 千	8,000	
			ぜん	ぜん 三 千	3,000	
52.	万	10,000	まん	まん 一万	10,000	Manji symbol (a religion from India)
				ひゃくまん 百　万	1,000,000 one million	
53.	円	yen, circle	えん	ひゃくえん 百　円	one hundred yen	Like a cottage, the round Japanese yen has windows.
				まんえん 一万 円	ten thousand yen	
54.	見	look, see	み(る)	み 見ます	look	A person standing sees well with his big eyes.

Illustration captions within the Examples/pictograph area:

- one (with pointing hand → 一 + 十)
- cottage + window = yen (円)

WORKBOOK   page 245

Recognition Kanji

いぬ	ふと(る)
1. 犬	**2.** 太
dog	fat

かいわ　Dialogue

🔊 **READ/LISTEN** What does Ken ask the teacher for permission to do?

しゅくだいを　だして　ください。

すみません。わすれました。ロッカーへ　行っても　いいですか。

はい、すぐ　行って、すぐ　かえって　ください。

はい、わかりました。

A Verb TE Form

The verb TE form is an important verb form used in many ways. When the TE form is followed by ください, it is a request form which means "Please do such and such." When the TE form is followed by もいいですか, it means "May I do such and such?" and is used to ask permission. The TE form is also used to string together sequences of verbs. The TE form also has many more functions.

The tense of the TE form is determined by the final tense of the sentence.

Example: たべて is the TE form of たべます.

◀)) MODELS

1. たべて　ください。   Please eat. (request)

2. たべても　いいですか。   May I eat? (permission)

3. たべて、ねました。   I ate and slept. (sequence)

How is the TE form derived from MASU form? Japanese verbs are divided into three groups according to the way they conjugate: Group 1 verbs, Group 2 verbs, and Irregular verbs.

1. Group 1 Verbs

Group 1 verbs are identified by the verb stem ending. The verb stem is that portion of the verb which remains after dropping the –ます. If there are two or more *hiragana* characters remaining in the verb stem after dropping the ます, and the final sound of the verb stem is an –*i* ending sound, the verb can usually be categorized as a Group 1 verb.

The TE form of Group 1 verbs are created by replacing the last –*i* syllable of the verb stem with a new ending. Different TE form endings are used depending on the original –*i* ending of the verb stem, as seen below.

Verb Stem Ending	TE Form Ending
み、に、び	んで
い、ち、り	って
き	いて
ぎ	いで
し	して

One exception in Group 1 is 行きます, which becomes 行って. See the chart on the next page for examples.

[-i ます]

	MASU form	Meaning	TE form
[み]	のみます	to drink	のんで
	よみます	to read	よんで
	やすみます	to rest, be absent	やすんで
[に]	しにます	to die	しんで
[び]	あそびます*	to play*	あそんで*
[い]	あいます	to meet	あって
[ち]	かちます	to win	かって
[り]	わかります	to understand	わかって
	しります	to get to know	しって
	かえります	to return (place)	かえって
	あります	to be (inanimate)	あって
	がんばります	to do one's best	がんばって
	はしります	to run	はしって
[き]	ききます	to listen, hear	きいて
	かきます	to write	かいて
	いきます	to go	いって**
	あるきます	to walk	あるいて
[ぎ]	およぎます*	to swim*	およいで*
[し]	はなします	to talk	はなして

* Not introduced yet.   ** Exception

2. Group 2 Verbs

Group 2 verbs can be identified by a verb stem (verb without ます) which ends in an "e-sounding" *hiragana*, or a verb stem which contains only one *hiragana*. See examples below. A few exceptions do exist. They must simply be learned as exceptions on a case by case basis. Group 2 verb TE forms are created simply by adding て after removing the – ます.

	MASU form	Meaning	TE form
[-e ます]	みえます	can be seen	みえて
	きこえます	can be heard	きこえて
	たべます	to eat	たべて
	ねます	to sleep	ねて
	まけます	to lose	まけて
[ます]	みます	to see, watch	みて
	います	to be (animate)	いて
[Exceptions]	おきます	to get up	おきて

3. Group 3 or Irregular Verbs

Only きます, します, and noun + します verbs belong to this group.

MASU form		Meaning	TE form	
	きます	to come		きて
	します	to do		して
べんきょう(を)	します	to study	べんきょう(を)	して
タイプ(を)	します	to type	タイプ(を)	して

READ/WRITE Write the correct TE form of the verbs in the ( ).

1. 先生：　早く　クラスに　__1__　ください。（来ます）

2. 生徒：　お水を　__2__　も　いいですか。（のみます）

3. 先生：　よく　かんじを　__3__　ください。（べんきょうします）

🔊 **READ/LISTEN** Read these sentences in Japanese. Which Group are the verbs in each sentence a part of? Answer in English.

名前を　かいて　ください。

これを　食べても　いいですか。

アクティビティー　Communicative Activities

🔊 A. Song ♪♪♪　♪♪♪

SPEAK TE Form Song (For Group 1 & Irregular verbs) Sing the tune of "O Christmas Tree."

Oh, み, に, び　Oh, み, に, び　み, に, び to んで！

Oh, い, ち, り　Oh, い, ち, り　い, ち, り to って！

き to いて　ぎ to いで　し to して　and きて, して

Oh, み, に, び　Oh, み, に, び　Now we know our TE forms!

B. Pair or Group Game

Visit the companion website (**cheng-tsui.com/adventuresinjapanese**) to find instructions and materials for playing a card game (see example cards below) to memorize verbs and their TE forms.

のみます	しにます	みます

WORKBOOK page 105

かいわ　Dialogue

🔊 **READ/LISTEN** What verb form does Ken use to ask the clerk for something?

すみません。　これを　見せて　ください。

これですか。　はい、　どうぞ。

たんご　Vocabulary

🔊

1. すわって
ください。

Please sit.

すわります
[すわる]

2. たって
ください。

Please stand.

たちます
[たつ]

3. だして
ください。

Please turn in
(something).

だします
[だす]

4. みせて
ください。

Please show me
(something).

みせます
[みせる]

5. まどを　あけて
ください。

Please open the window.

あけます
[あける]　'

6. ドアを　しめて
ください。

Please close the door.

しめます
[しめる]

7. しずかに　して
ください。

Please be quiet.

しずかに　します
[する]

8. もう　いちど
いってください。

もう　一ど
言って　ください。

9. ちょっと
まって
ください。

10. (お)みせ

11. すみません。

Please say it one more
time.

Please wait a minute.

store

Excuse me! (to get
attention)

いいます [いう]　　まちます [まつ]

よみましょう　Language in Context

🔊 **READ/LISTEN/SPEAK** Read these sentences in Japanese. Make your own request using the
TE form.

すみません、あれを　みせて
ください。

もう　一ど　言って　ください。

この　かんじを　よんで
ください。

ぶんぽう　Grammar

A　Making Requests with the Verb TE Form

Verb TE form ＋ください。

MODELS

The Verb TE form + extender ください is used to express a request: "Please do . . ."

1.　「ゆっくり　はなして　ください。」　　"Please speak slowly."

　　「はい、わかりました。」　　　　　　　"Yes, I understand."

2.　「まどを　あけて　ください。」　　　"Please open the window."

　　「はい、今　あけます。」　　　　　　　"Yes, I will open it now."

3.　「すみません。この　シャツを　みせて　ください。」
　　　　　　　　　　　　　　　　　　"Excuse me. Please show me this shirt."

　　「はい、どうぞ。」　　　　　　　　　　"Yes, here it is."

READ/WRITE Write the correct TE form of the verbs in the ( ).

1. 先生：　日本ごを＿＿1＿＿　ください。　　（はなします）

2. 先生：　しゅくだいを＿＿2＿＿　ください。　　（みせます）

3. 生徒：　すみません、もう　一ど＿＿3＿＿　ください。　　（いいます）

ぶんかノート　Culture Notes

Service in Japanese Stores

Japanese sales clerks are trained to be extremely polite and formal with their customers, not only in action but also in their language. Department stores in Japan usually hire many more clerks, thus providing more service to their customers. Customers are met at the door at opening time by employees who welcome them with a greeting and a bow. After shopping, purchases are wrapped free of charge at all sales counters. Many department stores are also equipped with playgrounds and nurseries where parents may entertain or rest with youngsters.

Due to the economic downturn in the 1990s, cost-cutting measures have scaled down some of the services provided. Large, upscale supermarkets offer stiff competition. For example, in the past all department stores hired numerous employees (often women) to greet customers, operate elevators, and provide information. These days they are mostly seen only at larger department stores in the major urban centers.

 Based on the information above, compare Japanese retail stores to retail stores in your own country. You may want to consider more than one store from your own country in your comparison. Create a Venn diagram listing similarities and differences you could present to a retail business considering opening a store in Japan.

アクティビティー　Communicative Activities

Pair Work

A. SPEAK/LISTEN You are hosting a Japanese student at your school. You bring the student to your Japanese class and request him/her to do the following. The Japanese student states that he/she understands you and does as you request.

1. Please wait here.

2. Please stand now.

3. Please introduce yourself.
   (じこしょうかいを　します)

4. Please write your name on the board
   (こくばん／ホワイトボード) in Japanese.

5. Please read your name.

6. Please observe (みます) our class.

Pair Work: Simon Says

B. SPEAK/LISTEN You ask your partner to act upon your request following the rules of "Simon Says." You may use these examples or create your own.

1. Please stand.

2. Please sit down.

3. Please open the door/window/book.

4. Please close the door/window.

5. Please show me your cellular phone.

6. Please say your name loudly.

7. Please write your name on the board
   (こくばん/ホワイトボード).

8. Please read this. (You write *kanji* or a short sentence on paper.)

9. Please look at (someone in your class). What color is his/her shirt?

WORKBOOK page 107

かいわ Dialogue

🔊 **READ/LISTEN** What does Ken want? What does Emi want?

ぶんけい Sentence Patterns

READ Find these patterns in the dialogue.

1. Noun 1 か Noun 2   Noun 1 or Noun 2

   ♻ Question 1 。(それとも) Question 2 。   Question 1. Or Question 2.

2. Verb (TE form) も いいですか。   [May I do 〜? (Asking for permission.)]

    はい、どうぞ。   [Yes, please.]

    いいえ、だめです。   [No, it is not all right.]

   ♻ Noun 1 も Noun 2 も 好きです。   [I like both Noun 1 and Noun 2.]

    Noun 1 も Noun 2 も 好きでは
ありません。   [I don't like either N1 or N2.]

たんご　Vocabulary

1. シャツ

shirt

2. ジャケット

jacket

3. パンツ

pants

ズボン is used by the older generation.

4. くつ

shoes

5. とけい

watch, clock

6. スーパー

supermarket

7. ほんや
本や

bookstore

8. はなや

flower shop

9. すしや

sushi shop/bar

10. きっさてん

coffee shop

11. かいます
[かう/かって]

to buy

ついか　たんご　Additional Vocabulary

1. コンビニ　　convenience store

READ/LISTEN/SPEAK Read these sentences in Japanese. Ask a partner what color shirt he/she wants to buy and respond.

あかい　シャツか　白い　シャツを
　　　　かいたいです。

あそこに　はなやが　あります。

ぶんぽう　Grammar

A Noun Connector か

Noun 1 か Noun 2　　　　　**Noun 1 or Noun 2**

か is used between two or more nouns. か is **not** used to conjoin adjectives, verbs or adverbs!

Compare to a previously learned form:

 Question 1。(それとも) Question 2。　　　Question 1. Or Question 2.

それとも is used to start a new sentence.

◄))) MODELS

1. ジュースか　お水を　のみます。　　I will drink juice or water.

2. 白か　みどりの　くつを　かいます。 I will buy white or green shoes.

3. スーパーで　かいましょうか。それとも、はなやで
かいましょうか。

Shall we buy it at a supermarket? Or at a flower shop?

READ/WRITE Write the correct particle in the ( ), using the English sentences as cues.

1. 本や (1)　きっさてん (2)　行きましょう。 Let's go to a bookstore or coffee shop.

2. ジャケット (3)　とけい (4)　かいました。 I bought a jacket and a watch.

3. すし (5)　てんぷらなど　たべました。 I ate sushi and tempura, etc.

B TE Form Verbs in Permission Questions

Verb (TE form) も　いいですか。 May I do such and such?

This structure is used when asking for permission. When granting permission, respond with はい、どうぞ。 When denying permission, say いいえ、だめです。 (いいえ、だめです is a strong response, and should only be used with people of lower status.)

◀)) MODELS

1. トイレへ　行っても　いいですか。 May I go to the restroom?

2. お水を　のんでも　いいですか。 May I drink (some) water?

READ/WRITE Write the correct TE form of the verbs in the ( ).

1. アニメを　__1__ も　いいですか。　（みます）

2. うちへ　早く __2__ も　いいですか。　（かえります）

3. えいごで　__3__ も　いいですか。　（はなします）

C Summary of Adjectives and Noun Modifiers

い Adjective + X + Noun	あかい　シャツ	red shirt
な Adjective + な + Noun	きれいな　シャツ	pretty shirt
Noun + の + Noun	あかと　しろの　シャツ	red and white shirt

READ Choose the correct particle from choices in the ( ). X means no particle is required.

1. しずか（X / な / の）　きっさてんです。

2. おいしい（X / な / の）　コーヒーです。

3. あかと　ピンク（X / な / の）　はなです。

Language Note

パンツ or ズボン?

As is the case with most modern languages, the Japanese language constantly experiences language shifts, especially in vocabulary. An example is the Japanese word for "trousers" which the older generation prefers to refer to as ズボン (or ずぼん). The younger generation prefers to use the word パンツ. This is unpopular among the older generation, who use the word パンツ to refer to underwear, which comes from British English.

アクティビティー Communicative Activities

Pair Work

A. SPEAK/LISTEN Interview your partner and find out what kind of items he/she wants to buy. Your partner describes two possible choices of colors he/she would like to buy. Write them down on a separate sheet of paper using a chart like the one at right.

Ex. A: どんな シャツを かいたいですか。

B: そうですねえ... 白か あかのシャツを かいたいです。

A: そうですか。

Purchase	Color
1. シャツ	or
2. ジャケット	or
3. くつ	or
4. パンツ	or
5. とけい	or
6. 車	or
7. ケータイ	or

B. SPEAK/LISTEN Your partner wants to do the following things. You are very accommodating and suggest a place where he/she can buy or get what he/she wants. You will accompany him/her to the appropriate place.

Ex.　　Person A:　おすしを　たべたいです。

　　　　Person B:　じゃ、今ばん　すしやへ　行きましょう。

　　　　Person A:　いいですねえ。

1. Wants to buy books

2. Wants to buy milk

3. Wants to drink some good coffee

4. Wants to buy a shirt

5. Wants to buy flowers

Writing

C. WRITE Write your teacher asking for permission to do the following things.

Ex.　トイレへ　行っても　いいですか。

1. Go to the locker

2. Drink water

3. Open the windows

4. Turn in today's homework tomorrow

WORKBOOK　page 109

かいわ　Dialogue

🔊 **READ/LISTEN** What color is the shirt Ken is looking at? How much is it?

ぶんけい　Sentence Patterns

READ Review these adjective + noun patterns and find them in the dialogue.

あかいの　　　　(that) red one

しずかなの　　　(that) quiet one

たんご　Vocabulary

	1. $	2. ¢	3. ¥ (yen)	4. 100	5. 1,000	6. 10,000
			いちえん	ひゃく	せん	いちまん
1	いちドル*	いっセント	一円	百**	千**	一万
2	にドル	ニセント	二円	二百	二千	二万
3	さんドル	三セント	三円	三びゃく	三ぜん	三万
4	よんドル	四セント	よえん	四百	四千	四万
5	ごドル	五セント	五円	五百	五千	五万
6	ろくドル	六セント	六円	ろっぴゃく	六千	六万
7	ななドル	七セント	七円	七百	七千	七万
8	はちドル	はっセント	八円	はっぴゃく	はっ千	八万
9	きゅうドル	九セント	九円	九百	九千	九万
10	じゅうドル	じゅっセント	十円			十万
?	なんドル	何セント	何円	何びゃく	何ぜん	何万

* All numbers follow the standard pronunciation shown in the first column, unless an exception is shown in black *hiragana*.

** One thousand is generally just せん. いっせん is not usually used.

One hundred is generally just ひゃく. いっぴゃく is not usually used.

7. (お)いくら	8. 〜ぐらい	9. どれ	10. どの〜
How much?	about 〜	Which one?	Which 〜?
[for cost, お adds politeness]	[not used for time]	[of more than 2]	

11.	じゅうまん	十万	100,000 (hundred thousand)
12.	ひゃくまん	百万	1,000,000 (one million)

よみましょう　Language in Context

🔊 **READ/LISTEN/SPEAK** Read these sentences in Japanese. Ask how much money a classmate has in his/her pocket and respond.

「いくら　ありますか。」
「765円　あります。」

この　むらさきの
セーターは　いくらですか。

ぶんぽう　Grammar

A A. Adjectives and Pronouns

い **Adjective** ＋の

な **Adjective** ＋ な ＋の

 MODELS

の is a noun that means "one," i.e., tall one, good one. In this case, の is not a particle.

1. 大きいのを　ください。　　　　Please give me a big one.

2. きれいなのを　ください。　　　Please give me a clean one.

READ/WRITE Write the correct Japanese equivalent of the English cues in the ( ).

1. シャツを　みせて　ください。あの＿**1**＿です。　　(white one)

2. この　チョコレートを　ください。この　__2__　です。($10)

3. あの　いぬを　みせて　ください。あの　__3__　を　みせて
　　ください。　　　(quiet)

B Summary of Pronouns

こ▮		そ▮		あ▮		ど▮	
ここ	here	そこ	there	あそこ	over there	どこ	where?
これ	this one	それ	that one	あれ	that one over there	どれ	which one?
この〜	this 〜	その〜	that 〜	あの〜	that 〜 over there	どの〜	which 〜 ?

READ Ken is working at a souvenir shop and Emi is his customer. Choose the correct word from the options in the ( ) based on the context.

エミ：シャツは　（どこ / どれ / どの）に　ありますか。

ケン：（あそこ / あれ / あの）です。（どこ / どれ / どの）が
　　　　好きですか。

エミ：（ここ / これ / この）シャツを　ください。いくらですか。

ケン：（これ / それ / あれ / どれ）は　20ドルです。

ぶんかノート　Culture Notes

A. Japanese Currency

The Japanese currency is the yen, and consists of both coins and bills. Small denominations are only available as coins: one yen, five yen, ten yen, fifty yen, a hundred yen and five hundred yen. Unlike the U.S., Japan no longer breaks the yen into cents or hundredths (called sen). Bills are available in 1,000 yen, 2,000 yen, 5,000 yen and 10,000 yen denominations. The value of the currency is clearly indicated on the coin or bill, and coins and bills graduate in size from small to large according to their value.

Japanese bills have many protections against counterfeiting. If one holds a Japanese bill to the light, one is able to see an image in the blank portion of the face of the bill. Although many Japanese now use credit cards and occasionally checks, most Japanese still prefer to pay for most things in cash. Therefore, it is not uncommon to see Japanese people carrying rolls of cash in their pockets.

The symbol ¥ is used to indicate yen. It appears before the numerical amount. Japanese also use the *kanji* 円, but it is only used after the number or numbers which are written in *kanji*. Compare: ¥500 and 五百円.

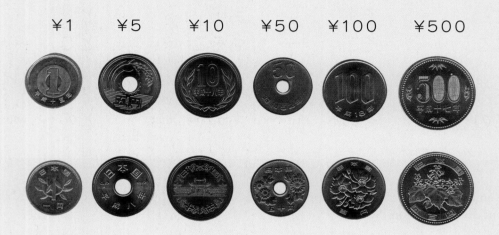

¥1　　¥5　　¥10　　¥50　　¥100　　¥500

B. Persons Featured on Japanese Currency

いちまんえん

ふくざわ ゆ きち
福沢諭吉 1835–1901

Fukuzawa Yukichi, a famed educator and writer of the Meiji Period, is regarded as one of the major forces who introduced Western thought to Japan in the late 1800s and early 1900s. He is best remembered as the founder of the Keio Gijuku University, now known as Keio University, one of the top private universities in Japan.

Born to a low-ranking samurai family in Osaka, Fukuzawa was fascinated by the West and studied Dutch and English. He eventually traveled to the U.S. and Europe as part of the first official missions to the Western world. Profoundly influenced by Western thought, Fukuzawa's prolific works cover a range of subjects from philosophy to women's rights.

ごせんえん

樋口一葉 (ひぐちいちよう) 1872–1896

Higuchi Ichiyo is the third woman to be featured on a Japanese note. She has graced the 5,000 yen note since 2004. Higuchi is known as one of the most famous female writers among modern literary writers in Japan. Born Higuchi Natsu to a family which traces its history to the samurai class, she lived a short and tragic life, but is remembered for the quality of her literary works.

Early in her life, Higuchi lost her father and brother, and her young family was left to fend for themselves. Higuchi decided to support her family by becoming a writer and became quite successful as she wrote her first novel at the age of 20. She is most famous for four major works, some of which have been translated into English. At the very young age of 24, Higuchi lost her battle with tuberculosis. Her short but dramatic life is remembered through her well recognized works.

にせんえん

紫式部 (むらさきしきぶ) 978–1014

In the summer of 2000, a new 2,000 yen note was issued by the Japanese government to mark the start of the new millenium. The design on the new bill features the Shurei no Mon, a historical landmark in Okinawa. The issuance of the bill coincided with a Summit Meeting of the leaders of eight major world powers held in July, 2000 in the city of Nago in Okinawa.

On the reverse side of the bill is a depiction of a portion of the world's oldest known novel, the *Genji Monogatari* (*Tales of Genji*) written on a scroll. Alongside this famous piece of literature is an illustration of its author, Murasaki Shikibu.

In order to prevent counterfeiting, it is said that the most high-tech form of printing is used to produce the bills. The 2,000 yen note is not commonly used.

せんえん

野口 英世 1876–1928

の ぐちひでよ

Noguchi Hideyo has been featured on the 1,000 yen note since 2004. Born Noguchi Seisaku in Fukushima Prefecture in northern Honshu, Noguchi suffered an accident as a child which determined his life path through adulthood.

At age 1 1/2, Noguchi fell into a burning fireplace and suffered a burn on his hand which remained deformed through his elementary school years. Through the efforts of one of his teachers and his friends, enough money was raised for him to have surgery on his hand. He was able to regain enough mobility to function at most daily tasks. He was so inspired by the dedication and craft of his surgeon that he decided to study to become a doctor himself. He changed his name to Noguchi Hideyo and began to pursue a career in reseearch.

Noguchi conducted much of his research abroad in the U. S., Central and South America. He is best known as a bacteriologist who is credited for his work in identifying the agent for syphillis. While doing research on yellow fever, he himself contracted the fever and succumbed to it at the age of 52.

 The exchange rate between the U.S. and Japan is constantly changing. Search for a currency converter online and calculate how much each of these amounts is in yen.

1) $1

2) $10

3) $50

4) $100

5) $5,000

6) $1,000,000

アクティビティー　Communicative Activities

Pair Work

A. SPEAK/LISTEN Ask about the price of your partner's shoes, bag, shirt, pants, watch, cap/hat, pencil, eraser, etc. Ask for prices in dollars and yen. Write your partner's answers on a separate sheet of paper, using a chart like the one below. Use the exchange rate of $1.00 = 100 yen as a guide.

Ex. You:　　その　くつは　いくらでしたか。

Partner:　　５０ドルぐらいでした。

You: 50ドルは　えんで　いくらですか。

Partner: 5せんえん　ぐらいです。

1. くつ	$	¥	5. ケータイ	$	¥		
2. バッグ	$	¥	6. ぼうし	$	¥		
3. シャツ	$	¥	7. えんぴつ	$	¥		
4. パンツ	$	¥	8. けしゴム	$	¥		

B. SPEAK/LISTEN Price each item pictured below. Ask your partner for his/her prices for each item and write them down on a separate sheet of paper using a chart like the one below. Compare your prices to check whether your communication was correct.

Ex. 「きいろい　シャツ or きいろいのは　いくらですか。」
「あおと　白の　シャツ or あおと　しろのは
いくらですか。」
「しずかな　いぬ or しずかなのは　いくらですか。」

My price				
Partner's price				

	 new	 old	 quiet	 noisy
My price				
Partner's price				

WORKBOOK page 111

かいわ　Dialogue

 READ/LISTEN How much is the chocolate? How many does Emi ask for?

> この　　チョコレートは　いかがですか。
> とても　おいしいですよ。
> それに、やすいです。

> いくらですか。

> 3ドルです。

> わあ、　やすいですねえ。一つ　ください。

たんご　Vocabulary

1. たかい
[い Adj]
expensive

2. やすい
[い Adj]
cheap

3. おいしい
[い Adj]
delicious

4. まずい
[い Adj]
unappetizing

5. すごい
[い Adj]

is terrific, terrible

Describes something
extreme

6. すばらしい
[い Adj]

is wonderful

7. ～は
いかがですか。

How about ～?

Polite equivalent of
どうですか

8. わあ！

Wow!

ついか　たんご　Additional Vocabulary

1. すてき   is nice (used by females)

2. かっこいい   is good looking, is stylish

よみましょう　Language in Context

READ/LISTEN/WRITE Read these sentences in Japanese. Write down what food you think is delicious and what food you think is unappetizing.

まずいです。

わあ、すばらしいですねえ！

ぶんかノート　Culture Notes

Compliments in Japan

In Japanese culture, it is generally considered impolite to
receive a compliment without trying to deny it. Often,
people will emphasize their humility by disparaging whatever was complimented.

Example:　A:　What a pretty sweater!

　　　　　B:　Oh no! It is quite old and the color does not suit me well.

This occurs not only with compliments about your possessions, but also about yourself and persons
belonging to your "in-group," deeds you have done, or decisions you have made. Despite these
denials, it is still polite to give compliments.

 Read the above description of the way the Japanese respond to compliments.
Write a short paragraph to a Japanese friend comparing the Japanese reaction to how
someone in your own culture would respond to a compliment. Note: there may
be more than one way to respond!

アクティビティー　Communicative Activities

Pair Work

A. SPEAK/LISTEN　You praise something your partner wears or has, such as his/her accessories,
clothing, etc. Your partner is very humble and denies it. You are curious and ask where he/she bought
the items. Your partner responds with information such as the store where he/she bought it, the price,
etc.

Ex.

Bさんの　とけいは　すごいですねえ。

いいえ、やすかったですよ。

どこで　かいましたか。

(Place)で　かいました。(Price)ドルでした。

そうですか。

B. SPEAK/LISTEN You are a salesperson and want to sell the following items to a customer. Describe each item and try to sell them as expensively as possible. Your partner is a customer and wants to bargain.

Ex. みせの人 (Clerk)： この　チョコレートは　いかがですか。

とても　おいしいですよ。　それに、

やすいです。

きゃく (Customer)： いくらですか。

みせの人： ２ドルです。

きゃく： それは　たかいですねえ。

みせの人： じゃ、１ドル４５セントです。

きゃく： そうですか。　一つ　ください。

Ex.

1.

2.

3.

4.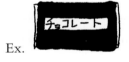

5.

6.

7.

WORKBOOK page 113

Lesson 11
Review

Review Questions

🔊 Ask your partner these questions or say these statements in Japanese. Your partner answers in Japanese. Check your answers using the audio.

Requests & Asking for Permission Review pages 349 and 354

1. Please read this. (Write a *kanji* on a sheet of paper for your partner to read.)

2. Please write your birthdate in *kanji* and read it aloud.

3. May I go to the restroom?

4. May I drink water?

5. May I turn in my homework tomorrow?

6. May I see this watch? [in a showcase in a department store]

Shopping Review pages 358, 364, and 372

7. Please buy one box of chocolate. [You are participating in a fund raising project.]

8. What kind of shirts do you want to buy?

9. Where did you buy your shirt and pants?

10. [Use the pictures below.] How much is the noisy dog?

11. [Use the pictures below.] Which TV is cheap?

12. [Use the pictures below.] Which one do you want to buy?

| $3,400 | $170 | $650 | $300 |

Text Chat

You will participate in a simulated exchange of text-chat messages. You should respond as fully and as appropriately as possible.

You will have a conversation with Keiko Sato, a Japanese high school student, about going to a coffee shop.

5月15日　01:34　PM

ともだちと　きっさてんに
行きますか。

Respond.

5月15日　01:38　PM

コーヒーが　好きですか。
それとも、ティーが
好きですか。

State preference.

5月15日　01:44　PM

日本の　コーヒーは　一ぱい
150円　ぐらいですよ。

Ask a question.

Can Do!
Now I can . . .

☐ make requests

☐ ask politely for permission

☐ count Japanese currency

☐ suggest items to purchase at a store

☐ ask the price of an item at a store

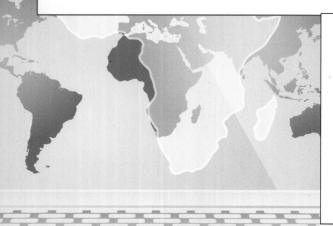

Cost of Living in Japan
にほんの　せいかつひ

RESEARCH Use books, the Internet, or interview a Japanese member of your community to answer the following.

The average income in Japan is roughly the same as the average income in the U.S. However, prices tend to be higher for many things in Japan, which results in a higher cost of living.

Determine

1. How much does an adult movie ticket cost in Japan?

2. How much does a cup of coffee from a きっさてん cost in Japan?

Compare

3. What is the average cost of a cellular phone or smartphone in your country?

4. What is the average cost of a cellular phone or smartphone in Japan?

5. What is the average cost of gasoline where you live?

6. What is the average cost of gasoline in Japan?
   (Note: Gas is sold in liters in Japan. 1 gallon = 3.7 liters)

7. How much does it cost to get a driver's license where you live?

8. How much does it cost to get a a driver's license in Japan?

Extend Your Learning
INFORMATION LITERACY AND PROBLEM SOLVING
Visit the companion website (**cheng-tsui.com/ adventuresinjapanese**) for links to information about average prices in Japan, or search online. Imagine that you are living in Japan with a monthly salary of ¥280,000. Using the information from the website, create a monthly budget. Consider rent, cost of transportation, utilities, food bills (groceries vs. eating out), and cost of entertainment, and allocate your funds appropriately.

ランチタイム
Lunch Time

✓ Can Do!
In this lesson you will learn to

- order food at a fast food restaurant
- use appropriate Japanese expressions when eating a meal
- offer food and drinks or ask for more
- communicate whether you have completed an activity or not
- describe things using multiple adjectives
- relate a sequence of events in one sentence

Online Resources

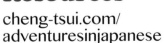

cheng-tsui.com/
adventuresinjapanese

- Audio
- Vocabulary Lists
- Vocabulary Flashcards
- *Kana* and *Kanji* Flashcards
- Activity Worksheets

Kanji
used in this lesson

In this lesson, you will learn several commonly used *kanji* to prepare you for the next level of study.

	Kanji	Meaning	Readings	Examples	
55.	天	heaven	てん	てん 天ぷら てん 天き	tempura weather a big man The Big Man in the sky waits in heaven.
56.	牛	cow	うし ぎゅう	おお うし 大きい牛 ぎゅうにゅう 牛乳	a big cow milk (cow)
57.	良	good	よ(い)	よ 良くないです	is not good A grain of rice and a person is good.
58.	食	to eat	た (べる) しょく	た 食べましょう。 しょくじ 食事を します	Let's eat. to have a meal A good thing for a person to do in his house is to eat rice.
59.	言	to say	い(う)	もう一ど い 言ってください。	Please say it again. Words come from the mouth.
60.	語	language	ご	ご 日本語 えいご 英語	Japanese language English 5 parts (2 eyes, 2 ears, 1 nose) and mouth People speak languages using their mouths and the five other parts of their head.

WORKBOOK page 249

Recognition Kanji

1. 何人〔なにじん〕　What nationality?
   何語〔なにご〕　What language?
   何人〔なんにん〕　How many people?
   何月〔なんがつ〕　What month?

Recognition Kanji

いっぱい
2. 一杯
one
(cupful, glassful, spoonful)

かいわ　Dialogue

 READ/LISTEN　How is Ken feeling? What does Emi suggest they do?

おなかが
ペコペコです。
エミさんは
もう　おひるを
食べましたか。

いいえ、
まだです。

じゃ、
いっしょに
食べませんか。

ええ、
食べましょう。
カフェテリアへ
行きましょう。

ぶんけい　Sentence Patterns

READ Find these patterns in the dialogue.

1. もう ＋ Verb -ました。 　　　　already ～

　　もう　たべました。 　　　　　[(I) already ate.]

2. まだ ＋ Verb (TE form) ＋ いません。 　　(not) yet ～

　　まだ　たべて　いません。 　　　[(I) have not eaten yet.]

3. まだです。 　　　　　　　　　　[Not yet.]

たんご　Vocabulary

1. おなかが　すきました。

I got hungry.

おなかが　ペコペコです。

I am hungry.

おなか means "stomach" and すきました means "became empty." ペコペコ is an onomatopoetic expression suggesting emptiness. 「おなかがすいています。」 also means "I am hungry."

2. のどが　かわきました。

I got thirsty.

のどが　カラカラです。

I am thirsty.

のど means "throat" and かわきました means "became dry." カラカラ is an onomatopoetic expression suggesting dryness. 「のどが　かわいています。」 also means "I am thirsty."

3. もう＋ Aff.

already

4. いいえ、
まだです。

No, not yet.

5. じゃ

Well then (informal)

6. では

Well then (formal)

よみましょう　Language in Context

🔊 **READ/LISTEN** Read these sentences in Japanese. Have you done your homework yet?

まだ　しゅくだいを　して
いません。

のどが　カラカラです。

ぶんぽう　Grammar

(A)　Adverbs

"Already" Adverb もう

もう ＋ **Verb** -ました。　　　　　　　**already**

まだです。　　　　　　　　　　　**not yet**

When used with an affirmative predicate, もう means "already." A simple negative response to a もう question is まだです。

🔊 MODELS

1. 「もう　おひるごはんを　食べましたか。」
   "Did you already eat lunch?"

   「いいえ、　まだです。」
   "No, not yet."

2. 「もう　しゅくだいを　だしましたか。」
   "Did you already turn in your homework?"

   「いいえ、　まだです。」
   "No, not yet."

"Not Yet" Adverb まだ

まだ ＋ **Verb (TE form)** ＋ いません。　(not) yet 〜

This is used to state that a certain action has not yet occured.

MODELS

1. 「もう　おひるごはんを　食べましたか。」
   "Did you already eat lunch?"

   「いいえ、まだ　食べて　いません。」
   "No, I have not eaten yet."

2. 「もう　しゅくだいを　しましたか。」
   "Did you already do your homework?"

   「いいえ、まだ　して　いません。」
   "No, I have not done it yet."

READ Choose the correct adverb or verb form from the options in the ( ) for each sentence.

1. ケン：（もう ／ まだ）　この　えいがを　見ましたか。

   エミ：いいえ、（もう ／ まだ）です。

2. 先生：（もう ／ まだ）　この　本を　よみましたか。

   ケン：いいえ、まだ　（よみませんでした／よんで　いません）。

ぶんかノート　Culture Notes

Fast Food in Japan

Because of the increasingly fast pace of life, fast food is very popular in Japan, especially among young people. Many famous fast-food franchises from the U.S. are common in urban areas and can even be found in remote towns throughout Japan. Other "native" fast food chains, which are designed and operated like their U.S. counterparts, are also very popular.

おべんとうやさん

The concept of "fast food," however, has long been a part of Japanese eating habits. Noodle shops near train stations are always crowded with people who literally drop in, gobble up a bowl of noodles while standing, and rush off in several minutes. おべんとう (boxed lunches) bought at stores can also be considered an early form of fast food.

 Choose a U.S. fast food chain that also operates in Japan to research online. Find five examples of how the menu in Japan differs from that of the U.S. and create a slideshow in Japanese with photos of the food to present to your class. You may give further explanation of the foods in English.

アクティビティー　Communicative Activities

Pair Work

A. SPEAK/LISTEN Ask your partner whether he/she has already done the following things.

Ex. Question: もう　おひるごはんを　食べましたか。

Yes Answer: はい、もう　食べました。

No Answers: いいえ、まだです。or いいえ、まだ　食べていません。

1. Eaten lunch
2. Seen a (movie title)
3. Read today's news (ニュース)
4. Listened to (music title)
5. Finished (project title)

B. SPEAK/LISTEN Say the following comments in Japanese. Your partner responds with an appropriate suggestion.

Ex. I am hungry.

おなかが　すきました。

じゃ、おひるごはんを　食べましょうか。

はい、そう　しましょう。

1. I am thirsty.
2. I have a headache.
3. I am tired.
4. I have lots of homework.
5. I have a big exam tomorrow.

WORKBOOK page 117

12か2
How much for everything?

かいわ　Dialogue

🔊 **READ/LISTEN** What does Ken order? How much is all the food?

ケン：　　　ピザを　二つと　コーラを
　　　　　　ください。

みせの人：のみものの　サイズは
　　　　　　S(エス)と　M(エム)と
　　　　　　L(エル)が　あります。

ケン：　　　M(エム)を　ください。

みせの人：ピザは　5ドルで、　コーラは
　　　　　1ドル25セントです。
　　　　　ぜんぶで　6ドル25セントです。

ぶんけい　Sentence Patterns

READ Find these sentence patterns in the dialogue.

1. Noun 1 は　Noun 2 / な Adjective で、Sentence 2 。

   ピザは　　5ドルで、コーラは　1ドル25セントです。

   [Pizza is $5 and cola is $1.25.]

2. 二つ／ぜんぶ で　for two/everything (total)

たんご　Vocabulary

1. ピザ

pizza

2. ハンバーガー

hamburger

3. ホットドッグ

hot dog

4. サンドイッチ

sandwich

5. サラダ

salad

6. フライドポテト

French fries

7. (お)べんとう

box lunch

8. (お)むすび or
(お)にぎり

rice ball

---

9. サイズ

size

10. S(エス)
サイズ

small size

11. M(エム)
サイズ

medium size

12. L(エル)
サイズ

large size

13. ぜんぶ

everything

14. ぜんぶで

for all

で is a totalizing particle.

---

15. Noun 1 は　　Noun 2/な Adjective で、Sentence 2。
Noun 1 is Noun 2/な Adj. **and** Sentence 2.

♻ Review: General counters are used to order foods and drinks.

1	ひとつ 一つ	2	ふたつ 二つ	3	みっつ 三つ	4	よっつ 四つ	5	いつつ 五つ
6	むっつ 六つ	7	ななつ 七つ	8	やっつ 八つ	9	ここのつ 九つ	10	とお 十

ついか　たんご　Additional Vocabulary

1. ラーメン	2. うどん	3. やきそば	4. にくまん
ramen	udon noodles	Chinese fried noodles	Chinese steamed pork bun

よみましょう　Language in Context

🔊 **READ/LISTEN/SPEAK** Read these sentences in Japanese. Say how much in total your lunch usually costs.

おべんとうは　一つ　いくらですか。

ピザは　$5で、コーラは $1.25です。　ぜんぶで $6.25です。

ぶんぽう　Grammar

A Conjoining な Adjective-Ending Sentences

Noun 1 は　　**Noun 2/** な **Adjective** で、**Sentence 2**。
＝**Noun1** は　　**Noun 2/** な **Adjective** です。　そして、**Sentence 2**。

で is the TE form of です and conjoins two sentences. It only can be used when the first sentence ends with a noun or な adjective, but never with a sentence ending with an い adjective or verb.

MODELS

1. あには　大学生で、　今　サンフランシスコに　います。
   My older brother is a college student and is now in San Francisco.

2. いもうとは　小学生で、　ねこが　大好きです。
   My younger sister is an elementary school student and loves cats.

3. 母は　テニスが　好きで、　父は　ゴルフが　好きです。
   My mother likes tennis and my dad likes golf.

4. この　レストランは　きれいで　しずかですね。
   This restaurant is clean and quiet, isn't it?

READ/WRITE Rewrite the following sets of two sentences as one sentence using the appropriate TE form of each adjective.

1. ぼくは　15さいです。そして、中学三年生です。

2. あれは　日本語が　上手です。そして、毎日　ともだちと　日本語で　話します。

B Totalizer で

Amount + Counter + で

で totalizes the quantity word it follows and may be translated as "for."

MODELS

1. この　シャツは　2まいで　30ドルです。 This shirt is $30 for two.

2. 「いくらですか。」 "How much is it?"

   「ぜんぶで　4ドル　50セントです。」 "It is $4.50 for all."

READ/WRITE Write the correct amount and counter or total in each blank and the correct particle in each ( ).

1. サンドイッチは　一つ　8ドルでした。＿1＿　（　）16ドルでした。

2. おむすびは　一つ　3ドルでした。＿2＿　（　）9ドルでした。

3. ピザは　5ドルで、コーラは　1ドル25セントでした。＿3＿　（　）6ドル25セントでした。

ぶんかノート　Culture Notes

A. Japanese Lunches

Lunch in Japan varies widely. Lunch may mean eating (お) べんとう (home lunches). (お) べんとう often consist of rice or rice balls, pickled and/or cooked vegetables, and some form of protein. Lunch may also mean eating at a company or school cafeteria that offers full hot meals and hot noodles. More and more, young Japanese enjoy fast food meals such as hamburgers and pizzas for lunch. Some people return home for lunch. Others may go out to a relaxing lunch at a restaurant. One can find almost any kind of food in the urban areas of Japan. Besides Japanese foods, Chinese, Italian, and American foods are popular.

ファストフードのおみせ

B. U.S. versus Japanese Sizes

Food portions and clothing sizes are generally smaller in Japan than in America. For example, at most fast food restaurants in Japan, medium sodas come in 16 oz (500 mL) cups; in the U.S. they come in 21 oz (620 mL) cups. When Japanese people order drinks at fast food stores in the U.S., they are often surprised that the portions are so large.

 There are approximately 11 calories in a fluid ounce of cola. Based on the information above, calculate how many calories are in an average medium cola in Japan and in the U.S.

Pair Work

A. SPEAK/LISTEN First, create a menu by determining prices for the items below with your partner. You and your partner will play a clerk and a customer at a snack bar. The customer orders lunch, a snack, and a drink. Then the clerk gives the price of each item, then the total cost. Take turns in each role.

メニュー

たべもの		スナック		のみもの	
ピザ	$____	ポテトチップ	$____	ミルク	$____
ハンバーガー	$____	コーンチップ	$____	オレンジジュース	$____
ホットドッグ	$____	プレッツル	$____		
サンドイッチ	$____	ケーキ	$____	コーラ	
フライドポテト	$____	ジェロ	$____	ソーダ	
サラダ	$____	アイスクリーム	$____	アイスティー	
フルーツサラダ	$____	チョコレート	$____	L	$____
べんとう	$____	キャンディ	$____	M	$____
にぎり	$____	ガム	$____	S	$____

Ex. 2 sandwiches, 1 large cola

Customer: サンドイッチを　二つと　L(エル)サイズの　コーラを　一つ　ください。

Worker: サンドイッチは　ふたつで　$__で、

(エル)サイズの　コーラは　ひとつ(で)　$__です。

ぜんぶで　$__です。

Order the following:

1. 2 slices of pizza, 1 bag of potato chips, 1 large size cola

2. 1 hot dog, 1 order of French fries, 1 medium soda

3. 1 salad, 2 rice balls, 1 orange juice

4. 1 *bento*, 1 jello, 1 small iced tea

5. (Your own choice)

WORKBOOK page 119

かいわ　Dialogue

🔊 **READ/LISTEN** What did Ken forget? What does Emi ask for?

あっ、　フォークを
わすれました。
エミさんも　フォークが
いりますか。

いいえ、　けっこうです。
私は　おはしで　食べます。
でも、お水を　一杯
おねがいします。

たんご　Vocabulary

🔊

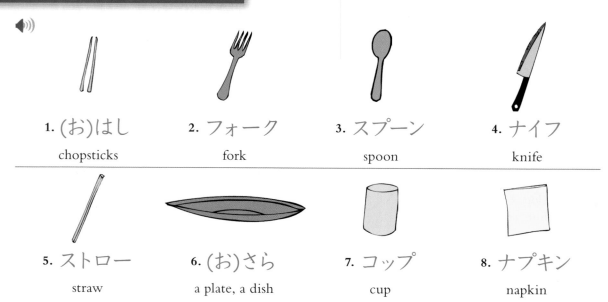

1. (お)はし
chopsticks

2. フォーク
fork

3. スプーン
spoon

4. ナイフ
knife

5. ストロー
straw

6. (お)さら
a plate, a dish

7. コップ
cup

8. ナプキン
napkin

9. cupful, glassful, bowlful, spoonful		
1	いっぱい	一杯
2	にはい	二杯
3	さんばい	三杯
4	よんはい	四杯
5	ごはい	五杯
6	ろっぱい	六杯
7	ななはい	七杯
8	はっぱい	八杯
9	きゅうはい	九杯
10	じゅっぱい	十杯
?	なんばい	何杯

10. フォークで

with a fork

11. いいえ、
けっこうです。

No, thank you.

12. わすれました
[わすれる/わすれて]

I forgot.

13. 〜が いります
[いる/いって]

need 〜

14. 〜を かして ください。
[かします/かす]

Please lend me 〜.

ついか たんご　Additional Vocabulary

1. (お)さとう　　　sugar

2. しお　　　　　　salt

3. こしょう　　　　pepper

4. ケチャップ　　　ketchup

5. ドレッシング　　dressing

READ/LISTEN/WRITE Read these sentences in Japanese. Write down what you eat with.

うどんを　おはしで　食べます。

お水を　一ぱい
おねがいします。

ぶんぽう Grammar

A Means Particle で ─────────

Means ＋で

This particle で is the same で used after a mode of transportation, a language, or any means of doing an action seen in earlier lessons (see Lessons 4 and 7). It tells how an action is done, or the means by which it is done.

 MODELS

1. この　しゅくだいを　えんぴつで　かきました。
   I wrote this homework with a pencil.

2. 「おはしで　食べますか。」　　　"Do you eat with chopsticks?"

   「いいえ、フォークで　食べます。」　"No, I eat with a fork."

READ Choose the best word to complete each sentence from the options in the ( ).

1. 私は　サラダを　（フォーク / スプーン / ナイフ）で
　食べます。

2. フライドポテトを　（手 / あし / はし）で　食べます。

3. 毎日　学校へ　（どれ / どこ / 何）で　行きますか。

ぶんかノート　Culture Notes

How to Hold Chopsticks (はし)

Hold the chopsticks slightly toward the thick end as shown above. Keeping the lower chopstick steady, move the upper one with a scissor-like action and pinch the food between the tip of the upper chopstick and the tip of the lower one.

 Follow the instructions above and practice picking up small objects with a pair of chopsticks (you can use a pair of pencils if no chopsticks are available). Once you've mastered using chopsticks, create a set of instructions and use them to teach your family members how to use chopsticks.

アクティビティー　Communicative Activities

Pair Work

A. SPEAK/LISTEN Ask your partner how he/she does the following things.

　Ex. eat rice.　You:　ごはんを　何で　食べますか。
　　　　　　Partner:　おはしで　食べます。

1. Eat spaghetti （スパゲッティ）

2. Eat steak （ステーキ）

3. Eat おべんとう

4. Eat stew （シチュー）

5. Drink milk

6. Eat むすび

7. Eat salad

B. SPEAK/LISTEN Offer the following items to your partner. He/she should accept or decline.

Ex. one rice ball. You: おむすびを　ひとつ　どうぞ。

Partner: どうも　ありがとう。 or いいえ、けっこうです。

1. One cup of tea
2. One piece of sushi
3. One cup of hot coffee
4. One piece of chocolate
5. One sandwich

C. SPEAK/LISTEN Say the following statements in Japanese. Your partner should respond appropriately with a helpful suggestion.

Ex. I forgot my money.

あっ、お金を　わすれました。

そうですか。　お金が　いりますか。

1. Please lend me money.
2. I need a car.
3. Oh, I forgot my homework.
4. Please lend me a pencil.

Class Work - Chopstick Race

D. SPEAK Bring chopsticks and dry beans to class. See how many beans each person can pick up with chopsticks in one minute. Count them in Japanese.

Reading

E. READ/WRITE Read the following e-mail from a Japanese student. Answer the questions below in Japanese using complete sentences.

私は　ピザや　スパゲッティが　大好きですが、サラダが
きらいです。ピザを　手で　食べますが、スパゲッティは
フォークで　食べます。でも、ラーメンは　おはしで　食べます。
今日　ばんごはんに　ピザを　三まい　食べたいです。

UNDERSTAND

1. What food does the writer like to eat?
2. How does the writer eat ramen?
3. What does the writer want to eat for dinner?

APPLY

4. How do you eat foods that you like?
5. Write an e-mail responding to the student. Describe the foods you like and how you eat them.

WORKBOOK page 121

かいわ　Dialogue

🔊 **READ/LISTEN** What does Ken say before eating? How does Emi describe her food?

ぶんけい　Sentence Patterns

READ Find this pattern in the dialogue.

Noun 1 は	い Adj. (-くて)、	Sentence 2 。	[The exam is long and difficult.]
しけんは	ながくて、	むずかしいです。	

1. つめたい [い Adj.]

cold (to the touch)

2. あたたかい [い Adj.]

warm

3. もう（いっぱい）

(one) more (cup)

4. いただきます。

Used before beginning a meal.

Literally means
"I will receive."

5. ごちそうさま。

Used upon finishing a meal.

Literally means
"It was a feast."

6. おなかが
いっぱいです。

I am full.

Literally means
"The stomach is full."

よみましょう　Language in Context

READ/LISTEN/SPEAK Read these sentences in Japanese. Offer a classmate a cup of tea or water.

おちゃを　もう　一ぱい　どうぞ。

コーヒーは
あたたかくて、おいしいです。

ぶんぽう　Grammar

A Conjoining い Adjective-Ending Sentences

い **Adjective** ＋くて、**Sentence2**。

When conjoining a sentence ending with an い adjective with another sentence, the final –*i* ending syllable of the adjective in the first sentence is dropped and replaced by –くて, then attached to the next sentence. The tense of the entire sentence is determined by the tense of the sentence ending. The TE form of いい is よくて.

🔊 MODELS

1. 日本語の　じゅぎょうは　おもしろくて、たのしいです。
   Japanese class is interesting and fun.

2. カフェテリアの　食べものは　すこし　まずくて、
   たかいですね。
   The cafeteria's food is a little unappetizing and expensive, isn't it?

3. きのうの　しけんは　ながくて、むずかしかったです。
   Yesterday's exam was long and difficult.

4. あの　先生は　やさしくて、いいです。
   That teacher is kind and (she is) good.

READ/WRITE Rewrite the following sets of two sentences as one sentence using the appropriate TE form of each adjective.

1. ジュースは　つめたいです。
   そして、おいしいです。

2. 日本語の　べんきょうは
   たのしいです。そして、
   大好きです。

3. この　レストランは　きれいです。
   そして、しずかです。

A. Eating Japanese Noodles

The many varieties of noodles in Japan make them a popular dish. Though noodles are also served fried, most noodles are prepared in soup. When eating noodles, Japanese people will often noisily slurp them down. While in the U.S. slurping is considered a sign of bad manners, in Japan it is a sign that you are enjoying your noodles.

うどん　noodles

B. いただきます and ごちそうさま

いただきます

An important pre-meal
Japanese ritual

Before and after meals, Japanese people always say the appropriate いただきます and ごちそうさま expressions. Sometimes, they will also briefly place their hands together as if in prayer and slightly bow their heads as they speak. By saying いただきます and bowing, you are humbly expressing gratitude for all of those who have contributed to making the meal possible, as well as all who have worked or sacrificed to provide the food.

Likewise, when closing the meal with ごちそうさま, you are expresses thanks for the preparation of the bountiful meal. When with family, you may simply say, ごちそうさま at the end of the meal. When eating alone, people often dispense with the expressions, but may still express thankfulness by bowing slightly and placing their hands together.

Does your family practice any before or after meal rituals or use expressions like those in Japan? Write a short essay comparing your family's eating rituals with those of Japan. Do they change when you are with your family, friends, or alone?

アクティビティー Communicative Activities

Pair Work

A. SPEAK/LISTEN Ask your partner for his/her opinion of the following. Your partner comments using two descriptive words in one sentence.

Ex. cafeteria food
カフェテリアの　食べものは　どうですか。

おいしくて、やすいです。

1. (Famous restaurant's) food
2. (Fast food restaurant's) food
3. School cafeteria's spaghetti
4. (Teacher)
5. (Class)

6. (School)
7. (Library)
8. (Someone's) house
9. (Japanese classroom)
10. (Friend)

B. SPEAK/LISTEN Role play the following skit with your partner.

A U.S. student stays over at his/her Japanese friend's house in Japan. The Japanese student's mother makes a Japanese-style breakfast for the U.S. student and serves it on the table. The Japanese mother speaks only Japanese. Use appropriate body language.

アメリカ人：　おはよう　ございます。

お母さん　：　おはよう。よく　ねましたか。

アメリカ人：　はい。 \<Sits at a table.\>

お母さん　：　あさごはんを　どうぞ。

アメリカ人：　ありがとう　ございます。いただきます。

\<Eats most of the food.\>

お母さん　：　ごはんを　もう　いっぱい　いかがですか。

アメリカ人：　いいえ、　けっこうです。もう　おなかが
　　　　　　　いっぱいです。ごちそうさま。

WORKBOOK page 123

12か5
I go to the library and do homework

かいわ　Dialogue

🔊 **READ/LISTEN**　What is Emi doing at 1:00? What will Ken do?

これから　何が　ありますか。

1時から　えい語の　じゅぎょうが
あります。

ぼくは　今　としょかんへ
行って、しゅくだいを　します。
じゃ、また　あとでね。

バイバイ。

ぶんけい　Sentence Patterns

READ Find this pattern in the dialogue.

Sentence 1　+　Verb (TE form)　、+　Sentence 2　。

テレビを　見て、　ねます。　[I will watch TV, and (then) go to bed.]

たんご　Vocabulary

1. じゃ、また　あとで。

Well then, see you later.

「では、また　あとで。」 is a formal
equivalent.

2. バイバイ。

Good–bye.

Used informally only.

3. これから

From now on

4. それから

And then

よみましょう　Language in Context

 READ/LISTEN Read these sentences in Japanese. Describe the function the TE form has in each sentence in English.

べんきょう　して、テレビを
見ます。

お水は　つめたくて、おいしいです。

ぶんぽう　Grammar

A Conjoining Verb-ending Sentences with the Verb TE Form

Sentence 1 (Verb TE form)、Sentence 2。

To conjoin two sentences with "and" when the first of the two sentences ends with a verb, convert the verb in the first sentence into its TE form and attach the second sentence.

A sequence of actions may be described using this construction. The first sentence occurs chronologically before the second. The tense of the sentence is determined by the last verb.

1. あさごはんを　食べて、しんぶんを　よみます。
   I eat breakfast and read the newspaper.

2. テレビを　見て、しゅくだいを　して、それから　ねます。
   I watch television, do homework, and then go to bed.

3. うちへ　かえって、それから　何を　しますか。
   You go home and then what do you do?

READ/WRITE Rewrite the following sets of two sentences as one sentence using the approriate TE form of each verb.

1. あさ　おきます。それから、あさごはんを　食べます。

2. うちへ　かえります。それから、テレビを　見ました。

3. 今　としょかんへ　行きます。そして、しゅくだいを　します。

B Summary of Conjoining Sentences

Sentence Endings	Conjoining Sentences
Noun ending	ピザは　2ドルで、べんとうは　5ドルです。 Pizza is $2 and *bento* is $5.
な Adjective ending	この　みせは　きれいで、しずかです。 This store is clean and quiet.
い Adjective ending	この　べんとうは　やすくて、おいしいです。 This box lunch is cheap and delicious.
Verb ending	うちへ　かえって、ねました。 I went home and went to bed.

READ/WRITE Rewrite the following sets of two sentences as one sentence using the appropriate noun, verb, or adjective form for each.

1. この　レストランは　おいしいです。そして、やすいです。

2. 私は　ごはんが　好きです。そして、毎日　食べます。

3. おべんとうは　7ドルでした。そして、おちゃは
   1ドル50セントでした。

4. レストランで　おひるを　食べました。そして、うちへ
かえりました。

ぶんかノート　Culture Notes

しょうゆ and みそ

Shoyu or "soy sauce" and *miso* "soy bean paste" are
two distinctive Japanese seasonings. みそ is made
by crushing boiled soybeans, adding salt and malted
rice, wheat, barley or beans. The paste is allowed to mature for as long as several years to draw
out its flavor. Different kinds of みそ are produced in the different regions of Japan. みそ is most
commonly used in the preparation of みそ soup. しょうゆ is the most common seasoning used in
Japanese cooking. It is made from soy beans also. The soybeans are steamed and mixed with roasted
wheat. The mixture is blended with brine and transferred to fermentation tanks for brewing.
しょうゆ is used as a seasoning and dipping sauce.

 Brainstorm a list of seasonings or sauces common in your own country. Then, research
one of the seasonings and describe the ingredients and process by which it is made in a
short paragraph. How do these ingredients and processes compare to those of *miso* and
soy sauce?

アクティビティー　Communicative Activities

Pair Work

SPEAK/LISTEN Interview your partner and ask what he/she has done today since getting up in the
morning. Keep asking questions until you get to the present.

Use 〜て、　〜。

You:　　けさ　おきて、何を　しましたか。

Partner:　けさ　おきて、あさごはんを　食べました。

You:　　あさごはんを　食べて、何を　しましたか。

　　　　　丶　　　　　丶

　　　　　丶　　　　　丶

You:　　これから、何を　しますか。

Partner:　これから、〜。

Lesson 12
Review

Review Questions

Ask your partner these questions in Japanese or say these statements. Your partner answers in Japanese. Check your answers using the audio.

Lunch Time   Review pages 382, 386, 392, and 397

1. Where do you usually eat hamburgers? [Name two places.]

2. Are you hungry? Are you thirsty?

3. Please give me two pizzas and one large size cola. [Give the total price.]

4. What do you eat *bento* with? (utensil)

5. Please have one cookie.

6. Please have a cup of hot coffee.

7. Where are the paper plates?

8. Did you forget your money today?

Japanese Class   Review pages 382 and 402

9. Have you already studied for tomorrow's Japanese exam?

10. Do we need our Japanese textbook today?

11. How is Japanese class? [Use two descriptive words in one sentence.]

12. What (class) do you have after this class?

Descriptives   Review page 404

13. What do Japanese people do at coffee shops? [List two things.]

14. How is the school cafeteria's food? [Use two adjectives in one sentence.]

15. How is your math class? [Use two adjectives in one sentence.]

16. What sports do your father and mother like? [Answer in one sentence.]

17. How is the school library? [Use two adjectives in one sentence.]

18. Do you like cola? Why? [Use two adjectives in one sentence.]

Your Schedule Review page 402

19. What did you do after getting up this morning?

20. Where did you go after you came to school today?

21. What did you do last night after you ate dinner?

Text Chat

You will participate in a simulated exchange of text-chat messages. You should respond as fully and as appropriately as possible.

You will have a conversation with Sachi Matsuda, a Japanese high school student, about lunch.

5月27日　03:45 PM

今日、もう　おひるごはんを
食べましたか。

Respond.

5月27日　03:48 PM

学校の　カフェテリアの
食べものは　どうですか。

Give at least two descriptions.

5月27日　03:54 PM

私は　毎日　母の
おべんとうを　食べますよ。

Ask a question.

Can Do!
Now I can . . .

☐ order food at a fast food restaurant

☐ use the appropriate Japanese expressions to begin or finish a meal

☐ offer more food or drinks to my friends or ask for more

☐ tell a friend whether I completed an activity or not

☐ describe my school, my classes, and more using multiple adjectives

☐ relate several activities I did in one sentence

Making Mochi
おもち Rice Cakes

What is Mochi?

Mochi, or rice cake, is made from a sticky variety of rice that is steamed, then kneaded by machine or pounded with a mallet in a mortar. It is usually formed into small round flattened mounds or cut into small rectangular blocks.

Mochi came to Japan from Southeast Asia at the same time rice cultivation was introduced. Originally, *mochi* was offered to the gods at shrines. Later, it was eaten on various festive occasions. *Mochi* first appeared at New Year's celebrations sometime during the eighth through tenth centuries. It was used primarily as a decoration called *kagamimochi*. One round *mochi* was placed on a slightly larger one, decorated festively with many symbolic foods and other items, and displayed in homes and businesses. Later, the tradition of eating *ozoni*, or *mochi* soup, on New Year's morning, began.

Because *mochi* is considered good luck, it is also part of other festive occasions including weddings, children's festivals, housewarmings, special birthdays, and other happy celebrations. Though there are many theories, *mochi* is considered a good luck symbol, because of its round, never-ending shape (like a wedding band), its sticky consistency (which symbolizes a family or a couple who will always "stick together"), and the sound of the word, (the verb *mochi*masu means "to have or possess," suggesting wealth). Also, rice in any form is traditionally considered a symbol of prosperity in Japan.

Mochi can be prepared in a variety of ways. It can be eaten plain, in soups, grilled, fried, flavored with various toppings, or most commonly, filled with sweetened red bean paste.

Microwave もち

Ingredients: 1 pkg. *mochiko* (a sweet rice flour—look for it online or in Asian groceries)
2 cups water
1 cup   sugar
1/4 tsp. vanilla
2 drops red or green food coloring
kinako (soy bean powder)/*katakuriko* (potato starch)

1. In a medium bowl, combine *mochiko*, water, sugar, vanilla and food coloring.

2. Mix until smooth.

3. Pour mixture into a greased 5-cup microwavable tube pan.

4. Cover with plastic wrap and cook on medium high for 10 minutes.

5. Pour *mochi* from tube pan into a rectangular baking pan and cool.

6. Loosen *mochi* by running a knife* around the inner and outer edges of the pan.

* Use a plastic knife or a knife wrapped in plastic wrap.

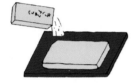

7. Remove to a board or platter dusted with *kinako* or *katakuriko* and cool.

8. Cut into serving pieces.

9. Coat with *kinako* or *katakuriko*.

Home-School Connection

Making Mochi
おもち Rice cake

My child made *mochi*!

Have fun!   Get your parent/guardian's signature.

Appendix A

Numbers and Counters

1か5 1～10	1か6 11～20	1か6 10～100
いち	じゅういち	じゅう
に	じゅうに	にじゅう
さん	じゅうさん	さんじゅう
し, よん	じゅうし	よんじゅう
ご	じゅうご	ごじゅう
ろく	じゅうろく	ろくじゅう
しち, なな	じゅうしち, じゅうなな	ななじゅう
はち	じゅうはち	はちじゅう
く, きゅう	じゅうく	きゅうじゅう
じゅう	にじゅう	ひゃく

	2か5 Flat Objects	2か5 Round or Unclassified Objects	3か1 People
1	いちまい	ひとつ	ひとり
2	にまい	ふたつ	ふたり
3	さんまい	みっつ	さんにん
4	よんまい	よっつ	よにん
5	ごまい	いつつ	ごにん
6	ろくまい	むっつ	ろくにん
7	ななまい	ななつ	ななにん
8	はちまい	やっつ	はちにん
9	きゅうまい	ここのつ	きゅうにん
10	じゅうまい	とお	じゅうにん
?	なんまい?	いくつ?	なんにん?

2か6 Days of the Month					
1	ついたち	11	じゅういちにち	21	にじゅういちにち
2	ふつか	12	じゅうににち	22	にじゅうににち
3	みっか	13	じゅうさんにち	23	にじゅうさんにち
4	よっか	14	じゅうよっか	24	にじゅうよっか
5	いつか	15	じゅうごにち	25	にじゅうごにち
6	むいか	16	じゅうろくにち	26	にじゅうろくにち
7	なのか	17	じゅうしちにち	27	にじゅうしちにち
8	ようか	18	じゅうはちにち	28	にじゅうはちにち
9	ここのか	19	じゅうくにち	29	にじゅうくにち
10	とおか	20	はつか	30	さんじゅうにち
?	なんにち?			31	さんじゅういちにち

	3か1 Ages	2か6 Months	3か3 Grades	2か7 Hours	7か2 Minutes
1	いっさい	いちがつ	いちねんせい	いちじ	いっぷん
2	にさい	にがつ	にねんせい	にじ	にふん
3	さんさい	さんがつ	さんねんせい	さんじ	さんぷん
4	よんさい	しがつ	よねんせい	よじ	よんぷん
5	ごさい	ごがつ		ごじ	ごふん
6	ろくさい	ろくがつ		ろくじ	ろっぷん
7	ななさい	しちがつ		しちじ	ななふん
8	はっさい	はちがつ		はちじ	はっぷん
9	きゅうさい	くがつ		くじ	きゅうふん
10	じゅっさい	じゅうがつ		じゅうじ	じゅっぷん
11	じゅういっさい	じゅういちがつ		じゅういちじ	
	20 はたち	12 じゅうにがつ		じゅうにじ	
?	なんさい?	なんがつ?	なんねんせい?	なんじ?	なんぷん?

	8か3 Large, Mechanized Goods	8か3 Birds	8か3 Small Animals	8か3 Long, Cylindrical Objects	12か3 Cupful, Spoonful, Etc.
1	いちだい	いちわ	いっぴき	いっぽん	いっぱい
2	にだい	にわ	にひき	にほん	にはい
3	さんだい	さんわ	さんびき	さんぼん	さんばい
4	よんだい	よんわ	よんひき	よんほん	よんはい
5	ごだい	ごわ	ごひき	ごほん	ごはい
6	ろくだい	ろくわ	ろっぴき	ろっぽん	ろっぱい
7	ななだい	ななわ	ななひき	ななほん	ななはい
8	はちだい	はちわ	はっぴき	はっぽん	はっぱい
9	きゅうだい	きゅうわ	きゅうひき	きゅうほん	きゅうはい
10	じゅうだい	じゅうわ	じゅっぴき	じゅっぽん	じゅっぱい
?	なんだい?	なんわ?	なんびき?	なんぼん?	なんばい?

Abbreviations of Grammar Term References

A	い Adjective	atsui, takai, shiroi
Adv	Adverb	totemo, amari, sukoshi
C	Copula	desu, de, na
Da	Adjectival Derivative	-tai
Dv	Verbal Derivative	masu, mashoo, masen
Exp	Expression	chotto matte kudasai
N	Noun	hana, kuruma, enpitsu
Na	な Adjective	kirei, joozu, suki, yuumei
Nd	Dependent Noun	-doru, -han
Ni	Interrogative Noun	dare, doko, ikura
Num	Number	ichi, juu, hyaku, sen
P	Particle	de, e, ni
Pc	Clause Particle	kara, ga
PN	Pre-Noun	donna, kono, ano
SI	Sentence Interjective	anoo, eeto
SP	Sentence Particle	ka, yo, ne, nee
V	Verb	
V1	Verb (group) 1	ikimasu, hanashimasu, nomimasu
V2	Verb (group) 2	tabemasu, nemasu, imasu
V3	Verb (group) 3 [irregular verb]	kimasu, shimasu

Japanese-English Glossary

Japanese (transliterated)	Japanese (かな)	Japanese (漢字)	Lesson	Type	English
A					
aimasu	あいます	会います	10-5	V1	meet
aka	あか	赤	5-5	N	red
akai	あかい	赤い	6-3	A	red
akemasu	あけます	開けます	11-2	V2	open
akete kudasai	あけてください	開けて下さい	2-2	Exp	Please open.
aki	あき	秋	10-4	N	autumn, fall
amari	あまり	余	5-4	Adv	(not) very
ame	あめ	雨	1-6	N	rain
ame	あめ	飴	2-5	N	candy
amerika	アメリカ		3-4	N	America
amerikajin	アメリカじん	アメリカ人	3-4	N	U.S. citizen
anata	あなた		2-4	N	you
anatano	あなたの		2-4	N	yours
ane	あね	姉	3-1	N	(my) older sister
ani	あに	兄	3-1	N	(my) older brother
ano	あの		2-4	PN	that ~ over there
anoo...	あのう...		2-1	SI	let me see ... , well ...
ao	あお	青	5-5	N	blue
aoi	あおい	青い	6-3	A	blue
arabiago	アラビアご	アラビア語	4-1	N	Arabic language
are	あれ		1-5	N	that one over there
arigatoo	ありがとう		1-4	Exp	Thank you.
arigatoo gozaimasu	ありがとうございます		1-4	Exp	Thank you very much.
arimasu	あります		8-1	V1	there is (inanimate obj.)
arimasu	あります		9-1	V1	have
aruite [arukimasu]	あるいて [あるきます]	歩いて [歩きます]	7-3	V1	walk
asa	あさ	朝	4-3	N	morning
asagohan	あさごはん	朝御飯	4-3	N	breakfast
asatte	あさって	明後日	9-3	N	day after tomorrow

Japanese (transliterated)	Japanese (かな)	Japanese (漢字)	Lesson	Type	English
ashi	あし	脚	6-1	N	leg
ashi	あし	足	6-1	N	foot
ashita	あした	明日	4-3	N	tomorrow
ashiyubi	あしゆび	足指	6-1	N	toe
asobimasu	あそびます	遊びます	9-5	V1	play, amuse (not for sports/music)
asoko	あそこ		2-5	N	over there
atama	あたま	頭	6-1	N	head
atarashii	あたらしい	新しい	8-4	A	new
atatakai	あたたかい	暖かい	12-4	A	warm
(-no) ato de	(〜の) あとで	(〜の) 後で	10-5	Pc	after ~
atsui	あつい	暑い	1-6	A	hot (temperature)

B

Japanese (transliterated)	Japanese (かな)	Japanese (漢字)	Lesson	Type	English
baibai	バイバイ		12-5	Exp	bye bye
baiten	ばいてん	売店	4-4	N	snack bar; kiosk
ban	ばん	晩	4-3	N	evening
bando	バンド		9-5	N	band
bangohan	ばんごはん	晩御飯	4-3	N	dinner, supper
baree(booru)	バレー(ボール)		5-3	N	volleyball
basu	バス		7-3	N	bus
basuketto(booru)	バスケット(ボール)		5-3	N	basketball
beddo	ベッド		8-5	N	bed
bengoshi	べんごし	弁護士	3-5	N	lawyer
benkyoo (o) shimasu	べんきょう	勉強(を)します	4-4	V3	study
bentoo	べんとう	弁当	12-2	N	box lunch
bijutsu	びじゅつ	美術	9-1	N	art
boku	ぼく	僕	1-1	N	I (used by males)
bokutachi	ぼくたち	僕達	10-3	N	we [used by males.]
boorupen	ボールペン		2-3	N	ballpoint pen
booshi	ぼうし	帽子	2-3	N	cap, hat
bosuton	ボストン		7-5	N	Boston
burajiru	ブラジル		3-4	N	Brazil
buta	ぶた	豚	8-5	N	pig
byooin	びょういん	病院	3-5	N	hospital
byooki	びょうき	病気	10-1	N	illness, sickness

C

Japanese (transliterated)	Japanese (かな)	Japanese (漢字)	Lesson	Type	English
chairo	ちゃいろ	茶色	5-5	N	brown color

Japanese (transliterated)	Japanese (かな)	Japanese (漢字)	Lesson	Type	English
chairoi	ちゃいろい	茶色い	6-3	A	brown
chakuseki	ちゃくせき	着席	1-3	Exp	Sit.
chichi	ちち	父	3-1	N	(my) father
chiimu	チーム		10-3	N	team
chiisai	ちいさい	小さい	6-2	A	small
chikai	ちかい	近い	8-5	A	near, close
chikatetsu	ちかてつ	地下鉄	7-3	N	subway
chikoku desu	ちこくです	遅刻です	1-3	Exp	tardy
chokoreeto	チョコレート		2-5	N	chocolate
chotto	ちょっと		4-1	Adv	a little [more colloquial than すこし]
chotto matte kudasai	ちょっとまってください	ちょっと待って下さい	1-4	Exp	Please wait a minute.
chuugaku	ちゅうがく	中学	3-3	N	intermediate school
chuugaku ichinensei	ちゅうがくいちねんせい	中学一年生	3-3	N	int. school 1st-year student (U.S. 7th grader)
chuugaku ninensei	ちゅうがくにねんせい	中学二年生	3-3	N	int. school 2nd-year student (U.S. 8th grader)
chuugaku sannensei	ちゅうがくさんねんせい	中学三年生	3-3	N	int. school 3rd-year student (U.S. 9th grader)
chuugakusei	ちゅうがくせい	中学生	3-3	N	int. school student
chuugoku	ちゅうごく	中国	3-4	N	China
chuugokugo	ちゅうごくご	中国語	4-1	N	Chinese language

D

Japanese (transliterated)	Japanese (かな)	Japanese (漢字)	Lesson	Type	English
~ dai	～だい	～台	8-3	Nd	[counter for mechanized goods]
daigaku	だいがく	大学	10-5	N	college, university
daigakusei	だいがくせい	大学生	10-5	N	college student
daiji	だいじ	大事	10-4	Na	important
daijoobu	だいじょうぶ	大丈夫	10-1	Na	all right
daikirai	だいきらい	大嫌い	5-2	Na	dislike a lot, hate
~ dashite kudasai	～だしてください	～出して下さい	2-2	Exp	Please turn in ~.
daisuki	だいすき	大好き	5-2	Na	like very much, love
dame	だめ	駄目	2-1	Na	no good
dansu	ダンス		5-1	N	dance, dancing
dare	だれ	誰	3-1	Ni	who
dashimasu	だします	出します	11-2	V1	turn in

Japanese (transliterated)	Japanese (かな)	Japanese (漢字)	Lesson	Type	English
[counter] de	[counter] で		12-2	N	[totalizing particle]
[place] de [action verb]	[place] で [action verb]		4-1	P	[doing something] at, in [a place]
[tool] de	[tool] で		12-3	P	with [tool]
[tool] de	[tool] で		4-5	P	by, with, on, in [tool particle]
[transportation] de	[transportation] で		7-3	P	by [transportation mode]
demo	でも		4-1	SI	But [at beginning of sentence]
densha	でんしゃ	電車	7-3	N	electric train
denwa	でんわ	電話	4-5	N	telephone
depaato	デパート		7-4	N	department store
desu	です		1-1	C	am, is, are
dewa	では		12-1	Exp	well then [formal]
doa	ドア		2-2	N	door
doko	どこ		3-4	Ni	where?
doko emo	どこへも		7-4	Ni+P	(not to) anywhere
dokusho	どくしょ	読書	5-1	N	reading
donna ~?	どんな~		5-2	PN	what kind of ~?
dono ~?	どの~		11-4	Nd	which ~?
doo desu ka	どうですか		7-5	Exp	how is it? [informal]
doo shimashita ka	どうしましたか		10-1	Exp	What happened?
doo itashimashite	どういたしまして		1-4	Exp	You are welcome.
doomo	どうも		1-4	Exp	Thank you.
dooshite?	どうして		9-3	Ni	why?
doozo yoroshiku	どうぞよろしく		1-1	N	Nice to meet you.
dore?	どれ		11-4	Ni	which one?
doru	ドル		11-4	Nd	dollar(s)
doyoobi	どようび	土曜日	2-7	N	Saturday

E

Japanese (transliterated)	Japanese (かな)	Japanese (漢字)	Lesson	Type	English
e	え	絵	5-1	N	painting, drawing
[place] e	[place] へ		7-2	P	to [place]
ee	ええ		1-5	SI	no [informal]
eeto...	ええと...		2-1	SI	let me see ... , well ...
eiga	えいが	映画	5-1	N	movie
eigo	えいご	英語	4-1	N	English
emu-saizu	エムサイズ		12-2	N	medium size

Japanese (transliterated)	Japanese (かな)	Japanese (漢字)	Lesson	Type	English
en	えん	円	11-4	Nd	yen
enjinia	エンジニア		3-5	N	engineer
enpitsu	えんぴつ	鉛筆	2-3	N	pencil
enpitsukezuri	えんぴつけずり	鉛筆削り	8-1	N	pencil sharpener
eru-saizu	エルサイズ		12-2	N	large size
esu-saizu	エスサイズ		12-2	N	small size
F					
fooku	フォーク		12-3	N	fork
~fun	～ふん	～分	7-1	Nd	minute
fune	ふね	船	7-3	N	boat, ship
furaidopoteto	フライドポテト		12-2	N	french fries
furansu	フランス		3-4	N	France
furansugo	フランスご	フランス語	4-1	N	French language
furorida	フロリダ		7-5	N	Florida
furui	ふるい	古い	8-4	A	old (not for person's age)
futari	ふたり	二人	3-1	N	two people
futatsu	ふたつ	二つ	2-5	N	two [general counter]
futotte imasu	ふとっています	太っています	6-4	V1	(is) fat
futsuka	ふつか	二日	2-6	N	2nd day of the month
futtobooru	フットボール		5-3	N	football
fuyu	ふゆ	冬	10-4	N	winter
G					
[sentence] ga	[sentence] が		5-3	Pc	but [less formal than でも]
[subject] ga	[subject] が		7-3	P	[subject particle]
gaikokugo	がいこくご	外国語	9-1	N	foreign language
gakkoo	がっこう	学校	3-3	N	school
gakusei	がくせい	学生	3-3	N	college student
ganbarimasu	がんばります	頑張ります	10-4	V1	do one's best
ganbatte	がんばって	頑張って	10-4	V1	Good luck.
gareeji	ガレージ		8-5	N	garage
~gatsu umare	～がつうまれ	～月生まれ	2-6	Nd	born in (month)
geemu	ゲーム		9-5	N	game
geemu(o)shimasu	ゲーム(を)します		9-5	V3	play a game
genki	げんき	元気	1-6	Na	fine, healthy
(o)genki desu ka	(お)げんきですか	(お)元気ですか	1-6	Exp	How are you?
getsuyoobi	げつようび	月曜日	2-7	N	Monday

Japanese (transliterated)	Japanese (かな)	Japanese (漢字)	Lesson	Type	English
giniro	ぎんいろ	銀色	5-5	N	silver color
gitaa	ギター		5-1	N	guitar
go	ご	五	1-4	Num	five
gochisoosama	ごちそうさま		12-4	Exp	[said after a meal]
gogatsu	ごがつ	五月	2-6	N	May
gogo	ごご	午後	7-1	N	p.m.
gohan	ごはん	御飯	4-2	N	(cooked) rice
go-juu	ごじゅう	五十	1-5	Num	fifty
gomi	ごみ		2-3	N	trash
gomibako	ごみばこ	ごみ箱	8-1	N	trash can
~goro	～ごろ		2-7	Nd	about (time)
gorufu	ゴルフ		5-3	N	golf
gozen	ごぜん	午前	7-1	N	a.m.
~gurai	～ぐらい		11-4	Nd	about ~ [Not used for time]
gurandokyanion	グランドキャニオン		7-5	N	Grand Canyon
guree	グレー		5-5	N	grey
gyuunyuu	ぎゅうにゅう	牛乳	4-2	N	(cow's) milk
H					
ha	は	歯	6-1	N	tooth
hachi	はち	八	1-4	Num	eight
hachigatsu	はちがつ	八月	2-6	N	August
hachi-juu	はちじゅう	八十	1-5	Num	eighty
haha	はは	母	3-1	N	(my) mother
hai	はい		1-2	Exp	Yes.
hai	はい		1-5	SI	yes
~hai	～はい	～杯	12-3	Nd	cupful, glassful, bowlful
hai doozo.	はい、どうぞ		2-5	Exp	Here, you are.
hajimemashite	はじめまして	初めまして	1-1	Exp	How do you do?/ Nice to meet you.
hajimemashoo	はじめましょう	始めましょう	1-3	Exp	Let's begin.
~han	～はん	～半	2-7	Nd	half
hana	はな	花	8-3	N	flower
hana	はな	鼻	6-1	N	nose
hanabi	はなび	花火	7-5	N	fireworks
hanashimasu	はなします	話します	4-1	V1	speak, talk
hanaya	はなや	花屋	11-3	N	flower shop
hanbaagaa	ハンバーガー		12-2	N	hamburger

Japanese (transliterated)	Japanese (かな)	Japanese (漢字)	Lesson	Type	English
haru	はる	春	10-4	N	spring
(o)hashi	(お)はし	(お)箸	12-3	N	chopsticks
hashirimasu	はしります	走ります	10-5	V1	run
hatachi	はたち	二十歳	3-1	N	twenty years old
hatsuka	はつか	二十日	2-6	N	20th day of the month
hawai	ハワイ		7-5	N	Hawaii
hayai	はやい	早い	7-1	A	early
hayaku	はやく	早く	10-2	Adv	early [used with a verb]
hayaku	はやく	早く	1-3	Exp	Hurry!
heta	へた	下手	5-3	Na	unskillful, poor at
heya	へや	部屋	8-5	N	room
hi	ひ	日	2-6	N	day
hidoi	ひどい	酷い	9-3	A	terrible
~hiki	~ひき	~匹	8-3	Nd	[counter for small animals]
hikooki	ひこうき	飛行機	7-3	N	airplane
hikui	ひくい	低い	6-1	A	short (height)
hiroi	ひろい	広い	8-5	A	wide, spacious
(o)hiru	(お)ひる	(お)昼	4-3	N	daytime
hirugohan	ひるごはん	昼御飯	4-3	N	lunch
hito	ひと	人	8-2	N	person
hitori	ひとり	一人	3-1	N	one person, alone
hitotsu	ひとつ	一つ	2-5	N	one [general counter]
hon	ほん	本	2-3	N	book
~hon	~ほん	~本	8-3	Nd	[counter for long cylindrical objects]
hontoo	ほんとう	本当	3-1	N	true
honya	ほんや	本屋	11-3	N	bookstore
hoomuruumu	ホームルーム		9-1	N	homeroom
hoshii	ほしい	欲しい	9-4	A	want (something)
hottodoggu	ホットドッグ		12-2	N	hotdog
hyaku	ひゃく	百	1-5	Num	hundred
hyaku-man	ひゃくまん	百万	11-4	Num	(one) million

I

Japanese (transliterated)	Japanese (かな)	Japanese (漢字)	Lesson	Type	English
ichi	いち	一	1-4	Num	one
ichigatsu	いちがつ	一月	2-6	N	January
ii	いい		2-1	A	good
ii desu nee	いいですねえ		9-3	Exp	How nice! [about a future event]

Japanese (transliterated)	Japanese (かな)	Japanese (漢字)	Lesson	Type	English
iie	いいえ		1-5	SI	no [formal]
iie, kekkoo desu	いいえ、けっこうです	いいえ、結構です	12-3	Exp	No, thank you.
iimasu	いいます	言います	11-2	V1	say
ikaga desu ka?	いかがですか	如何ですか	11-5	Ni	How about ~? [Polite exp. of どうですか]
ike	いけ	池	8-3	N	pond
ikimasu	いきます	行きます	7-2	V1	go
(o)ikura?	(お)いくら		11-4	Ni	How much?
ikutsu	いくつ		2-5	Ni	how many? [general counter]
(o)ikutsu?	(お)いくつ		3-1	Ni	How old?
ima	いま	今	2-7	N	now
imasu	います		8-1	V2	there is (animate object)
imooto	いもうと	妹	3-1	N	(my) younger sister
imootosan	いもうとさん	妹さん	3-2	N	(SO's) younger sister
indo	インド		3-4	N	India
inu	いぬ	犬	8-1	N	dog
irimasu	いります	要ります	12-3	V1	need
iro	いろ	色	5-5	N	color
isha	いしゃ	医者	3-5	N	(medical) doctor [informal]
isogashii	いそがしい	忙しい	7-4	A	busy
issho ni	いっしょに	一緒に	4-4	Adv	together
isu	いす	椅子	8-1	N	chair
itadakimasu	いただきます	頂きます	12-4	Exp	[before a meal]
itai	いたい	痛い	10-1	A	painful, sore
itsu	いつ		2-6	Ni	when
itsuka	いつか	五日	2-6	N	5th day of the month
itsumo	いつも		4-2	Adv	always
itsutsu	いつつ	五つ	2-5	N	five [general counter]

J

Japanese (transliterated)	Japanese (かな)	Japanese (漢字)	Lesson	Type	English
ja	じゃ		12-1	Exp	well then [informal]
jaketto	ジャケット		11-3	N	jacket
jama	じゃま	邪魔	6-5	Na	hindrance, nuisance, is in the way
~ji	～じ	～時	2-7	Nd	o'clock
jidoosha	じどうしゃ	自動車	7-3	N	car, vehicle

Japanese (transliterated)	Japanese (かな)	Japanese (漢字)	Lesson	Type	English
jimusho	じむしょ	事務所	8-4	N	office
jisho	じしょ	辞書	2-3	N	dictionary
jitensha	じてんしゃ	自転車	7-3	N	bicycle
jogingu	ジョギング		5-1	N	jogging
joozu	じょうず	上手	5-3	Na	skillful, (be) good at
jugyoo	じゅぎょう	授業	9-1	N	class, instruction
juu	じゅう	十	1-4	Num	ten
juugatsu	じゅうがつ	十月	2-6	N	October
juu-go	じゅうご	十五	1-5	Num	fifteen
juu-hachi	じゅうはち	十八	1-5	Num	eighteen
juu-ichi	じゅういち	十一	1-5	Num	eleven
juuichigatsu	じゅういちがつ	十一月	2-6	N	November
juu-ku	じゅうく	十九	1-5	Num	nineteen
juu-kyuu	じゅうきゅう	十九	1-5	Num	nineteen
juu-man	じゅうまん	十万	11-4	Num	hundred thousand
juu-nana	じゅうなな	十七	1-5	Num	seventeen
juu-ni	じゅうに	十二	1-5	Num	twelve
juunigatsu	じゅうにがつ	十二月	2-6	N	December
juu-roku	じゅうろく	十六	1-5	Num	sixteen
juu-san	じゅうさん	十三	1-5	Num	thirteen
juu-shi	じゅうし	十四	1-5	Num	fourteen
juu-shichi	じゅうしち	十七	1-5	Num	seventeen
juusu	ジュース		4-2	N	juice
juu-yokka	じゅうよっか	十四日	2-6	N	14th day of the month
juu-yon	じゅうよん	十四	1-5	Num	fourteen
K					
ka	か		1-3	SP	[question particle]
kachimasu	かちます	勝ちます	10-3	V1	win
kaerimasu	かえります	帰ります	7-2	V1	return (to a place)
kafeteria	カフェテリア		4-4	N	cafeteria
kagaku	かがく	科学	9-1	N	science
kaimasu	かいます	買います	11-3	V1	buy
kaimono	かいもの	買い物	7-4	N	shopping
kaimono(o)shimasu	かいもの（を）します	買い物（を）します	7-4	V3	go shopping
kaisha	かいしゃ	会社	7-2	N	company
kaishain	かいしゃいん	会社員	3-5	N	company employee
kaite kudasai	かいてください	書いて下さい	2-2	Exp	Please write.

Japanese (transliterated)	Japanese (かな)	Japanese (漢字)	Lesson	Type	English
kakimasu	かきます	書きます	4-5	V1	write
kami	かみ	紙	2-3	N	paper
kami(no ke)	かみ(のけ)	髪(の毛)	6-1	N	hair
kamoku	かもく	科目	9-1	N	subject
kanashii	かなしい	悲しい	9-3	A	sad
(o)kane	(お)かね	(お)金	2-3	N	money
kankoku	かんこく	韓国	3-4	N	Korea
kankokugo	かんこくご	韓国語	4-1	N	Korean language
kao	かお	顔	6-1	N	face
[sentence] kara	[sentence] から		9-3	Pc	because~, since~, ~so
~kara	～から		7-5	P	from~
karada	からだ	体	6-1	N	body
kashite kudasai	かしてください	貸して下さい	12-3	V1	(please) lend me
kata	かた	方	8-2	Nd	person [polite form of ひと]
kawa	かわ	川	7-4	N	river
kawaii	かわいい	可愛い	6-5	A	cute
kawaisoo ni	かわいそうに	可愛そうに	10-1	Exp	How pitiful.
kayoobi	かようび	火曜日	2-7	N	Tuesday
kaze	かぜ	風邪	10-1	N	(a) cold
kazoku	かぞく	家族	3-1	N	(my) family
(go)kazoku	(ご)かぞく	(御)家族	3-2	N	(someone's) family
keetai	ケータイ/けいたい	携帯	4-5	N	cellular phone
keikan	けいかん	警官	3-5	N	police officer
kesa	けさ	今朝	10-2	N	this morning
keshigomu	けしごむ	消しゴム	2-3	N	(rubber) eraser
ki	き	木	8-3	N	tree
kibishii	きびしい	厳しい	6-4	A	strict
kiiro	きいろ	黄色	5-5	N	yellow color
kiiroi	きいろい	黄色い	6-3	A	yellow
kiite kudasai	きいてください	聞いて下さい	2-2	Exp	Please listen.
kikimasu	ききます	聞きます	4-4	V1	listen, hear
kikoemasen	きこえません	聞こえません	2-1	V2	cannot hear
kikoemasu	きこえます	聞こえます	2-1	V2	can hear
kimasu	きます	来ます	7-2	V3	come
kiniro	きんいろ	金色	5-5	N	gold color
kinoo	きのう	昨日	4-3	N	yesterday
kinyoobi	きんようび	金曜日	2-7	N	Friday

Japanese (transliterated)	Japanese (かな)	Japanese (漢字)	Lesson	Type	English
kirai	きらい	嫌い	5-2	Na	dislike
kirei	きれい		6-5	Na	pretty, clean, neat, nice
kiritsu	きりつ	起立	1-3	Exp	Stand.
kissaten	きっさてん	喫茶店	11-3	N	coffee shop
kitanai	きたない	汚い	6-5	A	dirty, messy
kochira	こちら		3-4	N	this one [polite form of これ]
kodomo	こども	子供	8-2	N	child
koe	こえ	声	6-1	N	voice
koko	ここ		2-5	N	here
kokonoka	ここのか	九日	2-6	N	9th day of the month
kokonotsu	ここのつ	九つ	2-5	N	nine [general counter]
kokoro	こころ	心	6-1	N	heart
konban	こんばん	今晩	7-1	N	tonight
konban wa	こんばんは	今晩は	7-1	Exp	Good evening.
kongetsu	こんげつ	今月	10-4	N	this month
konnichi wa	こんにちは	今日は	1-2	Exp	Hello. Hi.
kono	この		2-4	PN	this
konpyuutaa	コンピューター		4-5	N	computer
konshuu	こんしゅう	今週	9-4	N	this week
koohii	コーヒー		4-2	N	coffee
kookoo	こうこう	高校	3-3	N	high school
kookoo ichinensei	こうこういちねんせい	高校一年生	3-3	N	H.S. 1st-year student (U.S. 10th grader)
kookoo ninensei	こうこうにねんせい	高校二年生	3-3	N	H.S. 2nd-year student (U.S. 11th grader)
kookoo sannensei	こうこうさんねんせい	高校三年生	3-3	N	H.S. 3rd-year student (U.S. 12th grader)
kookoosei	こうこうせい	高校生	3-3	N	high school student
koora	コーラ		4-2	N	cola
koppu	コップ		12-3	N	cup
kore	これ		1-3	N	this one
korekara	これから		12-5	SI	from now on
koto	こと	事	5-3	N	thing [intangible]
kotoshi	ことし	今年	9-5	N	this year
ku	く	九	1-4	Num	nine
kubi	くび	首	6-1	N	neck
kuchi	くち	口	6-1	N	mouth
(~o) kudasai	(〜を)ください	(〜を)下さい	2-5	Exp	Please give me ~.

Japanese (transliterated)	Japanese (かな)	Japanese (漢字)	Lesson	Type	English
kugatsu	くがつ	九月	2-6	N	September
~kurai	～くらい	～位	11-4	Nd	about ~ [Not used for time]
kurasu	クラス		9-1	N	class, instruction
kuro	くろ	黒	5-5	N	black
kuroi	くろい	黒い	6-3	A	black
kuruma	くるま	車	7-3	N	car, vehicle
kusuri	くすり	薬	10-2	N	medicine
kutsu	くつ	靴	11-3	N	shoes
kyandii	キャンディ		2-5	N	candy
kyanpu	キャンプ		7-4	N	camp
kyonen	きょねん	去年	9-5	N	last year
kyoo	きょう	今日	2-6	N	today
kyoodai	きょうだい	兄弟	3-1	N	(my) sibling(s)
kyookasho	きょうかしょ	教科書	2-3	N	textbook
kyooshitsu	きょうしつ	教室	8-4	N	classroom
kyuu	きゅう	九	1-4	Num	nine
kyuu-juu	きゅうじゅう	九十	1-5	Num	ninety

M

Japanese (transliterated)	Japanese (かな)	Japanese (漢字)	Lesson	Type	English
maamaa	まあまあ		5-4	Adv	so-so
machimasu	まちます	待ちます	11-2	V1	wait
mada desu [+neg.]	まだです[+neg.]		12-1	Exp	not yet
~made	～まで		7-5	P	to~; until ~
mado	まど	窓	8-1	N	window
mae	まえ	前	3-5	N	before
(~no) mae ni	(～の)まえに	(～の)前に	10-5	Pc	before ~
~mai	～まい	～枚	2-5	Nd	[counter for flat objects]
mainen	まいねん	毎年	9-5	N	every year
mainichi	まいにち	毎日	4-2	N	every day
maishuu	まいしゅう	毎週	9-4	N	every week
maitoshi	まいとし	毎年	9-5	N	every year
maitsuki	まいつき	毎月	10-4	N	every month
makemasu	まけます	負けます	10-3	V2	lose
(ichi)man	(いち)まん	(一)万	11-4	N	ten thousand
[verb] masen ka	[verb] ませんか		7-1	Dv	Won't you ~? [invitation]
[verb] mashoo	[verb] ましょう		7-1	Dv	Let's do ~. [suggestion]

Japanese (transliterated)	Japanese (かな)	Japanese (漢字)	Lesson	Type	English
mata	また	又	8-1	Adv	again
(ja) mata ato de	(じゃ)またあとで		12-5	Exp	(Well,) see you later.
mazui	まずい	不味い	11-5	A	unappetizing
me	め	目	6-1	N	eye
midori	みどり	緑	5-5	N	green
miemasen	みえません	見えません	2-1	V2	cannot see
miemasu	みえます	見えます	2-1	V2	can see
mijikai	みじかい	短い	6-2	A	short [not for height]
mikka	みっか	三日	2-6	N	3rd day of the month
mimasu	みます	見ます	4-5	V2	watch, look, see
mimi	みみ	耳	6-1	N	ear
miruku	ミルク		4-2	N	milk
(o)mise	(お)みせ	(お)店	11-2	N	store
misemasu	みせます	見せます	11-2	V2	show
misete kudasai	みせてください	見せて下さい	2-2	Exp	Please show me.
mite kudasai	みてください	見て下さい	2-2	Exp	Please look.
mittsu	みっつ	三つ	2-5	N	three [general counter]
(o)mizu	(お)みず	(お)水	4-2	N	water
mokuyoobi	もくようび	木曜日	2-7	N	Thursday
mono	もの	物	5-2	N	thing [tangible]
moo (ippai)	もう(いっぱい)	もう(一杯)	12-4	Adv	(one) more (cup)
moo [+past aff. V]	もう[+past aff. V]		12-1	Exp	already
mooichido	もういちど	もう一度	1-4	Adv	one more time
muika	むいか	六日	2-6	N	6th day of the month
murasaki	むらさき	紫	5-5	N	purple
mushiatsui	むしあつい	蒸し暑い	1-6	A	hot and humid
(o)musubi	(お)むすび	(お)結び	12-2	N	rice ball
muttsu	むっつ	六つ	2-5	N	six [general counter]
muzukashii	むずかしい	難しい	9-2	A	difficult

N

Japanese (transliterated)	Japanese (かな)	Japanese (漢字)	Lesson	Type	English
nado	など		9-5	Nd	etc.
nagai	ながい	長い	6-2	A	long
naifu	ナイフ		12-3	N	knife
namae	なまえ	名前	3-1	N	name
(o)namae	(お)なまえ	(お)名前	3-2	N	(SO's) name
nan	なん	何	1-3	Ni	what?
nana	なな	七	1-4	Num	seven
nana-juu	ななじゅう	七十	1-5	Num	seventy

Japanese (transliterated)	Japanese (かな)	Japanese (漢字)	Lesson	Type	English
nanatsu	ななつ	七つ	2-5	Num	seven [general counter]
nan-bai	なんばい	何杯	12-3	Ni	how many cups?
nanbiki	なんびき	何匹	8-3	Ni	how many [small animals]?
nanbon	なんぼん	何本	8-3	Ni	how many [long cylindrical objects]?
nandai	なんだい	何台	8-3	Ni	how many [mechanized goods]?
nan-gatsu	なんがつ	何月	2-6	Ni	what month?
nani	なに	何	1-3	Ni	what?
nanigo	なにご	何語	4-1	Ni	what language?
naniiro	なにいろ	何色	5-5	N	what color?
nani-jin	なにじん	何人	3-4	Ni	what nationality?
nanimo [+ Neg. V]	なにも [+ Neg. V]	何も [+ Neg. V]	4-3	Ni+P	(not) anything
nanji	なんじ	何時	2-7	Ni	what time?
nan-nensei	なんねんせい	何年生	3-3	N	what grade?
nan-nichi	なんにち	何日	2-6	Ni	what day of the month?
nan-nin	なんにん	何人	3-1	Ni	how many people?
nanoka	なのか	七日	2-6	N	7th day of the month
nan-sai	なんさい	何歳／何才	3-1	Ni	how old?
nanwa	なんわ	何羽	8-3	Ni	how many [birds]?
nan-yoobi	なんようび	何曜日	2-7	Ni	what day of the week?
napukin	ナプキン		12-3	N	napkin
natsu	なつ	夏	10-4	N	summer
naze	なぜ		9-3	Ni	why?
ne	ね		6-5	SP	isn't it? [sentence ending particle]
neko	ねこ	猫	8-1	N	cat
nemasu	ねます	寝ます	7-2	V2	sleep, go to bed
nemui	ねむい	眠い	10-2	A	sleepy
~nen	～ねん	～年	9-5	Nd	year
netsu	ねつ	熱	10-1	N	fever
nezumi	ねずみ	鼠	8-5	N	mouse
ni	に	二	1-4	Num	two
[activity] ni	[activity] に		7-2	P	to, for [activity]
[place] ni [+ direction V]	[place] に [+ direction V]		7-2	P	to [place]
[place] ni [+ existance V]	[place] に [+ existance V]		8-1	P	in, at [place]

Japanese (transliterated)	Japanese (かな)	Japanese (漢字)	Lesson	Type	English
[specific time] ni	[specific time] に		4-3	P	at [specific time]
~nichi	〜にち	〜日	2-6	Nd	day of the month
nichiyoobi	にちようび	日曜日	2-7	N	Sunday
nigate	にがて	苦手	5-3	Na	(be) weak in
nigatsu	にがつ	二月	2-6	N	February
(o)nigiri	(お)にぎり	(お)握り	12-2	N	rice ball
nihon	にほん	日本	3-4	N	Japan
nihongo	にほんご	日本語	4-1	N	Japanese language
(~wa) nihongo de nan to iimasu ka	(〜は)にほんごでなんといいますか	(〜は)日本語で何と言いますか	2-1	Exp	How do you say ~ in Japanese?
nihonjin	にほんじん	日本人	3-4	N	Japanese citizen
ni-juu	にじゅう	二十	1-5	Num	twenty
~nin	〜にん	〜人	3-1	Nd	[counter for people]
niwa	にわ	庭	8-5	N	garden, yard
no	の		3-1	P	[possessive and descriptive particle]
nodo	のど	喉	6-1	N	throat
nodo ga karakara desu	のどがカラカラです	喉がカラカラです	12-1	Exp	I am thirsty.
nodo ga kawaki-mashita	のどがかわきました	喉が渇きました	12-1	Exp	I got thirsty.
nomimasu	のみます	飲みます	10-2	V1	take (medicine)
nomimasu	のみます	飲みます	4-2	V2	drink
nomimono	のみもの	飲み物	5-2	N	beverage
nooto	ノート		2-3	N	notebook
nyuuyooku	ニューヨーク		7-5	N	New York

O

Japanese (transliterated)	Japanese (かな)	Japanese (漢字)	Lesson	Type	English
obaasan	おばあさん		3-2	N	grandmother, elderly woman
ocha	おちゃ	お茶	4-2	N	tea
ohayoo	おはよう		1-2	Exp	Good morning. (informal)
ohayoo gozaimasu	おはようございます		1-2	Exp	Good morning. (formal)
oishasan	おいしゃさん	お医者さん	3-5	N	(medical) doctor (formal)
oishii	おいしい	美味しい	11-5	A	delicious
ojiisan	おじいさん		3-2	N	grandfather, elderly man

Japanese (transliterated)	Japanese (かな)	Japanese (漢字)	Lesson	Type	English
okaasan	おかあさん	お母さん	3-2	N	(SO's) mother
okimasu	おきます	起きます	7-2	V2	wake up, get up
omedetoo gozaimasu	おめでとうございます		2-6	Exp	Congratulations.
omoshiroi	おもしろい	面白い	9-2	A	interesting
onaka	おなか	お腹	6-1	N	stomach
onaka ga ippai desu	おなかがいっぱいです	お腹が一杯です	12-4	Exp	(I am) full
onaka ga pekopeko desu	おなかがペコペコです	お腹がペコペコです	12-1	Exp	I am hungry.
onaka ga sukimashita	おなかがすきました	お腹が空きました	12-1	Exp	I got hungry.
oneesan	おねえさん	お姉さん	3-2	N	(SO's) older sister
onegaishimasu	おねがいします	お願いします	1-4	Exp	please [request]
ongaku	おんがく	音楽	4-4	N	music
oniisan	おにいさん	お兄さん	3-2	N	(SO's) older brother
onna	おんな	女	8-2	N	female
onna no hito	おんなのひと	女の人	8-2	N	woman, lady
onna no ko	おんなのこ	女の子	8-2	N	girl
ooi	おおい	多い	9-4	A	many, much
ookii	おおきい	大きい	6-2	A	big
orenji(iro)	オレンジ(いろ)	オレンジ(色)	5-5	N	orange (color)
osoi	おそい	遅い	7-1	A	late
osoku	おそく	遅く	10-2	Adv	late [used with a verb]
otoko	おとこ	男	8-2	N	male
otoko no hito	おとこのひと	男の人	8-2	N	man
otoko no ko	おとこのこ	男の子	8-2	N	boy
otoosan	おとうさん	お父さん	3-2	N	(SO's) father
otooto	おとうと	弟	3-1	N	(my) younger brother
otootosan	おとうとさん	弟さん	3-2	N	(SO's) younger brother
ototoi	おととい	一昨日	9-3	N	day before yesterday
owarimashoo	おわりましょう	終わりましょう	1-3	Exp	Let's finish.
oyogimasu	およぎます	泳ぎます	9-5	V1	swim
P					
paatii	パーティー		7-4	N	party
~pai	～ぱい	～杯	12-3	Nd	cupful, glassful, bowlful, spoonful
pan	パン		4-2	N	bread
pantsu	パンツ		11-3	N	pants

Japanese (transliterated)	Japanese (かな)	Japanese (漢字)	Lesson	Type	English
pasokon	パソコン		4-5	N	personal computer
piano	ピアノ		5-1	N	piano
pikunikku	ピクニック		7-4	N	picnic
pinku	ピンク		5-5	N	pink
piza	ピザ		12-2	N	pizza
~pon	～ぽん	～本	8-3	Nd	[counter for long cylindrical objects]
puuru	プール		8-2	N	pool
R					
raigetsu	らいげつ	来月	10-4	N	next month
rainen	らいねん	来年	9-5	N	next year
raishuu	らいしゅう	来週	9-4	N	next week
rajio	ラジオ		4-5	N	radio
rei	れい	礼	1-3	Exp	Bow.
renshuu	れんしゅう	練習	9-5	N	practice
renshuu(o)shimasu	れんしゅう(を)します	練習(を)します	10-5	V3	practice
repooto	レポート		4-5	N	report, paper
resutoran	レストラン		7-4	N	restaurant
rokkaa	ロッカー		8-4	N	locker
roku	ろく	六	1-4	Num	six
rokugatsu	ろくがつ	六月	2-6	N	June
roku-juu	ろくじゅう	六十	1-5	Num	sixty
rosanzerusu	ロサンゼルス		7-5	N	Los Angeles
ryokoo	りょこう	旅行	7-4	N	trip, traveling
ryokoo(o)shimasu	りょこう(を)します	旅行(を)します	7-4	V3	travel
ryukku	リュック		2-2	N	backpack
S					
~sai	～さい	～才／～歳	3-1	Nd	[counter for age]
saizu	サイズ		12-2	N	size
sakana	さかな	魚	8-3	N	fish
sakkaa	サッカー		5-3	N	soccer
samui	さむい	寒い	1-6	A	cold
san	さん	三	1-4	Num	three
~san	～さん		1-2	Nd	Mr./Mrs./Ms.
sandoitchi	サンドイッチ		12-2	N	sandwich
sanfuranshisuko	サンフランシスコ		7-5	N	San Francisco
sangatsu	さんがつ	三月	2-6	N	March

Japanese (transliterated)	Japanese (かな)	Japanese (漢字)	Lesson	Type	English
san-juu	さんじゅう	三十	1-5	Num	thirty
(o)sara	(お)さら	(お)皿	12-3	N	plate, dish
sarada	サラダ		12-2	N	salad
sayoonara	さようなら		1-2	Exp	Good-bye.
se(i)	せ(い)	背	6-1	N	height
seiseki	せいせき	成績	9-3	N	grade
seito	せいと	生徒	3-3	N	student [non-college]
semai	せまい	狭い	8-5	A	narrow, small (area)
sen	せん	千	11-4	N	thousand
sengetsu	せんげつ	先月	10-4	N	last month
sensei	せんせい	先生	1-2	N	teacher, Mr./Ms./Dr.
senshuu	せんしゅう	先週	9-4	N	last week
~sento	～セント		11-4	Nd	cent(s)
shakai	しゃかい	社会	9-1	N	social studies
shashin	しゃしん	写真	2-3	N	photo
shatsu	シャツ		11-3	N	shirt
shefu	シェッフ		3-5	N	chef, cook
shi	し	四	1-4	Num	four
shiai	しあい	試合	10-3	N	(sports) game
shichi	しち	七	1-4	Num	seven
shichigatsu	しちがつ	七月	2-6	N	July
shichi-juu	しちじゅう	七十	1-5	Num	seventy
shigatsu	しがつ	四月	2-6	N	April
(o)shigoto	(お)しごと	(お)仕事	3-5	N	job
shiken	しけん	試験	2-5	N	exam
shimasu	します		4-4	V3	do
shimemasu	しめます	閉めます	11-2	V2	close
shimete kudasai	しめてください	閉めて下さい	2-2	Exp	Please close.
shinbun	しんぶん	新聞	4-4	N	newspaper
shinimasu	しにます	死にます	10-1	V1	die
shirimasen	しりません	知りません	2-1	V1	do not know
shiro	しろ	白	5-5	N	white color
shiroi	しろい	白い	6-3	A	white
shizuka	しずか	静か	6-5	Na	quiet
shizuka ni shimasu	しずかにします	静かにします	11-2	V3	quiet down
shizukani shite kudasai	しずかにしてください	静かにして下さい	2-2	Exp	Please be quiet.
shokudoo	しょくどう	食堂	4-4	N	cafeteria

Japanese (transliterated)	Japanese (かな)	Japanese (漢字)	Lesson	Type	English
shokuji	しょくじ	食事	7-4	N	meal, dining
shokuji(o)shimasu	しょくじ(を)します	食事(を)します	7-4	V3	dine, have a meal
shoobooshi	しょうぼうし	消防士	3-5	N	firefighter
shootesuto	しょうテスト	小テスト	2-5	N	quiz
shufu	しゅふ	主婦	3-5	N	housewife
shukudai	しゅくだい	宿題	2-5	N	homework
shumi	しゅみ	趣味	5-1	N	hobby
shuumatsu	しゅうまつ	週末	9-4	N	weekend
soko	そこ		2-5	N	there
sono	その		2-4	PN	that ~
soo desu	そうです		1-5	Exp	it is
soo desu nee...	そうですねえ...		1-6	Exp	Yes it is!
soo desu nee...	そうですねえ...		5-1	Exp	Let me see ...
soo desuka	そうですか		3-1	Exp	Is that so? / I see.
soo dewa arimasen	そうではありません		1-5	Exp	It is not so. [formal]
soo ja arimasen	そうじゃありません		1-5	Exp	It is not so. [informal]
sore	それ		1-5	N	that one
sorekara	それから		7-2	SI	and then
soreni	それに		9-4	SI	moreover, besides
soretomo	それとも		6-4	SI	or
soshite	そして		3-2	SI	and
soto	そと	外	8-1	N	outside
subarashii	すばらしい	素晴らしい	11-5	A	wonderful
~sugi	~すぎ	~過ぎ	7-1	Nd	after ~
sugoi	すごい	凄い	11-5	A	terrible, terrific
suiei	すいえい	水泳	5-1	N	swimming
suiyoobi	すいようび	水曜日	2-7	N	Wednesday
suki	すき	好き	5-2	Na	like
sukoshi	すこし	少し	8-3	Adv	a few, a little
sukoshi	すこし	少し	4-1	Adv	a little [formal]
sukunai	すくない	少ない	9-4	A	is few, little
sumaatofon	スマートフォン		4-5	N	smartphone
sumimasen	すみません		1-4	Exp	excuse me
supein	スペイン		3-4	N	Spain
supeingo	スペインご	スペイン語	4-1	N	Spanish language
supootsu	スポーツ		5-1	N	sports
supuun	スプーン		12-3	N	spoon
sushiya	すしや	寿司屋	11-3	N	sushi shop/bar

Japanese (transliterated)	Japanese (かな)	Japanese (漢字)	Lesson	Type	English
sutoroo	ストロー		12-3	N	straw
suugaku	すうがく	数学	9-1	N	math
suupaa	スーパー		11-3	N	super market
suwarimasu	すわります	座ります	11-2	V1	sit
suwatte kudasai	すわってください	座って下さい	2-2	Exp	Please sit.
suzushii	すずしい	涼しい	1-6	A	cool [temperature]
T					
tabemasu	たべます	食べます	4-2	V2	eat
tabemono	たべもの	食べ物	5-2	N	food
~tachi	～たち	～達	8-3	Nd	[suffix for animate plurals]
tachimasu	たちます	立ちます	11-2	V1	stand
~tai	～たい		10-2	Da	want (to do something)
taigo	タイご	タイ語	4-1	N	Thai language
taihen	たいへん	大変	9-4	Na	hard, difficult
taiiku	たいいく	体育	9-1	N	P.E.
taipu(o)shimasu	タイプ(を)します		4-5	V3	type
taitei	たいてい	大抵	4-2	Adv	usually
takai	たかい	高い	11-5	A	expensive
takai	たかい	高い	6-1	A	tall
takusan	たくさん	沢山	8-3	Adv	a lot, many
takushii	タクシー		7-3	N	taxi
(o)tanjoobi	(お)たんじょうび	(お)誕生日	2-6	N	birthday
tanoshii	たのしい	楽しい	9-2	A	fun, enjoyable
(~o) tanoshimi ni shite imasu	(～を)たのしみにしています	(～を)楽しみにしています	7-5	Exp.	I am looking forward to (something)
tatemono	たてもの	建物	8-4	N	building
tatte kudasai	たってください	立って下さい	2-2	Exp	Please stand.
te	て	手	6-1	N	hand
(o)tearai	(お)てあらい	(お)手洗い	8-2	N	bathroom, restroom
tegami	てがみ	手紙	4-5	N	letter
tekisuto	テキスト		2-3	N	textbook
tenisu	テニス		5-3	N	tennis
(o)tenki	(お)てんき	(お)天気	1-6	N	weather
terebi	テレビ		4-5	N	TV
terebigeemu	テレビゲーム		5-1	N	video game
tisshu	ティッシュ		2-5	N	tissue
to	と	戸	8-1	N	door

Japanese (transliterated)	Japanese (かな)	Japanese (漢字)	Lesson	Type	English
to	と		3-2	P	and [between two nouns]
to (issho ni)	と(いっしょに)	と(一緒に)	4-4	P	(together) with (a person)
toire	トイレ		8-2	N	bathroom, restroom
tokei	とけい	時計	11-3	N	watch, clock
tokidoki	ときどき	時々	4-2	Adv	sometimes
tokui	とくい	得意	5-3	Na	strong in, can do well
tomodachi	ともだち	友達	4-1	N	friend
too	とお	十	2-5	Num	ten [general counter]
tooi	とおい	遠い	8-5	A	far
tooka	とおか	十日	2-6	N	10th day of the month
toranpu	トランプ		5-1	N	(playing) cards
tori	とり	鳥	8-3	N	bird
toshi o totteimasu	としをとっています	年を取っています	6-4	V1	(is) old (age)
toshokan	としょかん	図書館	4-4	N	library
totemo	とても		5-4	Adv	very
tsugi	つぎ	次	9-2	N	next
tsuitachi	ついたち	一日	2-6	N	first day of the month
tsukaremashita	つかれました	疲れました	10-2	V2	(got) tired
tsukarete imasu	つかれています	疲れています	10-2	V2	tired
tsukue	つくえ	机	8-1	N	desk
tsumaranai	つまらない		9-2	A	boring, uninteresting
tsumetai	つめたい	冷たい	12-4	A	cold (to the touch)
tsuyoi	つよい	強い	10-3	A	strong

U

Japanese (transliterated)	Japanese (かな)	Japanese (漢字)	Lesson	Type	English
uchi	うち		4-1	N	house
ude	うで	腕	6-1	N	arm
ueetaa	ウェイター		3-5	N	waiter
ueetoresu	ウェイトレス		3-5	N	waitress
umi	うみ	海	7-4	N	beach, ocean, sea
ureshii	うれしい	嬉しい	9-3	A	glad, happy
urusai	うるさい	煩い	6-5	A	noisy
uta	うた	歌	5-1	N	song, singing
utaimasu	うたいます	歌います	9-5	V1	sing
utsukushii	うつくしい	美しい	8-4	A	beautiful

Japanese (transliterated)	Japanese (かな)	Japanese (漢字)	Lesson	Type	English
W					
wa	は		1-1	P	[sentence topic-marking particle]
~wa	～わ	～羽	8-3	Nd	[counter for birds]
waa	わあ		11-5	SI	Wow!
waakushiito	ワークシート		2-5	N	worksheet
wakai	わかい	若い	6-4	A	young
wakarimasen	わかりません	分かりません	2-1	V1	do not understand
wakarimasu	わかります	分かります	2-1	V1	understand
warui	わるい	悪い	6-2	A	bad
wasuremasu	わすれます	忘れます	12-3	V2	forget
watashi	わたし	私	1-1	N	I (used by anyone)
watashino	わたしの	私の	2-4	N	mine
watashitachi	わたしたち	私達	10-3	N	we
Y					
[N1] ya [N2]	[N1] や [N2]		9-5	P	[Noun1] and [N2], etc.
yakyuu	やきゅう	野球	5-3	N	baseball
yama	やま	山	7-4	N	mountain
yasashii	やさしい	易しい	9-2	A	easy
yasashii	やさしい	優しい	6-4	A	nice, kind
yasete imasu	やせています	痩せています	6-4	V2	thin
yasui	やすい	安い	11-5	A	cheap
(o)yasumi	(お)やすみ	(お)休み	7-5	N	day off, vacation
(o)yasumi desu	(お)やすみです	(お)休みです	1-3	Exp	absent
yasumijikan	やすみじかん	休み時間	9-1	N	(a) break
yasumimasu	やすみます	休みます	10-2	V2	rest
(~o) yasumimasu	(～を)やすみます	(～を)休みます	10-2	V2	(be) absent (from ~)
yattsu	やっつ	八つ	2-5	N	eight [general counter]
[sentence] yo	[sentence] よ		6-5	SP	you know [sentence ending particle]
yoi	よい	良い	6-2	A	good
yokatta desu nee	よかったですねえ	良かったですねえ	9-3	Exp	How nice! [about a past event]
yokka	よっか	四日	2-6	N	4th day of the month
yoku	よく	良く	4-1	Adv	well, often
yoku dekimashita	よくできました	良く出来ました	2-2	Exp	Well done.
yomimasu	よみます	読みます	4-4	V1	read
yon	よん	四	1-4	Num	four

Japanese (transliterated)	Japanese (かな)	Japanese (漢字)	Lesson	Type	English
yonde kudasai	よんでください	読んで下さい	2-2	Exp	Please read.
yon-juu	じょんじゅう	四十	1-5	Num	forty
yooka	ようか	八日	2-6	N	8th day of the month
yoru	よる	夜	4-3	N	night
yottsu	よっつ	四つ	2-5	N	four [general counter]
yowai	よわい	弱い	10-3	A	weak
yubi	ゆび	指	6-1	N	finger
yukkuri	ゆっくり		1-4	Adv	slowly
yuube	ゆうべ	夕べ／昨夜	10-2	N	last night
yuugata	ゆうがた	夕方	4-3	N	late afternoon, early evening
yuumei	ゆうめい	有名	8-4	Na	famous

Z

Japanese (transliterated)	Japanese (かな)	Japanese (漢字)	Lesson	Type	English
zannen deshita nee	ざんねんでしたねえ	残念でしたねえ	9-3	Exp	How disappointing! [about a past event]
zannen desu nee	ざんねんですねえ	残念ですねえ	9-3	Exp	How disappointing! [about a future event]
zasshi	ざっし	雑誌	4-4	N	magazine
zenbu	ぜんぶ	全部	12-2	N	everything
zenbude	ぜんぶで	全部で	12-2	N	for everything / all
zenzen [+ Neg. V]	ぜんぜん [+ Neg. V]	全然 [+ Neg. V]	5-4	Adv	(not) at all

Appendix D

English-Japanese Glossary

English	Lesson	Type	Japanese (transliterated)	Japanese (かな)	Japanese (漢字)
Counters and Particles					
[counter for age]	3-1	Nd	~sai	～さい	～才／～歳
[counter for birds]	8-3	Nd	~wa	～わ	～羽
[counter for cupful, glassful, bowlful]	12-3	Nd	~hai	～はい	～杯
[counter for flat objects]	2-5	Nd	~mai	～まい	～枚
[counter for hours]	2-7	Nd	~ji	～じ	～時
[counter for long cylindrical objects]	8-3	Nd	~hon	～ほん	～本
[counter for long cylindrical objects]	8-3	Nd	~pon	～ぽん	～本
[counter for mechanized goods]	8-3	Nd	~dai	～だい	～台
[counter for people]	3-1	Nd	~nin	～にん	～人
[counter for small animals]	8-3	Nd	~hiki	～ひき	～匹
[possessive and descriptive particle]	3-1	P	no	の	
[question particle]	1-3	SP	ka	か	
[sentence ending particle] isn't it?	6-5	SP	ne	ね	
[sentence ending particle] you know	6-5	SP	[sentence] yo	[sentence] よ	
[sentence topic-marking particle]	1-1	P	wa	は	
[subject particle]	7-3	P	[subject] ga	[subject] が	
[tool particle] by, with, on, in	4-5	P	[tool] de	[tool] で	
[totalizing particle]	12-2	P	[counter] de	[counter] で	
in, at [place]	8-1	P	[place] ni [+ existance V]	[place] に [+ existance V]	
to [place]	7-2	P	[place] e	[place] へ	
to [place]	7-2	P	[place] ni [+ direction V]	[place] に [+ direction V]	
to, for [activity]	7-2	P	[activity] ni	[activity] に	

English	Lesson	Type	Japanese (transliterated)	Japanese (かな)	Japanese (漢字)
A					
a few, a little	8-3	Adv	sukoshi	すこし	少し
a little [formal]	4-1	Adv	sukoshi	すこし	少し
a little [more colloquial than すこし]	4-1	Adv	chotto	ちょっと	
a lot, many	8-3	Adv	takusan	たくさん	沢山
a.m.	7-1	N	gozen	ごぜん	午前
absent	1-3	Exp	(o)yasumi desu	(お)やすみです	(お)休みです
(be) absent (from ~)	10-2	V2	(~o) yasumimasu	(〜を)やすみます	(〜を)休みます
about (time)	2-7	Nd	~goro	〜ごろ	
about ~ [Not used for time]	11-4	Nd	~gurai, ~kurai	〜ぐらい, 〜くらい	〜位
after ~	7-1	Nd	~sugi	〜すぎ	〜過ぎ
after ~	10-5	Pp	(-no) ato de	(〜の) あとで	(〜の) 後で
again	8-1	Adv	mata	また	又
airplane	7-3	N	hikooki	ひこうき	飛行機
all right	10-1	Na	daijoobu	だいじょうぶ	大丈夫
already	12-1	Exp	moo [+past aff. V]	もう[+past aff. V]	
always	4-2	Adv	itsumo	いつも	
am, is, are	1-1	C	desu	です	
America	3-4	N	amerika	アメリカ	
and	3-2	SI	soshite	そして	
and [between two nouns]	3-2	P	to	と	
[Noun1] and [N2], etc.	9-5	P	[N1] ya [N2]	[N1] や [N2]	
and then	7-2	SI	sorekara	それから	
(not) anything	4-3	Ni+P	nanimo [+ Neg. V]	なにも[+ Neg. verb]	何も[+ Neg. verb]
(not to) anywhere	7-4	Ni+P	doko emo	どこへも	
April	2-6	N	shigatsu	しがつ	四月
Arabic language	4-1	N	arabiago	アラビアご	アラビア語
arm	6-1	N	ude	うで	腕
art	9-1	N	bijutsu	びじゅつ	美術
at [specific time]	4-3	P	[specific time] ni	[specific time] に	
[doing something] at, in [a place]	4-1	P	[place] de [action V]	[place] で [action V]	
(not) at all	5-4	Adv	zenzen [+ Neg. V]	ぜんぜん [+ Neg. V]	全然 [+ Neg. V]
August	2-6	N	hachigatsu	はちがつ	八月
autumn, fall	10-4	N	aki	あき	秋

English	Lesson	Type	Japanese (transliterated)	Japanese (かな)	Japanese (漢字)
B					
backpack	2-2	N	ryukku	リュック	
bad	6-2	A	warui	わるい	悪い
ballpoint pen	2-3	N	boorupen	ボールペン	
band	9-5	N	bando	バンド	
baseball	5-3	N	yakyuu	やきゅう	野球
basketball	5-3	N	basuketto(booru)	バスケット(ボール)	
bathroom, restroom	8-2	N	(o)tearai	(お)てあらい	(お)手洗い
bathroom, restroom	8-2	N	toire	トイレ	
beach, ocean, sea	7-4	N	umi	うみ	海
beautiful	8-4	A	utsukushii	うつくしい	美しい
because~, since~, ~so	9-3	Pc	[sentence] kara	[sentence] から	
bed	8-5	N	beddo	ベッド	
before	3-5	N	mae	まえ	前
before ~	10-5	Pp	(~no) mae ni	(〜の)まえに	(〜の)前に
beverage	5-2	N	nomimono	のみもの	飲み物
bicycle	7-3	N	jitensha	じてんしゃ	自転車
big	6-2	A	ookii	おおきい	大きい
bird	8-3	N	tori	とり	鳥
birthday	2-6	N	(o)tanjoobi	(お)たんじょうび	(お)誕生日
black	6-3	A	kuroi	くろい	黒い
black	5-5	N	kuro	くろ	黒
blue	6-3	A	aoi	あおい	青い
blue	5-5	N	ao	あお	青
boat, ship	7-3	N	fune	ふね	船
body	6-1	N	karada	からだ	体
book	2-3	N	hon	ほん	本
bookstore	11-3	N	honya	ほんや	本屋
boring, uninteresting	9-2	A	tsumaranai	つまらない	
born in (month)	2-6	Nd	~gatsu umare	〜がつうまれ	〜月生まれ
Boston	7-5	N	bosuton	ボストン	
Bow.	1-3	Exp	rei	れい	礼
box lunch	12-2	N	bentoo	べんとう	弁当
boy	8-2	N	otoko no ko	おとこのこ	男の子
Brazil	3-4	N	burajiru	ブラジル	
bread	4-2	N	pan	パン	
(a) break	9-1	N	yasumijikan	やすみじかん	休み時間
breakfast	4-3	N	asagohan	あさごはん	朝御飯

English	Lesson	Type	Japanese (transliterated)	Japanese (かな)	Japanese (漢字)
brown	6-3	A	chairoi	ちゃいろい	茶色い
brown color	5-5	N	chairo	ちゃいろ	茶色
building	8-4	N	tatemono	たてもの	建物
bus	7-3	N	basu	バス	
busy	7-4	A	isogashii	いそがしい	忙しい
But [begins sentence]	4-1	SI	demo	でも	
but [less formal than でも]	5-3	Pc	[sentence] ga	[sentence] が	
by [transportation mode]	7-3	P	[transportation] de	[transportation] で	
buy	11-3	V1	kaimasu	かいます	買います
bye bye	12-5	Exp	baibai	バイバイ	

C

English	Lesson	Type	Japanese (transliterated)	Japanese (かな)	Japanese (漢字)
cafeteria	4-4	N	kafeteria	カフェテリア	
cafeteria	4-4	N	shokudoo	しょくどう	食堂
camp	7-4	N	kyanpu	キャンプ	
can hear	2-1	V2	kikoemasu	きこえます	聞こえます
can see	2-1	V2	miemasu	みえます	見えます
candy	2-5	N	ame	あめ	飴
candy	2-5	N	kyandii	キャンディ	
cannot hear	2-1	V2	kikoemasen	きこえません	聞こえません
cannot see	2-1	V2	miemasen	みえません	見えません
cap, hat	2-3	N	booshi	ぼうし	帽子
car, vehicle	7-3	N	jidoosha	じどうしゃ	自動車
car, vehicle	7-3	N	kuruma	くるま	車
(playing) cards	5-1	N	toranpu	トランプ	
cat	8-1	N	neko	ねこ	猫
cellular phone	4-5	N	keetai	ケータイ/けいたい	携帯
cent(s)	11-4	Nd	~sento	～セント	
chair	8-1	N	isu	いす	椅子
cheap	11-5	A	yasui	やすい	安い
chef	3-5	N	sheffu	シェッフ	
child	8-2	N	kodomo	こども	子供
China	3-4	N	chuugoku	ちゅうごく	中国
Chinese language	4-1	N	chuugokugo	ちゅうごくご	中国語
chocolate	2-5	N	chokoreeto	チョコレート	
chopsticks	12-3	N	(o) hashi	(お)はし	(お)箸
class, instruction	9-1	N	jugyoo	じゅぎょう	授業
class, instruction	9-1	N	kurasu	クラス	
classroom	8-4	N	kyooshitsu	きょうしつ	教室

English	Lesson	Type	Japanese (transliterated)	Japanese (かな)	Japanese (漢字)
close	11-2	V2	shimemasu	しめます	閉めます
coffee	4-2	N	koohii	コーヒー	
coffee shop	11-3	N	kissaten	きっさてん	喫茶店
cola	4-2	N	koora	コーラ	
cold	1-6	A	samui	さむい	寒い
cold (to the touch)	12-4	A	tsumetai	つめたい	冷たい
(a) cold	10-1	N	kaze	かぜ	風邪
college student	10-5	N	daigakusei	だいがくせい	大学生
college, university	10-5	N	daigaku	だいがく	大学
color	5-5	N	iro	いろ	色
come	7-2	V3	kimasu	きます	来ます
company	7-2	N	kaisha	かいしゃ	会社
company employee	3-5	N	kaishain	かいしゃいん	会社員
computer	4-5	N	konpyuutaa	コンピューター	
Congratulations.	2-6	Exp	omedetoo gozaimasu	おめでとうございます	
cool [temperature]	1-6	A	suzushii	すずしい	涼しい
cup	12-3	N	koppu	コップ	
cute	6-5	A	kawaii	かわいい	可愛い

D

English	Lesson	Type	Japanese (transliterated)	Japanese (かな)	Japanese (漢字)
dance, dancing	5-1	N	dansu	ダンス	
day	2-6	N	hi	ひ	日
day after tomorrow	9-3	N	asatte	あさって	明後日
day before yesterday	9-3	N	ototoi	おととい	一昨日
day of the month	2-6	Nd	~nichi	～にち	～日
day off, vacation	7-5	N	(o)yasumi	(お)やすみ	(お)休み
daytime	4-3	N	(o)hiru	(お)ひる	(お)昼
December	2-6	N	juunigatsu	じゅうにがつ	十二月
delicious	11-5	A	oishii	おいしい	美味しい
department store	7-4	N	depaato	デパート	
desk	8-1	N	tsukue	つくえ	机
dictionary	2-3	N	jisho	じしょ	辞書
die	10-1	V1	shinimasu	しにます	死にます
difficult	9-2	A	muzukashii	むずかしい	難しい
dine, have a meal	7-4	V3	shokuji(o) shimasu	しょくじ(を)します	食事(を)します
dinner, supper	4-3	N	bangohan	ばんごはん	晩御飯
dirty, messy	6-5	A	kitanai	きたない	汚い
dislike	5-2	Na	kirai	きらい	嫌い

English	Lesson	Type	Japanese (transliterated)	Japanese (かな)	Japanese (漢字)
dislike a lot, hate	5-2	Na	daikirai	だいきらい	大嫌い
do	4-4	V3	shimasu	します	
do not know	2-1	V1	shirimasen	しりません	知りません
do not understand	2-1	V1	wakarimasen	わかりません	分かりません
do one's best	10-4	V1	ganbarimasu	がんばります	頑張ります
(medical) doctor	3-5	N	isha	いしゃ	医者
(medical) doctor (formal)	3-5	N	oishasan	おいしゃさん	お医者さん
dog	8-1	N	inu	いぬ	犬
dollar(s)	11-4	Nd	doru	ドル	
door	2-2	N	doa	ドア	
door	8-1	N	to	と	戸
drink	4-2	V2	nomimasu	のみます	飲みます

E

English	Lesson	Type	Japanese (transliterated)	Japanese (かな)	Japanese (漢字)
ear	6-1	N	mimi	みみ	耳
early	7-1	A	hayai	はやい	早い
early [used with a verb]	10-2	Adv	hayaku	はやく	早く
easy	9-2	A	yasashii	やさしい	易しい
eat	4-2	V2	tabemasu	たべます	食べます
eight	1-4	N	hachi	はち	八
eight [general counter]	2-5	N	yattsu	やっつ	八つ
eighteen	1-5	?	juu-hachi	じゅうはち	十八
8th day of the month	2-6	N	yooka	ようか	八日
eighty	1-5	?	hachi-juu	はちじゅう	八十
electric train	7-3	N	densha	でんしゃ	電車
eleven	1-5	?	juu-ichi	じゅういち	十一
engineer	3-5	N	enjinia	エンジニア	
English	4-1	N	eigo	えいご	英語
eraser (rubber)	2-3	N	keshigomu	けしごむ	消しゴム
etc.	9-5	Nd	nado	など	
evening	4-3	N	ban	ばん	晩
every month	10-4	N	maitsuki	まいつき	毎月
every week	9-4	N	maishuu	まいしゅう	毎週
every year	9-5	N	mainen	まいねん	毎年
every year	9-5	N	maitoshi	まいとし	毎年
every day	4-2	N	mainichi	まいにち	毎日
everything	12-2	N	zenbu	ぜんぶ	全部
exam	2-5	N	shiken	しけん	試験
excuse me	1-4	Exp	sumimasen	すみません	
expensive	11-5	A	takai	たかい	高い

English	Lesson	Type	Japanese (transliterated)	Japanese (かな)	Japanese (漢字)
[expression before a meal]	12-4	Exp	itadakimasu	いただきます	頂きます
[expression said after a meal]	12-4	Exp	gochisoosama	ごちそうさま	
eye	6-1	N	me	め	目
F					
face	6-1	N	kao	かお	顔
(my) family	3-1	N	kazoku	かぞく	家族
(someone's) family	3-2	N	(go)kazoku	(ご)かぞく	(御)家族
famous	8-4	Na	yuumei	ゆうめい	有名
far	8-5	A	tooi	とおい	遠い
(is) fat	6-4	V1	futotte imasu	ふとっています	太っています
(my) father	3-1	N	chichi	ちち	父
(someone's) father	3-2	N	otoosan	おとうさん	お父さん
February	2-6	N	nigatsu	にがつ	二月
female	8-2	N	onna	おんな	女
fever	10-1	N	netsu	ねつ	熱
fifteen	1-5	?	juu-go	じゅうご	十五
5th day of the month	2-6	N	itsuka	いつか	五日
fifty	1-5	?	go-juu	ごじゅう	五十
fine, healthy	1-6	Na	genki	げんき	元気
finger	6-1	N	yubi	ゆび	指
firefighter	3-5	N	shoobooshi	しょうぼうし	消防士
fireworks	7-5	N	hanabi	はなび	花火
1st day of the month	2-6	N	tsuitachi	ついたち	一日
fish	8-3	N	sakana	さかな	魚
five	1-4	N	go	ご	五
five [general counter]	2-5	N	itsutsu	いつつ	五つ
Florida	7-5	N	furorida	フロリダ	
flower	8-3	N	hana	はな	花
flower shop	11-3	N	hanaya	はなや	花屋
food	5-2	N	tabemono	たべもの	食べ物
foot	6-1	N	ashi	あし	足
football	5-3	N	futtobooru	フットボール	
for everything / all	12-2	N	zenbude	ぜんぶで	全部で
foreign language	9-1	N	gaikokugo	がいこくご	外国語
forget	12-3	V2	wasuremasu	わすれます	忘れます
fork	12-3	N	fooku	フォーク	
forty	1-5	?	yon-juu	じょんじゅう	四十

English	Lesson	Type	Japanese (transliterated)	Japanese (かな)	Japanese (漢字)
four	1-4	N	shi, yon	し, よん	四
four [general counter]	2-5	N	yottsu	よっつ	四つ
fourteen	1-5	?	juu-shi, juu-yon	じゅうし, じゅうよん	十四
4th day of the month	2-6	N	yokka	よっか	四日
France	3-4	N	furansu	フランス	
french fries	12-2	N	furaidopoteto	フライドポテト	
French language	4-1	N	furansugo	フランスご	フランス語
Friday	2-7	N	kinyoobi	きんようび	金曜日
friend	4-1	N	tomodachi	ともだち	友達
from~	7-5	P	~kara	~から	
from now on	12-5	SI	korekara	これから	
(I am) full.	12-4	Exp	onaka ga ippai desu	おなかがいっぱいです	お腹が一杯です
fun, enjoyable	9-2	A	tanoshii	たのしい	楽しい

G

English	Lesson	Type	Japanese (transliterated)	Japanese (かな)	Japanese (漢字)
game	9-5	N	geemu	ゲーム	
(sports) game	10-3	N	shiai	しあい	試合
garage	8-5	N	gareeji	ガレージ	
garden, yard	8-5	N	niwa	にわ	庭
girl	8-2	N	onna no ko	おんなのこ	女の子
glad, happy	9-3	A	ureshii	うれしい	嬉しい
go	7-2	V1	ikimasu	いきます	行きます
go shopping	7-4	V3	kaimono(o)shi-masu	かいもの (を)します	買い物 (を)します
gold color	5-5	N	kiniro	きんいろ	金色
golf	5-3	N	gorufu	ゴルフ	
good	6-2	A	yoi	よい	良い
good	2-1	A	ii	いい	
Good evening.	7-1	Exp	konban wa	こんばんは	今晩は
Good luck.	10-4	V1	ganbatte	がんばって	頑張って
Good morning. (formal)	1-2	Exp	ohayoo gozaimasu	おはようございます	
Good morning. (informal)	1-2	Exp	ohayoo	おはよう	
Good-bye.	1-2	Exp	sayoonara	さようなら	
grade	9-3	N	seiseki	せいせき	成績
Grand Canyon	7-5	N	gurandokyanion	グランドキャニオン	
grandfather, elderly man	3-2	N	ojiisan	おじいさん	
grandmother, elderly woman	3-2	N	obaasan	おばあさん	

English	Lesson	Type	Japanese (transliterated)	Japanese (かな)	Japanese (漢字)
green	5-5	N	midori	みどり	緑
grey	5-5	N	guree	グレー	
guitar	5-1	N	gitaa	ギター	
H					
hair	6-1	N	kami(no ke)	かみ(のけ)	髪(の毛)
half	2-7	Nd	~han	～はん	～半
hamburger	12-2	N	hanbaagaa	ハンバーガー	
hand	6-1	N	te	て	手
hard, difficult	9-4	Na	taihen	たいへん	大変
have	9-1	V1	arimasu	あります	
Hawaii	7-5	N	hawai	ハワイ	
head	6-1	N	atama	あたま	頭
heart	6-1	N	kokoro	こころ	心
height	6-1	N	se(i)	せ(い)	背
Hello. Hi.	1-2	Exp	konnichi wa	こんにちは	今日は
here	2-5	N	koko	ここ	
Here, you are.	2-5	Exp	hai doozo.	はい、どうぞ	
high school	3-3	N	kookoo	こうこう	高校
high school (H.S.) student	3-3	N	kookoosei	こうこうせい	高校生
H.S. 1st-year student (U.S. 10th grader)	3-3	N	kookoo ichinensei	こうこういちねんせい	高校一年生
H.S. 2nd-year student (U.S. 11th grader)	3-3	N	kookoo ninensei	こうこうにねんせい	高校二年生
H.S. 3rd-year student (U.S. 12th grader)	3-3	N	kookoo sannensei	こうこうさんねんせい	高校三年生
hindrance, nuisance	6-5	Na	jama	じゃま	邪魔
hobby	5-1	N	shumi	しゅみ	趣味
homeroom	9-1	N	hoomuruumu	ホームルーム	
homework	2-5	N	shukudai	しゅくだい	宿題
hospital	3-5	N	byooin	びょういん	病院
hot (temperature)	1-6	A	atsui	あつい	暑い
hot and humid	1-6	A	mushiatsui	むしあつい	蒸し暑い
hotdog	12-2	N	hottodoggu	ホットドッグ	
house	4-1	N	uchi	うち	
housewife	3-5	N	shufu	しゅふ	主婦
How about ~? [Polite exp. of どうですか]	11-5	Ni	ikaga desu ka?	いかがですか	如何ですか
How are you?	1-6	Exp	(o)genki desu ka	(お)げんきですか	(お)元気ですか

English	Lesson	Type	Japanese (transliterated)	Japanese (かな)	Japanese (漢字)
How disappointing! [about a future event]	9-3	Exp	zannen desu nee	ざんねんですねえ	残念ですねえ
How disappointing! [about a past event]	9-3	Exp	zannen deshita nee	ざんねんでしたねえ	残念でしたねえ
How do you do? / Nice to meet you.	1-1	Exp	hajimemashite	はじめまして	初めまして
How do you say ~ in Japanese?	2-1	Exp	(~wa) nihongo de nan to iimasu ka	(~は)にほんごで なんといいますか	(~は)日本語で何と 言いますか
how is it? [informal]	7-5	Exp	doo desu ka	どうですか	
how many [birds]?	8-3	Ni	nanwa	なんわ	何羽
how many [long cylindrical objects]?	8-3	Ni	nanbon	なんぼん	何本
how many [mechanized goods]?	8-3	Ni	nandai	なんだい	何台
how many [small animals]?	8-3	Ni	nanbiki	なんびき	何匹
how many cups?	12-3	Ni	nan-bai	なんばい	何杯
how many people?	3-1	Ni	nan-nin	なんにん	何人
how many? [general counter]	2-5	Ni	ikutsu	いくつ	
How much?	11-4	Ni	(o)ikura?	(お)いくら	
How nice! [about a future event]	9-3	Exp	ii desu nee	いいですねえ	
How nice! [about a past event]	9-3	Exp	yokatta desu nee	よかったですねえ	良かったですねえ
How old?	3-1	Ni	(o)ikutsu?	(お)いくつ	
How old?	3-1	Ni	nan-sai	なんさい	何歳／何才
How pitiful.	10-1	Exp	kawaisoo ni	かわいそうに	可愛そうに
hundred	1-5	Num	hyaku	ひゃく	百
hundred thousand	11-4	Num	juu-man	じゅうまん	十万
Hurry!	1-3	Exp	hayaku	はやく	早く

I

English	Lesson	Type	Japanese (transliterated)	Japanese (かな)	Japanese (漢字)
I (used by anyone)	1-1	N	watashi	わたし	私
I (used by males)	1-1	N	boku	ぼく	僕
I am hungry.	12-1	Exp	onaka ga pekopeko desu	おなかがペコペコ です	お腹がペコペコです
I am looking forward to (something)	7-5	Exp.	(~o)tanoshimi ni shite imasu	(~を)たのしみにして います	(~を)楽しみにして います
I am thirsty.	12-1	Exp	nodo ga karakara desu	のどがカラカラです	喉がカラカラです

English	Lesson	Type	Japanese (transliterated)	Japanese (かな)	Japanese (漢字)
I got hungry.	12-1	Exp	onaka ga sukimashita	おなかがすきました	お腹が空きました
I got thirsty.	12-1	Exp	nodo ga kawakimashita	のどがかわきました	喉が渇きました
illness, sickness	10-1	N	byooki	びょうき	病気
important	10-4	Na	daiji	だいじ	大事
India	3-4	N	indo	インド	
interesting	9-2	A	omoshiroi	おもしろい	面白い
intermediate school	3-3	N	chuugaku	ちゅうがく	中学
int. school student	3-3	N	chuugakusei	ちゅうがくせい	中学生
int. school 1nd-year student (U.S. 7th grader)	3-3	N	chuugaku ichinensei	ちゅうがくいちねんせい	中学一年生
int. school 2nd-year student (U.S. 8th grader)	3-3	N	chuugaku ninensei	ちゅうがくにねんせい	中学二年生
int. school 3rd-year student (U.S. 9th grader)	3-3	N	chuugaku sannensei	ちゅうがくさんねんせい	中学三年生
is few, little	9-4	A	sukunai	すくない	少ない
Is that so? / I see.	3-1	Exp	soo desuka	そうですか	
it is	1-5	Exp	soo desu	そうです	
It is not so. [formal]	1-5	Exp	soo dewa arimasen	そうではありません	
It is not so. [informal]	1-5	Exp	soo ja arimasen	そうじゃありません	

J

English	Lesson	Type	Japanese (transliterated)	Japanese (かな)	Japanese (漢字)
jacket	11-3	N	jaketto	ジャケット	
January	2-6	N	ichigatsu	いちがつ	一月
Japan	3-4	N	nihon	にほん	日本
Japanese citizen	3-4	N	nihonjin	にほんじん	日本人
Japanese language	4-1	N	nihongo	にほんご	日本語
job	3-5	N	(o)shigoto	(お)しごと	(お)仕事
jogging	5-1	N	jogingu	ジョギング	
juice	4-2	N	juusu	ジュース	
July	2-6	N	shichigatsu	しちがつ	七月
June	2-6	N	rokugatsu	ろくがつ	六月

K

English	Lesson	Type	Japanese (transliterated)	Japanese (かな)	Japanese (漢字)
knife	12-3	N	naifu	ナイフ	
Korea	3-4	N	kankoku	かんこく	韓国

L

English	Lesson	Type	Japanese (transliterated)	Japanese (かな)	Japanese (漢字)
Korean language	4-1	N	kankokugo	かんこくご	韓国語
large size	12-2	N	eru-saizu	エルサイズ	
last month	10-4	N	sengetsu	せんげつ	先月

English	Lesson	Type	Japanese (transliterated)	Japanese (かな)	Japanese (漢字)
last night	10-2	N	yuube	ゆうべ	夕べ／昨夜
last week	9-4	N	senshuu	せんしゅう	先週
last year	9-5	N	kyonen	きょねん	去年
late	7-1	A	osoi	おそい	遅い
late [used with a verb]	10-2	Adv	osoku	おそく	遅く
late afternoon, early evening	4-3	N	yuugata	ゆうがた	夕方
lawyer	3-5	N	bengoshi	べんごし	弁護士
leg	6-1	N	ashi	あし	脚
(please) lend me	12-3	V1	kashite kudasai	かしてください	貸して下さい
Let me see ...	5-1	Exp	soo desu nee...	そうですねえ...	
let me see ... , well ...	2-1	SI	anoo...	あのう...	
let me see ... , well ...	2-1	SI	eeto...	ええと...	
Let's begin.	1-3	Exp	hajimemashoo	はじめましょう	始めましょう
Let's do ~. [suggestion]	7-1	Dv	[verb] mashoo	[verb] ましょう	
Let's finish.	1-3	Exp	owarimashoo	おわりましょう	終わりましょう
letter	4-5	N	tegami	てがみ	手紙
library	4-4	N	toshokan	としょかん	図書館
like	5-2	Na	suki	すき	好き
like very much, love	5-2	Na	daisuki	だいすき	大好き
listen, hear	4-4	V1	kikimasu	ききます	聞きます
locker	8-4	N	rokkaa	ロッカー	
long	6-2	A	nagai	ながい	長い
Los Angeles	7-5	N	rosanzerusu	ロサンゼルス	
lose	10-3	V2	makemasu	まけます	負けます
lunch	4-3	N	hirugohan	ひるごはん	昼御飯

M

English	Lesson	Type	Japanese (transliterated)	Japanese (かな)	Japanese (漢字)
magazine	4-4	N	zasshi	ざっし	雑誌
male	8-2	N	otoko	おとこ	男
man	8-2	N	otoko no hito	おとこのひと	男の人
many, much	9-4	A	ooi	おおい	多い
March	2-6	N	sangatsu	さんがつ	三月
math	9-1	N	suugaku	すうがく	数学
May	2-6	N	gogatsu	ごがつ	五月
meal, dining	7-4	N	shokuji	しょくじ	食事
medicine	10-2	N	kusuri	くすり	薬
medium size	12-2	N	emu-saizu	エムサイズ	
meet	10-5	V1	aimasu	あいます	会います

English	Lesson	Type	Japanese (transliterated)	Japanese (かな)	Japanese (漢字)
milk	4-2	N	miruku	ミルク	
(cow's) milk	4-2	N	gyuunyuu	ぎゅうにゅう	牛乳
(one) million	11-4	N	hyaku-man	ひゃくまん	百万
mine	2-4	N	watashino	わたしの	私の
minute	7-1	Nd	~fun	～ふん	～分
Monday	2-7	N	getsuyoobi	げつようび	月曜日
money	2-3	N	(o)kane	(お)かね	(お)金
moreover, besides	9-4	SI	soreni	それに	
(one) more (cup)	12-4	Adv	moo (ippai)	もう(いっぱい)	もう(一杯)
morning	4-3	N	asa	あさ	朝
Mr./Mrs./Ms.	1-2	Nd	~san	～さん	
(my) mother	3-1	N	haha	はは	母
(SO's) mother	3-2	N	okaasan	おかあさん	お母さん
mountain	7-4	N	yama	やま	山
mouse	8-5	N	nezumi	ねずみ	鼠
mouth	6-1	N	kuchi	くち	口
movie	5-1	N	eiga	えいが	映画
music	4-4	N	ongaku	おんがく	音楽

N

English	Lesson	Type	Japanese (transliterated)	Japanese (かな)	Japanese (漢字)
name	3-1	N	namae	なまえ	名前
(SO's) name	3-2	N	(o)namae	(お)なまえ	(お)名前
napkin	12-3	N	napukin	ナプキン	
narrow, small (area)	8-5	A	semai	せまい	狭い
near, close	8-5	A	chikai	ちかい	近い
neck	6-1	N	kubi	くび	首
need	12-3	V1	irimasu	いります	要ります
new	8-4	A	atarashii	あたらしい	新しい
New York	7-5	N	nyuuyooku	ニューヨーク	
newspaper	4-4	N	shinbun	しんぶん	新聞
next	9-2	N	tsugi	つぎ	次
next month	10-4	N	raigetsu	らいげつ	来月
next week	9-4	N	raishuu	らいしゅう	来週
next year	9-5	N	rainen	らいねん	来年
Nice to meet you.	1-1	N	doozo yoroshiku	どうぞよろしく	
nice, kind	6-4	A	yasashii	やさしい	優しい
night	4-3	N	yoru	よる	夜
nine	1-4	N	ku	く	九
nine	1-4	N	kyuu	きゅう	九

English	Lesson	Type	Japanese (transliterated)	Japanese (かな)	Japanese (漢字)
nine [general counter]	2-5	N	kokonotsu	ここのつ	九つ
nineteen	1-5	?	juu-ku	じゅうく	十九
nineteen	1-5	?	juu-kyuu	じゅうきゅう	十九
ninety	1-5	?	kyuu-juu	きゅうじゅう	九十
9th day of the month	2-6	N	kokonoka	ここのか	九日
no [formal]	1-5	SI	iie	いいえ	
no [informal]	1-5	SI	ee	ええ	
no good	2-1	Na	dame	だめ	駄目
No, thank you.	12-3	Exp	iie, kekkoo desu	いいえ、けっこうです	いいえ、結構です
noisy	6-5	A	urusai	うるさい	煩い
nose	6-1	N	hana	はな	鼻
not yet	12-1	Exp	mada desu [+neg.]	まだです[+neg.]	
notebook	2-3	N	nooto	ノート	
November	2-6	N	juuichigatsu	じゅういちがつ	十一月
now	2-7	N	ima	いま	今

O

English	Lesson	Type	Japanese (transliterated)	Japanese (かな)	Japanese (漢字)
o'clock	2-7	Nd	~ji	～じ	～時
October	2-6	N	juugatsu	じゅうがつ	十月
office	8-4	N	jimusho	じむしょ	事務所
(is) old (age)	6-4	V1	toshi o totteimasu	としをとっています	年を取っています
old (not for person's age)	8-4	A	furui	ふるい	古い
(my) older brother	3-1	N	ani	あに	兄
(SO's) older brother	3-2	N	oniisan	おにいさん	お兄さん
(my) older sister	3-1	N	ane	あね	姉
(SO's) older sister	3-2	N	oneesan	おねえさん	お姉さん
one	1-4	N	ichi	いち	一
one [general counter]	2-5	N	hitotsu	ひとつ	一つ
one more time	1-4	Adv	mooichido	もういちど	もう一度
one person, alone	3-1	N	hitori	ひとり	一人
open	11-2	V2	akemasu	あけます	開けます
or	6-4	SI	soretomo	それとも	
orange (color)	5-5	N	orenji(iro)	オレンジ(いろ)	オレンジ(色)
outside	8-1	N	soto	そと	外
over there	2-5	N	asoko	あそこ	

P

English	Lesson	Type	Japanese (transliterated)	Japanese (かな)	Japanese (漢字)
P.E.	9-1	N	taiiku	たいいく	体育
p.m.	7-1	N	gogo	ごご	午後
painful, sore	10-1	A	itai	いたい	痛い

English	Lesson	Type	Japanese (transliterated)	Japanese (かな)	Japanese (漢字)
painting, drawing	5-1	N	e	え	絵
pants	11-3	N	pantsu	パンツ	
paper	2-3	N	kami	かみ	紙
party	7-4	N	paatii	パーティー	
pencil	2-3	N	enpitsu	えんぴつ	鉛筆
pencil sharpener	8-1	N	enpitsukezuri	えんぴつけずり	鉛筆削り
person	8-2	N	hito	ひと	人
person [polite form]	8-2	Nd	kata	かた	方
personal computer	4-5	N	pasokon	パソコン	
photo	2-3	N	shashin	しゃしん	写真
piano	5-1	N	piano	ピアノ	
picnic	7-4	N	pikunikku	ピクニック	
pig	8-5	N	buta	ぶた	豚
pink	5-5	N	pinku	ピンク	
pizza	12-2	N	piza	ピザ	
plate, dish	12-3	N	(o)sara	(お)さら	(お)皿
play a game	9-5	V3	geemu(o)shimasu	ゲーム(を)します	
play, amuse (not for sports/music)	9-5	V1	asobimasu	あそびます	遊びます
please [request]	1-4	Exp	onegaishimasu	おねがいします	お願いします
Please be quiet.	2-2	Exp	shizukani shite kudasai	しずかにしてください	静かにして下さい
Please close.	2-2	Exp	shimete kudasai	しめてください	閉めて下さい
Please give me ~.	2-5	Exp	(~o) kudasai	(〜を)ください	(〜を)下さい
Please listen.	2-2	Exp	kiite kudasai	きいてください	聞いて下さい
Please look.	2-2	Exp	mite kudasai	みてください	見て下さい
Please open.	2-2	Exp	akete kudasai	あけてください	開けて下さい
Please read.	2-2	Exp	yonde kudasai	よんでください	読んで下さい
Please show me.	2-2	Exp	misete kudasai	みせてください	見せて下さい
Please sit.	2-2	Exp	suwatte kudasai	すわってください	座って下さい
Please stand.	2-2	Exp	tatte kudasai	たってください	立って下さい
Please turn in ~.	2-2	Exp	~ dashite kudasai	〜だしてください	〜出して下さい
Please wait a minute.	1-4	Exp	chotto matte kudasai	ちょっとまってください	ちょっと待って下さい
Please write.	2-2	Exp	kaite kudasai	かいてください	書いて下さい
police officer	3-5	N	keikan	けいかん	警官
pond	8-3	N	ike	いけ	池
pool	8-2	N	puuru	プール	
practice	9-5	N	renshuu	れんしゅう	練習
practice	10-5	V3	renshuu(o)shimasu	れんしゅう(を)します	練習(を)します

English	Lesson	Type	Japanese (transliterated)	Japanese (かな)	Japanese (漢字)
pretty, clean, neat, nice	6-5	Na	kirei	きれい	
purple	5-5	N	murasaki	むらさき	紫

Q

English	Lesson	Type	Japanese (transliterated)	Japanese (かな)	Japanese (漢字)
quiet	6-5	Na	shizuka	しずか	静か
quiet down	11-2	V3	shizuka ni shimasu	しずかにします	静かにします
quiz	2-5	N	shootesuto	しょうテスト	小テスト

R

English	Lesson	Type	Japanese (transliterated)	Japanese (かな)	Japanese (漢字)
radio	4-5	N	rajio	ラジオ	
rain	1-6	N	ame	あめ	雨
read	4-4	V1	yomimasu	よみます	読みます
reading	5-1	N	dokusho	どくしょ	読書
red	6-3	A	akai	あかい	赤い
red	5-5	N	aka	あか	赤
report, paper	4-5	N	repooto	レポート	
rest	10-2	V2	yasumimasu	やすみます	休みます
restaurant	7-4	N	resutoran	レストラン	
return (to a place)	7-2	V1	kaerimasu	かえります	帰ります
(cooked) rice	4-2	N	gohan	ごはん	御飯
rice ball	12-2	N	(o)musubi	(お)むすび	(お)結び
rice ball	12-2	N	(o)nigiri	(お)にぎり	(お)握り
river	7-4	N	kawa	かわ	川
room	8-5	N	heya	へや	部屋
run	10-5	V1	hashirimasu	はしります	走ります

S

English	Lesson	Type	Japanese (transliterated)	Japanese (かな)	Japanese (漢字)
sad	9-3	A	kanashii	かなしい	悲しい
salad	12-2	N	sarada	サラダ	
San Francisco	7-5	N	sanfuranshisuko	サンフランシスコ	
sandwich	12-2	N	sandoitchi	サンドイッチ	
Saturday	2-7	N	doyoobi	どようび	土曜日
say	11-2	V1	iimasu	いいます	言います
school	3-3	N	gakkoo	がっこう	学校
science	9-1	N	kagaku	かがく	科学
2nd day of the month	2-6	N	futsuka	ふつか	二日
(Well,) see you later.	12-5	Exp	(ja) mata ato de	(じゃ)またあとで	
September	2-6	N	kugatsu	くがつ	九月
seven	1-4	Num	shichi	しち	七
seven	1-4	Num	nana	なな	七

English	Lesson	Type	Japanese (transliterated)	Japanese (かな)	Japanese (漢字)
seven [general counter]	2-5	N	nanatsu	ななつ	七つ
seventeen	1-5	Num	juu-nana	じゅうなな	十七
seventeen	1-5	Num	juu-shichi	じゅうしち	十七
7th day of the month	2-6	N	nanoka	なのか	七日
seventy	1-5	Num	nana-juu	ななじゅう	七十
seventy	1-5	Num	shichi-juu	しちじゅう	七十
shirt	11-3	N	shatsu	シャツ	
shoes	11-3	N	kutsu	くつ	靴
shopping	7-4	N	kaimono	かいもの	買い物
short (height)	6-1	A	hikui	ひくい	低い
short [not for height]	6-2	A	mijikai	みじかい	短い
show	11-2	V2	misemasu	みせます	見せます
(my) sibling(s)	3-1	N	kyoodai	きょうだい	兄弟
silver color	5-5	N	giniro	ぎんいろ	銀色
sing	9-5	V1	utaimasu	うたいます	歌います
sit	11-2	V1	suwarimasu	すわります	座ります
Sit.	1-3	Exp	chakuseki	ちゃくせき	着席
six	1-4	Num	roku	ろく	六
six [general counter]	2-5	N	muttsu	むっつ	六つ
sixteen	1-5	Num	juu-roku	じゅうろく	十六
6th day of the month	2-6	N	muika	むいか	六日
sixty	1-5	Num	roku-juu	ろくじゅう	六十
size	12-2	N	saizu	サイズ	
skillful, (be) good at	5-3	Na	joozu	じょうず	上手
sleep, go to bed	7-2	V2	nemasu	ねます	寝ます
sleepy	10-2	A	nemui	ねむい	眠い
slowly	1-4	Adv	yukkuri	ゆっくり	
small	6-2	A	chiisai	ちいさい	小さい
small size	12-2	N	esu-saizu	エスサイズ	
smartphone	4-5	N	sumaatofon	スマートフォン	
snack bar; kiosk	4-4	N	baiten	ばいてん	売店
so-so	5-4	Adv	maamaa	まあまあ	
soccer	5-3	N	sakkaa	サッカー	
social studies	9-1	N	shakai	しゃかい	社会
sometimes	4-2	Adv	tokidoki	ときどき	時々
song, singing	5-1	N	uta	うた	歌
Spain	3-4	N	supein	スペイン	
Spanish language	4-1	N	supeingo	スペインご	スペイン語
speak, talk	4-1	V1	hanashimasu	はなします	話します

English	Lesson	Type	Japanese (transliterated)	Japanese (かな)	Japanese (漢字)
spoon	12–3	N	supuun	スプーン	
sports	5–1	N	supootsu	スポーツ	
spring	10–4	N	haru	はる	春
stand	11–2	V1	tachimasu	たちます	立ちます
Stand.	1–3	Exp	kiritsu	きりつ	起立
stomach	6–1	N	onaka	おなか	お腹
store	11–2	N	(o)mise	(お)みせ	(お)店
straw	12–3	N	sutoroo	ストロー	
strict	6–4	A	kibishii	きびしい	厳しい
strong	10–3	A	tsuyoi	つよい	強い
strong in, can do well	5–3	Na	tokui	とくい	得意
student [college]	3–3	N	gakusei	がくせい	学生
student [non-college]	3–3	N	seito	せいと	生徒
study	4–4	V3	benkyoo (o) shi-masu	べんきょう	勉強(を)します
subject	9–1	N	kamoku	かもく	科目
subway	7–3	N	chikatetsu	ちかてつ	地下鉄
summer	10–4	N	natsu	なつ	夏
Sunday	2–7	N	nichiyoobi	にちようび	日曜日
super market	11–3	N	suupaa	スーパー	
sushi shop/bar	11–3	N	sushiya	すしや	寿司屋
swim	9–5	V1	oyogimasu	およぎます	泳ぎます
swimming	5–1	N	suiei	すいえい	水泳

T

English	Lesson	Type	Japanese (transliterated)	Japanese (かな)	Japanese (漢字)
TV	4–5	N	terebi	テレビ	
take (medicine)	10–2	V1	nomimasu	のみます	飲みます
tall	6–1	A	takai	たかい	高い
tardy	1–3	Exp	chikoku desu	ちこくです	遅刻です
taxi	7–3	N	takushii	タクシー	
tea	4–2	N	ocha	おちゃ	お茶
teacher, Mr./Ms./Dr.	1–2	N	sensei	せんせい	先生
team	10–3	N	chiimu	チーム	
telephone	4–5	N	denwa	でんわ	電話
ten	1–4	Num	juu	じゅう	十
ten [general counter]	2–5	N	too	とお	十
ten thousand	11–4	Num	(ichi)man	(いち)まん	(一)万
tennis	5–3	N	tenisu	テニス	
10th day of the month	2–6	N	tooka	とおか	十日

English	Lesson	Type	Japanese (transliterated)	Japanese (かな)	Japanese (漢字)
terrible	9-3	A	hidoi	ひどい	酷い
terrible, terrific	11-5	A	sugoi	すごい	凄い
textbook	2-3	N	kyookasho	きょうかしょ	教科書
textbook	2-3	N	tekisuto	テキスト	
Thai language	4-1	N	taigo	タイご	タイ語
Thank you very much.	1-4	Exp	arigatoo gozaimasu	ありがとうございます	
Thank you.	1-4	Exp	arigatoo	ありがとう	
Thank you.	1-4	Exp	doomo	どうも	
that ~	2-4	PN	sono	その	
that ~ over there	2-4	PN	ano	あの	
that one	1-5	N	sore	それ	
that one over there	1-5	N	are	あれ	
there	2-5	N	soko	そこ	
there is (animate obj.)	8-1	V2	imasu	います	
there is (inanimate obj.)	8-1	V1	arimasu	あります	
thin	6-4	V2	yasete imasu	やせています	痩せています
thing [intangible]	5-3	N	koto	こと	事
thing [tangible]	5-2	N	mono	もの	物
3rd day of the month	2-6	N	mikka	みっか	三日
thirteen	1-5	Num	juu-san	じゅうさん	十三
thirty	1-5	Num	san-juu	さんじゅう	三十
this	2-4	PN	kono	この	
this month	10-4	N	kongetsu	こんげつ	今月
this morning	10-2	N	kesa	けさ	今朝
this one	1-3	N	kore	これ	
this one [polite form]	3-4	N	kochira	こちら	
this week	9-4	N	konshuu	こんしゅう	今週
this year	9-5	N	kotoshi	ことし	今年
thousand	11-4	Num	sen	せん	千
three	1-4	Num	san	さん	三
three [general counter]	2-5	N	mittsu	みっつ	三つ
throat	6-1	N	nodo	のど	喉
Thursday	2-7	N	mokuyoobi	もくようび	木曜日
tired	10-2	V2	tsukarete imasu	つかれています	疲れています
(got) tired	10-2	V2	tsukaremashita	つかれました	疲れました
tissue	2-5	N	tisshu	ティッシュ	
today	2-6	N	kyoo	きょう	今日
to~; until ~	7-5	P	~made	～まで	

English	Lesson	Type	Japanese (transliterated)	Japanese (かな)	Japanese (漢字)
toe	6-1	N	ashiyubi	あしゆび	足指
together	4-4	Adv	issho ni	いっしょに	一緒に
tomorrow	4-3	N	ashita	あした	明日
tonight	7-1	N	konban	こんばん	今晩
tooth	6-1	N	ha	は	歯
trash	2-3	N	gomi	ごみ	
trash can	8-1	N	gomibako	ごみばこ	ごみ箱
travel	7-4	V3	ryokoo(o) shimasu	りょこう(を)します	旅行(を)します
tree	8-3	N	ki	き	木
trip, traveling	7-4	N	ryokoo	りょこう	旅行
true	3-1	N	hontoo	ほんとう	本当
Tuesday	2-7	N	kayoobi	かようび	火曜日
turn in	11-2	V1	dashimasu	だします	出します
twelve	1-5	Num	juu-ni	じゅうに	十二
20th day of the month	2-6	N	hatsuka	はつか	二十日
twenty	1-5	Num	ni-juu	にじゅう	二十
twenty years old	3-1	N	hatachi	はたち	二十歳
two	1-4	Num	ni	に	二
two [general counter]	2-5	N	futatsu	ふたつ	二つ
two people	3-1	N	futari	ふたり	二人
type	4-5	V3	taipu(o)shimasu	タイプ(を)します	

U

English	Lesson	Type	Japanese (transliterated)	Japanese (かな)	Japanese (漢字)
U.S. citizen	3-4	N	amerikajin	アメリカじん	アメリカ人
unappetizing	11-5	A	mazui	まずい	不味い
understand	2-1	V1	wakarimasu	わかります	分かります
unskillful, poor at	5-3	Na	heta	へた	下手
usually	4-2	Adv	taitei	たいてい	大抵
very	5-4	Adv	totemo	とても	
(not) very	5-4	Adv	amari	あまり	余

V

English	Lesson	Type	Japanese (transliterated)	Japanese (かな)	Japanese (漢字)
video game	5-1	N	terebigeemu	テレビゲーム	
voice	6-1	N	koe	こえ	声
volleyball	5-3	N	baree(booru)	バレー(ボール)	

W

English	Lesson	Type	Japanese (transliterated)	Japanese (かな)	Japanese (漢字)
wait	11-2	V1	machimasu	まちます	待ちます
waiter	3-5	N	ueetaa	ウェイター	
waitress	3-5	N	ueetoresu	ウェイトレス	

English	Lesson	Type	Japanese (transliterated)	Japanese (かな)	Japanese (漢字)
wake up, get up	7-2	V2	okimasu	おきます	起きます
walk	7-3	V1	aruite (arukimasu)	あるいて (あるきます)	歩いて (歩きます)
want (something)	9-4	A	hoshii	ほしい	欲しい
want (to do something)	10-2	Da	~tai	～たい	
warm	12-4	A	atatakai	あたたかい	暖かい
watch, clock	11-3	N	tokei	とけい	時計
watch, look, see	4-5	V2	mimasu	みます	見ます
water	4-2	N	(o)mizu	(お)みず	(お)水
we	10-3	N	watashitachi	わたしたち	私達
we [used by males]	10-3	N	bokutachi	ぼくたち	僕達
weak	10-3	A	yowai	よわい	弱い
weak in	5-3	Na	nigate	にがて	苦手
weather	1-6	N	(o)tenki	(お)てんき	(お)天気
Wednesday	2-7	N	suiyoobi	すいようび	水曜日
weekend	9-4	N	shuumatsu	しゅうまつ	週末
Well done.	2-2	Exp	yoku dekimashita	よくできました	良く出来ました
well then [formal]	12-1	Exp	dewa	では	
well then [informal]	12-1	Exp	ja	じゃ	
well, often	4-1	Adv	yoku	よく	良く
what color?	5-5	N	naniiro	なにいろ	何色
what day of the month?	2-6	Ni	nan-nichi	なんにち	何日
what day of the week?	2-7	Ni	nan-yoobi	なんようび	何曜日
what grade?	3-3	N	nan-nensei	なんねんせい	何年生
What happened?	10-1	Exp	doo shimashita ka	どうしましたか	
what kind of ~?	5-2	PN	donna~?	どんな～	
what language?	4-1	Ni	nanigo	なにご	何語
what month?	2-6	Ni	nan-gatsu	なんがつ	何月
what nationality?	3-4	Ni	nani-jin	なにじん	何人
what time?	2-7	Ni	nanji	なんじ	何時
what?	1-3	Ni	nan	なん	何
what?	1-3	Ni	nani	なに	何
when?	2-6	Ni	itsu	いつ	
where?	3-4	Ni	doko	どこ	
which ~?	11-4	Nd	dono~?	どの～	
which one?	11-4	Ni	dore?	どれ	
white	6-3	A	shiroi	しろい	白い
white color	5-5	N	shiro	しろ	白
who?	3-1	Ni	dare	だれ	誰

English	Lesson	Type	Japanese (transliterated)	Japanese (かな)	Japanese (漢字)
why?	9-3	Ni	dooshite?	どうして	
why?	9-3	Ni	naze	なぜ	
wide, spacious	8-5	A	hiroi	ひろい	広い
win	10-3	V1	kachimasu	かちます	勝ちます
window	8-1	N	mado	まど	窓
winter	10-4	N	fuyu	ふゆ	冬
with [tool]	12-3	P	[tool] de	[tool] で	
woman, lady	8-2	N	onna no hito	おんなのひと	女の人
wonderful	11-5	A	subarashii	すばらしい	素晴らしい
Won't you ~? [invitation]	7-1	Dv	[verb] masen ka	[verb] ませんか	
worksheet	2-5	N	waakushiito	ワークシート	
Wow!	11-5	SI	waa	わあ	
write	4-5	V1	kakimasu	かきます	書きます

Y

English	Lesson	Type	Japanese (transliterated)	Japanese (かな)	Japanese (漢字)
year	9-5	Nd	~nen	～ねん	～年
yellow	6-3	A	kiiroi	きいろい	黄色い
yellow color	5-5	N	kiiro	きいろ	黄色
yen	11-4	Nd	en	えん	円
yes	1-2	Exp	hai	はい	
yes	1-5	SI	hai	はい	
Yes it is!	1-6	Exp	soo desu nee...	そうですねえ...	
yesterday	4-3	N	kinoo	きのう	昨日
you	2-4	N	anata	あなた	
You are welcome.	1-4	Exp	doo itashimashite	どういたしまして	
young	6-4	A	wakai	わかい	若い
(my) younger brother	3-1	N	otooto	おとうと	弟
(SO's) younger brother	3-2	N	otootosan	おとうとさん	弟さん
(my) younger sister	3-1	N	imooto	いもうと	妹
(SO's) younger sister	3-2	N	imootosan	いもうとさん	妹さん
yours	2-4	N	anatano	あなたの	

Hiragana

	W	R	Y	M	H	N	T	S	K	
ん n	わ	ら	や	ま	は	な	た	さ	か	あ A
		り		み	ひ	に	ち chi	し shi	き	い I
		る	ゆ	む	ふ	ぬ	つ tsu	す	く	う U
		れ		め	へ	ね	て	せ	け	え E
	を ○	ろ	よ	も	ほ	の	と	そ	こ	お O

(Particle)

P	B
ぱ	ば
ぴ	び
ぷ	ぶ
ぺ	べ
ぽ	ぼ

D	Z	G	
だ	ざ	が	A
ぢ ji	じ ji	ぎ	I
づ zu	ず zu	ぐ	U
で	ぜ	げ	E
ど	ぞ	ご	O

Katakana

	W	R	Y	M	H	N	T	S	K	
ン n	ワ	ラ	ヤ	マ	ハ	ナ	タ	サ	カ	ア A
		リ		ミ	ヒ	ニ	チ chi	シ shi	キ	イ I
		ル	ユ	ム	フ	ヌ	ツ tsu	ス	ク	ウ U
		レ		メ	ヘ	ネ	テ	セ	ケ	エ E
ヲ O	ワ	ロ	ヨ	モ	ホ	ノ	ト	ソ	コ	オ O

(Particle)

P	B	
パ	バ	
ピ	ビ	
プ	ブ	
ペ	ベ	
ポ	ボ	

D	Z	G	
ダ	ザ	ガ	A
ヂ ji	ジ ji	ギ	I
ヅ zu	ズ zu	グ	U
デ	ゼ	ゲ	E
ド	ゾ	ゴ	O

Appendix G

Kanji 漢字

Kanji with a + before them are new readings.

3か	**1** 一 イチ, ひと (つ)	**2** 二 ニ, ふた (つ)	**3** 三 サン, みっ(つ)	**4** 四 シ, よ, よん, よっ (つ)	**5** 五 ゴ, いつ (つ)	**6** 日 ニ, ニチ, ひ, び, か	名前 なまえ	
4か	**7** 六 ロク, むっ (つ)	**8** 七 なな, シチ, なな(つ)	**9** 八 ハチ, やっ(つ)	**10** 九 きゅう, ク, ここの(つ)	**11** 十 ジュウ, とお	**12** 月 ガツ, ゲツ, つき	明日 あした	
5か	**13** 火 ひ, カ	**14** 水 みず, スイ	**15** 木 き, モク	**16** 金 かね, キン	**17** 土 つち, ド	**18** 本 もと, ホン, ポン, ボン	曜 ヨウ	
6か	**19** 口 くち, ぐち,コウ	**20** 目 め, モク	**21** 耳 みみ	**22** 手 て, シュ	**23** 父 ちち, とう	**24** 母 はは, かあ	上手 じょうず	下手 へた

7か	25 分	26 行	27 来	28 車	29 山	30 川	時	
	わ (かります), フン, プン, ブン	い (きます), コウ	き(ます)	くるま, シャ	やま, サン	かわ, がわ	ジ	
8か	31 人	32 子	33 女	34 好	35 田	36 男	私	
	ひと, ニン, ジン	こ	おんな	す(き)	た, だ	おとこ	わたし	
9か	37 先	38 生	39 今	40 毎	41 年	42 休	生徒	＋来
	セン	セイ	いま, コン	マイ	とし, ネン	やす(み)	せいと	ライ
10か	43 大	44 小	45 中	46 早	47 学	48 校	高校	
	おお (きい), ダイ	ちい (さい), ショウ	チュウ, なか	はや(い)	ガク, がっ	コウ	こうこう	
11か	49 白	50 百	51 千	52 万	53 円	54 見	犬	太
	しろ(い)	ヒャク, ピャク, ビャク	セン, ゼン	マン	エン	み(る)	いぬ	ふと(る)
12か	55 天	56 牛	57 良	58 食	59 言	60 語	何	＋一
	テン	ギュウ, うし	よ(い)	た(べる), ショク	い(う)	ゴ	なに, なん	いっ

Sapporo

Hokkaido

Aomori

Akita

Sendai

Niigata

Kyoto   Kanazawa

Kobe

Honshu

Hiroshima

Mt Fuji   Chiba

Fukuoka

Tokyo

Nagoya   Yokohama

Nara

Kochi   Osaka

Shikoku

Nagasaki

Matsuyama

Kyushu

Kagoshima

Okinawa

Naha